voices of a people's history
of the UNITED STATES
IN THE 21ST CENTURY

voices of a people's history
of the UNITED STATES
IN THE 21ST CENTURY

documents of hope and resistance

EDITED BY

Anthony Arnove
& Haley Pessin

SEVEN STORIES PRESS
New York • Oakland • London

SEVEN STORIES PRESS
www.sevenstories.com

Library of Congress Cataloging-in-Publication Data

Names: Arnove, Anthony, 1969- editor. | Pessin, Haley, editor.
Title: Voices of a people's history of the United States in the 21st century :
    documents of resistance and hope, 2000-2023 / edited by Anthony Arnove
    and Haley Pessin.
Other titles: Voices of a people's history of the United States in the twenty-first century
Description: Regular edition (RG). | New York : Seven Stories Press, 2023.
    | Includes bibliographical references and index.
Identifiers: LCCN 2022053229 | ISBN 9781644212974 (paperback) | ISBN
    9781644212981 (electronic)
Subjects: LCSH: United States--History--21st century--Sources. | United
    States--Social conditions--21st century--Sources. | Minorities--United
    States--Social conditions--21st century--Sources. | Race
    relations--United States--History--21st century--Sources.
Classification: LCC E891 .A17 2023 | DDC 973.93--dc23/eng/20221107
LC record available at https://lccn.loc.gov/2022053229

College professors and high school and middle school teachers may order free examination copies of Seven Stories Press titles. Visit https://www.sevenstories.com/pg/resources-academics or email academics@sevenstories.com.

Printed in the USA.

9 8 7 6 5 4 3 2 1

Contents

CHAPTER 2: THE STRUGGLE FOR JUSTICE IN THE AFTERMATH OF HURRICANE KATRINA

CHAPTER 3: OCCUPY OPENS A NEW ERA

CHAPTER 4: STANDING UP FOR EACH OTHER

CHAPTER 5: THE FERGUSON UPRISING, BARACK OBAMA, AND THE LIMITS OF "EQUALITY"

CHAPTER 6: "1,459 DAYS OF RESISTANCE": RESISTING TRUMPISM AND THE FAR RIGHT

CHAPTER 7: "WE WILL NOT BE SILENCED": #METOO AND THE ONGOING RESISTANCE TO TRUMP

CHAPTER 8: "OUR RESISTANCE MUST BE INTERSECTIONAL"

CHAPTER 9: "THE REAL PANDEMIC HERE IS CAPITALISM"

CHAPTER 10: ABOLITION AND THE UPRISING FOR BLACK LIVES

CHAPTER 11: "TRUMPISM CAN'T BE VOTED AWAY"

CHAPTER 12: THE STRUGGLE CONTINUES

"What I'm challenging us to do, in the spirit of solidarity, is not to embrace optimism but to embrace radical hope. Radical hope is a belief that despite the odds, despite the considerable measures against justice and peace, despite the legacy of hatred and imperialism and white supremacy and patriarchy and homophobia, despite these systems of power that have normalized settler colonialism, despite these structures, we can still win. We can still prevail."

—MARC LAMONT HILL

Introduction

This project continues work by Howard Zinn (1922–2010) in the book *Voices of a People's History of the United States* and, before that, *A People's History of the United States*, first published in 1980. In both books, Howard took inspiration and distilled critical lessons from countless people who worked to challenge oppression, exploitation, and injustice, participating in social movements that brought about changes many did not live to see in their own lifetime. Howard understood the power of listening to how these voices speak to our present and provide, in the words of Raymond Williams, "resources of hope."

The book *Voices of a People's History of the United States* has three editions. Howard worked on the first edition, published in 2004, and an updated second edition, published in 2009. For the third edition, published in 2014, Anthony Arnove updated the book with selections from the period after Howard's death in 2010, seeking to foreground voices that spoke to Howard's passions and concerns.

In beginning work on a fourth edition, especially inspired by the remarkable upsurge of activism for Black lives and liberation, which galvanized perhaps the largest protests in US history, our publisher, Dan Simon of Seven Stories Press, suggested a bold and compelling idea. Given that there were so many voices to add to this new edition, and given our wish to preserve all the selections of the original text, we would be severely limited by space. Could we create a new companion book focused on the voices of the people's movements of the United

States in the twenty-first century? So, while a fourth edition of *Voices of a People's History of the United States* is forthcoming, we are extremely excited to have the opportunity here to delve more deeply into the many voices of protest and dissent in the United States in the twenty-first century.

In gathering these selections, we benefited tremendously from the work of the many people associated with the organization Voices of a People's History of the United States, which has been working on stages and in schools since 2003 to bring primary-source texts of people's history to new audiences. For these staged readings and classroom workshops, Voices has developed a living body of new texts beyond those gathered in the first and later editions of the book. We are extremely grateful to the actors, spoken word artists, musicians, teachers, students, librarians, researchers, and others who helped us source these documents and show us their resonance.

Some of the texts here were first identified in our work on the documentary film *The People Speak*, which Howard Zinn wrote, directed, and produced. We are excited that some of these now appear in a *Voices* book for the first time.

Today, battle lines over how we understand US history are being drawn in real time. Following the 2020 protests against anti-Black racism and police brutality, right-wing politicians have sought to ban educators from teaching the 1619 Project and Critical Race Theory. Both serve as a catch-all for any acknowledgement that this country was founded through the genocide of Indigenous people and the kidnapping and enslavement of Africans whose labor produced the wealth of this country and served as the basis of its global empire.

Howard's own work continues to be targeted by political forces threatened by an honest conversation of our history and an independent-minded population informed about the history of people speaking out for change. President Donald Trump invoked Howard Zinn a full decade after his death at the 2020 White House Conference on American History, attacking his work as "propaganda." Without a hint of irony, Trump went on to call for the restoration of "patriotic education" in the nation's schools. We couldn't ask for a better endorsement to pick up a copy of or re-read *A People's History of the United States* and other works by Howard Zinn.

Young people are not empty vessels, passively accepting whatever ideas they are taught. They deserve the opportunity to engage critically with the world and to decide what they think for themselves. Alongside teacher-activist Jesse Hagopian, whose speech "I'm Not Alone in Pledging to #TeachTruth" is featured in this collection, we stand with all educators who continue to teach the genuine history of this country and its traditions of resistance.

As we write this introduction, tens of thousands of people are taking to the streets around the country to protest the Supreme Court's decision to overturn *Roe v. Wade*, culminating a decades-long effort by Republicans and the religious right to eliminate abortion rights in the United States. Just as mass movements in Argentina, Mexico, and Ireland have succeeded in expanding reproductive rights, the United States is headed in the opposite direction. In his concurring opinion, Clarence Thomas made clear that overturning *Roe* opens the door for the conservative-stacked court to take aim at other rights, such as those protecting contraception, gay marriage, and same-sex relationships.

All of this is a sober reminder that progress is not linear. Any positive reforms that workers, poor people, and the oppressed have wrested from the powerful can be taken away unless we organize to defend them. This is precisely why those who benefit most from the status quo are so fixated on controlling what we learn and how we talk about the past. They understand the power of history, because when we understand the past from the perspective of the oppressed, rather than the powerful, this calls into question the idea that this country has ever been committed to "liberty and justice for all" or that we could ever rely on the Supreme Court to protect our rights.

History told from this vantage, critically, also reveals the ways that, time and again, ordinary people have refused to accept unjust conditions. They spoke out, they fought back—and, sometimes, they won.

The last twenty-two years have witnessed historic concentrations of wealth and political power into fewer and fewer hands. As the COVID-19 pandemic claimed the lives of more than one million people in the United States and millions more globally, the wealth of the ten richest people on earth—nine of whom are from the United States—doubled from $700 billion to a staggering $1.5 trillion, according to a 2022 Oxfam report. This growing economic inequality has been accompanied by efforts to shift blame for mass unemployment and declining living standards away from the 1 percent—or, perhaps more accurately, the 0.1 percent—and onto some of the most disenfranchised communities, especially immigrants and those who are queer, trans, and people of color. It is a classic case of divide and conquer, and it has emboldened white supremacists to act violently, as in the mass shootings of Asian women at a spa in Atlanta, Georgia, or the targeted killing of Black people at a supermarket in Buffalo, New York.

But this same period has also been one of explosive protest, from the antiwar movement against the invasions and occupations of Afghanistan and Iraq; to the massive 2006 Day Without an Immigrant, which brought a million people into the streets under the slogan "Undocumented and Unafraid"; to Occupy Wall Street, which reintroduced the concept of class into collective consciousness and popularized the language of the 99 percent versus the 1 percent (which Howard Zinn had used in *A People's History of the United States*); to the Black Lives Matter movement and the "new abolitionists" (to borrow another phrase from Zinn), who insist that we imagine a society without police or prisons; to the explosive struggle at Standing Rock to defend Indigenous land and stop catastrophic climate change; to the teachers' strike wave that revived the labor movement, even in so-called red states where striking is illegal; to the #MeToo movement against misogyny and systemic sexism, which gave voice to survivors of sexual violence; to the Brooklyn March for Black Trans Lives, which brought out fifteen thousand people, the largest such march to date.

The United States is far from alone in this regard: a 2021 study found that the number of protests in 101 countries and across borders more than tripled between 2006 and 2020, including some of the largest protests in history. What these protests had in common is that they emerged in response to "failures of democracy and of economic and social development, fueled by discontent and a lack of faith in the official political processes." Protests in the United States during the pandemic further confirmed these sentiments, as employers attempted to force low-wage "essential workers" to risk their lives for the sake of profit. That burden fell disproportionately on Black people—already the targets of police brutality—who died at higher rates as the pandemic raged on.

Despite and because of the failure of federal and state governments to stop the chaos of disease and death, people came together in unexpected ways to do what the government would not. Communities created mutual aid groups to provide food, masks, and essential supplies for older, immunocompromised, and disabled people who could not afford to risk leaving their homes and potentially contracting the virus. Neighbors organized to keep those facing eviction from being kicked out onto the street as unemployment reached historic heights. Workers demanded the right to health and safety on the job, and refused to return to conditions that were intolerable long before the pandemic. People risked their own health and safety by mobilizing in massive, militant, multiracial protests to denounce anti-Black racism. Their actions embody Howard's contention that

> to be hopeful in bad times is not just foolishly romantic. It is based on the fact that human history is a history not only of cruelty but also of compassion, sacrifice, courage, kindness. What we choose to emphasize in this complex history will determine our lives. If we see only the worst, it destroys our capacity to do something. If we remember those times and places—and there are so many—where people have behaved magnificently, this gives us the energy to act, and at least the possibility of sending this spinning top of a world in a different direction.

By highlighting the voices of key activists and organizers who participated in the movements of this new century, we aim to show how social change has come about not through the actions of extraordinary individuals, but through ordinary people acting on their own behalf and in solidarity with each other. As Alicia Garza rightly points out in her speech "Why Black Lives Matter," included in chapter 5, "It is important to us that we understand that movements are not begun by any one person."

A number of the speeches, poems, and writings in this book feature the voices of activists and advocates with whom readers will likely be familiar. Others are by people who deserve to be more widely known. We are deeply honored to feature the text of Angela Y. Davis's speech to the Women's March on Washington; Chelsea E. Manning's statement read aloud by her attorneys ahead of her prison sentence for leaking classified documents that exposed US war crimes in Iraq; Naomi Klein's message delivered at Zuccotti Park at the height of Occupy Wall Street; the words of Bree Newsome, who scaled the flagpole outside the South Carolina State Capitol building to remove the Confederate Flag; and the open letter to Amazon CEO Jeff Bezos by Christian Smalls, the Amazon worker who was fired for organizing during the pandemic, only to become the leader of the first successful effort to unionize Amazon, among others. But we are equally excited for readers to encounter, perhaps for the first time, other voices, including Airickca Gordon-Taylor, the cousin of Emmett Till; Toni Smith-Thompson, the college basketball player who refused to stand for the National Anthem twelve years before Colin Kaepernick took a knee in protest against police murders of Black people; Naomi Wadler, who at eleven years old was the youngest speaker at the March for Our Lives and spoke on behalf of Black girls whose deaths by gun violence rarely make headlines; Steven Salaita, who was fired from his university for speaking out against Israel's brutality toward Palestinians; and Xiuhtezcatl Tonatiuh Martinez, a young Indigenous activist who offers a powerful vision of a just future for people and the planet.

Thanks to these and countless other rebels, today's movements are far less likely to be single-issue and more likely to see struggles against capitalism, racism, sexism, homophobia, transphobia, ableism, colonialism, and imperialism as linked. Our ability to more readily make these connections reflects the fact that movements are rarely self-contained: they cross-pollinate, build upon each other, and open space for activists to draw new connections and work across division. We owe to all of these activists a debt of gratitude for putting us on firmer ground to forge the solidarity needed to build a better world.

What unites these selections is that each person spoke out, took action, or intervened at a critical juncture. They were not merely identifying unjust conditions, but resisting them, sometimes at great personal risk. By breaking a silence, by picking a side, the voices we have gathered have individually and collectively generated the potential for another person, and then another, and then another to stand up and take meaningful action, often in ways they could not have anticipated. They remind us that what we do matters, that there is hope in resistance, and that in speaking out, we are never alone.

—Anthony Arnove and Haley Pessin

Acknowledgments

First and foremost, we want to acknowledge and thank the people whose words are featured in this anthology and all the people who made their expression possible, whether it was the event organizers for public speeches, the websites and newspapers that originally published them, the editors who helped to craft them, the radio producers and hosts, and all the other unnamed but vital contributors to the social movements that supported them.

We also want to thank all of the people who made the first three editions of *Voices of a People's History of the United States* possible. The list is too long to produce here but appears in the third edition of *Voices*.

At Seven Stories Press, Dan Simon was critical to planting and nurturing the seed that made the first edition of *Voices* possible and had the idea for this edition, as well. We are grateful for his vision and keen editorial eye, as well as the hard work of Jon Gilbert, Ruth Weiner, Stewart Cauley, Claire Zuo, Kristen Steenbeeke, and Tal Mancini.

Thanks to Myla Kabat-Zinn and Jeff Zinn for their belief in this project and encouragement to publish this volume, and the Zinn Education Project for their important work.

The Voices of a People's History nonprofit organization provided invaluable support that made this project possible. Thanks to Shade Adeyemo, Anna Strout, Róisín Davis, Jordana Leigh, Brian P. Jones, David Johnson, Martha Redbone, Matthew Covey, Sandra Garcia Betancourt, Said Rifai, and our cofounder Brenda Coughlin. Jocelyn Bonadio-de Freitas placed her immense organizational talents in the service of this project and offered valuable insights that informed our selection process. Susan Pourfar and Leta Levy workshopped a number of these readings and gave clarifying input on the editing and selection process. Claire Mooney deftly managed the immense challenge of clearing permissions for the book.

Many of the readings here were first read and workshopped on stages and in classrooms. We want to thank the numerous actors, musicians, spoken word artists, teachers, and students who helped us identify many of the speeches and other documents gathered here. We especially want to thank Lincoln Center for the Performing Arts, Viviana Benitez, Meera Dugal, Godfrey Palaia, Brianna Henry, Roshni Lavelle, Shanta Thake, Jeffrey Ellis-Lee, The Maxine Greene High School for Imaginative Inquiry, Stephen Noonan, Judith S. Kaye School, New York City Lab School for Collaborative Studies, New York University, National Nurses United, Ken Zinn, Brooklyn Academy of Music, Violaine Huisman, City Parks Foundation and SummerStage, Erika Elliott, Paula Abreu, Staceyann Chin, Morgan Spector, and Margaret Odette.

Numerous librarians, historians, archivists, and people's historians of all stripes gave invaluable advice to us in our research and selections and assisted with permissions. We want to thank Keeanga-Yamahtta Taylor, Dao X. Tran, Laurel Mei-Singh, Nick Estes, Dave Zirin, Sarah Jaffe, Imani Perry, Donna Murch, Walter Johnson, Kayla Reed, Ken Zinn, Christopher Petrella, Marc Pessin, Claudette Green-Pessin, Sandi Pessin Boyd, Astra Taylor, Sunaura Taylor, Cassandra Shaylor, Jackie Joiner, Tony Montenieri, Charlotte Sheedy, Regula Noetzli, Julie Wadler, Jen Marshall, Gustavo Mejias Morales, Patty Berne, Sean Larson, John McDonald, Ben Tarnoff, Michelle Fawcett, Arun Gupta, Ellen Adler, Justin Akers Chacón, Lama El Homaïssi, Esailama Artry-Diouf, Sarisa Howard Middleton, Narmeen Maria, Mily Treviño-Sauceda, Ginette Sims, Dana Blanchard, Jen Marlowe, Kimberly Davis, Lee Wengraf, Rebekah Barber, Keith Rosenthal, brian bean, Alan Maass, Keegan O'Brien, Eric Kerl, Dana Blanchard, David Whitehouse, Monique Dols, Brian Ward, Ryan Easterly, Carmela Mungcal, Alexandra Harido-polos, Jacob Nardone, Bill Roberts, Priyanka Ray, Ria Julien, Rebekah

Ward, Sean Joseph, Rory Fanning, Jia Lee, Joel Sronce, Anderson Bean, Gwenette Robertson, Keisha Williams, Ollie Gordon, Tanesha Grant, Jodi Schoenbrun Carter, Kay Sweeney, Shireen Akram-Boshar, Octavia Ridout, Denis Moynihan, John Stickney, Alexander Smith, James Edwards, Sarah Bandy, Eric Canepa, Khury Petersen-Smith, LaToya Hargrove, Jacob Blake Sr., Ashley Cook, Tanishia Lavette Williams, Noelle Hanrahan, Matthew Lasar, Melissa Nasson, Jill Dougan, Eric Ruder, Dana Cloud, Jisu Kim, Feminist Press, Rachel Ossip, Cory Silverberg, Daphne Kolader, Katrina Barilla, Gary Morris, Christopher Shay, *The Nation*, Judge Kevin Sharp, Liz Bierly, Nicole Eisenbraun, Ana Lara Lopez, Rosa Moore, Fran Shuler, Alianza Nacional de Campesinas, Savannah Ioakimedes, Karina Camarena Heredia, Liz Scott, Mary Beth Jarrad, Lucy Simpson, Jawaher Al Wadei, Sandra Mullings, Alia Tyner, Michael Tyner, Eshe Glover, Chad Payne, Dan DiMaggio, Moira Muntz, Victor Pate, Alison Cooper, Jacqueline Gares, Ashna Ali, Vaughan Fielder, Victoria Phillips, Michael DeVaul, CommunicateHealth, Robert Shatzkin, Stephany Evans, Cindy Li, Kiana Marsan, Alana Yu-lan Price, *Truthout*, Yin Q, Alex Y. Ding, Talya Sokoll, Siham B. Tinhinan, Jesse L. London, Elizabeth Jane Cole, Evil Twin Booking, Shannon Harmer, John Crowley, *The New Republic*, Melissa Gira Grant, Sarah Burns, and Sophie Pugh-Sellers. Thanks also to Francesca Ruggiero and Eric Soucy, who generously donated their time and talents to take our author photographs.

Our deepest appreciation and love to Naomi Murakawa and Vikramjit Gill for their solidarity, support, and comradeship throughout the many challenges of editing this book.

And a note on the text: In this edition, per Seven Stories house style, "African American" has been left without a hyphen and "Black," "Brown," and "Indigenous" have been capitalized throughout.

—Anthony Arnove and Haley Pessin

Prologue

We begin with the words of people's historian Howard Zinn (1922–2010), who inspired this book. In 1963, Howard Zinn was fired from Spelman College, where he was chair of the history department, because of his support for students' civil rights activism. In 2005, he was invited back to give the commencement address. Here is the text of that speech.

Howard Zinn, "Against Discouragement" (May 15, 2005)

I am deeply honored to be invited back to Spelman after forty-two years. I would like to thank the faculty and trustees who voted to invite me, and especially your president, Dr. Beverly Tatum. And it is a special privilege to be here with Diahann Carroll and Virginia Davis Floyd.

But this is your day—the students graduating today. It's a happy day for you and your families. I know you have your own hopes for the future, so it may be a little presumptuous for me to tell you what hopes I have for you, but they are exactly the same ones that I have for my grandchildren.

My first hope is that you will not be too discouraged by the way the world looks at this moment. It is easy to be discouraged, because our nation is at war—still another war, war after war—and our government seems determined to expand its empire even if it costs the lives of tens of thousands of human beings. There is poverty in this country, and homelessness, and people without health care, and crowded classrooms, but our government, which has trillions of dollars to spend, is spending its wealth on war. There are a billion people in Africa, Asia, Latin America, and the Middle East who need clean water and medicine to deal with malaria and tuberculosis and AIDS, but our government, which has thousands of nuclear weapons, is experimenting with even more deadly nuclear weapons. Yes, it is easy to be discouraged by all that.

But let me tell you why, in spite of what I have just described, you must not be discouraged.

I want to remind you that, fifty years ago, racial segregation here in the South was entrenched as tightly as was apartheid in South Africa. The national government, even with liberal presidents like Kennedy and Johnson in office, was looking the other way while Black people were beaten and killed and denied the opportunity to vote. So Black people in the South decided they had to do something by themselves. They boycotted and sat in and picketed and demonstrated, and were beaten and jailed, and some were killed, but their cries for freedom were soon heard all over the nation and around the world, and the president and Congress finally did what they had previously failed to do—enforce the Fourteenth and Fifteenth Amendments to the Constitution. Many people had said: The South will never change. But it did change. It changed because ordinary people organized and took risks and challenged the system and would not give up. That's when democracy came alive.

I want to remind you also that when the war in Vietnam was going on, and young Americans were dying and coming home paralyzed, and our government was bombing the villages of Vietnam—bombing schools and hospitals and killing ordinary people in huge numbers—it looked hopeless to try to stop the war. But just as in the Southern movement, people began to protest and soon it caught on. It was a national movement. Soldiers were coming back and denouncing the war, and young people were refusing to join the military, and the war had to end.

The lesson of that history is that you must not despair, that if you are right, and you persist, things will change. The government may try to deceive the people, and the newspapers and television may do the same, but the truth has a way of coming out. The truth has a power greater than a hundred lies. I know you have practical things to do—to get jobs and get married and have children. You may become prosperous and be considered a success in the way our society defines success, by wealth and standing and prestige. But that is not enough for a good life.

Remember Tolstoy's story, "The Death of Ivan Ilyich." A man on his deathbed reflects on his life, how he has done everything right, obeyed the rules, become a judge, married, had children, and is looked upon as a success. Yet, in his last hours, he wonders why he feels a failure. After becoming a famous novelist, Tolstoy himself had decided that this was not enough, that he must speak out against the treatment of the Russian peasants, that he must write against war and militarism.

My hope is that whatever you do to make a good life for yourself— whether you become a teacher, or social worker, or business person, or lawyer, or poet, or scientist—you will devote part of your life to making this a better world for your children, for all children. My hope is that your generation will demand an end to war, that your generation will do something that has not yet been done in history and wipe out the national boundaries that separate us from other human beings on this earth.

Recently I saw a photo on the front page of the *New York Times*, which I cannot get out of my mind. It showed ordinary Americans sitting on chairs on the southern border of Arizona, facing Mexico. They were holding guns and they were looking for Mexicans who might be trying to cross the border into the United States. This was horrifying to me—the realization that, in this twenty-first century of what we call "civilization," we have carved up what we claim is one world into two hundred artificially created entities we call "nations" and are ready to kill anyone who crosses a boundary.

Is not nationalism—that devotion to a flag, an anthem, a boundary, so fierce it leads to murder—one of the great evils of our time, along with racism, along with religious hatred? These ways of thinking, cultivated, nurtured, indoctrinated from childhood on, have been useful to those in power, deadly for those out of power.

Here in the United States, we are brought up to believe that our nation is different from others, an exception in the world, uniquely moral; that we expand into other lands in order to bring civilization, liberty, democracy. But if you know some history you know that's not true. If you know some history, you know we massacred American Indians on this continent, invaded Mexico, sent armies into Cuba and the Philippines. We killed huge numbers of people, and we did not bring them democracy or liberty. We did not go into Vietnam to bring democracy; we did not invade Panama to stop the drug trade; we did not invade Afghanistan and Iraq to stop terrorism. Our aims were the aims of all the other empires of world history—more profit for corporations, more power for politicians.

The poets and artists among us seem to have a clearer understanding of the disease of nationalism. Perhaps the Black poets especially are less enthralled with the virtues of American "liberty" and "democracy," their people having enjoyed so little of it. The great African American poet Langston Hughes addressed his country as follows:

> You really haven't been a virgin for so long.
> It's ludicrous to keep up the pretext
> You've slept with all the big powers
> In military uniforms,
> And you've taken the sweet life
> Of all the little brown fellows
> Being one of the world's big vampires,
> Why don't you come on out and say so
> Like Japan, and England, and France,
> And all the other nymphomaniacs of power.

I am a veteran of the Second World War. That was considered a "good war," but I have come to the conclusion that war solves no fundamental problems and only leads to more wars. War poisons the minds of soldiers, leads them to kill and torture, and poisons the soul of the nation.

My hope is that your generation will demand that your children be brought up in a world without war. If we want a world in which the people of all countries are brothers and sisters, if the children all over the world are considered as our children, then war—in which children are always the greatest casualties—cannot be accepted as a way of solving problems.

I was on the faculty of Spelman College for seven years, from 1956 to 1963. It was a heartwarming time, because the friends we made in those years have remained our friends all these years. My wife Roslyn and I and our two children lived on campus. Sometimes when we went into town, white people would ask: How is it to be living in the Black community? It was hard to explain. But we knew this—that in downtown Atlanta, we felt as if we were in alien territory, and when we came back to the Spelman campus, we felt that we were at home.

Those years at Spelman were the most exciting of my life, the most educational certainly. I learned more from my students than they learned from me. Those were the years of the great movement in the South against racial segregation, and I became involved in that in Atlanta; in Albany, Georgia; in Selma, Alabama; in Hattiesburg, Mississippi; and Greenwood and Itta Bena and Jackson. I learned something about democracy: that it does not come from the government, from on high, it comes from people getting together and struggling for justice. I learned about race. I learned something that any intelligent person realizes at a certain point—that race is a manufactured thing, an artificial thing, and while race does matter (as Cornel West has written), it only matters because certain people want it to matter, just as nationalism is something artificial. I learned that what really matters is that all of us—of whatever so-called race and so-called nationality—are human beings and should cherish one another.

I was lucky to be at Spelman at a time when I could watch a marvelous transformation in my students, who were so polite, so quiet, and then suddenly they were leaving the campus and going into town, and sitting in, and being arrested, and then coming out of jail full of fire and rebellion. You can read all about that in Harry Lefever's book *Undaunted by the Fight*. One day Marian Wright (now Marian Wright Edelman), who was my student at Spelman, and was one of the first arrested in the Atlanta sit-ins, came to our house on campus to show us a petition she was about to put on the bulletin board of her dormitory. The heading on the petition epitomized the transformation taking place at Spelman College. Marian had written on top of the petition: "Young Ladies Who Can Picket, Please Sign Below."

My hope is that you will not be content just to be successful in the way that our society measures success; that you will not obey the rules, when the rules are unjust; that you will act out the courage that I know is in you. There are wonderful people, Black and white, who are models. I don't mean African Americans like Condoleezza Rice, or Colin Powell, or Clarence Thomas, who have become servants of the rich and powerful. I mean W. E. B. Du Bois and Martin Luther King and Malcolm X and Marian Wright Edelman, and James Baldwin and Josephine Baker and good white folk, too, who defied the Establishment to work for peace and justice.

Another of my students at Spelman, Alice Walker, who, like Marian, has remained our friend all these years, came from a tenant farmer's family in Eatonton, Georgia, and became a famous writer. In one of her first published poems, she wrote:

> It is true—
> I've always loved
> the daring
>> ones
> Like the black young
> man
> Who tried
> to crash
> All barriers
> at once,
>> wanted to
> swim
> At a white
> beach (in Alabama)
> Nude.

I am not suggesting you go that far, but you can help to break down barriers, of race certainly, but also of nationalism; that you do what you can—you don't have to do something heroic, just something, to join with millions of others who will just do something, because all of those somethings, at certain points in history, come together, and make the world better.

That marvelous African American writer Zora Neale Hurston, who wouldn't do what white people wanted her to do, who wouldn't do what Black people wanted her to do, who insisted on being herself, said that her mother advised her: Leap for the sun—you may not reach it, but at least you will get off the ground.

By being here today, you are already standing on your toes, ready to leap. My hope for you is a good life.

Chapter 1

Fighting War and Injustice in the New Millennium

• • •

9

In the wake of massive protests against corporate globalization in Seattle in 1999, the new millennium began with activists making advances on a number of fronts. But they quickly faced two major setbacks. In 2000, George W. Bush was installed as president by the Supreme Court. The court refused a full recount of the votes in the state of Florida, where enormous voting problems had occurred, and gave Bush the election. Then on September 11, 2001, in one of the most horrific events in US history, terrorists hijacked passenger planes and flew them into the Twin Towers of downtown New York, and into the Pentagon, killing close to three thousand people. Bush immediately declared a "war on terror," and invaded and bombed Afghanistan.

Soon after, the Bush administration began a propaganda campaign asserting that Iraq had "weapons of mass destruction" and was an imminent threat. When the other countries in the United Nations were not entirely persuaded, the Bush administration, which had declared its right to wage a "pre-emptive" war unilaterally, attacked Iraq in March 2003. A majority of people in the United States at first supported the war, but disillusionment grew as it was revealed that the Bush administration had misled the public about Iraq's weapons capability and its alleged links to the September 11 attacks. Families of people who had died on September 11 organized to protest the idea that war was the way to deal with terrorism. GIs in Iraq began to speak out against the war. By summer 2004, a national poll showed that a majority of the US public opposed the war.

• • •

The organization ADAPT (Americans Disabled for Attendant Programs Today) began as a part of the civil rights struggle to gain access to public transportation. It was also instrumental in forcing the government to pass the Americans with Disabilities Act of 1990. But the act hardly resolved all of the problems facing the disabled, including forced institutionalization, inadequate health care, continued lack of access to buildings, and workplace discrimination. Here Denver-based activist Anita Cameron describes a protest against builders who refused to comply with federal regulations for constructing accessible homes.

Anita Cameron, "And the Steps Came Tumbling Down—ADAPT's Battle with the HBA" (2000)

Thursday, March 2, as the Home Builders Association was having their Home Solutions 2000 Expo at Denver's Currigan Hall, ADAPT held its own Home Solutions Expo out front on its first of four days of protest against the Home Builders Association of Metropolitan Denver. ADAPT had tried to work with the HBA for about a year trying to get them to comply with the Fair Housing Law and build homes with access. Meetings, letters, and committee work were to no avail. It is apparent that the HBA does not want their members building homes with access. The HBA actually wants the Fair Housing Law repealed! They feel that access should be provided on an as-needed basis, and feel that single-family detached homes, townhomes, and condos should continue to be exempted from accessibility requirements. Something had to be done.

That is why about eighty ADAPT members from Colorado and Kansas were at Currigan Hall on that cold Thursday evening, sending the HBA a strong message. We had great exhibits of our own to show. There was an accessible Barbie doll house, complete with an elevator. We had two doorways—one accessible, and the other inaccessible, which we went through to demonstrate the usefulness of one, and uselessness of the other. There were pictures of the buildings that Atlantis had bought and remodeled for access, as well as educational materials on accessibility. We even had petitions and flyers with ADAPT's demands—30 percent of all new homes to be accessible, 30 percent of all new homes to be visitable, meaning a no-step entrance and an accessible bath on the first floor, and clear enforcement mechanisms in Colorado's Fair Housing Law. We marched, sang, and chanted, and several ADAPT members spoke of the need for accessible homes and told stories of being forced to buy inaccessible homes, or even move out of state due to the lack of accessible housing. The cops came around trying to get us to leave, but there wasn't much they could do since we were on the sidewalk for the most part.

Friday, we were back with more awesome ADAPT stuff, including some gorgeous Styrofoam steps that Pat [King], our wheelchair repair guy, had made. After Dawn [Russell]'s rousing speech, everyone had a chance to tear down the steps with a wooden mallet. Afterward, we formed a gauntlet in front of the steps to the front doors and passed out flyers. Later we made a human chain, chanting, "The People United Will Never Be Defeated."

On Saturday, back again, we saw that the cops had put up barricades, which we quickly removed and got down to the business of letting the HBA know that they weren't going to "turn us around." Joe Ehman, an ADAPT member who is on the AIA [Architectural Inclusion and Access] committee, did a cool mock-up of Roger Reinhardt, the HBA vice president who had insulted ADAPT in a meeting a few weeks earlier by calling us simple-minded. Several of us gave interviews with the press; some of us paid to get inside the exhibit to speak with the various builders and contractors about access and pass out a couple of flyers, if we could. Only one small exhibit out of hundreds that had anything remotely to do with access. This time, the cops sent out a trained negotiator to tell us the police wanted ADAPT to stay in this "area" that they had designated by the barricades. We told him that if he brought Roger Reinhardt out to speak to us, we would leave. A few minutes later, he brought Roger out, but he had nothing to offer us but the same tired old discriminatory solutions that ADAPT would not accept. We kept our word, though, and left with a warning from the police that if we came back tomorrow, and did not stay within the barricades, we would be arrested. Little did they know . . .

On Sunday, we swept in, meaning nothing but business. We quickly sped up the ramps and began blocking and handcuffing ourselves to doors. The cops were there, but not quick enough to stop us. They began yelling out warnings, and soon, the arrests began. When the dust cleared, seventeen ADAPT members were arrested and charged with blocking and refusing to obey a lawful order.

The Home Builders Association tour of homes was another target of protests in July. After ignoring ADAPT's call for an accessible house in the Tour of Homes, for which the home builders build a series of new homes, this showcase even became an action-packed showcase. Crawling into homes, picketing outside, and eventually committing civil disobedience, Colorado ADAPT members sent the home builders a message that access can no longer be blown off. Challenging the Home builders to stop ignoring access to housing for people with disabilities, ADAPT continues their drive to end the excuses.

• • •

Manning Marable (1950–2011) authored fifteen books, including *Malcolm X: A Life of Reinvention*, for which he won the Pulitzer Prize for History, and the classic study *How Capitalism Underdeveloped Black America*. He delivered this prescient speech at the opening plenary of the 2001 Socialist Scholars Conference in New York City, "Rebuilding the Left for a New Century."

Manning Marable, "Race, Class, and Globalization: The Global Struggle for Democracy" (April 13, 2001)

Two great strategic tasks are required of the social justice movements and especially from activists of color in the United States today. The first is to make the political connections between the interlocking dynamics of institutionalized oppression, such as the relationship between mass incarceration, the dismantling of nearly all public institutions like schools and public hospitals, and the declining standard of living for most working families. We need to ask ourselves hard questions, like why does America imprison two million human beings, and, on any given day, supervise 5.4 million people who are either in jail, in prison, on parole, on probation, or awaiting trial? What impact does mass incarceration, and related issues like the privatization of prisons and the growing use of prison labor by powerful corporations, have on organized labor?

The second task is to foster the strategic recognition among oppressed people that what we're up against inside the United States is actually a global problem. Inequality is not just "Made in America." Structural racism and economic underdevelopment are not confined solely to the United States. The current national debate over reparations must be viewed through a global lens—linked to discussions about the cancellation of third-world debt to the International Monetary Fund and to European and North American banks, and linked to struggles for Holocaust reparations owed by Swiss banks.

Looking first inside the US situation, we can observe that many of the most serious problems we find in our neighborhoods—underfunded schools, deteriorating public transportation, closed libraries, public health clinics shut—are caused by class inequality. There's a simple reason that millions of Americans feel that they are working harder and harder, yet falling further and further behind. Since the 1980s, there has been a vast transfer of wealth to the upper 2 percent of all US households and a declining real standard of living for millions of working-class and low-income people. . . .

The escalation of class inequality has had a direct impact on the growing numbers of poor and working people pushed into prisons. What are the economic costs for American society of the vast expansion of our prison industrial complex? According to criminal justice researcher David Barlow at the University of Wisconsin at Milwaukee, between 1980 and 2000, the combined expenditures of federal, state, and local governments on police have increased about 400 percent. Corrections expenditures for building new prisons, upgrading existing facilities, hiring more guards, and related costs increased approximately 1,000 percent. Although it currently costs about $70,000 to construct a typical prison cell and about $25,000 annually to supervise and maintain each prisoner, the United States is currently building 1,725 new prison beds per week.

The driving ideological and cultural force that rationalized and justifies mass incarceration is the white American public's stereotypical perceptions about race and crime. . . .

The greatest victims of these racialized processes of unequal justice, of course, are African American and Latino young people. In April 2000, utilizing national and state data compiled by the FBI, the Justice

Department and six leading foundations issued a comprehensive study that documented vast racial disparities at every level of the juvenile justice process. African Americans under age eighteen comprise 15 percent of their national age group, yet they currently represent 26 percent of all those who are arrested. After entering the criminal justice system, white and Black juveniles with the same records are treated in radically different ways. According to the Justice Department's study, among white youth offenders, 66 percent are referred to juvenile courts, while only 31 percent of the African American youth are taken there.

Blacks comprise 44 percent of those detained in juvenile jails, 46 percent of all those tried in adult criminal courts, as well as 58 percent of all juveniles who are warehoused in adult prisons. In practical terms, this means that for young African Americans who are arrested and charged with a crime, they are more than six times more likely to be assigned to prison than white youth offenders. For those young people who have never been to prison before, African Americans are nine times more likely than whites to be sentenced to juvenile prisons. For youths charged with drug offenses, Blacks are forty-eight times more likely than whites to be sentenced to juvenile prison. White youths charged with violent offenses are incarcerated on average for 193 days after trial; by contrast, African American youths are held 254 days, and Latino youths are incarcerated 305 days.

There are today over two million Americans currently incarcerated, and while African Americans and Latinos comprise the majority of that population, the reality of racism should not obscure the equally important class dimensions of mass incarceration. About one-third of all prisoners were unemployed at the time of their arrests. Only 55 percent of the prison population held full-time jobs. Seventy percent of all prisoners earned less than a $15,000 annual income in the year prior to their arrest, with 32 percent earning under $5,000. Two-thirds of all prisoners have less than a high school level of education, and few have marketable skills to be competitive for employment once they are released. In effect, our prison system has become the chief means of warehousing the unemployed, the unskilled, and the poor.

US progressives can no longer afford the false luxury of economic determinism and rigid definitions of what constitutes "class struggle." ... The concept of class struggle becomes abstract and meaningless unless it is interwoven with the real experiences oppressed people encounter in their sites of resistance around racial, gender, and sexuality issues. In the United States, what comprises the class struggle is in many respects most clearly expressed by the devastating reality of, and struggles to overturn, structural racism. Class struggle can never be "color-blind" in a rigidly color-coded society.

African Americans and Latinos comprise 25 percent of the US population, but represent nearly two-thirds of the two million Americans currently in prison. Statistically, Blacks account for only 14 percent of all illegal drug users. Yet we are 35 percent of all drug arrests, 55 percent of all drug convictions, and 75 percent of all prison admissions for violating drug laws. Are Blacks just unlucky in the courts, or is something else at work here?

White Americans in 1995 had an infant mortality rate of 6.3 deaths per 1,000 births. The African American infant mortality rate in 1995 was 15.1 deaths per 1,000 live births—a higher rate than in Taiwan, Portugal, Cuba, Chile, or Bulgaria. Are Black babies just unlucky, or are their deaths an inevitable consequence of inadequate health care, poor housing, and the destructive impacts of poverty, unemployment, and extreme stress on pregnant Black women?

In several recent studies, major insurance companies have been found to charge Black homeowners significantly higher rates than whites to insure homes of identical value. Supermarket chains routinely charge higher prices for most groceries in minority urban neighborhoods than in predominantly white upper-class suburbs. Are African American consumers in the marketplace just unlucky, or is it the logical result of "equity inequity," the racial profiling of credit and capital investment in our communities? "Luck" clearly has nothing to do with our oppression.

Just examine the evidence of structural racism today. In the state of New Jersey, Black motorists are almost five times more likely to be stopped by that state's highway patrol than are whites. On one section of the New Jersey Turnpike in 1999, investigators found that 34 percent of all police stops of vehicles involved either Latinos or Blacks. Only 1 percent of all stops led to vehicle searches. Guess who was searched? More than 75 percent of all motorists searched were either Latino or African American.

An April 2000 study found that Blacks in New York City are denied loan applications at banks at twice the rate of whites, even when they have identical incomes. Even African Americans who earn more than $60,000 a year have a higher rejection rate than whites who earn under $40,000 a year. The racial profiling on our highways, the crime of "DWB"—driving while Black—is mirrored in the economic redlining of the ghettoes and barrios of central cities, denying credit and capital to people of color.

In the Bronx in 1999, Amadou Diallo was shot at forty-one times by the New York police, not for what he said, not for what he did, but for what he looked like. Amadou Diallo was not murdered because of his behavior, but because of the racialized image of him in the heads of four white police officers. Haitian immigrant Abner Louima was raped by New York police officers in a Brooklyn precinct bathroom in 1998 because as white men they were absolutely convinced they could get away with it. . . .

Oppressed people now find themselves increasingly pitted against each other, as they scramble to seize the crumbs that have fallen off the national banquet table. All too often, we compete against each other at the margins, refusing to recognize that it was our labor power that built the table, the banquet hall, and the kitchen. Instead of asking just for access and opportunity, we should be collectively fighting for power.

Finally, we must also understand that the gross economic inequality here in the United States is actually part of a larger global system of labor exploitation. "Neoliberalism" is the name of the political philosophy that now defines the dynamics of global inequality. Neoliberal policies in governments have meant fiscal and monetary measures to reduce wages, eliminating social welfare and health care expenditures, privatizing everything from public schools to public utilities, and getting rid of environmental and safety standards to protect consumers. . . .

Since the 1999 protests against globalization in Seattle, more people have begun making the clear connections between unemployment at home and economic underdevelopment abroad; between our underfunded inner-city public schools and the widespread illiteracy and absence of formal education in third-world countries; between homeless shelters in our cities and the homeless masses of Calcutta, Rio de Janeiro, and Lagos; between struggling Black dockworkers in Charleston, South Carolina, fighting for jobs and justice, and exploited workers of color in the sweatshops of Latin America, Asia, and the Caribbean. . . .

We are indeed in an economic struggle for the world's future. We cannot defeat corporate capital by concentrating our energies in one nation alone. What is required is "globalization from below," the unity of the most exploited and marginalized, the working poor, and the homeless. The struggles of poultry workers are identical, whether they are African Americans in North Carolina or Guatemalans. Unity comes through active solidarity, from building bridges of international cooperation. We should always remember that in the global village, there are only sixty of them, and nine hundred and forty of us.

• • •

On January 19, 2000, five members of the International Longshoremen's Association in Charleston, South Carolina, were indicted after police attacked their picket line as they protested the unloading of a ship by nonunion labor. The workers—who came to be known as the Charleston Five—were placed under house arrest and faced years in prison. The union's president, Kenny Riley, spoke about the need for solidarity with the workers in Madison, Wisconsin, before the South Central Federation of Labor and the Coalition of Black Trade Unionists. The struggle ended in victory in November 2001.

Kenny Riley, "We Won't Rest Until They're Vindicated" (July 4, 2001)

I thought it was tough being Black in South Carolina, but it's much tougher being union. South Carolina has a lot going for itself as far as the beauty of the state—the mountains, the ocean. But when it comes down to real-life issues, there's a lot to be desired.

South Carolina is dead last in every category you want to be first in, and first in every category you want to be last in. Just recently, we were successful in taking down the Confederate flag from the State House dome. But many of us are still not satisfied, because it's still flying in a place of sovereignty right there in front of the State House.

The flag is just symbolic of some of the things that are going on in our state with regard to working people, poor people, Black people, and other minorities.

We had [Gary McClain], who about a year ago was arrested for speaking up and requesting union representation at his plant. He was coming into work one morning, and his truck was surrounded by police cars. He was dragged out at gunpoint, thrown up against the truck, searched, and arrested. He was injected with drugs against his will and then transported to a mental institution, where he stayed for two weeks.

We have a plant in South Carolina where workers are becoming sterile because of the amount of lead contamination in their bodies. We had one worker who died as a result.

Because the union was becoming active in that campaign to fight lead contamination, [management] had a decertification vote scheduled. Our local as well as some other locals went down and rallied around that little local down there, and we were able to save the union.

Four years ago, when I took office, we started to take a look at these sorts of issues, and we wanted to make a difference in our state.

When you decide to do the kind of things that really start to make a difference and get people listening to you, and you have an impact, it starts to make some people a little bit nervous. And you find yourself starting to become a target.

When the now-governor decided that he wanted to seek our union's endorsement back in 1998, we gave him that endorsement. We got a Democratic governor in South Carolina for the first time in twelve years.

And when that governor tried to reward labor for its efforts by nominating me to the State Ports Authority Board, that was a serious mistake on his part, according to the right-wingers.

They launched a grassroots alert to every single business in the state of South Carolina, asking them to defeat this nomination because "we cannot afford to send the wrong message to the world that South Carolina was open to labor unions."

South Carolina was marketing its workers as third-world—productive workers who earn 26 percent less than the national average. They were saying, "Don't take your corporations and businesses to South America or Mexico or the Philippines. Bring them to South Carolina—we've got third-world conditions right here."

Plants are closing down in union states, and guess where they're coming? South Carolina and North Carolina.

There's no better-paying blue-collar job in South Carolina than the longshoreman. Then [Nordana] brought in a workforce that took that standard back thirty years. They offered eight dollars an hour with no benefits whatsoever.

We put up informational pickets to tell people what was going on. We were starting to have a real impact. So about two weeks before a Nordana vessel came to port, I got a call from the state law enforcement division. They were expecting six hundred cops to crush that demonstration, which they did. And it looked like a war zone leading up to that night.

The police officers started it. They started beating on their shields and making racial slurs to our workers. We got out there and had reestablished calm when, for no apparent reason, I got struck in the head with a [police officer's] baton. I received twelve stitches that night. Nine men were arrested, thrown into jail, and charged with trespassing.

We got them out of jail about 3:00 p.m. the next day and went on with our business—with the sole pleasure that we were going to be out there the next time the ship came.

Then the state attorney general [Charlie Condon] came in. He over-stepped the solicitor's office and local authorities and instituted felony charges that carry up to five years in prison.

To make matters worse, he placed these guys under house arrest—the usual restrictions for a hardened criminal.

Now we've got to provide the defense for twenty-seven men who have been named in a [$1.5 million] civil lawsuit. Here again, if we don't raise the money to defend them, they'll have to go on their own personal resources. Then, who's going to go on the picket line, knowing that they're putting their families' resources in jeopardy?

We've just become too vocal and outspoken in a state where you're supposed to stay in your place.

As far as the work is concerned, the Port of Charleston is pretty much back to normal, because after five months, we had gotten our work back. When we signed a contract [with Nordana], they dropped all interest in any lawsuit that they had previously filed.

And that was due to the help of our brothers in the International Dockworkers Council. They went aboard [Nordana] vessels and handed them letters to let them know that if those ships come back to their ports and the ship wasn't loaded with our labor, they wouldn't work in the port of Valencia, in the port of Barcelona, and the port of Tenerife.

That's what happens when you have that kind of international sol-idarity. They got the message real quick. They intended to destroy the movement, but what this is doing is inspiring the movement.

The rally in South Carolina [on June 9] was just out of this world. It got the attention of some of the right people in the state. Our state attorney general has said that he isn't going to be dictated to by union "comrades" coming into our state. But some of the business people are getting the message.

Think about an International Day of Action [on the first day of the trial], and the impact that it could have on our state economy and the economy of the world on just one day.

We're living in a time of just-in-time delivery to our factories. So you're not only talking about ships being out, but trucking being idled, warehouses being idled, plants maybe becoming idled.

The [International Longshore and Warehouse Union] on the West Coast says that they're going out, and European ports are going to participate in this International Day of Action. Right now, the [shipping] lines are becoming very nervous.

We won't rest, we won't stop until every one of these guys has been vindicated and exonerated. And that's why we're out here toiling night and day, traveling around the country—around the world sometimes—to try to build support.

We appreciate all you're doing for us. And we're standing by ready to reciprocate whenever you may need us.

• • •

On the morning of September 11, 2001, more than three thousand people perished when hijackers flew two planes into the World Trade Center in New York City, another into the Pentagon in Washington, and a fourth that crashed, after passenger resistance disrupted the hijackers, in Pennsylvania. In the wake of the attacks, President Bush and many other politicians voiced loud calls for retaliation, and it was soon clear that Afghanistan would be their target, even though a majority of the hijackers were from Saudi Arabia, and even though there was no clear evidence linking the government of Afghanistan to the attacks. There was widespread grief in the United States and some calls for revenge, but a number of family members who lost loved ones on September 11 spoke out against this course of action. A group of them gathered together to form an organization called September Eleventh Families for Peaceful Tomorrows. Two of the first people to speak out against the use of September 11 as a pretext for war were Orlando and Phyllis Rodriguez. Their son, Gregory, then only thirty-one years old, was killed that day while working on the 103rd floor of One World Trade Center. The Rodriguezes sent this open letter to the *New York Times* and other newspapers four days after the attack.

Orlando Rodriguez and Phyllis Rodriguez, "Not in Our Son's Name" (September 15, 2001)

Our son Greg is among the many missing from the World Trade Center attack. Since we first heard the news, we have shared moments of grief, comfort, hope, despair, fond memories with his wife, the two families, our friends and neighbors, his loving colleagues at Cantor Fitzgerald/ eSpeed, and all the grieving families that daily meet at the Pierre Hotel.

We see our hurt and anger reflected among everybody we meet. We cannot pay attention to the daily flow of news about this disaster. But we read enough of the news to sense that our government is heading in the direction of violent revenge, with the prospect of sons, daughters, parents, friends in distant lands dying, suffering, and nursing further grievances against us. It is not the way to go. It will not avenge our son's death. Not in our son's name.

Our son died a victim of an inhuman ideology. Our actions should not serve the same purpose. Let us grieve. Let us reflect and pray. Let us think about a rational response that brings real peace and justice to our world. But let us not as a nation add to the inhumanity of our times.

• • •

In the aftermath of the September 11 attacks, the government passed a number of measures restricting civil liberties, most notoriously the USA PATRIOT Act (the Uniting and Strengthening America by Providing Appropriate Tools Required to Intercept and Obstruct Terrorism Act of 2001). Approved overwhelmingly by Democrats and Republicans in Congress, many of whom acknowledged not reading the bill, it gave the government broad powers to wiretap, arrest, and detain people suspected of having ties to terrorists. Although President Bush disavowed anti-Muslim prejudice, it was clear that Muslims, South Asians, and other people of color were being targeted. These same groups were also subjected to verbal abuse and physical assaults on the streets, in workplaces, and in their homes. Monami Maulik, then a community organizer of the Queens-based DRUM (Desis Rising Up and Moving), wrote this essay on organizing after

September 11 for *Manavi*, a South Asian newsletter based in New Brunswick, New Jersey.

Monami Maulik, "Organizing in Our Communities Post–September 11th" (2001)

Since the tragic loss of lives on September 11th, I find the need for organizing in my community is even greater in the coming years. But this is not because September 11th was or will be the only mass-scale loss of human lives. Since the Gulf War, thousands of Iraqi children have suffered or lost their life stemming from economic sanctions imposed on Iraq. Are the lives of these children any less valuable? In the midst of realizing the mass-scale inhumanity of war, grassroots organizing can be the source of hope for building a world centered on peace and social justice. What distinguishes organizing from services, advocacy, and relief work is that organizing seeks to change the root causes of social injustice as opposed to responding to its symptoms. But the question becomes whether we are organizing to challenge the systems that perpetuate oppressions or to maintain the statu quo?

The tragedies of September 11th continue to deeply hurt the South Asian and immigrant communities at large on multiple levels. First, we lost members of our community in the World Trade Center. Moreover, a number of those missing were low-wage and/or undocumented immigrant service workers whose families do not qualify for federal aid and benefits. Second, during this period of grief, we have had to endure wide-scale anti-Arab, anti–South Asian, and anti-Muslim hate crimes. Hundreds of incidents ranging from threats to beatings and worse have been reported around the country. And these are only the incidents that are reported. Moreover, this anti-immigrant backlash is currently being institutionalized via new, ill-conceived legislation, racial profiling, and the suspension of hard-won civil rights. Deportations and detentions have increased for Arab, South Asian, and/or Muslim immigrants.

Third, the war in Afghanistan has many concerned with the possible devastation of communities back home.

Given this negative climate nationally for immigrant communities, particularly for undocumented immigrants in the years to come, there is an urgent need now more than ever to organize to reverse the growing conservatism that can undo years of racial justice, feminist, anti-homophobic, and pro-working-class struggle. Our short-term objectives should be to rebuild security in our communities to end racial injustice and provide relief to affected, including undocumented, families. Our long-term objectives need to challenge systemic racism and xenophobia, organize to end biased impacts of harsh legislation, and to build the emerging peace movement with the leadership of immigrant and people of color communities, particularly those whose voices are historically marginalized, such as women, queer people, undocumented immigrants, and low-wage workers.

But as socially conscious South Asians, perhaps our biggest challenge in organizing our communities in the coming years will be to counter the growing conservative backlash we are witnessing. In the past several weeks, some South Asian organizations have followed the harmful path of uncritical patriotism that has fueled wars and passage of broadly punitive legislation. At the same time, conservative and communalist forces that have fueled anti-Muslim, anti-Dalit, and anti-Christian violence in India have been utilizing the climate to increase communal tensions.

This is the moment that we must ask ourselves what side of the fence do we stand on? The side that will perpetuate more oppression of Global South people around the world like that we have glimpsed so close to home on September 11th? Or the side that is for peace with justice both within the United States, for all people including immigrants, working and poor people, women, queer people, and people of color, and outside the United States, for the people of Afghanistan and other nations impacted by militarism? DRUM and the community organizing we practice stands for the latter.

• • •

Boots Riley is a communist rapper, filmmaker, and activist based in Oakland, California. His lyrics to the song "Heven Tonite," which appears on the album *Party Music* by The Coup, advocate that the feeling of contentment and wholeness that religion's focus on the afterlife gives to some can be better achieved by fighting for justice and power in the here and now.

Boots Riley, "Heven Tonite" (November 6, 2001)

Preacher man wanna save my soul
Don't nobody wanna save my life
People we done lost control
Let's make heaven tonite
Preacher man wanna save my soul
Don't nobody wanna save my life
People we done lost control
Let's make heaven tonite

Now as I sleep may the oxygen inflate my lungs
May my arteries and heart oscillate as one
If police come may I awake
escape
and run
In the morning may I have the sake to scrape the funds
And if I take the plunge
May it be said that I wasn't afraid to shake my tongue
Show the state was scum
Makin' sure that the callin' bell of fate was
rung
Cuz if they could they would
And probly tried to
Rape the sun
Someone said that this is just my body
Wait for the Afterparty

Where ain't no shut-off note
And every wallet there is knotty
Feet are on the asphalt
Dick in the dirt
This system take vickin' to work
Listen alert
Check out the introvert
In the corner with the rip in her skirt
Stomach pains so she grippin' her shirt
Ain't never had dinner
So she know she ain't gettin' dessert
Don't try to tell me it's her mission to hurt
I got faith in the people and they power to fight
We gon' make the struggle blossom
Like a flower to light
I know that we could take power tonight
Make 'em cower from might
And get emergency clearance from the tower for flight
I ain't sittin' in your pews less you helpin' me resist and refuse
Show me a list of your views
If you really love me
Help me tear this muthafucka up
Consider this my tithe for the offer cup

Preacher man wanna save my soul
Don't nobody wanna save my life
People we done lost control
Let's make heaven tonite
Preacher man wanna save my soul
Don't nobody wanna save my life
People we done lost control
Let's make heaven tonite

I used to think about infinity
And how my memory is finna be

Invisibly slim in that vicinity
And though the stars are magnificent
Whisky and the midnight sky can make you feel insignificant
The revolution in this tune and verse
Is a bid for my love to touch the universe
Strugglin' over wages and funds
Let the movement get contagious and run
Through the end when it's gauges and guns
And if we win in the ages to come
We'll have a chapter where the history pages are from
They won't never know our name or face
But feel our soul in free food they taste
Feel our passion when they heat they house
When they got power on the streets
And the police don't beat 'em about
Let's make health care centers on every block
Let's give everybody homes and a garden plot
Let's give all the schools books
Ten kids a class
And give 'em truth for their pencils and pads
Retail clerk—"love ballads" where you place
this song
Let's make heaven right here
Just in case they wrong

Preacher man wanna save my soul
Don't nobody wanna save my life
People we done lost control
Let's make heaven tonite
Preacher man wanna save my soul
Don't nobody wanna save my life
People we done lost control
Let's make heaven tonite

• • •

Rita Lasar, a founding member of September Eleventh Families for Peaceful Tomorrows, lost her brother Avrame ("Abe") Zelmanowitz on September 11, 2001. He could have escaped, but stayed behind to help a quadriplegic coworker, Ed Beyea. When President Bush mentioned Abe's heroic actions in a speech at the National Cathedral in Washington, DC, Lasar expressed outrage that her brother's sacrifice was being used to justify the invasion of Afghanistan. After the assault on Afghanistan began, Lasar joined a delegation to visit families who lost loved ones in the US assault and to witness first hand the impact of the bombings. Just before the one-year anniversary of her brother's death, she wrote this commentary.

Rita Lasar, "To Avoid Another September 11, United States Must Join the World" (September 5, 2002)

When the planes hit the World Trade Center last September 11, my brother Avrame, who was in the North Tower, refused to join the evacuation because he was concerned for the safety of his close friend and fellow worker, a quadriplegic who could not easily leave. So Avrame stayed, hoping that help would arrive. When it didn't, he and his life-long associate died together, along with thousands of other innocent New Yorkers.

That day changed my life. It changed the lives of all those who lost loved ones in the towers.

It changed the lives of the relatives of those on the flight that crashed in Pennsylvania. It changed the lives of hundreds of families who lost loved ones in the Pentagon. And, perhaps to a lesser extent, it changed the lives of most people living in the United States.

In the months after the disaster, I often heard how September 11 changed the world. But I don't think the attacks changed the world. And to the extent that Americans believe that September 11 changed the world, it is because they don't know much about the world in which they live.

I have never heard anyone say that the horrific massacres of 1994 in Rwanda—which took more than five hundred thousand lives—

changed the world. Nor have I ever been told that Indonesia's massacre of two hundred thousand East Timorese during a twenty-year span changed the world. I have not even heard that the daily loss of eight thousand souls in sub-Saharan Africa due to AIDS changed the world. Were these people less important than my dear brother?

Despite my own personal grief, I must conclude that, in light of these far greater calamities, September 11 did not change the world. What it did, in its own terrible way, was invite Americans to join the world, which is already a very troubled place. The question is whether we will accept that invitation.

Sadly, President Bush has no interest in doing so. He does not want the United States to join, or even cooperate with, the new International Criminal Court. He has also withdrawn the United States from the long-standing Anti-Ballistic Missile Treaty with Russia, even as India and Pakistan shudder on the verge of nuclear war. He refuses to support international agreements that would alleviate global warming, and he will not seek to ratify the treaty banning land mines, leaving the United States in the company of Iraq, Iran, and North Korea, Bush's "axis of evil."

And now the president is planning for a war against Iraq. Never mind that Iraq has committed no act of aggression against us that justifies war, that there has been no evidence linking Iraq to the September 11 attacks. Neither does the president seem to care that the world is opposed to an invasion of Iraq.

The international coalition that fought the first Gulf War was cemented by the principle that one country cannot invade another without provocation. Now the White House is poised to dismiss the coalition to launch an unprovoked invasion of Iraq.

An isolated United States is an unsafe country. As September 11 showed, there are no barricades high enough, no bombs big enough, no intelligence sophisticated enough to make America invulnerable.

We Americans have a choice.

We can conclude that we are alone, that we owe the world nothing and that the world owes us everything. This is the assumption implicit in Bush's "you're either with us or against us" stance, which is a shortsighted and self-centered philosophy. Or we can open our eyes and see the abundance of opportunities for making the planet a safer and more just place, by actively participating in international organizations, multilateral treaties, and protocols that advocate peace and social equality.

We can no longer afford a go-it-alone approach. If we want the world's help in getting at the roots of terrorism, we are going to have to start helping the rest of the world. We are going to have to comprehend that there are millions of people around the globe who understand all too well the horror of tragedies like September 11.

When that realization occurs, only then will we glimpse how September 11 changed the world.

• • •

Rachel Corrie, a student at The Evergreen State College and member of the Olympia Movement for Justice and Peace, traveled to the Gaza Strip in Palestine in early 2003 as a volunteer with the International Solidarity Movement (ISM). On March 16, 2003, she was killed when she was run over by a Caterpillar bulldozer while trying to block the destruction of a Palestinian home. The bulldozer was operated by two Israeli soldiers, but built in the United States. Neither the commander nor the driver could have failed to see Corrie, who was wearing a bright orange jacket and signaled her presence by waving her arms as the slow-moving bulldozer approached. After her death, Corrie's family and friends released copies of her moving letters describing the struggle against the US-backed occupation of Palestinian lands. Here is one of the letters she sent home.

Rachel Corrie, Letter from Palestine (February 7, 2003)

Hi friends and family, and others,

I have been in Palestine for two weeks and one hour now, and I still have very few words to describe what I see. It is most difficult for me to think about what's going on here when I sit down to write back to the United States. Something about the virtual portal into luxury. I don't know if many of the children here have ever existed without tank-shell holes in their walls and the towers of an occupying army surveying them constantly from the near horizons. I think, although I'm not entirely sure, that even the smallest of these children understand that life is not like this everywhere. An eight-year-old was shot and killed by an Israeli tank two days before I got here, and many of the children murmur his name to me—Ali—or point at the posters of him on the walls. The children also love to get me to practice my limited Arabic by asking me, "Kaif Sharon?" "Kaif Bush?" and they laugh when I say, "Bush majnoon," "Sharon majnoon" back in my limited Arabic. (How is Sharon? How is Bush? Bush is crazy. Sharon is crazy.) Of course this isn't quite what I believe, and some of the adults who have the English correct me: "Bush mish majnoon"—Bush is a businessman. Today I tried to learn to say, "Bush is a tool," but I don't think it translated quite right. But anyway, there are eight-year-olds here much more aware of the workings of the global power structure than I was just a few years ago.

Nevertheless, no amount of reading, attendance at conferences, documentary viewing and word of mouth could have prepared me for the reality of the situation here. You just can't imagine it unless you see it—and even then you are always well aware that your experience of it is not at all the reality: what with the difficulties the Israeli army would face if they shot an unarmed US citizen, and with the fact that I have money to buy water when the army destroys wells, and the fact, of course, that I have the option of leaving. Nobody in my family has been shot, driving in their car, by a rocket launcher from a tower at the end of a major street in my hometown. I have a home. I am allowed to go see the ocean. When I leave for school or work I can be relatively certain that there will not be a heavily armed soldier waiting halfway between Mud Bay and downtown Olympia at a checkpoint with the power to decide whether I can go about my business, and whether I can get home again when I'm done. As an afterthought to all this rambling, I am in Rafah: a city of about 140,000 people, approximately 60 percent of whom are refugees— many of whom are twice or three times refugees. Today, as I walked on top of the rubble where homes once stood, Egyptian soldiers called to me from the other side of the border, "Go! Go!" because a tank was coming. And then waving and "What's your name?" Something disturbing about this friendly curiosity. It reminded me of how much, to some degree, we are all kids curious about other kids. Egyptian kids shouting at strange women wandering into the path of tanks. Palestinian kids shot from the tanks when they peek out from behind walls to see what's going on. International kids standing in front of tanks with banners. Israeli kids in the tanks anonymously—occasionally shouting and also occasionally waving—many forced to be here, many just aggressive—shooting into the houses as we wander away.

I've been having trouble accessing news about the outside world here, but I hear an escalation of war on Iraq is inevitable. There is a great deal of concern here about the "reoccupation of Gaza." Gaza is reoccupied every day to various extents but I think the fear is that the tanks will enter all the streets and remain here instead of entering some of the streets and then withdrawing after some hours or days to observe and shoot from the edges of the communities. If people aren't already thinking about the consequences of this war for the people of the entire region then I hope you will start.

• • •

More than ten million people around the globe demonstrated against war on Iraq on February 15, 2003, in the largest coordinated international protest in human history. More than one million across the United States joined the demonstration, with some five hundred thousand coming out in New York, despite police edicts and barricades keeping people from marching. Two days after the demonstrations, a reporter wrote on the front page of the *New York Times*, "The fracturing of the Western alliance over Iraq and the huge antiwar demonstrations around the world this weekend are reminders that there may still be two superpowers on the planet: the United States and world public opinion. In his campaign to disarm Iraq, by war if necessary, President Bush appears to be eyeball to eyeball with a tenacious new adversary: millions of people who flooded the streets of New York and dozens of other world cities to say they are against war based on the evidence at hand." On February 15, dozens of activists addressed the demonstration in New York. Here is the speech of the actor and Black activist Danny Glover.

Danny Glover, Speech During the World Day of Protest Against the War (February 15, 2003)

We come here to reclaim our right as citizens of the world to peacefully protest! We must all stand as one voice to demand that the real users of weapons of mass destruction—our own country—dismantle them. That those who manufactured this climate of fear stop their lies, and heed the will of the people and the nation and the rest of the world to say no to war. That's why we come here!

We've overcome many obstacles in order to stand here this afternoon. For one, nature's unyielding and unforgiving reminder that this is February, and it's cold! But Mother Earth has smiled on us because she understands clearly that our voice must be heard. She knows that she is sick and only we, we the people, can heal her. She knows that.

We've overcome the obstacles that have been placed in our path on this journey by the city of New York and the state of New York and the federal institutions. Yet we've overcome our own fear to be here today because only with the acknowledgement of that fear do we demonstrate our real courage to stand up today. We stand here because our right to dissent and our right to be participants in a true democracy has been hijacked by an administration of liars and murderers who curse us because we stand in the way of their tyranny, who curse us because we stand in the way of their unholy and brutal agenda. An administration whose villainy and greed is insatiable. We stand at this threshold of history and say to them, "Not in our name! Not in our name!"

We stand here, and our stand is critical because inevitably in the future we'll have to challenge US policy in the Gulf of Guinea. We'll have to challenge US policy in other places and other oil-producing countries in Africa. We'll have to do that. We have to challenge the potential recolonization of Africa.

But we stand here because we stand on the shoulders of others who have come before us and who have called for peace and justice. Men and women like Fannie Lou Hamer, Harriet Tubman, Martin and Malcolm, W. E. B. Du Bois, Toussaint Louverture. Toussaint Louverture, who at forty-seven years old led an assault against slavery on the island of Haiti two hundred years ago. And we stand here, yes, we stand here, because Paul Robeson would be proud for us to stand here. And he would say to us that we are climbing Jacob's ladder! We are climbing Jacob's ladder! We are climbing Jacob's ladder!

• • •

In the past few decades, media institutions have become concentrated in fewer and fewer hands. In response, activists have sought ways to build independent media outlets that will not sacrifice truth for profit. Among the most important of these efforts is the television and radio program *Democracy Now!* The show, co-hosted by Juan González and Amy Goodman, features many stories largely excluded from the corporate media, and played an especially critical role in the period after September 11, when establishment media outlets rallied around the flag to support the "war on terror," including the invasion of Afghanistan in October 2001 and the subsequent build-up to invading and occupying Iraq in March 2003. Here journalist Amy Goodman discusses the importance of independent media soon after the invasion of Iraq.

Amy Goodman, "Independent Media in a Time of War" (April 21, 2003)

A *Newsday* reporter asked me the other day, am I opposed to "embedded" reporters? You know they say it in the mainstream media: "Our reporter embedded with the Marines."

Even Walter Cronkite the other day raised some objections. "What an unfortunate choice of words," he said. And he was critical. You rarely hear that criticism in the mainstream media, the working journalists today. What kind of critical reporting do we get?

It's this parade of retired generals that are on the network's payrolls. We now have people like Wesley Clark, General Wesley Clark, on the payroll of CNN, who is questioning their embedded reporter on the front line. He is questioning the reporter and the reporter is saying, "Yes, sir. No, sir."

This is journalism in America today. They have redefined "general news," and we have got to challenge that.

Why is it that if they have these retired generals on the payroll, they don't have peace activists and peace leaders also on the payroll? So let's have the same number of reporters embedded with Iraqi families, let's have reporters embedded in the peace movement all over the world, and maybe then we'll get some accurate picture of what's going on. Aaron Brown had some interesting comments. He said he admits CNN *NewsNight* came "a little late" to the peace movement. But once the war started, those voices are irrelevant because then the war is on.

We're seeing these romanticized pictures of soldiers against sunsets and the planes on those aircraft carriers that the embedded photographers are getting at the sunrise hour.

Think about Dan Rather the night that the bombs started falling on Iraq. He said, "Good morning, Baghdad." And Tom Brokaw said, "We don't want to destroy the infrastructure of Iraq, because we're going to own it in a few days." And Peter Jennings was interviewing Chris Cuomo, who is a reporter for ABC, and he was out on the street, where we were, Times Square, with thousands of people in the freezing rain who had come out to protest the war. They had all sorts of signs that were sopping wet, and people were trying to keep the umbrellas up and the police charged a part of the crowd. Jennings said to Cuomo, "What are they doing out there? What are they saying?" And he said, "Well, they have these signs that say 'No Blood for Oil,' but when you ask them what that means, they seem very confused. I don't think they know why they're out here." I guess they got caught in a traffic jam.

Why not have Peter Jennings, instead of asking someone who clearly doesn't understand why they're out there, invite one of them into the studio, and have a discussion like he does with the generals?

Why don't they also put doctors on the payroll? That way, you can have the general talking about the bomb that Lockheed Martin made, and the kind of plane that drops it, and whether it was precision guided or not. And then you can have the doctor talking about the effect of the bomb. Not for or against the war, just how a cluster bomb enters your skin and what it means when your foot is blown off, if you're lucky and you're not killed. So why not have doctors and generals at least? But this is just to show how low the media has gone.

You have not only Fox, but MSNBC and NBC—yes, owned by General Electric, one of the major nuclear weapons manufacturers in the world. MSNBC and NBC, as well as Fox, titling their coverage taking the name of what the Pentagon calls the invasion of Iraq: "Operation Iraqi Freedom." So that's what the Pentagon does, and you expect that. They research the most effective propagandistic name to call their operation. But for the media to name their coverage what the Pentagon calls it—every day seeing "Operation Iraqi Freedom"—you have to ask: if this were state media, how would it be any different?

Even now, the media has had to start reporting a little bit on the protest. But it's not those events that we're talking about. It's the daily drumbeat coverage, who's interviewed on the front pages of the *New York Times* and the *Washington Post*, who gets the headline stories in the network newscast, that matters. They're the ones shaping foreign policy.

Fairness and Accuracy in Reporting did a study. In the week leading up to General Colin Powell going to the Security Council to make his case for the invasion and the week afterward—this was the period where more than half of the people in this country were opposed to an invasion—they did a study of CBS *Evening News*, NBC *Nightly News*, ABC *World News Tonight*, and the *NewsHour with Jim Lehrer* on PBS. The four major newscasts. Two weeks. Three hundred and ninety-three interviews on war. Three were antiwar voices. Three of almost four hundred, and that included PBS. This has to be changed. It has to be challenged.

We are not the only ones—Pacifica Radio, National Public Radio stations—we are not the only ones that are using the public airwaves. They are, too. And they have to provide the diversity of opinion that fully expresses the debate and the anguish and the discussions that are going on all over this country. That is media serving a democratic society.

For a while in talks before the invasion, I've been saying as we see the full-page pictures of the target on Saddam Hussein's forehead that it would be more accurate to show the target on the forehead of a little Iraqi girl, because that's who dies in war. The overwhelming majority of people who die are innocent civilians. And then what happens on the first night of the invasion? Missile strikes a residential area in Baghdad. They say they think they've taken out Saddam Hussein. Independent reporter May Ying Welsh, who stayed there as the bombs fell, who you heard on *Democracy Now!* on a regular basis, went to the hospital right after that first attack, and there was a four-year-old girl critically injured from that missile attack and her mother critically injured and her mother's sister. That's who dies, that's who gets injured in war. . . .

Our mission is to make dissent commonplace in America, so you're not surprised when you're at work, someone walks over to the water cooler and makes a comment, and someone isn't shocked and says, "What's that all about?" but that it comes out of the finest tradition that built this country. People engaged in dissent. We have parallel worlds in this country. For some, it's the greatest democracy on earth. There is no question about that. But for others, immigrants now in detention facilities, they have no rights, not even to a lawyer. And we have to be there and we have to watch and we have to listen. We have to tell their stories until they can tell their own. That's why I think *Democracy Now!* is a very good model for the rest of the media, as is the Indy Media Center all over the country and the world. Built on almost nothing except the goodwill and the curiosity and the interest and the passion of people who are tired of seeing their friends and neighbors through a corporate lens, and particularly tired and afraid of the fact that that image is being projected all over the world. That is very dangerous. Dissent is what makes this country healthy. And the media has to fight for that, and we have to fight for an independent media.

• • •

Speaking at the same pulpit at New York City's Riverside Church from which Martin Luther King Jr. delivered his famous "Beyond Vietnam" speech in 1967, the writer Arundhati Roy challenged the US invasion of Iraq before the more than two thousand people who attended the event. She shared the stage that night with Howard Zinn.

Arundhati Roy, "Instant-Mix Imperial Democracy (Buy One, Get One Free)" (May 13, 2003)

We might as well accept the fact that there is no conventional military force that can successfully challenge the American war machine. Terrorist strikes only give the US government an opportunity that it is eagerly awaiting to further tighten its stranglehold. Within days of an attack you can bet that Patriot II would be passed. To argue against US military aggression by saying that it will increase the possibilities of terrorist strikes is futile. It's like threatening Brer Rabbit that you'll throw him into the bramble bush. Anybody who has read the document called The Project for the New American Century can attest to that. The government's suppression of the Congressional Committee Report on September 11th, which found that there was intelligence warning of the strikes that was ignored, also attests to the fact that, for all their posturing, the terrorists and the Bush regime might as well be working as a team. They both hold people responsible for the actions of their governments. They both believe in the doctrine of collective guilt and collective punishment. Their actions benefit each other greatly.

The US government has already displayed in no uncertain terms the range and extent of its capability for paranoid aggression. In human psychology, paranoid aggression is usually an indicator of nervous insecurity. It could be argued that it's no different in the case of the psychology of nations. Empire is paranoid because it has a soft underbelly.

Its homeland may be defended by border patrols and nuclear weapons, but its economy is strung out across the globe. Its economic outposts are exposed and vulnerable. Already the Internet is buzzing with elaborate lists of American and British government products and companies that should be boycotted. Apart from the usual targets—Coke, Pepsi, McDonald's—government agencies like USAID, the British DFID, British and American banks, Arthur Andersen, Merrill Lynch, American Express could find themselves under siege. These lists are being honed and refined by activists across the world. They could become a practical guide that directs the amorphous but growing fury in the world. Suddenly, the "inevitability" of the project of Corporate Globalization is beginning to seem more than a little evitable.

It would be naïve to imagine that we can directly confront Empire. Our strategy must be to isolate Empire's working parts and disable them one by one. No target is too small. No victory too insignificant. We could reverse the idea of the economic sanctions imposed on poor countries by Empire and its Allies. We could impose a regime of Peoples' Sanctions on every corporate house that has been awarded with a contract in postwar Iraq, just as activists in this country and around the world targeted institutions of apartheid. Each one of them should be named, exposed, and boycotted. Forced out of business. That could be our response to the Shock and Awe campaign. It would be a great beginning.

Another urgent challenge is to expose the corporate media for the boardroom bulletin that it really is. We need to create a universe of alternative information. We need to support independent media like *Democracy Now!*, *Alternative Radio*, South End Press.

The battle to reclaim democracy is going to be a difficult one. Our freedoms were not granted to us by any governments. They were wrested from them by us. And once we surrender them, the battle to retrieve them is called a revolution. It is a battle that must range across continents and countries. It must not acknowledge national boundaries, but, if it is to succeed, has to begin here. In America. The only institution more powerful than the US government is American civil society. The rest of us are subjects of slave nations. We are by no means powerless, but you have the power of proximity. You have access to the Imperial Palace and the Emperor's chambers. Empire's conquests are being carried out in your name, and you have the right to refuse. You could refuse to fight. Refuse to move those missiles from the warehouse to the dock. Refuse to wave that flag. Refuse the victory parade.

You have a rich tradition of resistance. You need only read Howard Zinn's *A People's History of the United States* to remind yourself of this.

Hundreds of thousands of you have survived the relentless propaganda you have been subjected to, and are actively fighting your own government. In the ultra-patriotic climate that prevails in the United States, that's as brave as any Iraqi or Afghan or Palestinian fighting for his or her homeland.

If you join the battle, not in your hundreds of thousands, but in your millions, you will be greeted joyously by the rest of the world. And you will see how beautiful it is to be gentle instead of brutal, safe instead of scared. Befriended instead of isolated. Loved instead of hated.

I hate to disagree with your president. Yours is by no means a great nation. But you could be a great people.

History is giving you the chance.

Seize the time.

• • •

In the preface to his classic book *Freedom Dreams: The Black Radical Imagination*, historian Robin D. G. Kelley asserted that for activists, there can be no separation between our theories of social change and our practice. Instead, we should view social movements as wellsprings of knowledge: by creating new possibilities for transcending our current, intolerable conditions, they allow us to imagine a world beyond the present.

Robin D. G. Kelley, *Freedom Dreams* (June 15, 2003)

My mother has a tendency to dream out loud. I think it has something to do with her regular morning meditation. In the quiet darkness of her bedroom her third eye opens onto a new world, a beautiful light-filled place as peaceful as her state of mind. She never had to utter a word to describe her inner peace; like morning sunlight, it radiated out to everyone in her presence. My mother knows this, which is why for the past two decades she has taken the name Ananda ("bliss"). Her other two eyes never let her forget where we lived. The cops, drug dealers, social workers, the rusty tapwater, roaches and rodents, the urine-scented hallways, and the piles of garbage were constant reminders that our world began and ended in a battered Harlem/Washington Heights tenement apartment on 157th and Amsterdam.

Yet she would not allow us to live as victims. Instead, we were a family of caretakers who inherited this earth. We were expected to help any living creature in need, even if that meant giving up our last piece of bread. . . . She wanted us to imagine a world free of patriarchy, a world where gender and sexual relations could be reconstructed. She wanted us to see the poetic and prophetic in the richness of our daily lives. She wanted us to visualize a more expansive, fluid, "cosmos-politan" definition of Blackness, to teach us that we are not merely inheritors of a culture but its makers.

So with her eyes wide open my mother dreamed and dreamed some more, describing what life could be for us. . . . She dreamed of land, a spacious house, fresh air, organic food, and endless meadows without boundaries, free of evil and violence, free of toxins and environmental hazards, free of poverty, racism, and sexism . . . just free. She never talked about how we might create such a world, nor had she connected her vision to any political ideology. But she convinced my siblings and me that change is possible and that we didn't have to be stuck there forever.

The idea that we could possibly go somewhere that exists only in our imaginations—that is, "nowhere"—is the classic definition of utopia. Call me utopian, but I inherited my mother's belief that the map to a new world is in the imagination, in what we see in our third eyes rather than in the desolation that surrounds us. . . .

What are today's young activists dreaming about? We know what they are fighting against, but what are they fighting for? These are crucial questions, for . . . the most powerful, visionary dreams of a new society don't come from little think tanks of smart people or out of the atomized, individualistic world of consumer capitalism where raging against the status quo is simply the hip thing to do. Revolutionary dreams erupt out of political engagement; collective social movements are incubators of new knowledge. While this may seem obvious, I am increasingly surrounded by well-meaning students who want to be activists but exhibit anxiety about doing intellectual work. They often differentiate the two, positioning activism and intellectual work as inherently incompatible. They speak of the "real" world as some concrete wilderness overrun with violence and despair, and the university as if it were some sanitized sanctuary distant from actual people's lives and struggles. At the other extreme, I have had students argue that the problems facing "real people" today can be solved by merely bridging the gap between our superior knowledge and people outside the ivy walls who simply do not have access to that knowledge. Unwitting advocates of a kind of "talented tenth" ideology of racial uplift, their stated goal is to "reach the people" with more "accessible" knowledge, to carry back to the 'hood the information folks need to liberate themselves. While it is heartening to see young people excited about learning and cognizant of the political implications of knowledge, it worries me when they believe that simply "droppin' science" on the people will generate new, liberatory social movements.

I am convinced that the opposite is true: Social movements generate new knowledge, new theories, new questions. The most radical ideas often grow out of a concrete intellectual engagement with the problems of aggrieved populations confronting systems of oppression. For example, the academic study of race has always been inextricably intertwined with political struggles. Just as imperialism, colonialism, and post-Reconstruction redemption politics created the intellectual ground for Social Darwinism and other manifestations of scientific racism, the struggle against racism generated cultural relativist and social constructionist scholarship on race. The great works by W. E. B. Du Bois, Franz Boas, Oliver Cox, and many others were invariably shaped by social movements as well as social crises such as the proliferation of lynching and the rise of fascism. Similarly, gender analysis was brought to us by the feminist movement, not simply by the individual genius of the Grimke sisters or Anna Julia Cooper, Simone de Beauvoir, or Audre Lorde. Thinking on gender and the possibility of transformation evolved largely in relationship to social struggle.

Progressive social movements do not simply produce statistics and narratives of oppression; rather, the best ones do what great poetry always does: transport us to another place, compel us to relive horrors and, more importantly, enable us to imagine a new society. We must remember that the conditions and the very existence of social movements enable participants to imagine something different, to realize that things need not always be this way. It is that imagination, that effort to see the future in the present, that I shall call "poetry" or "poetic knowledge." I take my lead from Aimé Césaire's great essay "Poetry and Knowledge," first published in 1945. Opening with the simple but provocative proposition that "poetic knowledge is born in the great silence of scientific knowledge," he then demonstrates why poetry is the only way to achieve the kind of knowledge we need to move beyond the world's crises. "What presides over the poem," he writes, "is not the most lucid intelligence, the sharpest sensibility or the subtlest feelings, but experience as a whole." This means everything, every history, every future, every dream, every life form from plant to animal, every creative impulse—plumbed from the depths of the unconscious. Poetry, therefore, is not what we simply recognize as the formal "poem," but a revolt: a scream in the night, an emancipation of language and old ways of thinking. Consider Césaire's third proposition regarding poetic knowledge: "Poetic knowledge is that in which man spatters the object with all of his mobilized riches."

In the poetics of struggle and lived experience, in the utterances of ordinary folk, in the cultural products of social movements, in the reflections of activists, we discover the many different cognitive maps of the future, of the world not yet born. Recovering the poetry of social movements, however, particularly the poetry that dreams of a new world, is not such an easy task. For obvious reasons, what we are against tends to take precedence over what we are for, which is always a more complicated and ambiguous matter. It is a testament to the legacies of oppression that opposition is so frequently contained, or that efforts to find "free spaces" for articulating or even realizing our dreams are so rare or marginalized. . . .

Another problem, of course, is that such dreaming is often suppressed and policed not only by our enemies but by leaders of social movements themselves. The utopian visions of male nationalists or so-called socialists often depend on the suppression of women, of youth, of gays and lesbians, of people of color. Desire can be crushed by so-called revolutionary ideology. I don't know how many times self-proclaimed leftists talk of universalizing "working-class culture," focusing only on what they think is uplifting and politically correct but never paying attention to, say, the ecstatic. I remember attending a conference in Vermont about the future of socialism, where a bunch of us got into a fight with an older generation of white leftists who proposed replacing retrograde "pop" music with the revolutionary "working-class" music of Phil Ochs, Woody Guthrie, preelectric Bob Dylan, and songs from the Spanish Civil War. And there I was, comically screaming at the top of my lungs, "No way! After the revolution, we STILL want Bootsy! That's right, we want Bootsy! We need the funk!"

• • •

Long before Colin Kaepernick made international headlines for taking a knee, Toni Smith-Thompson, the captain of the women's basketball team at Manhattanville College, turned her back during the playing of the National Anthem to protest the buildup toward the US war against Iraq in 2003. One year later, she spoke to author Dave Zirin about her reasons for taking this stand.

Toni Smith-Thompson, "If They Don't Want Politics in Sports Then They Need to Take the National Anthem Out" (March 12, 2004)

I'm from a mixed racial and ethnic background. . . . I was learning about the prison industrial complex and the wars against Native Americans. It made me very angry but I never paid attention to how this history played out on the court. I never thought about the National Anthem because I went to alternative schools. I never had to say the pledge. I never had to stand and salute anything before class. On the court I would just stand and let the time go by.

So last year I was talking with my boyfriend. His family's very politically active also. They don't ever stand for the National Anthem, and they're very clear on their position. We were talking about all the policies we dislike, and he said, "Why do you stand for the anthem at your games?" And I said, "Well I never really thought about it. I'm the captain of the team, and I have to be a team leader and a good role model." He said, "But that has nothing to do with who you are. This is not what you believe in. You just told me how much you dislike this flag and what it stands for. . . . This flag represents the slaughter of our ancestors," and I said, "You're absolutely right."

We had a game a few days later, and as we stood up to sing the National Anthem I said no. I thought, "No, this is not more important than my beliefs. This [ritual] has nothing to do with who I am." I didn't tell anyone. I didn't really think of it as something that should be made public. It went unnoticed even by my teammates and family. Then one day the president of the school came up to me and said, "If anyone gives you any trouble, send them to me." I said, "All right, but it's not an issue." And then he told me that there was this huge uproar, that there were several parents of the team who were furious and were threatening to go to the NCAA.

A few of the parents went to the president of the school. The next thing that happened was one of my teammates called my dorm room and said, "You have to look on instant messenger. You have to see what our teammates are writing about you." There was this back and forth IM battle saying, "I can't believe Toni's doing this, what kind of a team captain is she?" All of this was done behind my back. No one asked me why, no one confronted me about it. The next day in the locker room I confronted the girl who began the IM discussion and that turned into an explosion within the team.

We were playing a game at St. Joseph's. Their assistant coach had just been sent over to serve. They were angry. Nothing really came about it at that game, but the next team we were scheduled to play was the Merchant

Marine Academy. People at St. Joseph's called and warned them about me. In addition to that a news reporter got ahold of it. The Merchant Marine Academy was the worst team in the league. They were something like 0 and 25. They don't have any fans, and let me tell you, this gym was packed. You can't even imagine what it was like. They had cadets lined up on the sidelines, each with their own flag that was about seven feet tall. Every single person in the stand was in uniform, with their own flag. They were shouting things at me—obscenities, curses, you name it. It was unbelievable. It was so bad that even the teammates who hated what I was doing had to put themselves in my place and defend my position. It came down to, "You're not going to disrespect my team." That news reporter captured how angry everyone was at that game, and at the next game the AP was there and the story took off.

Half of my teammates were completely against me. Completely against everything I was doing. There were four girls who were very against me and tried to make my life a living hell. The one who started the instant messenger drama sent a petition around the school, saying, "Sign this to demand that Toni Smith return all her financial aid, because she is disrespecting our school." What's the point in that? We were teammates in the middle of the season, one of the best seasons our school has ever had, and it just didn't make any sense. They talked to reporters when we were asked not to by the coach and by the president. When I finally decided to talk to the press it was because my teammates were speaking out without permission. It got to the point where either they're going to have lies out there or I speak up.

[D]uring World War II, when America decided that we needed to show our superiority to other countries, they implemented the National Anthem before sporting events and when they did that they put politics in the middle of sports. The question is not why did I choose to turn my back on the flag. It's why do we have to do this at basketball games? If they don't want politics in sports then they need to take the National Anthem out because that is inherently political.

I was aware of Muhammad Ali, and I was aware of Tommie Smith and John Carlos. But I didn't connect myself to them. I saw one article that had my picture right next to theirs, and I was completely blown away. That was the first time I connected the two. I didn't feel in any way like it was on the same scale. I will say that like [Smith and Carlos] the point was not to put myself forward but to get people to talk about these issues. Last year people didn't want to acknowledge that we were going to war. They wanted to hide it. It can become really easy to not acknowledge the fact that we are killing people in other countries because it's not here. A big issue I had with September 11th was that was the first event since Pearl Harbor where there was an attack of such magnitude on this country. And you could see this all over the place, people going, "Never forget, never forget 9/11." 9/11 was terrible, but that level of destruction is every single day for other people in other countries. I think that it is unbelievably arrogant to say, "Now we can do whatever we want." It has sent the message that "we are better than you. We are superior human beings to everyone else in the world." It's really appalling.

I got one letter in the mail that was a death threat. It said, "I've seen you, I've been close enough to touch you, I'm a disabled veteran, I'll find you again, you won't be able to disrespect my country anymore, I'll make sure that it's an end for you." That scared me. I was a little bit frightened after that, and I was more cautious about where I went for a little while.

But the way I felt at the time was that there were many protests during the Vietnam War that outraged people. Then when circumstances came to light about how illegal the war was and how many killed and died senselessly, people said, "Oh, now I get it." I think that's what's happening now. There are stories now that have been done about me—because it's the end of the year and people are recapping—and the tone is more supportive. There are a lot of people who were angry at the time, saying, "How dare you not support my son, he's going off to war." And now either their son has died or their son is still over there, and they realize that this war is bogus and they don't have any health insurance or have to wait online for food. Now they say, "Oh, I get it. Now I get what you were trying to say. And now my son is over there, my daughter's over there, and I can't help when I could have helped before." So I think a lot of that has come to light, as we knew it would, because they couldn't keep it hidden forever. If that validates it for other people then I'm glad. They don't have to agree with me but at least they can understand why.

I'm really big on not living with regrets. There are always things in your life you're not going to be happy with, choices you've made that you're not pleased with, but every choice you make you make it for a reason and you might not know what that reason is until later, and it might hurt you at the time, but eventually it pans out and it shapes who you are as a person. Anything that I would have done differently would have altered who I am now.

• • •

After the US government, ignoring protests and world opinion, launched the attack on Iraq on March 20, 2003, some of the most important voices of dissent were soldiers and their families. Where, they asked, was the threatening Iraq arsenal of the weapons of mass destruction that allegedly was the cause of the war? None could be found. In a stage-managed event, President Bush declared an end to "major combat operations" on May 1, but deaths of soldiers continued to mount, soon exceeding those who had died during the invasion. US soldiers came to be seen not as liberators, but as an occupying army. In August 2003, while serving in Mosul, Iraq, Camilo Mejía was the first US soldier who served in Iraq to go public with his refusal to continue fighting George Bush's war. A military court forced Mejía to serve seven months' confinement for his decision. After his release, Mejía dedicated himself to building the antiwar movement and organizing counter-recruitment efforts. In July 2005, he gave this speech in Chicago.

Camilo Mejía, "I Pledge My Allegiance to the Poor and Oppressed" (July 3, 2005)

Those of us in the GI antiwar movement, whether we know it or not, face a powerful enemy. When I say antiwar movement, it is assumed that I mean the war in Iraq, but the war in Iraq should be seen as part of something far bigger and far more devastating.

The powerful enemy is the corporations that finance congressional and presidential campaigns, the corporations in control of our privatized government. This is the same enemy that charges the American people a billion dollars per week to send their children to fight a criminal war against the children of Iraq.

Our struggle is the struggle against those who say "support our troops" while turning their backs on returning veterans. Support the troops by waving flags and slapping yellow ribbons on the bumpers of SUVs. Support the troops while they are killing their brothers and sisters in Iraq— meanwhile, hiding the flag-draped coffins some of them are coming home in, and keeping the horror of their wounds out of the public's view.

We struggle against those who create terrorism through the spread of hunger and poverty so they can spread war and reap the profits. We struggle against those who invade and occupy a land for its resources, and then call its people terrorists for refusing to be conquered.

No longer able to rely on the rhetoric of the Cold War, the corporate warmongers need this global terrorism to justify the spread of its empire. So the war we oppose is the war waged by corporations on the billions of people around the world who live in utter misery.

The so-called American Dream, to many poor people, is tied to the obligation to fight in a war for corporate domination. They call it an all-volunteer army. But to them, I say: Show me a society where everyone has access to healthcare. Show me a society where everyone has access to an education. Show me a society where everyone has access to decent wages, where everyone lives a dignified life, and then I will show you an all-volunteer army.

Poverty and oppression around the world provide the building blocks for an empire. Poverty and oppression at home provide the building blocks to build an imperial army. In saying no to that imperial army—in refusing to fight an imperial war against our brothers and sisters of Iraq—I pledge my allegiance to the poor and oppressed of the world. In saying no to an imperial army and in refusing to fight an imperial war against our brothers and sisters of Iraq, I pledge my allegiance to the working class of the world. Their struggle—which is my struggle—is your struggle too.

• • •

Cindy Sheehan's son Casey was killed in action in Iraq on April 4, 2004. This is a speech she delivered in August 2005 at the Veterans for Peace convention in Dallas, Texas, just before heading down to camp outside of Bush's vacation home in Crawford, Texas. President Bush refused to meet with her, but Sheehan helped galvanize sentiment against the occupation of Iraq.

Cindy Sheehan, "It's Time the Antiwar Choir Started Singing" (August 5, 2005)

I said to my son not to go. I said, "You know it's wrong. You know you're going over there. You know your unit might have to kill innocent people, you know you might die." And he says, "My buddies are going. If I don't go, my buddies will be in danger."

Thirty of our bravest young men have already died this month, and it's only the fifth of August. And the tragedy of the Marines in Ohio is awful.

But do you think George Bush will interrupt his vacation and go visit the families of the twenty Marines that have died in Ohio this week? No, because he doesn't care, he doesn't have a heart. That's not enough to stop his little "playing cowboy" game in Crawford for five weeks.

So, as you can imagine, every day, the grieving parents that have lost—lost, I don't like to use that word—[the parents] whose child was murdered—it's extremely difficult, you can't even get a small scab on our wound, because every day it's ripped open.

So anyway, when that filth-spewer and warmonger George Bush was speaking after the tragedy of the Marines in Ohio, he said a couple things that outraged me—seriously outraged me. George Bush was talking and he never mentioned the terrible incident of those Marines, but he did say that the families of the ones who have been killed can rest assured that their loved ones died for a "noble cause."

He also said—he says this often, and this really drives me crazy—he said that we have to stay in Iraq and complete the mission, to honor the sacrifices of the ones who have fallen.

And I say, why should I want one more mother to go through what

I've gone through because my son is dead? You know what, the only way he can honor my son's sacrifice is to bring the rest of our troops home. To make my son's death count for peace and love, and not war and hatred like [Bush] stands for.

I don't want him using my son's death or my family's sacrifice to continue the killing. I don't want him to exploit the honor of my son and others to continue the killing.

And I just had this brainstorm: I'm going to Crawford. I don't know where Crawford is. But I don't care, I'm going. And I'm going to go, and I'm going to tell them, "You get that evil maniac out here, because a Gold Star Mother, somebody whose son's blood is on his hands, has questions for him."

And I'm going to say, "Okay, listen here, George. Number one: I demand, every time you get up and spew the filth that you're continuing the killing in Iraq to honor my son's sacrifice, honoring the fallen heroes by continuing the mission, you say, 'except Casey Sheehan.'"

You don't have my permission to use my son's name.

And I'm going to say, "And you tell me, what the noble cause is that my son died for." And if he even starts to say "freedom and democracy," I'm going to say, "bullshit." You tell me the truth. You tell me that my son died for oil. You tell me that my son died to make your friends rich. You tell me my son died so you can spread the cancer of Pax Americana, imperialism, in the Middle East.

You get America out of Iraq, you get Israel out of Palestine, and you'll stop the terrorism.

And if you think I won't say "bullshit" to the president, then you're wrong, because I'll say what's on my mind.

So anyway, I'm going to go to Crawford tomorrow, and I'm going to say, "Get George here." And if they say, "No, he's not coming out." Then I'm going to say, "OK, I'm going to put up my tent here and I'm staying until he comes and talks to me."

Another thing that I'm doing is—my son was killed in 2004, so I'm not paying my taxes for 2004. And I tell everybody that. If I get a letter from the IRS, I'm going to say, "You killed my son for this. I don't owe you anything."

I live in Vacaville, California. If you can find me there, come and get me and put me on trial.

It's up to us, as moral people, to break immoral laws, and resist. As soon as the leaders of a country lie to you, they have no authority over you. These maniacs have no authority over us. And they might be able to put our bodies in prison, but they can't put our spirits in prison.

When I was growing up, it was "communists." Now it's "terrorists." So you always have to have somebody that's our enemy to be afraid of, so the war machine can build more bombs, and guns, and bullets, and everything.

But I do see hope. I see hope in this country. Fifty-eight percent of the American public are with us. We're preaching to the choir, but not everybody in the choir is singing. If all of the 58 percent started singing, this war would end.

Chapter 2

The Struggle for Justice in the Aftermath of Hurricane Katrina

Patricia Thompson, Kalamu Ya Salaam, and Father Jerome Ledoux, *Voices from the Storm* (Fall 2005)
Howard Zinn, "Don't Despair about the Supreme Court" (October 21, 2005)
Elvira Arellano, Statement of Elvira Arellano in Sanctuary (August 15, 2006)
Evann Orleck-Jetter, Statement on Marriage Equality (March 18, 2009)
Moustafa Bayoumi, "My Arab Problem" (October 24, 2010)
Gustavo Madrigal-Piña, "Undocumented and Unafraid" (August 22, 2011)
Troy Davis, Letter Given to His Lawyers Before His Execution (September 21, 2011)

● ● ●

One of the darkest moments in the Bush II presidency came when Hurricane Katrina made landfall in New Orleans and the Gulf Coast in August 2005, leading to massive destruction and loss of life, especially for poor Black and Brown people. The government's inaction spoke volumes.

The anger over Katrina and antiwar sentiment helped propel an Illinois senator named Barack Obama to the presidency in November 2008. Obama became the first Black president in US history, in part because he had voted against the war in Iraq. Obama's 2008 election prompted mainstream commentators to speculate that the United States was now a "post-racial" society. But Obama continued and even expanded many of the extraordinary war powers claimed by Bush II, and racial and economic divides continued to grow. Social problems of health, housing, joblessness, and the lack of equality for gays and lesbians and other oppressed groups persisted. Against that backdrop, new movements emerged.

• • •

When Hurricane Katrina devastated New Orleans and the Gulf Coast in August 2005, millions watched in anger as the national government failed to help people trapped in the floodwaters of the Mississippi Delta. Katrina devastated the gulf coasts of Louisiana and Mississippi, destroying whole neighborhoods and causing thousands of deaths. The US government was shamefully slow to give help. It became clear that people's urgent needs were being neglected because the government did not care about its impact on the most vulnerable communities, particularly poor people of color. Here, three survivors of the disaster speak out about their experiences in the aftermath of the storm.

Patricia Thompson, Kalamu Ya Salaam, and Father Jerome Ledoux, *Voices from the Storm* (Fall 2005)

PATRICIA THOMPSON

When Hurricane Katrina hit, I was in a state of desperation. I was doing work for my church for two hundred dollars a month. We were getting paid once a month, the last day of the month. The hurricane hit August 29.

I know you've heard all of this foolishness about the people that just did not want to leave: those are bald-faced lies. I had one dollar in my pocket. I did not have a vehicle, so there was no way for us to get out. It was two people living in my house when the storm hit, me and my youngest daughter.

My son went with his girlfriend and her family, and my second-oldest daughter and her kids left with her job—she's a supervisor at a convalescent home. But my oldest daughter, my third-oldest daughter, my fourth-oldest daughter, and my baby daughter were also stuck in New Orleans.

We was hearing on the news and everything that the hurricane was coming. I was watching the meteorologist on the news, listening at the radio and everything. I remember seeing one particular weatherman who had a very, very worried look on his face, and he was explaining that what we were about to encounter we were not ready for. And if I could understand what the man was saying, then I knew the mayor, I knew the governor, and I knew the president knew what time it was. We got a mandatory evacuation order less than twenty-four hours before the storm made landfall. Less than twenty-four hours.

I know the race card was being played. I don't know exactly what percentage of the city had evacuated, but there were masses and masses and masses of Black folk left in this city. There were some whites, but I guarantee that for every white person they had in New Orleans, they had a few hundred Blacks.

So anyway, once we got the mandatory evacuation order, right now you're like crazy, you don't know what to do, you can't evacuate, you don't have any way. So now this leaves desperation. People are trying to get water, people are trying to get food. People are trying to steal cars, whatever they can do to help themselves and get out of that city. . . .

I had two other sisters and a son that lived on the other side of the Mississippi River bridge. Over across the river is Jefferson Parish. Where we live was Orleans Parish. Jefferson Parish was nowhere near in the condition that Orleans was. It's a better community to live in. It's got better drainage systems, and everything is better across the river. So in New Orleans, looking like a war-torn country, if you could just get across the bridge, you could get to safety, and I had family members over there. . . .

Before we were rescued, we attempted to try to cross the bridge. This is where we met with the resistance. We were told to turn around or risk being shot. The police! The police told us this. That's the way we were treated trying to cross that bridge. . . .

[Y]ou see, the sheriff, Mr. Harry Lee—and I say Mr. Harry Lee because I can't even tell you what I'd like to call him because he's an egotistical, racist somebody—he definitely has no love for Blacks. It's just blatant. The politicians have been doing what they want to do and getting away with it for so long now, it's the normal thing to do. . . .

They had police all over the place. They had military all over the place. FEMA was all over the place. And nobody was doing anything to help us. They were just there to keep us in line. They boxed us in that city. They wouldn't let us out. They said if we tried to get out, they'd shoot to kill.

Let me tell you something. That is nothing new for New Orleans. The police been doing that. And I hate to say it, but the Black police are just as bad as the whites. That's the way I read it, anyway.

KALAMU YA SALAAM

The troops did not come into the city until Friday afternoon. I figured out what the problem was. They waited until they had enough troops so they could come in and apply the whole "shock and awe" routine and take the city back. They needed thirty thousand armed troops with weapons at the ready. . . .

Within two days after the troops arrived, the Superdome and the Convention Center were all cleared out. People were forced out by gunpoint. People think that the rescue mission was not a military mission, but this was a military operation.

FATHER JEROME LEDOUX

The police were omnipresent, but not in places like the Lower Nine. . . .

I was very angry. See, at any given moment, you had a staging area possible on the West Bank. There was no water there. How many buses do we have in the United States? How many hundreds? Let's say the presidential family and retinue just happen to be in the area and got trapped into such an environment, I bet the whole hacienda and the whole ranch that it would not have been even close to the same. They would've gone beyond hell and high water, literally, to change things. They have sea planes, they have all kinds of hovercraft and sea craft, amphibious craft. Everyone would have been gone from New Orleans.

PATRICIA THOMPSON

But I thank God for one thing. Mr. Bush, he's got a soul and he's gotta pay. I wouldn't want to be him for nothing in the world. He's got a soul. It ain't the right kind, but he's got one to be accountable for. This man knew well what we were in for.

● ● ●

In this essay, people's historian Howard Zinn argued we should never depend on the Supreme Court to defend the rights of poor people, women, people of color, or dissenters.

Howard Zinn, "Don't Despair about the Supreme Court" (October 21, 2005)

John Roberts sailed through his confirmation hearings as the new Chief Justice of the Supreme Court, with enthusiastic Republican support, and a few weak mutterings of opposition by the Democrats. Then, after the far right deemed Harriet Miers insouciantly doctrinaire, Bush nominated arch conservative Samuel Alito to replace Sandra Day O'Connor. This has caused a certain consternation among people we affectionately term "the left."

I can understand that sinking feeling. Even listening to pieces of Roberts's confirmation hearings was enough to induce despair: the joking with the candidate, the obvious signs that, whether Democrats or Republicans, these are all members of the same exclusive club.

Roberts's proper "credentials," his "nice guy" demeanor, his insistence to the Judiciary Committee that he is not an "ideologue" (can you imagine anyone, even Robert Bork or Dick Cheney, admitting that he is an "ideologue"?) were clearly more important than his views on equality, justice, the rights of defendants, the war powers of the president.

At one point in the hearings, the *New York Times* reported, Roberts "summed up his philosophy." He had been asked, "Are you going to be on the side of the little guy?" (Would any candidate admit that he was on the side of "the big guy"? Presumably serious "hearings" bring out idiot questions.)

Roberts replied: "If the Constitution says that the little guy should win, the little guy's going to win in court before me. But if the Constitution says that the big guy should win, well, then the big guy's going to win, because my obligation is to the Constitution."

If the Constitution is the holy test, then a justice should abide by its provision in Article VI that not only the Constitution itself but "all Treaties made, or which shall be made, under the Authority of the United States, shall be the supreme Law of the Land." This includes the Geneva Convention of 1949, which the United States signed, and which insists that prisoners of war must be granted the rights of due process.

A district court judge in 2004 ruled that the detainees held in Guantanamo for years without trial were protected by the Geneva Convention and deserved due process. Roberts and two colleagues on the Court of Appeals overruled this.

There is enormous hypocrisy surrounding the pious veneration of the Constitution and "the rule of law." The Constitution, like the Bible, is infinitely flexible and is used to serve the political needs of the moment. When the country was in economic crisis and turmoil in the thirties and capitalism needed to be saved from the anger of the poor and hungry and unemployed, the Supreme Court was willing to stretch to infinity the constitutional right of Congress to regulate interstate commerce. It decided that the national government, desperate to regulate farm production, could tell a family farmer what to grow on his tiny piece of land.

When the Constitution gets in the way of a war, it is ignored. When the Supreme Court was faced, during Vietnam, with a suit by soldiers refusing to go, claiming that there had been no declaration of war by Congress, as the Constitution required, the soldiers could not get four Supreme Court justices to agree to even hear the case. When, during World War I, Congress ignored the First Amendment's right to free speech by passing legislation to prohibit criticism of the war, the imprisonment of dissenters under this law was upheld unanimously by the Supreme Court, which included two presumably liberal and learned justices: Oliver Wendell Holmes and Louis Brandeis.

It would be naive to depend on the Supreme Court to defend the rights of poor people, women, people of color, dissenters of all kinds. Those rights only come alive when citizens organize, protest, demonstrate, strike, boycott, rebel, and violate the law in order to uphold justice.

The distinction between law and justice is ignored by all those senators—Democrats and Republicans—who solemnly invoke as their highest concern "the rule of law." The law can be just; it can be unjust. It does not deserve to inherit the ultimate authority of the divine right of the king.

The Constitution gave no rights to working people: no right to work less than twelve hours a day, no right to a living wage, no right to safe working conditions. Workers had to organize; go on strike; defy the law, the courts, the police; create a great movement which won the eight-hour day, and caused such commotion that Congress was forced to pass a minimum-wage law, and Social Security, and unemployment insurance.

The Brown decision on school desegregation did not come from a sudden realization of the Supreme Court that this is what the Fourteenth Amendment called for. After all, it was the same Fourteenth Amendment that had been cited in the Plessy case upholding racial segregation. It was the initiative of brave families in the South—along with the fear by the government, obsessed with the Cold War, that it was losing the hearts and minds of colored people all over the world—that brought a sudden enlightenment to the Court.

The Supreme Court in 1883 had interpreted the Fourteenth Amendment so that nongovernmental institutions—hotels, restaurants, etc.—could bar Black people. But after the sit-ins and arrests of thousands of Black people in the South in the early sixties, the right to public accommodations was quietly given constitutional sanction in 1964 by the Court. It now interpreted the interstate commerce clause, whose wording had not changed since 1787, to mean that places of public accommodation could be regulated by congressional action and be prohibited from discriminating.

Soon this would include barbershops, and I suggest it takes an ingenious interpretation to include barbershops in interstate commerce.

The right of a woman to an abortion did not depend on the Supreme Court decision in *Roe v. Wade*. It was won before that decision, all over the country, by grassroots agitation that forced states to recognize the right. If the American people, who by a great majority favor that right, insist on it, act on it, no Supreme Court decision can take it away.

The rights of working people, of women, of Black people have not depended on decisions of the courts. Like the other branches of the political system, the courts have recognized these rights only after citizens have engaged in direct action powerful enough to win these rights for themselves.

This is not to say that we should ignore the courts or the electoral campaigns. It can be useful to get one person rather than another on the Supreme Court, or in the presidency, or in Congress. The courts, win or lose, can be used to dramatize issues.

On St. Patrick's Day, 2003, on the eve of the invasion of Iraq, four antiwar activists poured their own blood around the vestibule of a military recruiting center near Ithaca, New York, and were arrested. Charged in state court with criminal mischief and trespassing (charges well suited to the American invaders of a certain Mideastern country), the St. Patrick's Four spoke their hearts to the jury. Peter DeMott, a Vietnam veteran, described the brutality of war.

Danny Burns explained why invading Iraq would violate the UN Charter, a treaty signed by the United States. Clare Grady spoke of her moral obligations as a Christian. Teresa Grady spoke to the jury as a mother, telling them that women and children were the chief victims of war, and that she cared about the children of Iraq. Nine of the twelve jurors voted to acquit them, and the judge declared a hung jury. (When the federal government retried them on felony conspiracy charges, a jury in September acquitted them of those and convicted them on lesser charges.)

Still, knowing the nature of the political and judicial system of this country, its inherent bias against the poor, against people of color, against dissidents, we cannot become dependent on the courts, or on our political leadership. Our culture—the media, the educational system—tries to crowd out of our political consciousness everything except who will be elected president and who will be on the Supreme Court, as if these are the most important decisions we make. They are not. They deflect us from the most important job citizens have, which is to bring democracy alive by organizing, protesting, engaging in acts of civil disobedience that shake up the system. That is why Cindy Sheehan's dramatic stand in Crawford, Texas, leading to 1,600 antiwar vigils around the country, involving one hundred thousand people, is more crucial to the future of American democracy than the mock hearings on Justice Roberts or the ones to come on Judge Alito.

That is why the St. Patrick's Four need to be supported and emulated. That is why the GIs refusing to return to Iraq, the families of soldiers calling for withdrawal from the war, are so important.

That is why the huge peace march in Washington on September 24 bodes well.

Let us not be disconsolate over the increasing control of the court system by the right wing.

The courts have never been on the side of justice, only moving a few degrees one way or the other, unless pushed by the people. Those words engraved in the marble of the Supreme Court, "Equal Justice Before the Law," have always been a sham.

No Supreme Court, liberal or conservative, will stop the war in Iraq, or redistribute the wealth of this country, or establish free medical care for every human being. Such fundamental change will depend, the experience of the past suggests, on the actions of an aroused citizenry, demanding that the promise of the Declaration of Independence—an equal right to life, liberty, and the pursuit of happiness—be fulfilled.

• • •

The criminalization of undocumented migrants and asylum seekers, particularly those who cross the southern US border, led to rising deportations, workplace raids, imprisonment, and family separations, regardless of which party controlled Congress and the White House. In response, a number of churches, unions, and cities created sanctuaries to protect people targeted by immigration authorities and police, as well as right-wing vigilantes. Elvira Arellano, an undocumented migrant from Mexico, took sanctuary at a Chicago church in August 2006. Though eventually deported in 2007, she returned as an asylum seeker in 2014 and has continued to organize in Chicago. Arellano gave this statement, speaking in Spanish except for the final paragraph, at Adalberto United Methodist Church.

Elvira Arellano, Statement of Elvira Arellano in Sanctuary (August 15, 2006)

Today, I was ordered by the Department of Homeland Security to turn myself in for deportation at 10 West Jackson Street in Chicago, Illinois.

I believe that this order is selective, vindictive, retaliatory, and inhumane. One year ago, I was granted a stay of deportation while private bills on my behalf were pending in the Congress. Nothing has changed since that stay was granted. Homeland Security has the legal power—and I believe, the obligation—to extend this stay of deportation.

In the three years since I was first arrested in my home in front of my son, I have struggled day in and day out for all of the 12 million undocumented in this country, for the families and for the children, many of who like mine are US citizens. I am not a criminal. I am not a terrorist. I am a mother and a worker.

I am also a person of faith and scripture. In the Book of Acts, Peter tells the authorities, "I leave it to you to judge whether I should obey you or obey God. For my part, I cannot deny what I have seen and heard."

What I have seen and heard is the injustices of a broken law heaped upon our families. We were welcomed here to work and pay taxes. Now we are being tortured and our families broken to serve the interest of racist politicians.

President Bush has said he is in favor of legalization. He has said that "Family values do not stop at the Rio Grande." And yet President

Bush is pursuing a relentless policy of raids, deportations, separation of families, and sanctions. This is hypocrisy.

I cannot submit to hypocrisy. My faith will not let me.

I have asked for and been granted sanctuary by my church. I am here and I will remain here for as long as necessary.

If Homeland Security chooses to send its agents on the Holy Ground to arrest me, then I will know that God wants me to be an example of the hatred and hypocrisy of the current policy of this government. I am at peace with my decision.

I have instructed my attorney to send a letter to Ms. Deborah Achim at Home[land] Security informing her of my decision and my location. I have done this because I do not wish my friends and community to be subjected to raids and harassment. Nor do I want Homeland Security to use me as an excuse to arrest and deport others like me and to try to destroy their families and the lives of their children.

Let this press conference put it on the public record that Homeland Security knows where I am.

I ask President Bush to pray and to listen to God. I ask him to stop his administration from doing what it is doing to all of the families and all of the children.

I am not criminal. I am not terrorist. I am mom.

• • •

On October 11, 2009, more than 250,000 people mobilized to Washington, DC, for the National Equality March organized by veteran and grassroots activists demanding full equality for lesbian, gay, bisexual, and transgender people. Despite skepticism from establishment figures (openly gay representative Barney Frank infamously opined, "The only thing [marchers are] going to be putting pressure on is the grass"), the turnout underscored the massive sea change in social attitudes around same-sex relationships since the modern gay rights movement began in earnest, following the 1969 Stonewall Rebellion and a refusal to accept the ongoing stigmatization and second-class status experienced by queer people. Earlier that spring, the movement for equal rights for lesbian and gay families achieved important victories in Iowa, Vermont, and a number of other states. In Vermont, legislators cited the moving testimony of Evann Orleck-Jetter, a middle school student who spoke before a Joint Senate and House Judiciary Committee public hearing. Here is her testimony.

Evann Orleck-Jetter, Statement on Marriage Equality
(March 18, 2009)

My name is Evann Orleck-Jetter. I'm twelve years old and I live in Thetford Center. I have a wonderful family. I live with my little brother, my grandma, and two moms who are with me all the time and support me in whatever I do. I love them very much and I wish that having to stand up here right now in front of this committee wasn't an issue anymore. We should be past this. I work really hard in school, I have good friends, and I am really happy with two loving parents who help me in everything I do.

I have been studying the civil rights movement in school, and I have learned all about the countless acts of bravery that Blacks performed to get their rights. But we still haven't reached the Promised Land that Martin Luther King wanted us to reach. Because, although Black boys and white boys, and Black girls and white girls, can play together now, we still don't accept that two people of the same gender can be together, married, with kids of their own.

On the day of Barack Obama's election, everyone was celebrating. And I was too. Except that on that same wonderful night, Proposition 8 was passed in California. That took away the rights of homosexuals in California to marry. We took a step back into the past.

We need to reach the Promised Land. Vermont's freedom to marry can help us get back on track. Feeling accepted in a society where gay and lesbian people aren't represented in daily life—like on television, in the media—is a real problem. There aren't any examples of a family like mine. If my parents could just have the right to get married, this would make such a difference. It hurts me sometimes when I feel invisible, because few people understand my feelings about my family, and few people want to ask about families with two moms. It's time to ask. It's time to understand. And it's time to accept and honor families like mine. Passing this law will make it easier for me to talk about my family openly, and the subject won't have to stay behind closed doors. This would mean so much to me, my brother, and many others. Thank you for your time and your consideration.

• • •

Here the Brooklyn writer and scholar Moustafa Bayoumi describes some of his experiences facing anti-Arab racism and Islamophobia and being targeted by right-wing media outlets.

Moustafa Bayoumi, "My Arab Problem" (October 24, 2010)

In August 2010, I briefly occupied a small corner of the culture wars, and I felt like a fish in a fishbowl. Everybody was staring at a distorted image of me, and all I could do was blink and blow bubbles.

I teach at Brooklyn College, where the undergraduate writing program has for several years assigned a "common reading" to all freshmen. This year the program selected my book *How Does It Feel to Be a Problem? Being Young and Arab in America*, in which I tell the stories of seven Arab-American men and women, all in their twenties and living in Brooklyn, coping in a post-9/11 world.

Everything was fine until about a week before classes began. That's when the chair of my department called me to report that the college had received complaints about the selection.

I hoped the noise would fade, but within days, tabloid news media had grabbed the issue from the right-wing blogosphere. I was ready to hide behind a piece of coral. Both the *New York Times* and the *New Yorker* pointed out that the controversy was driven almost entirely by off-campus conservatives, but it didn't matter. Now I—not those manufacturing the storm—had become the "controversial" one, and Brooklyn College was "pushing" an "anti-American, pro-Islam" book, at least according to rightwingnews.com.

I might have found the fracas amusing were it not unpleasant to be called all kinds of names in public. I certainly didn't recognize my book or myself in the descriptions being tossed about. I mean, the only radical organization I belong to is the Park Slope Food Coop (from which, I must confess, I've been suspended several times).

Opposition to my book seems more symptomatic of our moment than produced by its contents. The Texas State Board of Education recently voted to limit references to Islam in their high-school textbooks.

Understanding this topsy-turvy world, where assailants driven by ideology paint their targets as the ideological ones, also explains the rhetoric around Park51, the so-called Ground Zero mosque (not at Ground Zero and not a mosque).

As soon as Muslims are on the cusp of entering the mainstream fully, we are hit with a wave of opposition attempting to render us or our work invisible. Never mind that we are, by all reasonable accounts, downright moderates on the political spectrum. The trick is simply to attach the word "radical" in front of a Muslim name, and, like a magician, make the actual person disappear in a cloud of suspicion.

At a time when *The Economist* reports that 55 percent of Americans hold unfavorable views of Islam, and *Time* found that nearly one-third of Americans say Muslims should not be permitted to run for president (too late!), I would like to think that the opposition to our work illustrates the need for it even more profoundly.

Ideology blinds people to the point where they won't even admit the experiences of others. To be invisible means to be twisted beyond recognition, to have others speak for you, or simply to be not seen. When our opponents approach us, they see only our surroundings, themselves, or figments of their imagination—indeed, anything except us.

We must ask questions about the direction American society has been taking since the inauguration of the War on Terror, a war that could possibly never end and that can also be self-justifying. It has created its own War on Terror culture, one that exploits people's fears and traffics liberally in stereotypes of others. War on Terror culture has meant that we are now regularly seen as dangerous outsiders, that our daily actions are constantly viewed with suspicion, that our complex histories in this country are neglected or occluded, and that our very presence and our houses of worship have become issues of local, regional, and national politics. This is a culture that too often rationalizes away unnecessary killing while supporting authoritarian-leaning practices. It thrives on secrecy and militarism. War on Terror culture is obsessed with exploiting fear and with shaping the realms of politics, and it feeds on the dubious and paranoid logic of scapegoating others.

Or maybe there's another source of the animus against me. A while back, I published a short essay in *The New York Times Magazine* describing my experiences as an Arab extra on the set of *Sex and the City 2*. I was mildly critical of the movie for the way it used the Middle East, yet again, as an exotic stage for American pop-culture fantasies. Maybe that set some people off. After all, the show has a lot of hard-core fans.

● ● ●

In May 2011, Georgia governor Nathan Deal signed HB 87, a harsh anti-immigrant law inspired by Arizona's notorious SB 1070. The year prior, the State Board of Regents banned undocumented students from attending the top five public universities in the state. This speech by Gustavo Madrigal-Piña was delivered on August 22, 2011, as part of the "Graduation of Resistance" organized by the Georgia Undocumented Youth Alliance. It was delivered on the steps of the University of Georgia Arch, where fifty years earlier Hamilton Holmes and Charlayne Hunter were the first Black students to matriculate, defying widespread protests against integrated schools.

Gustavo Madrigal-Piña, "Undocumented and Unafraid" (August 22, 2011)

Hello everyone. My name is Gustavo. I am undocumented and I am unafraid.

I was brought here to this country at the age of nine by my parents. Ever since, many people have asked me what brought my family to this country. The answer has always been simple and always been the same: poverty.

Poverty meaning an uncertain one to two meals a day, if there were ever any second meals.

Poverty meaning walking forty-five minutes downhill to go to school and an hour and a half back uphill to go back home because we were too poor to afford the bus fare.

Poverty meaning that my parents had to make a choice. A life-or-death choice between living in the same conditions that you'd been living in—in poverty—or [to] go out and search for a better life. And I'm eternally grateful to my parents for the choice they made.

I said life-or-death choice because our journey to the [United] States brought us a couple of times close to death. I remember the second time of walking through the desert, my mom collapsed from the heat. Now, we were very lucky to have such generous people traveling with us who gave up their water so that my mom could drink it, get back up, and keep walking. I'm eternally grateful to them for that, even though that meant they had to go without water.

At the end of our journey, we were kidnapped by a gang. Me and my sister, we were nine and eight years old, respectively, at that time. They didn't care. That didn't matter to them. They stripped all of us of our clothes, our money, and our dignity.

Luckily we were let go and we eventually made it to Griffin, Georgia, which would become my family's home for the next ten years.

I don't blame my parents for the situation that I'm in. I am grateful to them. I realize that they made the responsible and courageous choices that they had to make, that any parent in that situation, in those shoes, would have made for their kids. For my mom and dad, *muchas gracias y los quiero mucho por todo lo que han hecho por mí.*

Why am I sharing this with you today? It's not to gain your sympathy but to obtain your support. To show you, but not only you—to show sympathetic and opposing politicians, and everyone—that I am not an "illegal alien," that I am indeed a human being, a human being with rights.

I would show everyone that I'm not just a number, that I'm not part of a quota that needs to be met by President Obama every year . . . who, as sympathetic as he may be, is no better than Nathan Deal, or Russell Pierce, or Matt Ramsey, with his program "Secure Communities."

In these troubled economic times, the State of Georgia has decided to make me and my fellow undocumented brothers and sisters an enemy and a scapegoat. How did they do this? First they banned us from the top five universities here in the State of Georgia, no matter how qualified we are to attend those institutions. And then they criminalized our very own existence and livelihood through HB 87. Well, I'm here to tell the State of Georgia that I'm not going down without a fight, that I'm here to fight for my brothers and sisters.

I'm here to tell the State of Georgia that I refuse to become a second-class citizen or anything below that. I want to tell the State of Georgia that I refuse to let anyone—anyone—become a second-class citizen or anything below that.

I will put up resistance as long as there is blood pumping through my veins. And I'm also here to ask you to join me and my undocumented brothers and sisters in the fight of our lives. We need to fight back. We need to organize through the struggles that we all share as part of the working class. And together we can beat HB 87, overturn the ban, and win social and educational equality for all.

I would like to wrap this up with a quote from one of my favorite people—you guys might know him—Malcolm X. I speak from a personal standpoint, but I'm pretty sure that I also speak for many of my undocumented brothers and sisters. To the State of Georgia, and I quote, "We declare our right on this earth to be a human being, to be respected as a human being, to be given the rights of a human being in this society, on this earth, in this day, which we intend to bring into existence by any means necessary."

My name is Gustavo Madrigal. I am undocumented, unafraid, and unashamed.

• • •

On September 21, 2011, Troy Davis, a Black man, was put to death by the State of Georgia, despite strong evidence of his innocence and the racism of the criminal legal system in Georgia and in death penalty cases more broadly. As Amnesty International observed, "The case against [Davis] primarily rested on witness testimony," yet "seven of key nine witnesses recanted or changed their testimony, some alleging police coercion." Davis's execution was protested by hundreds of thousands across the globe. In the campaign to free him, activists proclaimed their solidarity with the powerful slogan "I Am Troy Davis." In this letter given to lawyers just before his murder, Davis spoke about his struggle for freedom and against the death penalty.

Troy Davis, Letter Given to His Lawyers Before His Execution (September 21, 2011)

I want to thank all of you for your efforts and dedication to Human Rights and Human Kindness, in the past year I have experienced such emotion, joy, sadness, and never-ending faith. It is because of all of you that I am alive today, as I look at my sister Martina I am marveled by the love she has for me and of course I worry about her and her health, but as she tells me she is the eldest and she will not back down from this fight to save my life and prove to the world that I am innocent of this terrible crime.

As I look at my mail from across the globe, from places I have never ever dreamed I would know about and people speaking languages and expressing cultures and religions I could only hope to one day see firsthand, I am humbled by the emotion that fills my heart with overwhelming, overflowing Joy. I can't even explain the insurgence of emotion I feel when I try to express the strength I draw from you all, it compounds my faith and it shows me yet again that this is not a case about the death penalty, this is not a case about Troy Davis, this is a case about Justice and the Human Spirit to see Justice prevail.

I cannot answer all of your letters but I do read them all, I cannot see you all but I can imagine your faces, I cannot hear you speak but your letters take me to the far reaches of the world, I cannot touch you physically but I feel your warmth every day I exist.

So Thank you and remember I am in a place where execution can only destroy your physical form but because of my faith in God, my family, and all of you I have been spiritually free for some time and no matter what happens in the days, weeks to come, this Movement to end the death penalty, to seek true justice, to expose a system that fails to protect the innocent must be accelerated.

There are so many more Troy Davises.

This fight to end the death penalty is not won or lost through me but through our strength to move forward and save every innocent person in captivity around the globe. We need to dismantle this Unjust system city by city, state by state, and country by country.

I can't wait to Stand with you, no matter if that is in physical or spiritual form, I will one day be announcing,

I AM TROY DAVIS, and I AM FREE!

Never Stop Fighting for Justice and We Will Win!

Chapter 3

Occupy Opens a New Era

• • •

Three years after the financial crisis of 2008, which further escalated economic inequality in the United States, hundreds—and then thousands—of people flooded Zuccotti Park in the heart of New York City's financial district on September 17, 2011. Catalyzed by the people's movements erupting around the globe, protesters occupied the square for weeks, uniting under the slogan "We are the 99 percent"—a phrase that Howard Zinn had used in his book *A People's History of the United States* many years earlier—and inspired similar encampments throughout the country. In one of the most creative periods of protest in years, activists organized in public spaces around the country—and the world—under the banner of the Occupy Wall Street movement. Sadly, Zinn, who died January 27, 2010, at age eighty-seven, did not live to see this movement, which so fully embodied his spirit, sense of humor, and lifelong commitment to bringing about fundamental change.

Though it was eventually cleared out by massive and coordinated police mobilizations, the Occupy Wall Street movement put economic inequality squarely into the mainstream of national discourse and helped galvanize numerous new organizations that would continue its work. The echoes of the Occupy movement still resonate today.

• • •

Here is the collective declaration issued by the Occupy New York City General Assembly the night of September 29, 2011.

Occupy NYC General Assembly, Declaration of the Occupation of New York City (September 29, 2011)

As we gather together in solidarity to express a feeling of mass injustice, we must not lose sight of what brought us together. We write so that all people who feel wronged by the corporate forces of the world can know that we are your allies.

As one people, united, we acknowledge the reality: that the future of the human race requires the cooperation of its members; that our system must protect our rights, and upon corruption of that system, it is up to the individuals to protect their own rights, and those of their neighbors; that a democratic government derives its just power from the people, but corporations do not seek consent to extract wealth from the people and the Earth; and that no true democracy is attainable when the process is determined by economic power. We come to you at a time when corporations, which place profit over people, self-interest over justice, and oppression over equality, run our governments. We have peaceably assembled here, as is our right, to let these facts be known.

They have taken our houses through an illegal foreclosure process, despite not having the original mortgage.

They have taken bailouts from taxpayers with impunity, and continue to give executives exorbitant bonuses.

They have perpetuated inequality and discrimination in the workplace based on age, the color of one's skin, sex, gender identity, and sexual orientation.

They have poisoned the food supply through negligence, and undermined the farming system through monopolization.

They have profited off of the torture, confinement, and cruel treatment of countless nonhuman animals, and actively hide these practices.

They have continuously sought to strip employees of the right to negotiate for better pay and safer working conditions.

They have held students hostage with tens of thousands of dollars of debt on education, which is itself a human right.

They have consistently outsourced labor and used that outsourcing as leverage to cut workers' health care and pay.

They have influenced the courts to achieve the same rights as people, with none of the culpability or responsibility.

They have spent millions of dollars on legal teams that look for ways to get them out of contracts in regard to health insurance.

They have sold our privacy as a commodity.

They have used the military and police force to prevent freedom of the press.

They have deliberately declined to recall faulty products endangering lives in pursuit of profit.

They determine economic policy, despite the catastrophic failures their policies have produced and continue to produce.

They have donated large sums of money to politicians supposed to be regulating them.

They continue to block alternate forms of energy to keep us dependent on oil.

They continue to block generic forms of medicine that could save people's lives in order to protect investments that have already turned a substantive profit.

They have purposely covered up oil spills, accidents, faulty book-keeping, and inactive ingredients in pursuit of profit.

They purposefully keep people misinformed and fearful through their control of the media.

They have accepted private contracts to murder prisoners even when presented with serious doubts about their guilt.

They have perpetuated colonialism at home and abroad.

They have participated in the torture and murder of innocent civilians overseas.

They continue to create weapons of mass destruction in order to receive government contracts.*

To the people of the world,

We, the New York City General Assembly occupying Wall Street in Liberty Square, urge you to assert your power.

Exercise your right to peaceably assemble, occupy public space, create a process to address the problems we face, and generate solutions accessible to everyone.

To all communities that take action and form groups in the spirit of direct democracy, we offer support, documentation, and all of the resources at our disposal.

Join us and make your voices heard!

• • •

One of the people active in Occupy Wall Street in New York City was Manissa Maharawal, who has studied and worked with urban social movements from Occupy Wall Street and anti-gentrification activism to Black Lives Matter. Here she speaks of the vital work she and others did to "take on the history and legacy of oppression" and "address the way these things play out within the [Occupy] movement and outside of it."

---

* These grievances are not all-inclusive.

Manissa Maharawal, "So Real it Hurts—Notes on Occupy Wall Street" (October 4, 2011)

I first went down to Occupy Wall Street almost a week after it had started. I hadn't gone down earlier because, like many of my Brown friends, I was wary of what I had heard or just intuited that it was mostly a young white male scene.

But after hearing about the arrests and police brutality on Saturday and after hearing that thousands of people had turned up for their march, I decided to see for myself. A friend and I biked over the Brooklyn Bridge around noon, dodging the tourists and cars on Chambers Street. We ended up at Ground Zero. For a moment we felt lost. The landscape was strange. We were in the shadow of half-built buildings. They glittered and twisted into the sky. But they also seemed so naked: rust-colored steel poking out of their tops, their sides, their guts spilling out for all to see. Finally we got to Liberty Plaza. At first it seemed so unassuming; we didn't entirely know what to do. We wandered around. We made posters and laid them on the ground. I didn't know anyone down there. Not one person.

There were a lot of young white kids. But there weren't only young white kids. There were older people, there were mothers with kids, and there were a lot more people of color than I expected. We sat on the stairs and watched everyone mill around us. There was the usual protest feeling of people moving around in different directions, not sure what to do, but within this there was also order: a food table, a library, a busy media area.

I stayed for a few hours, impressed and energized by what I saw: people seemed to be taking care of each other. There seemed to be a general feeling of solidarity and it was less disorganized than I expected.

When I left, walking my bike back through the streets of the Financial District, fighting the crowds of tourists and men in suits, I felt something pulling me back to that space. I started telling my friends to go down there and check it out. I started telling people that it was a pretty awesome thing, that just having a space to have these conversations mattered, that it was more diverse than I expected. And I went back.

The next night I showed up at Occupy Wall Street with a group that had just attended a South Asians for Justice meeting, and the [General Assembly] was in session. People were passing around the Declaration of the Occupation of Wall Street, which I had heard read the night before. I hadn't realized that it was going to be finalized as *the* declaration of the movement right then and there. When I heard it the night before with my friend Sonny, we noted that a line about the eradication of race, class, and gender divisions seemed strange. Did they really think these problems were behind us? But Sonny and I had shrugged it off as the ramblings of one of the many working groups at Occupy Wall Street.

Now we realized that this was actually a really important document, that it was going to be sent into the world and read by thousands of people. And that if we let it go into the world the way it was, it would mean that people like me would shrug this movement off. It would keep people like me and my friends and my community from joining this movement. So this was urgent. This movement was about to send a document into the world about who and what it was that included a line that erased the memory of all power relations and ignored decades of oppression. I didn't want to walk away from this. I couldn't walk away. And that night I was with people who also couldn't walk away.

There is something intense about speaking in front of hundreds of people, but there is something even more intense about speaking in front of hundreds of people with whom you feel aligned and you are saying something that they do not want to hear. And then it is even more intense when that crowd is repeating everything you say, which is the way the General Assemblies or any announcements at Occupy Wall Street work. But hearing yourself in an echo chamber means that you make sure your words mean something, because they are being said back to you as you say them. And so when we finally got everyone's attention I carefully explained the issue. We wanted a small change in language, a change representative of a larger ethical concern: to act like oppression is a thing of the past, we argued, is wrong.

After the meeting we found a man who had helped write the document and told him that he needed to change or take out the first line of the declaration: "As one people, formerly divided by the color of our skin, gender, sexual orientation, religion or lack thereof, political party, and cultural background, we acknowledge the reality: that there is only one race, the human race."

But it's "scientifically true," he told us. There was only one race. Were we advocating for there being different races?

No, we said. Of course we weren't. What we were trying to say was that by beginning a document that was going to be the declaration of Occupy Wall Street in a way that sounded as if racism, classism, religious oppression, patriarchy, homophobia, and transphobia no longer existed, in a way that sounded as if this movement didn't need to take on the history and legacy of oppression or address the way these things play out within the movement and outside of it, was naïve and alienating to people who felt these things on a daily basis. That in fact we felt some of these things on a daily basis. That in order for this movement to be inclusive it needed to acknowledge these realities and find creative ways to work through them instead of ignoring them.

And so, there in that circle, on that street corner, we did a crash course on white privilege, structural racism, and oppression. We did a course on history and the Declaration of Independence and colonialism and slavery. And let me tell you what it feels like to stand in front of a white man and explain privilege to him. It hurts. It makes you tired. Sometimes it makes you want to cry. Sometimes it is exhilarating. Every single time it is hard.

But people listened. We had to fight for it, but it felt worth it. It felt worth it to sit down on a street corner in the Financial District at 11:30 p.m. on a Thursday night, after working all day long, and argue for changing the first line of Occupy Wall Street's official Declaration of the Occupation of New York City. It felt worth it not only because we got the line changed but also because standing there, speaking up—carefully and slowly spelling out that I experience the world differently from him, that this was not about him being personally racist but about relations of power, that he urgently needed to listen and believe me about this—felt like a victory for the movement on its own.

The line was removed. We sat down and re-wrote the opening of the Declaration, and it has been published with our re-write. And when we walked away, I felt like something important had just happened, that we had just pushed the movement a little bit closer to the movement I would like to see, one that takes into account historical and current inequalities, oppressions, racisms, relations of power, one that doesn't just reinforce privilege but confronts it head on.

Later that night I biked home over the Brooklyn Bridge and I somehow felt like, just maybe, at least in that moment, the world belonged to me as well as to everyone dear to me and everyone who needed and wanted more from the world. I somehow felt like maybe the world could be all of ours.

• • •

Canadian American author and activist Naomi Klein delivered this speech articulating the hope and promise of the Occupy movement in Zuccotti Park on October 6, 2011.

Naomi Klein, "Occupy Wall Street: The Most Important Thing in the World Now" (October 6, 2011)

I love you.

And I didn't just say that so that hundreds of you would shout "I love you" back, though that is obviously a bonus feature of the human microphone. Say unto others what you would have them say unto you, only way louder.

Yesterday, one of the speakers at the labor rally said: "We found each other." That sentiment captures the beauty of what is being created here. A wide-open space (as well as an idea so big it can't be contained by any space) for all the people who want a better world to find each other. We are so grateful.

If there is one thing I know, it is that the 1 percent loves a crisis. When people are panicked and desperate and no one seems to know what to do, that is the ideal time to push through their wish list of pro-corporate policies: privatizing education and social security, slashing public services, getting rid of the last constraints on corporate power. Amid the economic crisis, this is happening the world over.

And there is only one thing that can block this tactic, and fortunately, it's a very big thing: the 99 percent. And that 99 percent is taking to the streets from Madison to Madrid to say, "No. We will not pay for your crisis."

That slogan began in Italy in 2008. It ricocheted to Greece and France and Ireland and finally it has made its way to the square mile where the crisis began.

"Why are they protesting?" ask the baffled pundits on TV. Meanwhile, the rest of the world asks: "What took you so long?" "We've been wondering when you were going to show up." And most of all: "Welcome."

Many people have drawn parallels between Occupy Wall Street and the so-called anti-globalization protests that came to world attention in Seattle in 1999. That was the last time a global, youth-led, decentralized movement took direct aim at corporate power. And I am proud to have been part of what we called "the movement of movements."

But there are important differences, too. For instance, we chose summits as our targets: the World Trade Organization, the International Monetary Fund, the G8. Summits are transient by their nature; they only last a week. That made us transient, too. We'd appear, grab world headlines, then disappear. And in the frenzy of hyper-patriotism and militarism that followed the September 11 attacks, it was easy to sweep us away completely, at least in North America.

Occupy Wall Street, on the other hand, has chosen a fixed target. And you have put no end date on your presence here. This is wise. Only when you stay put can you grow roots. This is crucial. It is a fact of the information age that too many movements spring up like beautiful flowers but quickly die off. It's because they don't have roots. And they don't have long-term plans for how they are going to sustain themselves. So when storms come, they get washed away.

Being horizontal and deeply democratic is wonderful. But these principles are compatible with the hard work of building structures and institutions that are sturdy enough to weather the storms ahead. I have great faith that this will happen.

Something else this movement is doing right: You have committed yourselves to nonviolence. You have refused to give the media the images of broken windows and street fights it craves so desperately. And that tremendous discipline has meant that, again and again, the story has been the disgraceful and unprovoked police brutality, which we saw more of just last night. Meanwhile, support for this movement grows and grows. More wisdom.

But the biggest difference a decade makes is that, in 1999, we were taking on capitalism at the peak of a frenzied economic boom. Unemployment was low, stock portfolios were bulging. The media was drunk on easy money. Back then it was all about start-ups, not shut downs.

We pointed out that the deregulation behind the frenzy came at a price. It was damaging to labor standards. It was damaging to environmental standards. Corporations were becoming more powerful than governments, and that was damaging to our democracies. But to be honest with you, while the good times rolled, taking on an economic system based on greed was a tough sell, at least in rich countries.

Ten years later, it seems as if there aren't any more rich countries. Just a whole lot of rich people. People who got rich looting the public wealth and exhausting natural resources around the world.

The point is, today everyone can see that the system is deeply unjust and careening out of control. Unfettered greed has trashed the global economy. And it is trashing the natural world, as well. We are over-fishing our oceans, polluting our water with fracking and deep-water drilling, turning to the dirtiest forms of energy on the planet, like the Alberta tar sands. And the atmosphere cannot absorb the amount of carbon we are putting into it, creating dangerous warming. The new normal is serial disasters: economic and ecological.

These are the facts on the ground. They are so blatant, so obvious, that it is a lot easier to connect with the public than it was in 1999 and to build the movement quickly.

We all know, or at least sense, that the world is upside down: we act as if there is no end to what is actually finite—fossil fuels and the atmospheric space to absorb their emissions. And we act as if there are strict and immovable limits to what is actually bountiful—the financial resources to build the kind of society we need.

The task of our time is to turn this around: to challenge this false scarcity. To insist that we can afford to build a decent, inclusive society—while at the same time respect the real limits to what the earth can take.

What climate change means is that we have to do this on a deadline. This time, our movement cannot get distracted, divided, burned out, or swept away by events. This time, we have to succeed. And I'm not talking about regulating the banks and increasing taxes on the rich, though that's important.

I am talking about changing the underlying values that govern our society. That is hard to fit into a single media-friendly demand, and it's also hard to figure out how to do it. But it is no less urgent for being difficult.

That is what I see happening in this square. In the way you are feeding each other, keeping each other warm, sharing information freely, and providing health care, meditation classes, and empowerment training. My favorite sign here says, "I care about you." In a culture that trains people to avoid each other's gaze, to say, "Let them die," that is a deeply radical statement.

A few final thoughts. In this great struggle, here are some things that don't matter:

- What we wear
- Whether we shake our fists or make peace signs
- Whether we can fit our dreams for a better world into a media sound bite

And here are a few things that do matter:

- Our courage
- Our moral compass
- How we treat each other

We have picked a fight with the most powerful economic and political forces on the planet. That's frightening. And as this movement grows from strength to strength, it will get more frightening. Always be aware that there will be a temptation to shift to smaller targets—like, say, the person sitting next to you at this meeting. After all, that is a battle that's easier to win.

Don't give in to the temptation. I'm not saying don't call each other on shit. But this time, let's treat each other as if we plan to work side by side in struggle for many, many years to come. Because the task before us will demand nothing less.

Let's treat this beautiful movement as if it is the most important thing in the world. Because it is. It really is.

• • •

A nine-day strike of the Chicago Teachers Union (CTU) in September 2012 ended with a historic victory against Mayor Rahm Emanuel and efforts to corporatize and defund the public education system. On October 6, organizers held a forum to draw lessons from the strike. Among the featured speakers was Kirstin Roberts, a preschool teacher and member of the CTU.

Kirstin Roberts, "We Stood Up to the Bullies" (October 6, 2012)

I began teaching in 2006. My first jobs were at social service agencies, contracting with Chicago Public Schools to provide preschool on the cheap. These were nonunion, very low benefits, very long working hours, high staff-turnover jobs.

They were also jobs working with some of the poorest and highest-needs kids in the city—kids with HIV, foster kids, kids with histories of extreme abuse, kids with cognitive and physical impairments.

This combination—kids with the greatest needs getting the least experienced and worst compensated teachers—is, of course, no coincidence. This is education policy in the richest country on Earth.

One of the great contributions of the Chicago Teachers Union strike of 2012 is that this realization about our public education system—and how the education deformers are transforming teaching into a short-term, lower-skill, lower-wage job—is now being discussed not by a few people, but by millions.

I started working in the Chicago Public Schools in January 2010. The timing of this was significant. A month after starting my job, an article in the *Chicago Tribune* identified the neighborhood where my school is located as having the second-highest home foreclosure rate in the city.

The impact of this social crisis is felt in our classrooms every day—children whose families have lost their homes suffer profoundly, and they bring this suffering with them to school.

This shows up in a thousand different ways, from minor behavior problems resulting from anxiety to what can only be described as depression. At work, we refer to them as the recession babies—children born in the last five years to moms and dads who have been laid off, lost their homes, and who have all the so-called personal problems that result from this kind of economic devastation.

Billionaire hedge fund managers or hotel heiresses take particular glee in lecturing teachers for using poverty as an "excuse" to explain away a "culture of failure" we've created through our ineptitude and selfishness. It's interesting that responsibility for the greatest economic downturn since the 1930s—a crisis created by bankers and corporate America's insatiable greed—isn't something they're willing to embrace.

There is no cottage industry of well-funded think tanks lecturing financiers regarding the culture of failure inside investment banks. There are no politicians screaming for accountability and merit pay for CEOs.

Instead of taking responsibility and preaching sacrifice for themselves, they instead look for creative new ways to divert public funds into their private coffers—through privatization schemes like charter schools, through taxpayer-funded bailouts, through "job creation incentives" (which rightfully should be called welfare for the rich)—thus further robbing the public schools of the resources we so desperately need.

Robbing the poor to pay the rich, and then having the nerve to blame the poor and the people who teach them for the very conditions the rich created—this is education policy in the richest country on Earth. The Chicago Teachers Union strike, I believe, has made an important contribution of pushing these crimes into the public spotlight, as well.

Yesterday at school, we ran out of hand soap. We took the children to the bathroom, and as they lined up to wash their hands, we realized our pump soap was running out. My heart sank, because I knew that I had no more soap in my supply locker.

This is a small thing—a minor thing—but it's also a big thing. See, we aren't provided soap in the bathrooms at our school. There isn't room in the budget. We beg our parents to donate soap to us, or we buy it out of our measly supply budget, or we pay for it out of pocket. It's hard to explain, but these are the daily, petty failures that add up over time.

The message becomes so clear: You and your students aren't worth it. If nobody had soap—if there was a worldwide soap shortage—then it wouldn't hurt. But it's obvious that some people's children will always have clean hands, and so much more.

Some people's children will go to schools with seven full-time art teachers; some children will go to school with none. Some children will go to schools where student-to-teacher ratios are nine-to-one, and some children will go to kindergarten with forty-two five-year-old friends and one teacher.

Some children will get world languages, social workers and counselors, iPads and music class, libraries, recreational activities, and beauty and joy. And some children simply will get tested, and tested again and again, as they sit in cold classrooms all winter and stifling classrooms during the spring and summer.

It's not hard to guess whose children get the things that make school worthwhile and enriching, and whose children don't. Again, this is education policy in the richest country on Earth. The greatest contribution of this strike is highlighting, for all to see, this injustice being perpetrated upon our children.

This strike alone couldn't solve this injustice, but by asserting that all children deserve what Emanuel's and Penny Pritzker's children get, we have contributed to the building of a movement that, in no small measure, will be able to mobilize the kind of power necessary to tackle these inequities.

Now, I want to talk about that power.

When it became clear over the last year that members of the CTU needed to prepare ourselves to strike, I was very nervous. In the building where I work, there was plenty of built-up anger and frustration, but most often, this was expressed through anxiety, people blaming themselves—and sometimes parents and coworkers—and cynicism.

I had a hard time imagining how this could change. . . . Truth be told, I hit the picket lines at 6:30 a.m. on day one of the strike exhilarated but also scared out of my mind. Would my coworkers and colleagues around the system stand strong? Would I? Most importantly, would the rest of Chicago stand with us?

About an hour into the picketing, most of my fears—as well as my hearing—were gone. The honking from the passing cars—filled with workers on their way to jobs, some of them scrambling to drop their kids off at hastily arranged childcare—was deafening.

Then the homemade tamales and boxes of doughnuts began arriving from our parents. They stood with us. They stood with us because they knew we were fighting to defend the right to a decent public education for their kids. But more than that, they stood with us because we were standing up to the same bullies that had caused so much misery for so many, for so long.

The outpouring of solidarity was matched by an outpouring of creativity on the picket lines and at the mass protests every afternoon. Teachers and staff who had long been stifled and forced to deliver rote lessons designed solely for test preparation began to paint and dance and sing their struggle.

Some of the teachers who had voiced the most reluctance about the strike in my building became the most vocal and outspoken chanters on the picket line. The imagination and the confidence unleashed during this strike gives us a tiny glimpse of the power of human creativity that can—and someday will—be utilized to transform our schools into places of true learning and development.

• • •

In spring 2013, Farea Al-Muslimi traveled from Yemen to speak about the impact of Obama's drone wars on his country. Here is an edited version of his testimony to the United States Senate Judiciary Committee Subcommittee on the Constitution, Civil Rights, and Human Rights.

Farea Al-Muslimi, "Drone Wars: The Constitutional and Counterterrorism Implications of Targeted Killing" (April 23, 2013)

My name is Farea Al-Muslimi. I am from Wessab, a remote mountain village in Yemen, about nine hours' drive from my country's capital, Sana'a. Most of the world has never heard of Wessab. But just six days ago, my village was struck by a drone, in an attack that terrified thousands of simple, poor farmers. The drone strike and its impact tore my heart, much as the tragic bombings in Boston last week tore your hearts and also mine.

I am here today to talk about the human costs and consequences of targeted killing by the United States in Yemen.

For almost all of the people in Wessab, I'm the only person with any connection to the United States. They called and texted me that night with questions that I could not answer: Why was the United States terrifying them with these drones? Why was the United States trying to kill a person with a missile when everyone knows where he is and he could have been easily arrested?

My village is beautiful, but it is very poor and in a remote part of Yemen. Even though the region it is in is about the same size of Bahrain, there isn't a single meter of asphalt road in it. Developmental projects by the central government rarely reach my village and humanitarian aid from international organizations like USAID never does. I know that most people have never heard of Wessab. But I could never have imagined that it would be the location of a drone strike.

My understanding is that Hameed Meftah, who is also known as Hameed Al-Radmi, was the target of the drone strike. Many people in Wessab know Al-Radmi. Earlier on the night he was killed, he was reportedly in the village meeting with the general secretary of local councillors, the head of the local government. A person in the village told me that Al-Radmi had also met with security and government officials at the security headquarters just three days prior to the drone strike. Yemeni officials easily could have found and arrested Al-Radmi.

After the strike, the farmers in Wessab were afraid and angry. They were upset because they know Al-Radmi but they did not know that he was a target, so they could have potentially been with him during the missile strike. Some of the people that were with Al-Radmi when he was killed were never affiliated with AQAP [Al-Qaeda in the Arabian Peninsula] and only knew Al-Radmi socially. The farmers in my village were angry because Al-Radmi was a man with whom government security chiefs had a close connection. He received cooperation from and had an excellent relationship with the government agencies in the village. This made him look legitimate and granted him power in the eyes of those poor farmers, who had no idea that being with him meant they were risking death from a US drone.

The people in my village wanted Al-Radmi to be captured, so that they could question him and find out what he was doing wrong so they could put an end to it. They still don't have an answer to that question. Instead, all they have is the psychological fear and terror that now occupies their souls. They fear that their home or a neighbor's home could be bombed at any time by a US drone.

In my work with foreign journalists, I have visited many areas struck by drones or warplanes that residents believe were dispatched as part of the targeted killing program conducted by the United States. I have traveled most frequently to Abyan, an area in southern Yemen, which had been seized in early 2011 by Ansar al-Sharia, a group aligned with AQAP. One of my trips to Abyan, with National Public Radio, was in mid-January 2012, just two days after the area was freed from AQAP. Traveling in the area was dangerous, both because some AQAP members had simply gone underground by shaving their beards and remaining in town, and because we did not know whether we might find ourselves in a place where a drone might strike next.

In Abyan and other places in Yemen, I visited many locations where local residents were suffering from the consequences of targeted killing operations. I have met with dozens of civilians who were injured during drone strikes and other air attacks. I have met with relatives of people who were killed by drone strikes as well as numerous eyewitnesses. They have told me how these air strikes have changed their lives for the worse.

In early March 2013, I was working with *Newsweek* in Abyan when I met the mother of a boy named Muneer Muhammed. Muneer, an eighteen-year-old boy, transported goods for shops via his donkey in the local souk of Ja'ar town. He had recently been engaged and was preparing for his wedding. Muneer was at work when a missile hit and killed him in May 2012.

At the time of strike, Muneer's mother was in Lahj. She told me that she could not attend her son's funeral or even see him before he was buried, due to the heavy fighting between the government forces and Ansar al-Sharia along the road between Lahj and Abyan. In fact, the last time this grieving mother saw her son was when she was shown his dead body on a video from a random eyewitness's phone. She told me, in tears, that if she ever meets the individual who shot the missile, she will "crunch him into pieces" in her mouth.

The people with whom we spoke in Abyan told us that Muneer was not a member of AQAP. But that has not stopped AQAP from trying to use his death to recruit supporters to their cause. Local residents told us that they approached one of Muneer's relatives, urging him to join AQAP in order to seek revenge for Muneer's death.

Days after Abyan was freed from AQAP control in June 2012, I met a fisherman named Ali Al-Amodi in a hospital in Aden. The day before, his house in Shaqra, on the seaside of Abyan, was targeted by a US air strike. Al-Amodi told me that he stood helplessly as his four-year-old son and six-year-old daughter died in his arms on the way to the hospital.

Al-Amodi had no links with AQAP. He and other locals said that his house was targeted by mistake. In that same strike, four other children and one woman were killed. Witnesses said none were militants.

Later in June 2012, I visited Al-Makhzan, a town outside of Ja'ar, where a drone strike targeting Nader Al-Shadadi took place. Al-Shadadi is identified by the Yemeni government as a terrorist and a leader of Ansar al-Sharia. He has been targeted at least three times in different places, but the strikes have missed him every time. This time, it targeted his aunt's house. Neighbors say he was not there, and his aunt's only son was killed. There is no evidence that the son was affiliated with AQAP.

Ma'mon, a twelve-year-old boy who lives next door and witnessed the aftermath of the strike, had tears in his eyes when he told me how the sound of the strike woke him up that morning. Referring to the drones, he told me how "we hear them every night" and that he is afraid each day that they "will come back."

In Aden, I spoke with Saleh Bin Fareed, one of the tribal leaders present on December 17, 2009, at the site where a US cruise missile targeted the village of Al-Majalah in Lawdar, Abyan. In the poor village that day, more than forty civilians were killed, including four pregnant women. Bin Fareed was one of the first people to the scene. He and others tried to rescue civilians. He told me their bodies were so decimated that it was impossible to differentiate between the children, the women, and their animals. Some of these innocent people were buried in the same grave as animals.

The killing of innocent civilians by US missiles in Yemen is helping to destabilize my country and create an environment from which AQAP benefits. Every time an innocent civilian is killed or maimed by a US drone strike or another targeted killing, it is felt by Yemenis across the country. These strikes often cause animosity toward the United States and create a backlash that undermines the national security goals of the United States. The US strikes also increase my people's hatred against the central government, which is seen as propped up by the Persian Gulf governments and the United States.

I know that some policymakers in the United States and Yemen claim that AQAP does not use drone strikes as a tool to recruit more people to their cause. This is incorrect. The case of the Toaiman family in Mareb, as reported by NPR based on a trip in which I participated, is one specific example. The Toaimans' oldest son joined AQAP hoping to avenge the death of his father, an innocent civilian killed by a drone strike in October 2011. The son has twenty-eight brothers waiting to do so as well. One of his youngest brothers, a nine-year-old, carries a picture of a plane in his pocket. The boy openly states that he wants revenge and identifies his father's killer as "America."

But the main issue is not whether AQAP recruits more terrorists because of drone strikes. AQAP's power and influence has never been based on the number of members in its ranks. AQAP recruits and retains power through its ideology, which relies in large part on the Yemeni people believing that America is at war with them.

Whether targeted killing strikes are carried out by US forces or Yemeni forces at the United States' request often makes little difference, especially when strikes kill innocent civilians. Yemenis already have a strained relationship with their own armed forces because of the internal conflicts in our country. (Even though I just turned twenty-three, I have lived through nine wars in my life: six in Sada, one in the southern provinces in 1994, the recent conflict in Abyan, and the 2011 conflict in Sana'a. The US targeted killing program is the tenth war I have lived through.) The fact that innocent civilians are dying and the Yemeni army is receiving so much support from the United States strains that relationship even more.

As someone who has lived and worked on this issue very closely, I cannot help but feel that the American and Yemeni governments are losing the war against AQAP. Even when drone strikes target and kill the right people, it is at the expense of creating the many strategic problems I have discussed today. Every tactical success is at the expense of creating more strategic problems. I do, however, believe that things can still be fixed. If the United States wants to win the battle against AQAP in Yemen, I strongly suggest that it consider taking the following steps:

- Stop all the targeted killing strikes.
- Announce the names of those already on the "kill list," so that innocent civilians can stay out of harm's way.
- Issue an official apology to the families of all civilians killed or injured by targeted killing strikes.
- Compensate the families of innocent civilians killed or injured by strikes conducted or authorized by the United States.
- In every village where there has been a targeted killing, build a school or hospital so that the villagers' only experience with America will not be the death and destruction caused by an American missile.

• • •

Barack Obama ran for president in 2008 with promises to reform US immigration law. By the middle of his second term, he had deported more than two million undocumented people, more than any president in US history. Roberto Meneses Marquez, the president of Day Laborers United (*Jornaleros Unidos*), a group working for the rights of workers in the precarious day labor industry, many of them undocumented, spoke out against these policies.

Roberto Meneses Marquez, "A Day Laborer" (April 30, 2013)

I am an undocumented day laborer in Queens who has worked in this country for almost twenty years. I do hard, dangerous jobs on construction sites such as demolition or carrying out the trash, when I can get any work at all. I have known many men who have been killed in workplace accidents or who have become gravely ill from breathing in dust due to a lack of adequate protective equipment.

We deserve the chance to become full members of the society we contribute to every day. For the past decade, I have heard much in the media about a possible immigration reform law. But, I have learned not to believe it.

In the early 2000s, there was talk of the United States and Mexico reaching a comprehensive deal to legalize all undocumented immigrants in return for a free trade deal that would allow private investment in Pemex, Mexico's state-owned oil company. Those talks fell apart after September 11.

During his 2004 re-election campaign, President George W. Bush once again raised hopes of immigration reform to woo the Latino vote, but it was an empty promise. In 2006, we went out into the streets by the millions, and our demands continued to be ignored.

President Barack Obama won the Hispanic vote in 2008 by promising that in his first one hundred days as president, he would put forth comprehensive immigration reform. Once in office, he said he was too busy dealing with the economic crisis to work on immigration reform.

Today, in Obama's second term as president, we hear the same promise of humane and comprehensive immigration reform.

But, I don't see it. As far as I can tell from what is being discussed, we are being asked to accept a process toward legalization that would take ten to fifteen years. The only thing being offered is a simple guest worker permit similar to what we already have with the H-2A and H-2B visas.

Far from being a solution, work permits are instruments of exploitation for immigrant workers on both sides of the border. In immigrants' countries of origin, unscrupulous brokers collect large fees, promising to help arrange work permits, and then disappear with people's money. On this side of the border, the bosses expose the workers to long hard hours of labor in unhealthy conditions and without necessary protections. If the workers don't like it, they can lose their jobs and their work permits.

Creating a new set of work permits, without a real path to permanent residency and citizenship, will only legalize the exploitation we live under while requiring us to go to "the back of the line" and pay thousands of dollars in fines and more taxes for the privilege of being treated this way.

The Senate's bipartisan "Gang of Eight" (which includes New York Senator Chuck Schumer) may think they are fooling us. But I can't swallow this deception. And I suspect there are many others like me among the eleven million undocumented people in this country who understand what is being proposed and will have no motivation to come "out of the shadows" to participate in this process.

The distrust that I feel comes from observing two successive presidential administrations, one Republican and the other Democrat. They speak from both sides of their mouth. From one side they spew words of legalization, but on the other side they generate more anti-immigration laws, increase deportations, build detention centers and jails, and pour more investments into policing the border.

I am over forty-five years old, as are many of the people I work with in construction. And it appears increasingly likely that we will not live long enough to be legalized. This is unjust. After almost two decades in this country, there are a couple of things I have learned: firstly, don't trust the politicians, and secondly, it will only be through our own ability to organize and collectively fight for our rights that we will see improvements in our lives.

• • •

Amber Kudla grew up in North Tonawanda, New York, a small city between Niagara Falls and Buffalo. In 2013, she graduated top of her high school class at North Tonawanda High School and delivered a speech at graduation as valedictorian, the same year New York State began implementing the Common Core testing system. Initially afraid of public speaking and cautious of making a political statement, she chose to address the proliferation of standardized testing and its impact on critical thinking, much to the dismay of her school principal. The title of her speech, which appeared in the graduation program, is the phone number of North Tonawanda's representative in the New York State Assembly, who Kudla encouraged her audience to call.

Amber Kudla, "518-455-4767" (June 23, 2013)

Mr. Woytila, Mr. Fisher, honored guests, parents, friends, families, and members of the class of 2013.

First and foremost, let's thank all of our families for their support and guidance over the past eighteen years and for never giving up on us. We also owe our teachers and administrators many thanks for motivating us to try our hardest and for giving up their free time to help us out. They have all provided us with many great opportunities and have served as excellent role models.

Now, I don't think I'm qualified to stand up here and give 250 students advice, and I'm sure you have received enough motivation and insight from Mike and Mr. Fisher, so I'll just take the opportunity to voice an opinion. What I would really like to address here is the current state of public education.

This year, New York has joined four other states in following the Common Core standards. The goal is for every student in New York to learn the same things as every student in all of the other states. And in order to do this, we apparently have to triple the number of standardized tests that students take, in exchange for state funding. This year we took assessments at the beginning, middle, and end of each course as part of this new system.

Some people think this will challenge our students to work harder and help the United States to rise above other countries in academic rankings. They say that once we adjust to the change, these tests will be beneficial. On the other hand, many teachers, principals, and administrators across the state have felt the need to retire early, since their job descriptions have changed so drastically that they hardly consider themselves educators anymore. Most say that it has become all about tests and numbers and that there is very little focus on the students.

Whether you are for or against these assessments seems to depend on how you define learning. Perhaps it is your perspective that better test scores mean your child understands more. To me, testing has little connection to learning, and knowledge is not something that can be definitively measured with grades.

Regardless, these state assessments sit kids down for an exam on the first day of school, testing things that will take them at least a year to learn. That's pretty discouraging in high school, and I can't imagine what that does to a first grader's motivation. Learning should be about discovery. Does it make sense to begin your discovery with a summary of the journey?

No, that's really just cheating yourself. You see, introducing subjects with the most difficult topics first is not a good way to get people excited about learning. We are students, not statistics. And these tests should have no effect on how we are taught. And they are affecting how we are taught.

The thing is, our educational system is built for the average student. Multiple choice means that answers need to be watered down, so they test the most general concepts. I believe that we all have far greater potential, but we are taught how to be average. And is that really going to help us when we enter the job market and we are vying for the same job as our brilliant exchange student, Quilin?

As for the argument that the assessments are challenging our students more, sure that's true. It's a challenge to fit the same amount of material into one year with more exams. It's a challenge to memorize loads of facts in time for the next test. It's also a challenge to eat a teaspoon of cinnamon in one bite without choking, but what are you really accomplishing?

How about some statistics? The dropout rate in some parts of the United States is about 25 percent. In Finland, it is less than 1 percent. Why? Because in Finland, teaching is left up to the teachers. Standardized tests are few and far between. And guess what? They consistently outperform the United States on international math, science, and literacy tests.

At this point, I'd like to throw a slightly relevant quote by a famous person into the mix to make my speech seem more legitimate. That appears to be how these things work. So Albert Einstein once said, "Everybody is a genius, but if you judge a fish by its ability to climb a tree, it will live its whole life believing that it is stupid." We can't judge someone's intelligence by how well he or she does in a small group of isolated classes. Everyone learns differently, so education is not something that can be successfully standardized.

Sure, we have to get a lot of people through the system, but there are more efficient ways of doing it. Maybe it's more cost-effective to have large impersonal classes, but to cram in so much meaningless information? We could learn a lot more if we could discover connections between biology and physics or English and history, instead of memorizing lists of isolated facts just long enough to pass tests.

I mean, you all know that kid in math class that would always ask the teacher, "When will we ever use this in real life?" To which the teacher responds, "You'll need it on the final exam." No, that is not the answer. You are learning math because it has useful applications. Yet the nation's mentality seems to be that we are learning these things just to pass tests. And why do we need to pass tests? To evaluate teachers and get funding.

But what good is this funding if we are not learning the things that will help us to reach our full potential? I once had a teacher who, after I asked a few too many questions, told me, "It's not something you can understand. You just have to memorize it." Don't ever let anyone tell you that. You are capable of understanding anything you set your minds to. It may take time, it may take patience, but if you really want to understand something, get out there and understand it. You can't let people try to tell you who you are and what you are worth. That you aren't as smart as someone else because you scored ten points lower than him on a standardized test. That doesn't mean anything—grades are just numbers. It's better to learn and to understand than to get good grades. And no, one does not imply the other.

Anyways, this is why I tried so hard to get out of this speech. Not because I don't respect all of you. I do. It's just that "valedictorian" is a label and I don't respect what it stands for. I am not the smartest person in our class. I could learn something new from every single one of you. I'm good at memorizing things, but that's not so useful outside of the standardized world of high school. And I'm pretty sure a lot of you have been more successful than I was, unless your standard for judging success is a Scantron.

Now you must be wondering why this is relevant. We're graduating, we're out of the system, it doesn't matter anymore. Well, it still matters to anyone you know that's growing up in New York State. School should not be about passing tests to get more funding. School should be about learning, understanding, thinking critically, and finding something that you are passionate about. Tell your younger siblings, friends, and neighbors to think, and to form their own opinions. To cautiously let their grades slide and do some actual learning.

Clearly my position is that most of the numbers you are given in high school are useless, but here's one that means something. The title of this speech, which you can find in your program, is the phone number of Robin Schimminger, our representative in the New York State Assembly. You can use this to share your opinion with Albany, whether you are for or against the state assessments. Let your voice be heard, and hopefully someday education will once again be about the joy of learning and discovery.

Well, that was the closest I could come to inspirational. I'm not very good at coming up with really deep stuff. So I'm going to end with one final quote from an author named John Green. He describes the one test, the only test in your life that matters. And spoiler alert: it is not a standardized state assessment. He says,

> The test will measure whether you are an informed, engaged, and productive citizen of the world; and it will take place in schools, and bars, and hospitals, and dorm rooms, and in places of worship. You will be tested on first dates, in job interviews, while watching football, and while scrolling through your Twitter feed.
>
> The test will judge your ability to think about things other than celebrity marriages, whether you'll be persuaded by empty political rhetoric, and whether you'll be able to place your life and your community in a broader context.
>
> The test will last your entire life, and it will be comprised of the millions of decisions that, when taken together make your life yours. And everything—everything—will be on it. So pay attention.

Thank you—and congratulations, class of 2013.

• • •

In 2010, Chelsea E. Manning, who was then an army intelligence analyst in Iraq, released hundreds of thousands of classified documents to the organization WikiLeaks. Manning's leak also included video of a 2007 US airstrike on Iraqi civilians that killed two Reuters journalists, as well as scores of State Department diplomatic cables that many credit with catalyzing the Arab Spring. Arrested several months later, Manning spent nearly a year in solitary confinement before facing court-martial on charges including "aiding the enemy." The following is a transcript of Manning's statement read by her lawyer David Coombs after she was sentenced to thirty-five years in federal prison. Manning spent seven years behind bars, where she twice attempted suicide, before being freed, only to then be jailed again from 2019 to 2020 for refusing to testify before a grand jury investigating WikiLeaks.

Chelsea E. Manning, "Sometimes You Have to Pay a Heavy Price to Live in a Free Society" (August 21, 2013)

The decisions that I made in 2010 were made out of a concern for my country, her citizens, and the wider world that we live in. Since the events of September 11, 2001, the United States has been involved in a war with an enemy that chose, and chooses, not to use a traditional battlespace. Due to this fact, we altered our methods for combating the risks posed to us, in America, and our way of life.

For a long time, I agreed with these methods. I chose to volunteer and help defend my country. However, it was not until I arrived in Iraq and was finally "connecting the dots" between the contents of often classified military and diplomatic documents that I worked with on a daily basis, and real flesh and blood—that I realized [in] our efforts to meet the risks posed to us by our enemies, we had completely forgotten about our humanity. We consciously, and repeatedly, elected to devalue human life—both in Iraq and Afghanistan, and now elsewhere. When we engaged those we perceived as the enemy, we often killed innocent civilians. And, whenever we killed innocent civilians, we chose to not accept responsibility for these failures and instead hid behind a complex and growing veil of "national security" and "classification" in order to avoid public accountability.

In our zeal to kill the enemy, we internally debated the definition of "torture." We held individuals in Guantánamo Bay for years without due process of law. We inexplicably turned a blind eye to torture and executions by our host-nation partners in Iraq and Afghanistan, and we stomached countless other, recorded and documented, acts in the name of our "War on Terror."

All too often, patriotism is the cry extolled when morally and ethically questionable acts are advocated by those in power. When these cries of patriotism drown out any logically based intentions—it is usually the eager and dedicated American soldier on the ground that is given orders to carry out an ill-conceived mission. As the late Howard Zinn once said, "There is not a flag large enough to cover the shame of killing innocent people."

I understand that my actions violated the law—but I acted only out of a desire to help people. When I chose to disclose classified information to the public, I did so out of a love for my country, her citizens, and a sense of duty to others.

I serve my time knowing that sometimes you have to pay a heavy price to live in a free society. I will gladly pay that price if it means we could have a country that is truly conceived in liberty and dedicated to the proposition that "all [women and] men are created equal."

Chapter 4

Standing Up for Each Other

Phillip Agnew, "#OurMarch" (August 28, 2013)
Airickca Gordon-Taylor, "No Justice, No Peace: Families of Police Brutality
   Victims Speak Out" (June 28, 2014)
Chrishaun "CeCe" McDonald, "Standing Up for Each Other" (March 10, 2014)
Michelle Farber, "We All Have to Be Brave" (May 14, 2014)
Michelle Alexander, "How to Dismantle the 'New Jim Crow'" (July 2014)
Ursula K. Le Guin, Speech in Acceptance of the National Book Foundation
   Medal for Distinguished Contribution to American Letters (November
   19, 2014)

• • •

When Obama was elected to a second term, many people hoped he would
pursue a more ambitious and progressive agenda. Yet the reality was much
different. The killing of a Florida youth, Trayvon Martin, by a racist vigilante in
early 2012 highlighted for many that racism persisted in this supposedly "colorblind" and "post-racial" society. "If the problem of the twentieth century was,
in W. E. B. Du Bois's famous words, 'the problem of the color line,' then the
problem of the twenty-first century is the problem of colorblindness, the refusal
to acknowledge the causes and consequences of enduring racial stratification,"
Naomi Murakawa wrote in her book *The First Civil Right: How Liberals Built
Prison America*.

   Organizations such as Dream Defenders emerged to organize in this new
period. Families of people killed by police violence continued to speak out.

Others campaigned for the rights of LGBTQ people and the right to abortion, against the cruelty of mass incarceration and "the New Jim Crow," and for a world that values people—not profit.

• • •

On August 28, 2013, tens of thousands of people poured onto the National Mall for the fiftieth anniversary of the historic March on Washington. Phillip Agnew, a leader of the youth activist group Dream Defenders, which launched in the aftermath of the murder of Florida teen Trayvon Martin in February 2012, was scheduled to speak but then was cut from the program. In a YouTube video posted later that day, Agnew shared the speech he was unable to deliver.

Phillip Agnew, "#OurMarch" (August 28, 2013)

By the time we finish our conversation this morning, another Black boy will lay bleeding in the streets of Chicago. And as we rest our heads tonight, three hundred thousand of our veterans will lay their heads homeless. And I would love to explain to you how the hate we spread abroad is the real reason that hatred washes upon our shores, but I only have two minutes.

And I can tell you that Philadelphia just closed twenty-three of its schools. At the same time it makes way for a $400 million state-of-the-art prison. And that North Carolina and Florida continue to silence their citizens at the ballot box, but I only have two minutes. I could tell you how even as we celebrate Dr. King's dream, over four hundred thousand of our immigrant brothers and sisters languish away in privately owned detention camps. And how we still find our queer brothers and sisters in prison in the shadows of their closets, but I only have two minutes.

And I'd tell you how our mothers, sisters, wives, and daughters still earn less, have no control over their bodies, and are traded and trafficked like slaves. And I could tell you how it's easier for someone to buy a gun and put it to their head than it is to diagnose the illness within it, but I only have two minutes. And if there was time, I would tell you that millions of young people, and queer people, and poor people, and people of color are asking what do we do with all of this anger, all this fear, this disappointment and frustration, this madness that we feel, but alas I only have one minute.

And with it, this last minute of our conversation, I tell you that, though all may seem lost, there is a generation of dreamers, and lovers, and defenders, and builders bubbling, bubbling, bubbling beneath the rubble. And beneath your feet, you may feel a collective quaking, tremors of a sleeping giant awakening, emanating from fault lines at the Arizona-Mexico border; and Raleigh; and in Austin; and in Cleveland, Ohio; and Chicago, Illinois; and even Tallahassee, Florida. And we've come here from every crack, crease, and crevice of our country to our Capitol to say that, for all those whose cares have been our concern, we are ready. To say to anybody who believes we will be coopted, or we will be bought, that we're ready. And for those that doubt our energy and our resolve and our discipline, we are ready.

For those that believe that future fingers may fail the torch, fear not: we're ready. For all those that believe in the power of nonviolence and love as unconquerable, we are ready.

Fifty years ago, a man told us of a promised land. And for fifty years, we've wandered and wondered: where are the youth? The constant whispers in our ears. And so we have come asking neither permission nor questions, but to answer one and say that we are here. Believing indeed that we have a beautiful history and the one that we will build in the future will truly astonish the world, we are ready.

May the outcome always prosper over income, peace over profit, revolution over revenue, and all peace and power to the people.

For anybody who doubts us, don't believe us—just watch. We are ready.

• • •

Airickca Gordon-Taylor was the cousin of Emmett Till (1941–55), whose brutal lynching in 1955 helped galvanize the civil rights movement. Gordon-Taylor served as the director of the Mamie Till Mobley Memorial Foundation, named after Till's mother. She spent her life educating new generations about her family's legacy and fiercely advocating for other victims of racist violence until her untimely death in 2020 at age fifty. She spoke at the Socialism Conference in Chicago alongside activists who had lost loved ones to police brutality. Two months later, the police murder of Michael Brown in Ferguson, Missouri, would launch the Black Lives Matter movement.

Airickca Gordon-Taylor, "No Justice, No Peace: Families of Police Brutality Victims Speak Out" (June 28, 2014)

I was just doing what I felt that I was supposed to do as one of the legacies of my family running the [Mamie Till Mobley Memorial] Foundation and continuing the traditions of Mamie Till-Mobley, Emmett's mother, and what she did, mentoring children and working with youth in the community.

But when Trayvon Martin was murdered, our children were very angry and they got out into the streets and they were pissed about the verdict that was rendered for Zimmerman. I couldn't stand by and just be a mentor and not really educate them about Emmett Till even more so. They really wanted to know about Emmett Till, they wanted to know about that not-guilty verdict that was rendered in 1955 to J. W. Milam and Roy Bryant, who murdered Emmett Till, and then sold their stories months later about how they intentionally were going to make an example out of him. And they tortured and beat and shot and tied a gin fan around his neck and tossed his body into the Tallahatchie River, never to be found again. And they got away with it.

Many of you might wonder, why am I sitting on a panel to discuss police violence. You might not think that Emmett was murdered by police. Well, let's think about Jim Crow. J. W. Milam and Roy Bryant and the KKK were the police, and the police were the KKK. So, technically, Emmett was murdered by the police. The police sat on the jury in 1955. The jury selection was by the police in 1955. The judge was a part of that whole systematic system down in Mississippi that rendered that not guilty verdict, even though there were witnesses and they got off, and double jeopardy. The whole system during that time was Jim Crow. So Emmett was murdered and never given justice by the same system that is doing the same thing almost sixty years later. Next year will be the 60th year anniversary of the murder of Emmett Till.

When I was six months old, I went to live with Mamie, Emmett's mother, and his grandmother, Alma Spearman, and Jeanie Mobley Jr., his stepdad. And as a young child, I used to share the same bed with his grandmother, and she would exchange bedtime stories with me. I would tell her my version of "The Three Little Pigs" and she would tell me about a little boy named "Bobo." And it wasn't until I became much older that I understood that the stories that she was sharing with me were true stories about her grandson, Emmett Till. And as I grew older, I start[ed] to see and understand the images all around me in the home were from a little boy that never got older. These were Emmett Till. The yardstick that I had to go fetch to get my whoopins, I was getting Emmett's whoopins. You know, I was like, why am I getting whooped for being just a rambunctious little kid? But I reminded Mamie of the rambunctious fourteen-year-old that she lost named Emmett Till.

How many of you know the story of Emmett Till? So you know that he whistled at a white woman because he didn't know the rules of Jim Crow when he went to Mississippi, and that whistle cost his life. In the middle of the night, J. W. Milam and Roy Bryant went to the home of his uncle and threatened to kill a house full of young people if they did not relinquish Emmett to them. And they never saw him again alive. Well, that black bayou river spilled the bitter taste of racism and covered Emmett's body right on up. He was never supposed to be found. And so, some young Caucasian boys were fishing, and they saw that little foot dangling, which happened to get caught right at the mouth [of the river]. A twig caught his foot, and that's the only thing that kept his body afloat, and kept him from being never seen again. But God had another plan. He wanted his body to be seen and to be found. And although the world was not supposed to see the corpse that they filled in that box that came to Chicago with a seal that was never to be broken, Mamie defied all the laws that they had set in place. She broke the seal, she broke open the padlock, and then she defied everything when she opened his casket to show the world what they had done.

I hear that I missed Amy Goodman talking about Emmett and Mamie the night before last, and that she talked about how Mamie inspired her and what she did. You'd be amazed how I read and I hear things about how Mamie's decision to open that casket has inspired people all over the world. There's a young boy, his name was Darius [Lane Jr.], sixteen. He was lynched. He was beaten by a lynch mob in France for what they thought he had done committing a burglary. And they printed his body next to the image of Emmett. The picture has since been removed from the article. I was looking at it before I came today, and the family requested that it be removed, but we receive images of brutally murdered or beaten and tortured children, as well as adults, with images next to Emmett all year long. People send them to us, requesting that we assist them and help them.

And to me, it's remarkable that Emmett's casket has never closed. It's been almost sixty years and we are still confronted with the same violent issues of racism. And people compare it to what happened to Emmett Till in 1955. And they ask us to please help them, they reach out to our family because they feel that we can identify or give them direction or just understand what they're going through, and to see these images.

Families across the country who have been victims of racial violence, we are coming together, we have come together, we are connected. We are no longer individually trying to fight this battle and fight this war. We have formed a collective unit, because collectively as a unit, we have more power, we have more force. And unfortunately more and more families are joining us, and we are growing the momentum and the power.

All of these mothers embody a portion or percentage of Emmett Till's mother. If I could just take a piece of Emmett's mom out of each one of these mothers, then I'm going back sixty years to the mother that started it when she lost her child, Emmett Till. That's how deep it is.

• • •

Chrishaun "Cece" McDonald is a Black trans woman and anti-PIC (prison industrial complex) activist. In 2011, at the age of twenty-three, she was charged with
murder after defending herself against a transphobic attacker. McDonald initially faced up to forty years in prison, but thanks to local LGBTQ activists, a
campaign to "Free CeCe" put a spotlight on violence against trans women and
their mistreatment by the criminal legal system. After serving nineteen months
in a men's prison, McDonald was finally released. In this excerpt from an interview conducted by Keegan O'Brien, McDonald tells her story.

Chrishaun "Cece" McDonald, "Standing Up for Each Other" (March 10, 2014)

A group of my friends and I were walking to the twenty-four-hour
grocery store around midnight. Prior to even getting into the incident, we were stopped by the police for what the officer said was a
noise complaint. But I knew that it was racial profiling, because he had
just driven by a bar that was open and where a bunch of people were
being loud and drunk—and we were just down the street, walking and
talking among ourselves.

As I was walking and talking with my boyfriend, some of my friends
were up ahead. And as I was talking to him, I saw this back-and-forth
conversation going on between my friends and some people. I didn't
know if it was an argument or anything at the time—I just saw them
talking.

Then, as I got closer to the scene, I saw this guy being really rude and
making really hurtful, derogatory statements—saying things like we're
"chicks with dicks" and "you niggers need to go back to Africa." It was
just a lot for me. That was the first time that I ever dealt with racism
like that.

It was crazy how things happened after that. Eventually, everyone
was arguing, and I was just sitting there, trying to figure it out, but
a part of me knew that this whole situation was petty—these people
were clearly drunk. As I was getting ready to walk off, this woman

comes out and yells, "I'll take all you bitches on," and she threw her drink at me and smashed her cup in my face—that's how my face got lacerated.

That's pretty much what initiated the whole big brawl. I kept telling them that I didn't want to fight anymore and to please just leave me alone.

But this same guy kept pursuing me. Other people were yelling at me to turn around, and when I did, here he comes, full of hate and anger and bitterness, and full of drugs and alcohol. He went from walking to almost jogging to sprinting. I felt like he was going to really hurt me—that he was going to try to kill me. So I felt, at that point, like I needed to defend myself. My intention wasn't to stab him, my intention was to walk away. I was trying to be the bigger person in the situation and let it go.

Eventually, he caught up to me. I was walking backward, making sure that he wasn't going to try anything. Eventually, he was within reach, and so I pulled out the scissors and told him, "I don't want to fight." He looked down at the scissors like he didn't even care. It was like he was possessed.

I remember saying one last time, "I don't want to fight," and he reached out, grabbed my hair and was trying to yank me down. My reflexes kicked in. It was my immediate reaction. I didn't even know I had stabbed him—it was just a reaction of having to defend myself.

Right after I stabbed him, he was yelling, "Bitch, you stabbed me," and, "This bitch stabbed me." I knew I needed to hurry up and leave because he was crazy and he was going to do something really bad— like go get a gun or something. So I ran and waited in the store parking lot.

After I was standing in the parking lot for a while, the police came, and I was thinking, "Finally!" But the first thing they did is get out the car and arrest me! When I asked for what, they said, "Someone called in saying that someone was stabbed," and I was like, "Yeah, clearly me!" My face and my clothes were covered in my blood! They were making it seem like I was the initial aggressor. And that wasn't at all the case. It was the exact opposite, but they instantly criminalized me.

Three days later, I found out that they were charging me with murder, and I had a full-blown panic attack, to the point that I blacked out. It was really scary. I called everybody I knew—that's how people got involved. A close friend of mine, Abby Beasley, who was a caseworker, connected me with Katie Burges, who works for the Trans Youth Support Network. They were pretty much the keystones of this whole movement that got built up.

It was a really, really troubling time for me, and I had my ups and downs—so low that at one point, I was on the brink of suicide. To have such loving and caring support from family and friends who just encompassed me with so much encouragement was a blessing, and it meant a lot.

Eventually, when it came time for the trial, they added another murder charge—so I was looking at two murder charges for one person. And because they charged me with a second charge, I was looking at eighty years! Honestly, that made me want to just give up.

But I knew that I wanted to fight this for as long as I could—especially after educating myself about the prison industrial complex and how the system targets certain groups of marginalized peoples. I was inspired by that knowledge, and decided that I wanted to be the person who fought this system—to let them know that I wasn't scared and that I'm going to do whatever I need to make sure my voice is heard.

I just feel like no matter what, prisons are bad for everybody. They aren't just bad for trans people—they're bad for all people. Yes, I had my issues. I dealt with extra discrimination and extra scrutiny. I had to deal with things that other people wouldn't have had to deal with in prison because I was a trans woman in a men's prison. Of course, it was upsetting, and it was hard.

But I was blessed to have the support of a team that was willing to support me in this fight against the system. Not everyone in there had that—not everyone had support or someone to help them or be there for them, to protect them or understand them or get them in touch with the right resources. I was blessed to have that.

What happened in my case is a blueprint for the LGBTQI community, African American community, cisgender community, and white community on how to work collectively and be a team. My case showed how many people can come together from different backgrounds and different groups, and contribute to a cause in whatever way they could. There were so many different aspects to this movement, and it made the organizing so much more dynamic.

When we're being targeted, people tend to stick to what they know, whether that's race or gender or whatever. But this showed people how to put aside their personal issues and come together to address a bigger issue. As long as people decide to keep segregating and separating themselves from the rest of the world, and allow ignorance and hatred to keep us apart, we'll never be able to come together and expand our horizons to address the bigger issues going on.

I also want to tell everybody that they should get involved. Because you're making a difference. You're making a difference for yourself and for someone else and for our future generations. I feel like the revolution is now. We're a generation that's making change, and what we do now will affect the kind of world that our children and grandchildren will inherit.

• • •

Across the nation, anti-choice activists and politicians have worked aggressively to roll back hard-won rights to abortion and other forms of reproductive care, an effort that culminated in 2022 with the Supreme Court overturning the landmark cases *Roe v. Wade* and *Planned Parenthood v. Casey*. Anti-choice forces often resorted to deadly violence, including the 2009 assassination of longtime Kansas abortion provider George Tiller. In 2014, Michelle Farber, a midwife at reproductive health clinics, described the impact of anti-choice protests on abortion providers and those seeking their services.

Michelle Farber, "We All Have to Be Brave" (May 14, 2014)

For the first time in my life, I gazed out of two large windows in my office and the thought drifted through my mind, "I wonder if these windows are bulletproof?" I am a nurse-midwife, and I work for a large system of clinics that provides all kinds of reproductive and primary health care, from birth control to well-woman exams. But we also provide another type of reproductive health service that makes us a target for anti-choice demonstrators: abortion.

I live and practice in a state where nurse practitioners, nurse-midwives, and physician's assistants can be medication abortion providers. I am proud to be an abortion provider and feel grateful to be able to provide this vital service to women who chose to terminate their pregnancies. Medication abortions account for roughly a quarter of all pregnancy terminations in the US today, after the "abortion pill" mifepristone (Mifeprex) came on the market in the United States in 2000.

Recently, the clinics I work for endured what is known as "Forty Days for Life," a biannual demonstration in which anti-choice activists picket abortion clinics for the forty days of Lent in the spring and again in the fall.

I started my first job as a midwife a few months before Forty Days for Life began. But that didn't mean that my clinic didn't encounter protesters. Somehow, the anti-choicers know which days are in-clinic abortion days, and I was still in my training period when I encountered them for the first time. I had arrived at the clinic before they got there, but I didn't need to look outside to know that they had arrived.

On in-clinic abortion days, my job is twofold, one medical and one emotional. My first task is generally straightforward: I see women to give them necessary medications before their procedure, talk to them about what to expect, and get them settled with a birth control method for afterward.

My second task, helping a woman through her emotions about the day, is anything but straightforward. The wide range of emotions I see is astounding, and I feel grateful for each woman who shares her story with me. We tell all women that any number of emotions, from sadness to relief, from grief to empowerment, are all normal and expected.

But there is one emotion that creeps into my exam room, which I know would not be there if the anti-choicers were not there.

"I'm scared," a tearful young woman confides in me.

"Tell me more about what you're scared of. Is it the procedure, or something else?" I try to coax out the crux of this woman's feelings.

"I'm scared I'll hate myself."

I hear this often.

"What if those people out there are right?"

"Do you think I'm going to hell for this?"

"They said this will hurt for the baby, is that true? Will the baby feel pain?"

I spend the precious few moments I have to try and undo the damage—the self-doubt, self-loathing, and slut-shaming that the anti-choicers have rolled into a science.

That first day was emotionally draining, and while I have gotten better at comforting women through these difficult emotions, I have not gotten used to it.

As I left the staff entrance that day, I had completely forgotten that the protesters might still be there. I looked up and saw their giant crosses and posters of "aborted" fetuses, and an unexpected shock of fear and intimidation shot through my core.

I stopped dead in my tracks as I locked eyes with an old man who was praying and singing. He watched me walk to my car. I watched him take a photograph of my license plate. I immediately wished I had removed my nametag before exiting the clinic.

I seethed in rage as I drove home. In all my days as a clinic defender, I held a healthy anger in my heart that pushed me and my comrades to stand up to this type of harassment. But that day I felt different. This was personal.

This man and all those like him were the reason many of my patients sat in puddles of tears in the chair next to mine throughout the day. He was protesting the individual choices of the women that I cared for that day. He was protesting my very existence as an abortion provider. He and those like him were not only there to harass and intimidate the patients and staff—one of his aims, I quickly realized, was to scare me.

After that day, I had a long talk with my partner about driving to the clinic in my easily recognizable car versus biking. My mother, to this day, tells me to leave the clinic with the rest of the staff.

The Supreme Court will decide in June whether or not a Massachu-setts law creating buffer zones around clinics is constitutional. These buffer zones, the opponents say, infringe on the right of free speech of anti-abortion protesters.

Over the past few decades, the radical anti-choice movement has shifted strategy from one of firebombs and threats (although these still occur with startling regularity) to one of peaceful "sidewalk coun-selors." Those who oppose the buffer zones paint the protesters as friendly old ladies, too fragile to hurt a fly and merely concerned about young women and babies.

I and the rest of the clinic staff felt a wide range of emotions over those forty days. Some days brought bloodcurdling anger due to the miniature grave one protester set up. Some days, we laughed at the fact that they have nothing better to do. And some days, we had patients walk right up to them and cuss them out.

Some days, I would catch one of them taking photographs of my license plate and the plates of other cars in the parking lot, and the fear I felt on that first day would creep back into my bones, unwittingly. One day, a sweet-looking child called me a "baby killer" as I rode past him and his parent, as I started my bike commute home.

Not all of the days were painful, though. Some of the most heart-ening experiences came when we received community support. An older lady brought by flowers and cookies, with a card detailing her knowledge of the years when abortion was illegal.

A few pro-choice clinic defenders stood out in the pouring rain for hours, and we each rotated going out and thanking them for standing up for what we do. That one day sticks out in my mind, because each of our spirits was so lifted, it was as though the heavy blanket of oppo-sition was made lighter, even if just for a moment.

One evening in late March, about halfway through the Forty Days for Life protests, I sat with a heavy heart on my commute home one evening. I was listening to the story about how Susan Cahill's clinic in Montana was vandalized and subsequently closed.

Cahill has been providing family medicine and abortion services in Montana for almost forty years, and the collective hearts of every abortion provider were broken along with hers that day. Her clinic had been vandalized in a violent manner by the son of one of the founders of a crisis pregnancy center, the so-called peaceful sidewalk counselors. The vandal "meticulously destroyed" everything in the office, from exam tables and the ultrasound machine, to art and family photos hanging on the clinic walls.

This act revealed something clarifying about the anti-choice movement today, and something that those of us who work in abortion services know all too well: that there is a thinly veiled cloak of "God's love" and "saving babies" that is backed with much more sinister propaganda and hate.

The kind of intimidation and harassment the clinic staff and I endure in order to provide a vital, life-saving service should be anything but legal, let alone condoned by the Supreme Court. Moreover, the kind of slut-shaming, judgment, and harassment that each and every one of my patients faces while attempting to access health care should not only require a buffer zone but, in my eyes, should be outlawed as hate speech altogether.

I debated whether or not to run this article under my own name and discussed with my partner what writing openly as an abortion provider means for our lives. I am lucky in that I am not targeted personally by the anti-choice attacks. They do not picket my place of worship or my children's schools, nor put my face on "Wanted: Dead or Alive" posters and circulate them throughout my community—all of which have been documented against other providers across the country.

In the end, I knew that I must step forward and make the call to all other abortion providers to speak out against the harassment and intimidation we face in order to do our jobs. I draw immense inspiration in the bravery of Dr. Willie Parker, a physician who flies down to Mississippi twice a month to keep the doors of the state's last clinic open and speaks publicly about his work often.

My wish is that we all be as brave—and feel as safe to be as brave—as he is. Not only to counter the narrative of the granny sidewalk counselor, but to shed light on what kind of fighting movement we need to battle back against such an organized, anti-choice, anti-woman movement. To shed light on what kind of harassment these so-called sidewalk counselors actually engage in, and to expose their greater political aims: to move the United States back to a time when abortion was illegal, an agenda they will try to push through by any means necessary.

We owe it to all the other abortion providers who have been targeted. We owe it to our patients and their families. We owe it to Susan Cahill. We owe it to George Tiller.

• • •

Michelle Alexander is a civil rights lawyer, advocate, and legal scholar and author of *The New Jim Crow: Mass Incarceration in the Age of Colorblindness*, which became a national bestseller and helped change the conversation about the criminal legal system, inspiring new organizing efforts to transform it. In this essay, she spoke about the urgency of organizing against mass incarceration, as well as other "system[s] of racial and social control."

Michelle Alexander, "How to Dismantle the 'New Jim Crow'" (July 2014)

I hear a stirring, a rumbling. An awakening. Sometimes the sound is so faint, I worry it's my imagination, my optimism getting the best of me. I pause, listen, and wait. Here it comes again. I want to rush to my window, fling it open, stick my head way out, and look around. Is it happening? For real this time? Is the sleeping giant finally waking up?

God knows we've slept too long.

Many of us—myself included—slept through a revolution. Actually, it was a counterrevolution that has blown back much of the progress that so many racial justice advocates risked their lives for. This counterrevolution occurred with barely a whimper of protest, even as a war was declared, one that purported to be aimed at "drugs."

Really, the war took aim at people—overwhelmingly poor people and people of color—who were taken prisoner en masse and then relegated to a permanent, second-class status, stripped of basic civil and human rights such as the right to vote, the right to serve on juries, and the right to be free from legal discrimination in employment, housing, and access to education and public benefits. Branded "criminals" or "felons," millions of people discovered that the very rights supposedly won in the civil rights movement no longer applied to them.

A penal system unprecedented in world history emerged in a few short decades; by the year 2000, two million people found themselves behind bars, and sixty million were saddled with criminal records that would condemn them for life—staggering statistics, given that in the 1970s there were only about 350,000 people in prison.

I am listening carefully at my window now. I hear that rumbling sound, signs of an awakening in the streets. My heart leaps for joy. People of all colors are beginning to raise their voices a little louder; people who have spent time behind bars are organizing for the restoration of their civil and human rights; young people are becoming bolder and more defiant in challenging the prison industrial complex; and people of faith are finally waking up to the uncomfortable reality that we have been complicit in the birth and maintenance of a system predicated on denying to God's children the very forms of compassion, forgiveness, and possibilities for redemption that we claim to cherish.

Even in the halls of power, winds of change have begun to blow. I turn on the news and I see the attorney general of the United States condemning felon disenfranchisement laws and harsh mandatory minimum sentences and expanding the criteria for clemency for those imprisoned for nonviolent offenses. For the first time in decades, it appears that the prison-building boom is slowing down, the numbers of people being locked in cages beginning to decline. State legislatures are reforming drug laws aimed at nonviolent drug offenders, marijuana legalization has taken hold in Colorado and Washington, and seventeen states have passed laws decriminalizing marijuana. Change is in the air.

It all looks so good from here, on my couch, with the remote control in one hand. How tempting it is to imagine that this problem is sorting itself out on its own. But as my thoughts drift toward complacency,

I hear that voice whispering to me again, a voice that returns whenever I get tired or lazy and begin to think maybe someone else will do my work, make my contribution for me. That inner voice repeats the words of Martin Luther King Jr. "[H]uman progress never rolls in on the wheels of inevitability," King said. "It comes through the tireless efforts and the persistent work of dedicated individuals who are willing to be co-workers with God. And without this hard work, time itself becomes an ally of the primitive forces of social stagnation."

Social stagnation. That is precisely the danger we face now: a little reform here, a little reform there, and then . . . nothing. A new normal that looks and feels much like the old. The sleeping giant may toss and turn but ultimately choose to stay in bed, imagining that someone else will do the work that is ours to do. Many of us have comfortable beds and simply don't want to be disturbed.

I remember my early stirrings. Although I was a civil rights lawyer and firmly committed to social justice, it took me a long while to see the bigger picture. Only after years of representing victims of racial profiling, investigating patterns of drug law enforcement, and attempting to assist people who had been released from prison "re-enter" society only to be faced with one legal barrier after another did I finally wake up to the reality that social justice advocates like me were not wrestling with mere social or legal problems. We were dealing with a vast new system of racial and social control—the rise of a new caste-like system in the United States. It is a system that cannot be "reformed" and thereby redeemed any more than it would have been possible to reform slavery or Jim Crow and thereby approach justice.

The system of mass incarceration is rotten to its core. . . .

The ultimate question for us, as people of faith and conscience, is whether we are willing to rise to the challenge this moment in our history presents. Are we willing to do the work? Are we willing to end the drug war in its entirety and shift to a public health model for dealing with drug addiction and abuse? Are we willing to abolish legal discrimination against people with criminal records—discrimination that denies them basic human rights to work, shelter, education, and food? Are we willing to organize for restorative, rehabilitative, and transformative models of justice that take seriously the interests of the victim, the offender, and the community as a whole? Are we willing to tell the truth—the whole truth—about the values and ideologies that brought us to this place and time? Or will we go back to sleep and tolerate a slightly downsized version of the prison industrial complex, one that still cages and perpetually controls millions, but on a slightly smaller scale? . . .

In the end, if our advocacy fails to build a new moral consensus— if it fails to cultivate an ethic of genuine care, compassion, and concern for every human being of every class, race, and nationality—the reforms we achieve will not bring an end to caste-like systems in the United States. Mass incarceration will remain, just downsized a bit, or a new system of racial and social control will emerge . . .

The evil of these systems lies not in their cost, inefficiency, or impracticality. The evil lies in the belief that some of us are disposable, unworthy of care, compassion, or concern. And until we challenge that core belief, systems of racial and social control will continue to be born and thrive in this country for a long, long time. . . .

All of us will need support and guidance as we find our voice and strength in building this movement, though some of us are facing truly desperate circumstances. Let us step forward, as we are, with arms open wide and ready to grow, challenge, and be challenged. We are all co-workers with God, together bending the arc of history toward justice.

May we rise up like a sleeping giant, awakening at last, and get to work making America and ourselves what we must become.

● ● ●

The award-winning author Ursula K. Le Guin (1929–2018), perhaps best known for her imaginative science fiction novels *The Dispossessed* and *The Left Hand of Darkness*, challenged readers to reimagine our understandings of gender, power, love, work, community, and much more. In 2014, Le Guin gave this remarkable speech in New York City after being honored for her Distinguished Contribution to American Letters.

Ursula K. Le Guin, Speech in Acceptance of the National Book Foundation Medal for Distinguished Contribution to American Letters (November 19, 2014)

To the givers of this beautiful reward, my thanks, from the heart. My family, my agents, my editors, know that my being here is their doing as well as my own, and that the beautiful reward is theirs as much as mine. And I rejoice in accepting it for, and sharing it with, all the writers who've been excluded from literature for so long—my fellow authors of fantasy and science fiction, writers of the imagination, who for fifty years have watched the beautiful rewards go to the so-called realists.

Hard times are coming, when we'll be wanting the voices of writers who can see alternatives to how we live now, can see through our fear-stricken society and its obsessive technologies to other ways of being, and even imagine real grounds for hope. We'll need writers who can remember freedom—poets, visionaries—realists of a larger reality.

Right now, we need writers who know the difference between production of a market commodity and the practice of an art. Developing written material to suit sales strategies in order to maximize corporate profit and advertising revenue is not the same thing as responsible book publishing or authorship.

Yet I see sales departments given control over editorial. I see my own publishers, in a silly panic of ignorance and greed, charging public libraries for an e-book six or seven times more than they charge customers. We just saw a profiteer try to punish a publisher for disobedience, and writers threatened by corporate fatwa. And I see a lot of us, the producers, who write the books and make the books, accepting this—letting commodity profiteers sell us like deodorant, and tell us what to publish, what to write.

Books aren't just commodities; the profit motive is often in conflict with the aims of art. We live in capitalism, its power seems inescapable—but then, so did the divine right of kings. Any human power can be resisted and changed by human beings. Resistance and change often begin in art. Very often in our art, the art of words.

I've had a long career as a writer, and a good one, in good company. Here at the end of it, I don't want to watch American literature get sold down the river. We who live by writing and publishing want and should demand our fair share of the proceeds; but the name of our beautiful reward isn't profit. Its name is freedom.

Chapter 5

The Ferguson Uprising, Barack Obama, and the Limits of "Equality"

Tef Poe, "Dear Mr. President" (December 1, 2014)
Ferguson Action, "About This Movement" (December 15, 2014)
Amanda Blackhorse, "This Is What Dehumanization Looks Like" (March 21, 2015)
Ross Gay, "A Small Needful Fact" (April 30, 2015)
Bree Newsome, "Now Is the Time for True Courage" (June 30, 2015)
Sins Invalid, "10 Principles of Disability Justice" (September 17, 2015)
Dream Defenders, "Social Media Blackout" (September 21, 2015)
Lindy West, "I Set Up #ShoutYourAbortion Because I Am Not Sorry, and I Will
    Not Whisper" (September 22, 2015)
Samaria Rice, "Why I Have Not Endorsed Any Candidate: Reflections from a
    Mom of the Movement" (March 15, 2016)
Alicia Garza, "Why Black Lives Matter" (March 18, 2016)
Chanel Miller, "Impact Statement" (June 3, 2016)
Nick Estes, "Native Liberation: The Way Forward" (August 13, 2016)
Kimberlé Williams Crenshaw, "The Urgency of Intersectionality" (October 27, 2016)
Leonard Peltier, "Our Day of Mourning" (November 30, 2016)

• • •

By 2014, the fantasy of a "post-racial" United States had been obliterated by the emergence of the Black Lives Matter movement following the police killings of Michael Brown in Ferguson, Missouri, and of Eric Garner in Staten Island, New York. Protesters took to the streets, shutting down highways in cities across the country as they marched against police killings of Black people and the fact that police rarely, if ever, faced consequences from the legal system. The rise of social media combined with activism on the ground meant that police brutality could no longer be dismissed as the work of a few "bad apples." Activists raised popular consciousness about the regularity and ease with which the police snuffed out Black life, from Tamir Rice in Cleveland, Ohio, to Rekia Boyd in Chicago, to Freddie Gray in Baltimore, to Alton Sterling in Baton Rouge, to Philando Castile in Minneapolis–St. Paul, and on and on.

Yet, if police racism was the catalyst for the movement, the struggle also opened space to discuss deeper inequalities throughout US society. As Keeanga-Yamahtta Taylor observed in her seminal book *From #BlackLivesMatter to Black Liberation*, it was no coincidence that the largest protests for racial justice since the civil rights movement coincided with the election of the nation's first Black president. While Black people faced an unemployment rate double that of whites and saw their wealth evaporate, having been deliberately targeted for predatory loans by the very banks that Obama had bailed out during the recession, "the reluctance of his administration to address any of the substantive issues facing Black communities . . . meant that suffering [had] worsened in those communities over the course of Obama's term in office." Meanwhile, Obama's promise of hope and change gave way to disillusionment, as immigrant rights activists dubbed Obama the "deporter-in-chief" for the three million deportations that occurred during his administration—more than under any other president.

While the movements of the 1960s had succeeded in removing formal barriers to social mobility, allowing a minority of middle-class women, Black and Latinx people, and others from historically marginalized groups to enter the political establishment, their success did not fundamentally change conditions for the majority within those groups. Activists were forced to grapple with the limits of formal equality and representation within the halls of power, given that the system they sought to access remained organized around social and economic inequality. Importantly, disillusionment with politicians of both parties in the face of unmitigated state violence meant that activists would have to take matters into their own hands, as exemplified by the defiance of Ferguson protesters, who faced down militarized police forces that resembled an occupying army; by the bravery of Bree Newsome, who scaled a flagpole to remove the long-standing Confederate flag from the South Carolina State Capitol; and by the heroic struggle to stop the construction of the Dakota Access Pipeline and defend Indigenous sovereignty at Standing Rock.

• • •

On August 9, 2014, police officer Darren Wilson shot and killed Michael Brown, an unarmed Black eighteen-year-old from Ferguson, Missouri. Brown's body was left in the street for four hours, prompting observers to call it a modern-day lynching. After a jury acquitted Wilson, the residents of Ferguson took to the streets in weeks of rebellion. When tanks, tear gas, and rubber bullets failed to stop the protests, Governor Jay Nixon sent in the National Guard. Rather than condemning the state's show of force, President Barack Obama instead lectured protesters about "violence" and "looting." In an open letter to the nation's first Black president, rapper and activist Tef Poe questioned Obama's response.

Tef Poe, "Dear Mr. President" (December 1, 2014)

Dear Mr. President,

I write this letter with high hopes that it reaches you with a sober heart and a pair of open ears.

In St. Louis, our police force has a history of abusing its power while torturing Black people. We have cried out for help, and your response earlier this summer basically condemned us. Like many other young people from my community, I was confused.

The police attacked us for taking to the streets to resist police brutality, and our beloved Black president seemingly endorsed it. I'm sure you will say this isn't the case, but as a young Black man in America I speak for a large demographic of us that has long awaited our Black president to speak in a direct tone while condemning our murders. From our perspective, the statement you made on Ferguson completely played into the racist connotations that we are violent, uneducated, welfare-recipient looters. Your remarks in support of the National Guard attacks upon us and our community devoured our dignity.

When an assault rifle is aimed at your face over nothing more than a refusal to move, you don't feel like the American experience is one that includes you. When the president your generation selected does not condemn these attacks, you suddenly begin to believe that this system is a fraudulent hoax—and the joke is on you. Racism is very much alive in America, but as a president with so much melanin in his skin, you seem to address it very bashfully.

Many of us, whether we admit it or not, looked to you for some form of moral support. We do not want to die. We do not want race riots in our city. We previously lived very normal lives outside the overly aggressive dealings we've often experienced with those who are sworn to uphold the law.

Police often kill us (every twenty-eight hours in this country, in fact) and go unpunished. Who holds them accountable if even our president has no official commitment to do so? As a community of young, responsible and politically engaged Black people, we have collectively decided that we will hold them accountable ourselves. We are committed and will continue to fight in a very fearless and openly broadcasted display of hope and audacity. We are a broad coalition of organizers and activists. Through the marvels of the Internet our reach has traveled across the world.

In Geneva, Switzerland, a few of us visited the US ambassador, yet unfortunately this display was a waste of time and energy. He did his job. He heard our concerns, but he was not emotionally moved to stop this massive act of violence from the state. And I say to you, Mr. President, your silence is consent as well. We will remember you according to your work. When you leave the Oval Office and return to society as one of us, we will judge you accordingly. Your party is being judged accordingly.

Governor Jay Nixon is your colleague, but through a lack of sound judgment and sincere analysis he has morphed into the everlasting enemy of oppressed Black people in Missouri. Senator Claire McCaskill has a bit more dignity than Nixon, but her decision to remain idle on this subject has also signified to the community that she is not one of us.

Right now we are being treated like enemies of the state while the racist police force continues to arm itself and occupy our communities.

We encountered the harsh nature of the militarized police force first-hand. We were tear-gassed and hoarded into jail cells like livestock, simply for chanting in honor of Mike Brown. Armored vehicles turned our neighborhood into a military encampment. Young women from Palestine have visited us and lectured us about constructing homemade gas masks. College students are actively searching online for affordable bulletproof vests.

I have never looted or violently struck a police officer. We do lift our voices to yell, and yes, we often use profanity. We are more aggressive than protesters in the past, primarily because we are in a state of emotional disbelief. Mike Brown spent four and a half hours in the street, baking and bleeding on the hot summer pavement. We know you know this is wrong, so the disconnect between your words and your personal convictions has raised many questions in the Black community.

Now we are organizing against you and members of your party as though we didn't vote for you to begin with. This saddens me, because we rooted for you. We love you and want to sing praises of you to our children, but first we need a statement of solidarity from you to the young Black people facing the perils of police brutality. We will not get this statement, and we know it.

I wish you could remember your days as a grassroots organizer in your own community. I beg you to find time to reflect back and remember when you were in the same position as we are. You are a career politician, so your opinions may not have been as radical as mine, but remember back to when you were organizing at this level.

If not for the protection provided by their last name, your beautiful Black daughters could also be considered human targets. If the malice of Darren Wilson would've left Sasha in the middle of the street with a bullet in her head, would you have responded to this matter with such a passive, unemotional tone? Would you go on camera and applaud the National Guard for attacking the citizens of your own neighborhood for demanding answers for the murder of your daughter?

Have you heard the sobs of our mothers as they suffer through these atrocities? What if Michelle had to look into a casket with one of your daughters inside it? What if a careless police officer attacked your family in this manner, and the only line of defense you have is the community?

Me and my friends are young. We voted for you because initially you spoke our language. We believed you would be more of an activist than a typical suit-and-tie teleprompter politician. Are you not outraged by the treatment of your own people by law enforcement? Why is it so difficult for you to display a moment of honesty and reflection to the public about your own Blackness?

Your children will grow up with Black skin. They have Black parents. We will want to champion them as honorable reflections of the Black American experience. Will your decisions to not address these issues play a role in their acceptance into the Black progressive community when they are older?

I address you respectfully and with great admiration for your accomplishments. As a Black man talking to another Black man, we can no longer afford to allow you, as our highest voice in the highest office, to remain idle on the issue of race and equality in America. We can no longer allow you, as one of the most respected and admired Black men on the planet, to ignore our cries for help. Most of us don't have the privilege of the Oval Office. Even with that privilege, at the wrong place and time, you too can become a victim of this violence. Please help us fight these monsters. The right side of history awaits you. I love you and respect you, like a younger brother watching his older brother from the bleachers.

I am simply asking you to help us.

● ● ●

The rebellion that followed the police killing of Michael Brown kicked off the largest anti-racist movement since the civil rights era. While police killings of Black people were the catalyzing issue, activists argued that real justice must address racism in all its forms. In a statement by the group Ferguson Action, activists laid out the stakes of these protests.

Ferguson Action, "About This Movement"
(December 15, 2014)

On the week of August 9, Black youth in Ferguson took to the streets and kicked off a wave of resistance against police violence that has spread across the country. In the last four months, we have stood united in a call for change in our system of policing and a new vision for Black lives, lived fully and with dignity.

Millions have answered that call with simple acts of civil disobedience. We are marching, shutting down streets, taking highways, stopping trains and yes, even tweeting. We have done all of this together. We've met in our homes, offices, and schools—and walked out of them, with our hands up. Many of you have organized small actions that when woven together, have tremendous impact.

And this weekend, over fifty thousand people took to the streets of New York City in the largest march yet, seeking justice for Eric Garner and all victims of police violence.

This movement belongs to all of us. It is broad and people-powered, made up of many places and parts. No one organization, group, or leader can claim this ongoing momentum, which was undeniably sparked by a group of young Black people in Ferguson who said: "Enough." These marches, sit-ins, and occupations continue a long tradition of civil disobedience in the pursuit of justice that has inspired the world to act. That is real leadership.

Together, we have made #BlackLivesMatter a dinner table conversation, and in doing so, opened a long-overdue national dialogue on what it takes for Black people to fully attain freedom. Because when we are out in the streets, we know that this movement is bigger than body cameras or civilian review boards. We are all asking important questions.

What is justice when police officers can kill and beat us with impunity, on and off camera.

What is justice when the policing system we aim to change feeds our nation's addiction to prisons, where many of our family members serve unjust sentences that do nothing to repair the fabric of our communities? Meanwhile, law enforcement officers and the departments that employ them are never held accountable for the damage they inflict in our neighborhoods.

What is justice when the promise of a living wage is beyond the reach of many in our communities? When our schools are broken and underfunded? When we are pushed out of our neighborhoods to make room for wealthier, whiter residents?

The truth is that justice eludes us: at our schools, in our streets, at our borders, in prison yards, on protest lines and even in our homes. It is that full freedom that we fight for when we say that #BlackLivesMatter.

This is a movement of and for *all* Black lives—women, men, transgender, and queer. We are made up of both youth *and* elders aligned through the possibilities that new tactics and fresh strategies offer our movement. Some of us are new to this work, but many of us have been organizing for years. We came together in Mike Brown's name, but our roots are also in the flooded streets of New Orleans and the bloodied BART stations of Oakland. We are connected online and in the streets. We are decentralized, but coordinated. Most importantly, we are organized.

Yet we are likely not respectable negroes. We stand beside each other, not in front of one another. We do not cast any one of ours to the side in order to gain proximity to perceived power. Because this is the only way we will win. We can't breathe. And we won't stop until Freedom.

• • •

The Diné activist and social worker Amanda Blackhorse, who is a member of the Navajo Nation, has been a key figure in the movement against the use of Indigenous names and cultural figures as sports team mascots. In July 2020, she and other organizers achieved a major victory when the National Football League franchise in Washington, DC, finally relented in its yearslong insistence that it would never change its offensive team name.

Amanda Blackhorse, "This Is What Dehumanization Looks Like" (March 21, 2015)

Quite often when speaking out and educating others about the mascot issue, the same question is asked, "Why are you people worried about mascots? Don't you have bigger issues to worry about on the reservations?"

Native people, likewise, will also ask, "Why are we (Indigenous peoples) fighting the mascot issue when there are bigger issues to fight?"

Oh yes, the bigger issues question. What most people seem to be referring to are the many issues which plague Native American communities. Societal problems such as violence against women, suicide, alcoholism, high unemployment rates on reservations, poverty, etc. Many of these issues have been highlighted throughout the history of Native American people, through various studies, articles, documentaries, movies, so on and so on.

I grew up in this ever-so-familiar way of poverty and destruction, in all those "bigger issues" people talk about. My very existence is a symptom of that. I understand it very well; I've been accustomed to it, and in many ways it has made me the very resilient person I am today. I understand the struggles of "poverty" and in many ways, I continue to live in that struggle.

So when people tell me we should be worrying about those "bigger issues," a part of me smiles within, not because it's funny, but because I empathize and further because I know it all too well.

Indeed, these are all very important issues to address and they should be addressed. Many Native American leaders, allies, and the like have worked on addressing these issues and, today, continue to address them. The mascot issue does not take away from the work happening toward making positive change; rather the mascot issue is allowing for those issues to be addressed in an easier way.

If we are not respected as human beings how can we be respected when dealing with politics and/or economics? It makes it harder to be seen as leaders, advocates, and people who want real change to happen in our communities if you are seen as just a person who dances at powwows and viewed as a mere relic of old cowboy and Indian movies. Of course this is not the case in every situation when dealing with non-Natives and government, but it seems to be a common misconception of Native people, which transcends into politics and government.

Not only are we looked at as just those Indians, but we don't seem to be heard by the viewer either. Native people have been struggling, advocating, protesting, and trying to invoke change in our communities, but, again, we are not heard!

The mascot issue has been going on for more than forty years and we are only now beginning to see our people and topics on the national level. Just because it doesn't make headlines does not mean the battles are not being fought somewhere in Native America. Our voice doesn't seem to be strong enough, so protest, lawsuits, and movements are necessary so that we can be heard, loud and clear.

By telling Native people they should be worried about more important issues tells Native people their voice and their feelings are not enough or they are unimportant. It tells Native people that the voice of the non-Native is far more important and more powerful than the true voice of the Indigenous population.

Native American people have been targeted for their race, their land, and their resources. So when the dominant culture believes they are superior to the Indigenous population they will dehumanize and dominate us for their own good. This includes the dehumanization of our entire being, especially our identity.

Dehumanization of Indigenous people is:

1. The land-grabbing of Indigenous lands
2. The raping, violence, and hatred directed at Indigenous women and children
3. The poisoning of our water
4. The desecration of our ancestors' bones and graves
5. Each "redskin" (hair, scalp, nose, ears, genitals, and skin) taken off of an Indigenous person
6. Each child taken from the arms of their parents and grandparents for the sake of "killing the Indian and saving the man"

7. Each treaty that was not honored
8. Every acre of land stolen from Indigenous people
9. Every law passed since the Doctrine of Discovery for the sake of manifest destiny
10. Every religion stuffed down the throats of Indigenous men and women for the sake of colonization
11. Each smallpox blanket
12. Every head of hair chopped off in boarding schools and residential schools
13. The forced mining, fracking, and desecration of Indigenous lands yesterday and today
14. The sterilization of Indigenous women by Indian Health Service
15. Each tribe which no longer exists due to the attempted extermination of Indigenous people
16. Each tribal person who was exiled and relocated to urban communities
17. Each person who has been subjected to alcoholism in the name of poor business or poor treaty deals
18. Each Native person who has been experimented on and exploited for their blood, bodies, and DNA

The dehumanization of Indigenous people continues today. Each example is how Native Americans, First Nations, and Indigenous peoples of this continent have been subjects for acts of genocide. Each example has occurred in some variation in Native American communities and Indigenous communities throughout North and South America. If you have no respect for a person's dignity, well-being, and physical well-being, you will not have respect for their identity, therefore making it easy to mascot them. As long as the populace refuses to see Native people as real, living, breathing, and resilient individuals, the easier it becomes to demean, degrade, and mascot them. If our very existence or presence has been stripped away it is easier to create a multimillion-, if not billion-dollar industry off of the very identity of these people for entertainment purposes.

What people don't realize is there are *real* Natives out there who have been truly affected and psychologically damaged by sports mascots. There are real children and youth out there who have fought with their blood, sweat, and tears to remove these racist mascots and names. Those children are real and are tribal members and citizens of nations. Although you may not see it or have been affected by it doesn't mean it doesn't exist. Just because it is out of sight and out of mind doesn't make it any less real, any less hurtful to those who have been affected by it.

Any attempt to humanize Indigenous people is a step in the right direction. Eliminating Native mascots may not be the complete answer, but it is a step in the right direction.

The mascot movement has empowered millions of Indigenous peoples around the world because for once we have a voice; for once they can stand at the national level and be proud to be Indigenous.

And allow me to drive home this point: using the "bigger issues" excuse is just that, an excuse. It is an excuse that is counterproductive and does nothing to solve the greater problem of the oppression of Native people and racism directed at Native people. It's an excuse to be apathetic and to deny a problem really exists. If you are not engaged in addressing those bigger issues you should not be using the bigger issues excuse. If you happen to be working on those bigger issues and still do not agree then let's agree to disagree, and also understand that just because this isn't your struggle, it doesn't mean it isn't a struggle for your fellow Native people.

The questions we should be asking ourselves are: "Why have we not achieved true self-determination as Indigenous people?" and "Why is it that in this day and age are we still fighting for common decency to be respected by our non-Native counterparts?" Those are the real questions.

● ● ●

In 2014, the name Eric Garner became synonymous with a rallying cry for help: "I can't breathe." As Garner was being choked to death on the sidewalks of Staten Island, he repeatedly told the police officers who were pinning him to the ground, "I can't breathe." But before his name became intertwined with this tragic plea, and sparked massive protest against police brutality across the country, he was many other things: Garner was a father to six, he was known around his community as a neighborhood peacemaker, and, perhaps less known, he was a horticulturalist. In this poem, first published on the *Split This Rock* blog, Ross Gay muses on Garner's life and work at the New York City Department of Parks and Recreation.

Ross Gay, "A Small Needful Fact" (April 30, 2015)

Is that Eric Garner worked
for some time for the Parks and Rec.
Horticultural Department, which means,
perhaps, that with his very large hands,
perhaps, in all likelihood,
he put gently into the earth
some plants which, most likely,
some of them, in all likelihood,
continue to grow, continue
to do what such plants do, like house
and feed small and necessary creatures,
like being pleasant to touch and smell,
like converting sunlight
into food, like making it easier
for us to breathe.

• • •

Bree Newsome became an overnight hero for daring to accomplish in a day what years of waiting on legislators had failed to do. With the help of fellow activists, she scaled the thirty-foot flagpole outside the South Carolina State Capitol building and took down the Confederate flag. The flag's origins lie in the Civil War, when states seceded from the Union in order to preserve the Southern system of slavery. It has remained a symbol of racist terror ever since. Three days after her bold action, which led to her arrest, Newsome described why she risked arrest to remove the flag and why she could not have succeeded alone.

Bree Newsome, "Now Is the Time for True Courage" (June 30, 2015)

For far too long, white supremacy has dominated the politics of America resulting in the creation of racist laws and cultural practices designed to subjugate non-whites. And the emblem of the Confederacy, the stars and bars, in all its manifestations, has long been the most recognizable banner of this political ideology. It's the banner of racial intimidation and fear whose popularity experiences an uptick whenever Black Americans appear to be making gains economically and politically in this country.

It's a reminder how, for centuries, the oppressive status quo has been undergirded by white supremacist violence with the tacit approval of too many political leaders.

The night of the Charleston Massacre, I had a crisis of faith. The people who gathered for Bible study in Emanuel AME Church that night—Cynthia Marie Graham Hurd, Susie Jackson, Ethel Lee Lance, Depayne Middleton-Doctor, Tywanza Sanders, Daniel Simmons, Sharonda Coleman-Singleton, Myra Thompson and Rev. Clementa Pinckney (rest in peace)—were only doing what Christians are called to do when anyone knocks on the door of the church: invite them into fellowship and worship.

The day after the massacre I was asked what the next step was and I said I didn't know. We've been here before and here we are again: Black people slain simply for being Black; an attack on the Black church as a place of spiritual refuge and community organization.

I refuse to be ruled by fear. How can America be free and be ruled by fear? How can anyone be?

So, earlier this week I gathered with a small group of concerned citizens, both Black and white, who represented various walks of life, spiritual beliefs, gender identities, and sexual orientations. Like millions of others in America and around the world, including South Carolina Governor Nikki Haley and President Barack Obama, we felt (and still feel) that the Confederate battle flag in South Carolina, hung in 1962 at the height of the civil rights movement, must come down.

We discussed it and decided to remove the flag immediately, both as an act of civil disobedience and as a demonstration of the power people have when we work together. Achieving this would require many roles, including someone who must volunteer to scale the pole and remove the flag. It was decided that this role should go to a Black woman and that a white man should be the one to help her over the fence as a sign that our alliance transcended both racial and gender divides. We made this decision because for us, this is not simply about a flag, but rather it is about abolishing the spirit of hatred and oppression in all its forms.

I removed the flag not only in defiance of those who enslaved my ancestors in the southern United States, but also in defiance of the oppression that continues against Black people globally in 2015, including the ongoing ethnic cleansing in the Dominican Republic. I did it in solidarity with the South African students who toppled a statue of the white supremacist, colonialist Cecil Rhodes. I did it for all the fierce Black women on the front lines of the movement and for all the little Black girls who are watching us. I did it because I am free.

To all those who might label me an "outside agitator," I say to you that humanitarianism has no borders. I am a global citizen. My prayers are with the poor, the afflicted and the oppressed everywhere in the world, as Christ instructs. If this act of disobedience can also serve as a symbol to other peoples' struggles against oppression or as a symbol of victory over fear and hate, then I know all the more that I did the right thing.

You see, I know my history and my heritage. The Confederacy is neither the only legacy of the South nor an admirable one. The Southern heritage I embrace is the legacy of a people unbowed by racial oppression. It includes towering figures of the civil rights movement like Ida B. Wells, Martin Luther King Jr., Fannie Lou Hamer, Rosa Parks, Medgar Evers, and Ella Baker. It includes the many people who rarely make the history books but without whom there is no movement. It includes pillars of the community like Rev. Clementa Pinckney and Emanuel AME Church.

As you are admiring my courage in that moment, please remember that this is not, never has been, and never should be just about one woman. This action required collective courage just as this movement requires collective courage. Not everyone who participated in the strategizing for this nonviolent direct action volunteered to have their names in the news so I will respect their privacy. Nonetheless, I'm honored to be counted among the many freedom fighters, both living and dead.

I see no greater moral cause than liberation, equality, and justice for all God's people. What better reason to risk your own freedom than to fight for the freedom of others? That's the moral courage demonstrated yesterday by James Ian Tyson who helped me across the fence and stood guard as I climbed. History will rightly remember him alongside the many white allies who, over the centuries, have risked their own safety in defense of Black life and in the name of racial equality.

It is important to remember that our struggle doesn't end when the flag comes down. The Confederacy is a Southern thing, but white supremacy is not. Our generation has taken up the banner to fight battles many thought were won long ago. We must fight with all vigor now so that our grandchildren aren't still fighting these battles in another fifty years. Black Lives Matter. This is non-negotiable.

I encourage everyone to understand the history, recognize the problems of the present, and take action to show the world that the status quo is not acceptable. The last few days have confirmed to me that people understand the importance of action and are ready to take such action. Whether the topic is trending nationally or it's an issue affecting our local communities, those of us who are conscious must do what is right in this moment. And we must do it without fear. New eras require new models of leadership. This is a multi-leader movement. I believe that. I stand by that. I am because we are. I am one of many.

This moment is a call to action for us all. All honor and praise to God.

• • •

Sins Invalid is an inclusive, pathbreaking disability justice project that "incubates and celebrates artists with disabilities, centralizing artists of color and LGBTQ/gender-variant artists as communities who have been historically marginalized" and is "committed to social and economic justice for all people with disabilities—in lockdowns, in shelters, on the streets, visibly disabled, invisibly disabled, sensory minority, environmentally injured, psychiatric survivors—moving beyond individual legal rights to collective human rights." In 2015, Sins Invalid clarified core principles that should animate movements for disability justice; in November 2022, they revised the text, which we include here.

Sins Invalid, "10 Principles of Disability Justice" (September 17, 2015)

From our vantage point within Sins Invalid, where we incubate the framework and practice of disability justice, this emerging framework has ten principles, each offering opportunities for movement building:

1. INTERSECTIONALITY

Simply put, this principle says that we are many things, and they all impact us.

We are not only disabled, we are also each coming from a specific experience of race, class, sexuality, age, religious background, geographical location, immigration status, and more. Depending on context, we all have areas where we experience privilege, as well as areas of oppression. The term "intersectionality" was first introduced by feminist theorist Kimberlé Crenshaw in 1989 to describe the experiences of Black women, who experience both racism and sexism in specific ways. We gratefully embrace the nuance that this principle brings to our lived experiences, and the ways it shapes the perspectives we offer.

2. LEADERSHIP OF THOSE MOST IMPACTED

By centering the leadership of those most impacted, "we are led by those who most know these systems" (Aurora Levins Morales). This means that as disabled BIPOC queer/trans/nonbinary economically exploited people with family and ancestors in the global South, we know in our very bodies the harm that these oppressions create and have deep understandings of how oppressive systems work to reinforce and recreate each other. This knowledge opens paths to understanding how we can undermine, transform, or outright abolish oppressive systems. Further, we create and hold visions for a world with life-affirming systems that work for us.

3. ANTI-CAPITALIST POLITICS

Our literal bodyminds conflict with capitalist methods and goals. We resist conforming to "normative" levels of productivity in a capitalist culture. Human activity and creation is so much more than labor as defined by capitalism. Our worth is not dependent on what and how much we can produce.

4. CROSS-MOVEMENT SOLIDARITY

Ableism is rooted in the hatred and fear of disabled bodyminds, but also in the terror of *all* forms of existence/embodiment and power that threaten the domination of white cis-hetero patriarchal colonial power. Undermining ableism necessarily and simultaneously demands that we oppose white supremacy, challenge cis-heteropatriarchy, and support the rematriation of Indigenous lands.

As we shift how social justice movements understand disability and contextualize ableism, disability justice lends itself to politics of alliance.

5. RECOGNIZING WHOLENESS

Each person is full of history and life experience. Each person has an internal experience composed of our own thoughts, sensations, emotions, sexual fantasies, perceptions, and quirks. Disabled people are whole people.

6. SUSTAINABILITY

We learn to pace ourselves, individually and collectively, to be sustained long-term. We value the teachings of our bodies and experiences and use them as a critical guide and reference point to help us move away from urgency and into a deep, slow, transformative, unstoppable wave of justice and liberation.

7. COMMITMENT TO CROSS-DISABILITY SOLIDARITY

We value and honor the insights and participation of all of our community members, even and especially those who are most often left out of political conversations. We are building a movement that breaks down isolation between people with physical impairments, people who are sick or chronically ill, psych survivors and people with mental health disabilities, neurodiverse people, people with intellectual or developmental disabilities, Deaf people, Blind people, people with environmental injuries and chemical sensitivities, and all others who experience ableism and isolation that undermines our collective liberation.

8. INTERDEPENDENCE

Before the massive colonial project of Western European expansion, we understood the nature of interdependence within our communities. We see the liberation of all living systems and the land as integral to the liberation of our own communities, as we all share one planet. We work to meet each other's needs as we build toward liberation, without always reaching for state solutions which inevitably extend state control further into our lives.

9. COLLECTIVE ACCESS

As Black and Brown and queer crips, we bring flexibility and creative nuance to our engagement with each other. We create and explore ways of doing things that go beyond able-bodied and neurotypical norms. Access needs aren't shameful—we all function differently depending on context and environment. Access needs can be articulated and met privately, through a collective, or in community, depending upon an individual's needs, desires, and the capacity of the group. We can share responsibility for our access needs; we can ask that our needs be met without compromising our integrity; we can balance autonomy while being in community; we can be unafraid of our vulnerabilities, knowing our strengths are respected.

10. COLLECTIVE LIBERATION

We move together as people with mixed abilities, multiracial, multi-gendered, mixed class, across the sexual spectrum, with a vision that leaves no bodymind behind.

This is disability justice. We honor the longstanding legacies of resilience and resistance which are the inheritance of all of us whose bodies and minds will not conform. Disability justice is a vision and practice of what is yet-to-be, a map that we create with our ancestors and our great-grandchildren onward, in the width and depth of our multiplicities and histories, a movement toward a world in which every body and mind is known as beautiful.

● ● ●

The Florida-based Dream Defenders have used bold organizing strategies and deployed savvy means of communicating their message to wide audiences. But in fall 2015, the group took a deliberate break from social media to focus on more personal methods of communication and organizing, in the process raising critical questions about ways some activists have confused Twitter followers and Facebook "likes" with base-building.

Dream Defenders, "Social Media Blackout" (September 21, 2015)

After three years of fighting, organizing, and building, we have spent the last eight months in deep collective reflection. With that has come great clarity, perspective, and the realization that many of our biggest supporters, fans, and followers don't truly know what we *do*, who our members *are*, and *how* we are building power for transformational change in the state of Florida.

Dream Defenders is an organization with membership throughout Florida committed to developing and nurturing strong community relationships, a deep understanding of the needs of our people, to facilitate the collective development and execution of transformational solutions. It is more than actions, protests, or occupations: though we do all three very well. The on-the-ground work that we do is tangible and transformational.

We have watched the growing debate about cultural influencers, social media/activist celebrities with larger followings and no accountability that comment on political issues. This is a worthwhile debate. Especially in this hypersensitive climate where discord and discourse is discouraged and attacked.

We have always used social media as a part of our organizing. Twitter, Instagram, and Facebook have created the unprecedented opportunity to contribute to and critique conversations and events as they happen. The emergence of a collective voice channeled online has helped us, and a host of others, develop a brand that people trust and believe relevant.

The answer is clear for us: Social media is a microphone—it amplifies the grassroots organizing work that we are doing to transform our circumstances. It does not, and never will, take the place of building deep relationships which are at the core of organizing. Everything outside of that—though important in shifting culture, changing policy, and transforming our communities—simply is *not* organizing.

To change our communities, we must have power, not just followers.

Our culture rewards folks for RTs [retweets] and posting the same information, articles, and snarky comments. Our profiles get more attention for talking about tragedies than they do for highlighting the work that our membership is doing day in and day out. We have attained social media popularity that doesn't necessarily support a growth in our membership, nor does it give them a strategic advantage in transforming their circumstances locally.

We appreciate the immense support and trust that has been shared with Dream Defenders over the past three years. We recognize that people trust and love our brand because we are led by the work that our members are doing. But, it troubles us that participating in Twitter conversations and television appearances are held up as "doing the work," when we know that so much more has to be done.

As our social media profile has grown so has its separation from the voice and work of our incredible membership. In keeping up with the latest hashtags or movement trends/moments we have lost our way at times and fallen victim to the schizophrenia of the times. We can blame the culture. We choose to blame ourselves.

That said, we as an organization have decided to take a step back and take a "social media sabbatical" of sorts—to adjust, re-center and get it right.

We will be back in November with a fresh voice; one that emanates from the grassroots and is a complement to movement work, not just characters.

● ● ●

Lindy West is a Seattle-based comedian, writer, and activist whose work focuses on feminism and combating fatphobia. She is the author of the best-selling memoir *Shrill: Notes from a Loud Woman* and is a producer on the Hulu TV series of the same title. In the following essay, she explains the motivation behind #ShoutYourAbortion, a campaign to destigmatize the procedure.

Lindy West, "I Set Up #ShoutYourAbortion Because I Am Not Sorry, and I Will Not Whisper" (September 22, 2015)

Almost exactly five years ago, in September 2010, I took one pill, and then another, and lay in my bed for a night and a day, and then I wasn't pregnant anymore. It was a fairly smooth experience, distressing only because my relationship was bad and I had no money. The procedure itself was a relief. Not being able to have it would have been the real trauma.

Suddenly, last week, in the thick of the right-wing, misogynist crusade to defund Planned Parenthood (a vital American nonprofit that provides a broad range of healthcare services, including pelvic exams, STI screenings, contraception, and abortion), a thought bowled me over: I never, ever talk about my abortion. I live in a progressive city, I have a fiercely pro-choice social circle and family, I write confessionally about myself for a living—so why is it that I never speak about abortion in anything beyond an abstract way, even with my closest friends? I know about who has a vagina infection, whose boyfriend's penis bends weird, who used to do drugs, who still does. And I know how all of them feel about abortion, policy-wise. But I don't know who has had one, and they don't know about mine. It's not a secret; it's just something we don't talk about.

Not talking about our personal experiences with abortion wasn't conscious—it felt like a habit, a flimsy ouroboros of obfuscation. We don't talk about it because we don't talk about it because we don't talk about it. So, on Saturday, when my friend Amelia Bonow posted this plainspoken, unapologetic announcement on her Facebook page, it felt simultaneously so obvious, so simple, and so revolutionary: "Like a year ago I had an abortion at the Planned Parenthood on Madison Ave, and I remember this experience with a near inexpressible level of gratitude . . . I am telling you this today because the narrative of those working to defund Planned Parenthood relies on the assumption that abortion is still something to be whispered about. Plenty of people still believe that on some level—if you are a good woman—abortion is a choice which should be accompanied by some level of sadness, shame, or regret. But you know what? I have a good heart and having an abortion made me happy in a totally unqualified way. Why wouldn't I be happy that I was not forced to become a mother?"

"The assumption that abortion is still something to be whispered about." That struck me hard. The fact that even progressive, outspoken, pro-choice feminists feel the pressure to keep our abortions under wraps—to speak about them only in corners, in murmurs, in private with our closest confidantes—means that opponents of abortion get to define it however suits them best. They can cast those of us who have had abortions as callous monstrosities, and seed fear in anyone who might need one by insisting that the procedure is always traumatic, always painful, always an impossible decision. Well, we're not, and it's not. The truth is that life is unfathomably complex, people with uteruses own their bodies unconditionally, and every abortion story is as unique as the person who lives it. Some are traumatic, some are even regretted, but plenty are like mine.

With her permission, I screen-grabbed Amelia's post and put it on Twitter, with a hashtag that seemingly wrote itself: Don't whisper, #ShoutYourAbortion.

The response was immediate and overwhelming—it felt, almost, as if many had been waiting for this moment to speak. People I've known for years told me stories I'd never heard before. Complete strangers shared a galaxy of personal experiences, from the harrowing to the mundane:

Leit Motif
@_leitmotif_
if ever pregnant, i will have an abortion. i lay claim to my own life. that life will not include giving birth. #ShoutYourAbortion
12:32 AM · Sep 21, 2015

Anne Carlin #JeSuisProle #VAW must end NOW!
@sacarlin48
I had to make the·choice at 45 yrs after a number of miscarriages. V. Difficult #shoutyourabortion
12:26 AM · Sep 21, 2015

msmanet🐾🐾
@msmanet
my abortion gave me my life back . . . started my healing from
rape. no regrets, not one.
#ShoutYourAbortion
11:33 PM · Sep 20, 2015

DreamMeanNormaJean
@MeanNormaJean
Without my abortion, I'd be forever tied to the man who would
go on to rape me 5 years into our relationship.
#ShoutYourAbortion
6:28 PM · Sep 20, 2015

Hot Spoon Trick Proponent
@Jomegsallan
No traumatic backstory: Didn't want kids. Couldn't afford
kids. Contraceptive failure with casual bf. Not one regret.
#ShoutYourAbortion
10:02 PM · Sep 20, 2015

All of those abortions are valid. None are shameful.

There are no "good" abortions and "bad" abortions, because an abortion is just a medical procedure, reproductive healthcare is healthcare, and it is a fact without caveat that a fetus is not a person. I own my body, and I decide what I allow to grow in it. Telling our stories at full volume chips away at stigma, at lies, at the climate of shame that destroys the lives (sometimes literally) of women and girls and anyone anywhere on the gender spectrum who can become pregnant, especially those living in poverty, in rural areas, and in hyper-religious and conservative households. (It's vital to remember, too, that being able to tell my abortion story without feeling unsupported and unsafe—beyond the general unease of knowing my country is full of heavily armed, anti-intellectual GOP wingnuts—is a privilege. I speak out because I can.)

There's a reason why #ShoutYourAbortion has been getting mountains of positive, mainstream press attention, while the people terrorizing us (my feed is clogged with pictures of bloody fetuses and death threats—this is Twitter, after all) are ignored on the fringe. It's because we are right, and however glacially society evolves, it is evolving in the right direction. Abortion is common. Abortion is happening. Abortion needs to be legal, safe, and accessible to everyone. Abortion is a thing you can say out loud.

I am not sorry.

• • •

After the murder of her twelve-year-old son, Tamir, by police in Cleveland, Ohio, in 2014, Samaria Rice founded the Tamir Rice Foundation and the Tamir Rice Afrocentric Cultural Center. Rice directly challenged the celebrity activists who invoked the name of her son and others in ways she found troubling, noting, "Families of those who are killed by the police—and whose loved ones' deaths spark mass movements—continue to navigate political misrepresentation, battle zones of police repression, homelessness, and poverty, while Black 'leadership' that has not been selected by the masses flourishes through celebrity status." Here she speaks about the limits of focusing on elections and piecemeal reform, when more meaningful change is needed.

Samaria Rice, "Why I Have Not Endorsed Any Candidate: Reflections from a Mom of the Movement" (March 15, 2016)

Over the past few weeks, I had been approached by many people all with the same question: Who will I endorse for president of the United States? I have heard this even more since the launch of the Justice for Tamir Speak Out Tour. I have watched as my fellow mothers that have lost children have chosen a candidate to invest their faith in and I support them in their pursuits of justice for their children, and the people want to know where I stand.

For over a year I have been fighting for justice for my son, Tamir, who was killed by Cleveland police officers Timothy Loehmann and Frank Garmback. For over a year, I've waited to see if any candidate or official, including my state's governor, would release a plan of action that addressed the failures and inhumane decisions responsible for my son's death. While I've waited, I've been speaking out for true action, with changes that would help prevent another tragedy like Tamir's murder, changes that truly hold these police accountable and give people power in the communities we live in.

As a resident of Cleveland, Ohio, my local and state governments have not only failed my family, they've caused us severe trauma. After shooting Tamir, Cleveland police neglected to call aid for my son and handcuffed my daughter, who was trying to help her brother. Then the City of Cleveland later tried to charge me for the ambulance ride that was too late to save my son's life. They said it was a mistake, and no one was held responsible for any of the pain they caused my family.

After Tamir's death, the county prosecutor, Timothy McGinty, an elected official, responsible for seeking justice for Tamir, instead blamed my twelve-year-old boy for his own death. All of this happened under the administration of Ohio governor John Kasich, a 2016 presidential nominee. Ohio's state government has shown me repeatedly that the people elected to serve have no interest in justice. The loss of Tamir has made it clear to me that Cleveland is deeply invested in a system of injustice. No one has been held responsible for any part of this entire traumatic experience. No one has at least apologized for killing my son. Not a single politician has offered me some substantial support.

While I've continued to push my state's officials toward real changes, several presidential candidates have said my son's name in their mouth, using his death as an example of what shouldn't happen in America. Twelve-year-old children should never be murdered for playing in a park. But not a single politician: local, state, or federal, has taken action to make sure it doesn't happen again.

Instead of plans for justice and accountability, I have been shown several plans for criminal justice reform, none that address my experience of the entire system being guilty. Those plans don't address the many ways elected officials become exempt to accountability and the legal flaws that allow them to extend that exemption to cops who kill. These plans do not get rid of the trauma of knowing that my tax dollars help pay the salaries of the police officers that killed my son.

As one of the Mothers of the Movement, I know the death of Tamir has shown many just how important police accountability is. I also know it must be a piece of a larger plan to address the deep corruptions that exist in America. The people should be the ones determining what accountability looks like, not prosecutors who work closely with police to deny the people justice. County prosecutors, whose job requires them to believe the police the majority of the time, should not be the same people prosecuting them. Police officers often lie about fearing for their life.

True community oversight of the police is one that evens the balance of power and allows the communities police serve to judge how well they are doing their job. My experience has let me know that the system is working just the way the people in power want it to. That is why I refuse to accept plans or support politicians that offer what they propose as solutions, not informed by us, the community. It's why I won't accept plans for more "community police" as positive solutions when it was the police that killed my son. I cannot settle for partial solutions and lip service. I know we need real action, and I refuse to endorse any candidate that offers less.

• • •

Alicia Garza is a Black queer political strategist, organizer, and a founding member of the Black Lives Matter Global Network. Along with Ayọ Tometi (formerly known as Opal Tometi) and Patrisse Cullors, Garza launched the hashtag #BlackLivesMatter in response to the 2013 acquittal of George Zimmerman for the murder of Trayvon Martin. The three went on to play a leading role in the national movement against anti-Black racism and police brutality. In 2016, Garza presented at the Citizen University National Conference on strategies and lessons for the struggle.

Alicia Garza, "Why Black Lives Matter" (March 18, 2016)

It is important to us that we understand that movements are not begun by any one person. That this movement actually was begun in 1619 when Black people were brought here in chains and at the bottoms of boats. And certainly we should be reminded that it is the combined effort of so many incredibly courageous and bold and fearless and wise people that some, you will never know their names. But you should know that they too are cocreators of what it is that we are experiencing and participating in today.

With that being said our role has been to remind us of our humanity. To remind us that Black Lives Matter, too. To remind us that we are still living in a time when that is a contested statement. And it should not be.

We've been living in an era where everything and nothing is about race. Where the [deaths and killing of Black people by police] are often cast aside as the result of a few bad apples, or an unfortunate consequence of what happens to people who don't try hard enough to succeed. We emerge from an era where talking about race and racial inequity and systemic racism has been deemed racist in and of itself.

You see, a cauldron has been bubbling under the surface for a very, very long time, occasionally expressing itself in instances of uprising. But none as sustained as what we are experiencing today. Indeed, the last decade of post-racialism, and the neoliberal assault on Black communities, has prompted a beautiful upsurge in Black resistance. And it is a resistance that has resulted in a new political order.

Each year, there are more than one thousand fatal shootings that occur by on-duty police officers. Each year, less than five of those shootings on average result in a charge of murder or manslaughter against those officers. Now, in the last few years the number of officers who are being held accountable has tripled, but let's put this into context: from five to fifteen every year. It's nowhere near close to enough. It is in no way the solution to police violence and police brutality. The solution to police violence and police brutality is not to lock up killer cops. The solution is to reimagine what kind of safety do we want and deserve.

Even still, even though it's not enough, and even though it is not the solution, those convictions would not have happened were it not for the organizing and disruptions of the last few years.

Were it not for the community of Ferguson, Missouri, who've refused to go home, who refuse to let the system work, Darren Wilson would still be patrolling that community. And the corrupt nature of policing and debtors' prisons, and all of the other things that we have learned about what's happening in Ferguson, Missouri, would still go unchecked.

Were it not for the years of organizing in Chicago to fire the officer who killed Rekia Boyd, to expose the collusion between the mayor and the prosecutor, we wouldn't have seen the recent unseating of Anita Alvarez, who was complicit in the cover-up of the shooting of Laquan McDonald, who was shot sixteen times in the back by Chicago police.

Were it not for the organizing that didn't get national attention, prosecutor Timothy McGinty, who refused to bring charges against the officers who killed twelve-year-old Tamir Rice playing alone in the park, would still have a job.

You see, Black people, Black resistance, and Black organizing has changed the landscape of what is politically possible. Whether or not you call it Black Lives Matter, whether or not you put a hashtag in front of it, whether or not you call it the Movement for Black Lives, all of that is irrelevant. Because there was resistance before Black Lives Matter, and there will be resistance after Black Lives Matter.

What's more important to acknowledge is that Black people today are determined to make the impossible possible. And that that work cannot be credited to either political party. When we say "no more business as usual," it is an indicator that we aim to transform this democracy into something that supports all of us, not just some of us.

This generation of Black resistance says that we are not satisfied with the crumbs that may fall from the table of power, and we are not satisfied with merely sitting at the tables of power. This generation of Black resistance, of Black organizing, says that we aim to completely transform the way that power is distributed, the way that power functions. And that we aim for a new kind of power that is in collaboration rather than in competition.

From my perspective, there are three critical lessons that we have learned about how social change happens. The first lesson, and this may be the most important one, is that organizing works. And that we must remain clear that organizing and protest are not the same thing. Protest is an important tactic, and it raises the stakes. But protest alone will not accomplish all that we seek.

At the same time, those of us who seek to upset the table of power cannot and must not continue to assert that somehow disruption is destructive to the aims that we seek. Frederick Douglass expressed this in a speech he delivered in 1857:

> If there is no struggle there is no progress. Those who profess to favor freedom and yet deprecate agitation are those who want crops without plowing up the ground; they want rain without thunder and lightning. They want the ocean without the awful roar of its many waters.
>
> This struggle may be a moral one, or it may be a physical one, and it may be both moral and physical, but it must be a struggle. Power concedes nothing without a demand. It never did and it never will. Find out just what any people will quietly submit to and you have found out the exact measure of injustice and wrong which will be imposed upon them, and these will continue till they are resisted either with words or blows, or with both.

Now, the final lesson here is actually one of foreshadowing. We are in the midst of a moment where mass shootings have increased. Where attacks on the centers that provide women much-needed health care, including but not limited to abortion, have increased. We are in an era where the number of people who are dying at the wrong end of a gun is increasing rapidly. And our faith in the sanctity of the political process is eroding before our eyes.

We must acknowledge that what we are experiencing is a powerful backlash to powerful movements in the making. That means that we must acknowledge and actively disrupt the processes that divide us. It means we should get comfortable not in sameness, but in difference. It means we should get comfortable knowing that while we are not all the same, we are all impacted by dangerous systems like white supremacy. It's not Donald Trump that we need to be afraid of. It's the system and the society that created him.

I believe deeply in our ability to succeed. I believe deeply in our creativity, in our courage, in our determination. Let us build the movement that says, "Not in our name." Let us build the movement that unites millions of us, brilliant and wise in our differences, and convicted in the belief that we are exactly what we need to free ourselves.

As our sister Arundhati Roy once said, "Another world is not only possible, she is on her way. On a quiet day, I can hear her breathing."

• • •

Chanel Miller, formerly known as "Emily Doe," is the author of the best-selling memoir *Know My Name*. She is a survivor of what was colloquially referred to as the "Stanford Rape Case." Originally published anonymously on Buzzfeed, Miller's words went viral. Below is an excerpt from her powerful statement.

Chanel Miller, "Impact Statement" (June 3, 2016)

Your Honor, if it is all right, for the majority of this statement I would like to address the defendant directly.

You don't know me, but you've been inside me, and that's why we're here today. . . .

This is not a story of another drunk college hookup with poor decision making. Assault is not an accident. Somehow, you still don't get it. Somehow, you still sound confused. I will now read portions of the defendant's statement and respond to them.

You said, Being drunk I just couldn't make the best decisions and neither could she.

Alcohol is not an excuse. Is it a factor? Yes. But alcohol was not the one who stripped me, fingered me, had my head dragging against the ground, with me almost fully naked. Having too much to drink was an amateur mistake that I admit to, but it is not criminal. Everyone in this room has had a night where they have regretted drinking too much, or knows someone close to them who has had a night where they have regretted drinking too much. Regretting drinking is not the same as regretting sexual assault. We were both drunk, the difference is I did not take off your pants and underwear, touch you inappropriately, and run away. That's the difference.

You said, If I wanted to get to know her, I should have asked for her number, rather than asking her to go back to my room.

I'm not mad because you didn't ask for my number. Even if you did know me, I would not want to be in this situation. My own boyfriend knows me, but if he asked to finger me behind a dumpster, I would slap him. No girl wants to be in this situation. Nobody. I don't care if you know their phone number or not.

You said, I stupidly thought it was okay for me to do what everyone around me was doing, which was drinking. I was wrong.

Again, you were not wrong for drinking. Everyone around you was not sexually assaulting me. You were wrong for doing what nobody else was doing, which was pushing your erect dick in your pants against my naked, defenseless body concealed in a dark area, where partygoers could no longer see or protect me, and my own sister could not find me. Sipping Fireball is not your crime. Peeling off and discarding my underwear like a candy wrapper to insert your finger into my body, is where you went wrong. Why am I still explaining this.

You said, During the trial I didn't want to victimize her at all. That was just my attorney and his way of approaching the case.

Your attorney is not your scapegoat, he represents you. Did your attorney say some incredulously infuriating, degrading things? Absolutely. He said you had an erection, because it was cold.

You said, you are in the process of establishing a program for high school and college students in which you speak about your experience to "speak out against the college campus drinking culture and the sexual promiscuity that goes along with that."

Campus drinking culture. That's what we're speaking out against? You think that's what I've spent the past year fighting for? Not awareness about campus sexual assault, or rape, or learning to recognize consent. Campus drinking culture. Down with Jack Daniels. Down with SKYY Vodka. If you want talk to people about drinking go to an AA meeting. You realize, having a drinking problem is different than drinking and then forcefully trying to have sex with someone? Show men how to respect women, not how to drink less.

Drinking culture and the sexual promiscuity that goes along with that. Goes along with that, like a side effect, like fries on the side of your order. Where does promiscuity even come into play? I don't see headlines that read, "Brock Turner, Guilty of drinking too much and the sexual promiscuity that goes along with that." Campus Sexual Assault. There's your first PowerPoint slide. Rest assured, if you fail to fix the topic of your talk, I will follow you to every school you go to and give a follow-up presentation.

Lastly you said, I want to show people that one night of drinking can ruin a life.

A life, one life, yours, you forgot about mine. Let me rephrase for you, I want to show people that one night of drinking can ruin two lives. You and me. You are the cause, I am the effect. You have dragged me through this hell with you, dipped me back into that night again and again. You knocked down both our towers, I collapsed at the same time you did. If you think I was spared, came out unscathed, that today I ride off into sunset, while you suffer the greatest blow, you are mistaken. Nobody wins. We have all been devastated, we have all been trying to find some meaning in all of this suffering. Your damage was concrete; stripped of titles, degrees, enrollment. My damage was internal, unseen, I carry it with me. You took away my worth, my privacy, my energy, my time, my safety, my intimacy, my confidence, my own voice, until today.

I am no stranger to suffering. You made me a victim. In newspapers my name was "unconscious intoxicated woman," ten syllables, and nothing more than that. For a while, I believed that that was all I was. I had to force myself to relearn my real name, my identity. To relearn that this is not all I am. That I am not just a drunk victim at a frat party found behind a dumpster, while you are the All-American swimmer at a top university, innocent until proven guilty, with so much at stake. I am a human being who has been irreversibly hurt, my life was put on hold for over a year, waiting to figure out if I was worth something.

My independence, natural joy, gentleness, and steady lifestyle I had been enjoying became distorted beyond recognition. I became closed off, angry, self-deprecating, tired, irritable, empty. The isolation at times was unbearable. You cannot give me back the life I had before that night either. While you worry about your shattered reputation, I refrigerated spoons every night so when I woke up, and my eyes were puffy from crying, I would hold the spoons to my eyes to lessen the swelling so that I could see. I showed up an hour late to work every morning, excused myself to cry in the stairwells, I can tell you all the best places in that building to cry where no one can hear you. The pain became so bad that I had to explain the private details to my boss to let her know why I was leaving. I needed time because continuing day to day was not possible. I used my savings to go as far away as I could possibly be. I did not return to work full-time as I knew I'd have to take weeks off in the future for the hearing and trial, that were constantly being rescheduled. My life was put on hold for over a year, my structure had collapsed.

I can't sleep alone at night without having a light on, like a five-year-old, because I have nightmares of being touched where I cannot wake up, I did this thing where I waited until the sun came up and I felt safe enough to sleep. For three months, I went to bed at six o'clock in the morning.

I used to pride myself on my independence, now I am afraid to go on walks in the evening, to attend social events with drinking among friends where I should be comfortable being. I have become a little barnacle always needing to be at someone's side, to have my boyfriend standing next to me, sleeping beside me, protecting me. It is embarrassing how feeble I feel, how timidly I move through life, always guarded, ready to defend myself, ready to be angry.

You have no idea how hard I have worked to rebuild parts of me that are still weak. It took me eight months to even talk about what happened. I could no longer connect with friends, with everyone around me. I would scream at my boyfriend, my own family whenever they brought this up. You never let me forget what happened to me. At the end of the hearing, the trial, I was too tired to speak. I would leave drained, silent. I would go home, turn off my phone, and for days I would not speak. You bought me a ticket to a planet where I lived by myself. Every time a new article come out, I lived with the paranoia that my entire hometown would find out and know me as the girl who got assaulted. I didn't want anyone's pity and am still learning to accept victim as part of my identity. You made my own hometown an uncomfortable place to be.

You cannot give me back my sleepless nights. The way I have broken down sobbing uncontrollably if I'm watching a movie and a woman is harmed, to say it lightly, this experience has expanded my empathy for other victims. I have lost weight from stress, when people would comment I told them I've been running a lot lately. There are times I did not want to be touched. I have to relearn that I am not fragile, I am capable, I am wholesome, not just livid and weak . . .

And finally, to girls everywhere, I am with you. On nights when you feel alone, I am with you. When people doubt you or dismiss you, I am with you. I fought everyday for you. So never stop fighting, I believe you. As the author Anne Lamott once wrote, "Lighthouses don't go running all over an island looking for boats to save; they just stand there shining." Although I can't save every boat, I hope that by speaking today, you absorbed a small amount of light, a small knowing that you can't be silenced, a small satisfaction that justice was served, a small assurance that we are getting somewhere, and a big, big knowing that you are important, unquestionably, you are untouchable, you are beautiful, you are to be valued, respected, undeniably, every minute of every day, you are powerful and nobody can take that away from you. To girls everywhere, I am with you.

• • •

Nick Estes, a citizen of the Lower Brule Sioux Tribe, is a cofounder of The Red Nation, an organization "dedicated to the liberation of Native peoples from capitalism and colonialism." Here is part of his speech at the first annual Native Liberation Conference at the Larry Casuse Center in Albuquerque, New Mexico.

Nick Estes, "Native Liberation: The Way Forward" (August 13, 2016)

The Red Nation formed in November 2014 out of a collective desire to create a platform for revolutionary Native organizing and to fight back against this settler colonial system that seeks our annihilation. That very summer, two Navajo men, our relatives Allison "Cowboy" Gorman and Kee "Rabbit" Thompson, were brutally murdered by three non-Native men. The story is familiar to most of us. Our relatives—our aunties, uncles, cousins, brothers, sisters, mothers, fathers, grandparents, and even ourselves—are cast as outsiders, exiles in our own homelands in places we call border towns, the white-dominated settlements that ring Indian reservations where persistent patterns of police brutality, rampant discrimination, and violence against Natives define everyday life. The men who murdered Cowboy and Rabbit later admitted to committing similar violent acts against fifty others in a one-year period. They told investigators they were looking for a "good time," and Native people were their playthings, just like the white boys in Farmington who attacked and murdered Navajo men "for fun" in what they call "Indian rolling," or like how rich, racist white men like Dan Snyder, the owner of the infamous Washington football team, use Natives as playthings for entertainment and mascots that celebrate the scalping and mutilating of Native bodies.

Natives become entertainment objects for sport and killing because in this society we are unreal and not fully human. Cowboy and Rabbit's killers spent more than an hour mutilating their bodies to the point they were unrecognizable. It was so bad authorities could not identify them and neither Cowboy nor Rabbit carried personal ID. All-too-common among Albuquerque's unsheltered community, the Albuquerque Police Department (APD) confiscated and destroyed the men's IDs—which included drivers' licenses and CIB cards—to prevent them from buying alcohol or receiving basic human rights, such as access to housing, food, medical care, and employment. Even before they were killed, the APD and this settler society had marked and sentenced Cowboy and Rabbit to a certain kind of death, a social death, where they were excluded, like most Natives, from the realm of the living and relegated to a place where they were considered killable and disposable.

When we founded The Red Nation, this was our primary concern, to address the common experience of Natives: four of every five Natives lives off-reservation in border towns, which include places like Gallup, Farmington, Winslow, Albuquerque, Denver, Rapid City, and Phoenix, to name just a few. Why is this significant? Typically, Natives living off-reservation are considered unauthentic or somehow less Native. They are derisively referred to as "Urban Indians." The truth is that reservations were created as open-air concentration camps, to contain and limit our movements across land that was rightfully ours.

Our ancestors did not choose reservation life; it was forced upon them. Natives who "went off the reservation" were the revolutionaries and rebels who refused confinement. In those days, those who willfully crossed the reservation borders were considered renegades, outlaws, or hostiles. They were usually hunted down, summarily shot, hanged, or imprisoned by law enforcement or by vigilantes. In other words, Natives off the reservation have always been deemed criminal, deviant, and in the way. Today, the recent police killings of Loreal Tsingine, Allen Locke, Sarah Lee Circle Bear, Jacquelyn Salyers, and many more are evidence that the criminalization and extermination of Native life is fundamental to settler society. And border towns literally thrive on Native death.

This is our common experience and our common struggle. This is why we formed The Red Nation.

In fact, police killings of Natives have increased in just the last year and some predict that number will double by the end of 2016, unless we take action now. Native women make up 30 percent of all the police killings of women just this year, even though Natives make up barely 1 percent of the national population. On top of this, Natives are killed by police at the highest rate. Some attempt to parse out these horrible statistics to suggest that Natives have it worse than other groups, as if being murdered by the police is a competition. The truth is that Natives, Blacks, and Latinxs have historically been the targets of the racist police state, the colonial system that enslaved Blacks for their labor, killed Indians for their land, and created a cheap, exploitable labor pool from Indigenous-descended people, now called Latinxs. And because of this reality . . . the Red Nation stands with all victims of police brutality. We recognize that undoing the system that oppresses everyone requires multinational unity and class solidarity among the racialized poor, colonized, and working-class peoples.

To understand why the Native struggle is essential, then, we must first begin with why Natives are targeted for elimination: to gain access to territory. Despite popular belief, Natives are not targeted and killed for our culture, spirituality, religion, or civilization. We are eliminated so that corporations and the settler state can gain access to our territory and resources. That requires the liquidation of our societies, the forced removal of our people from the land, the creation of a blood quantum system that dilutes our identity and decreases our population, the confinement to reservations or prisons, the breaking up of our land base and collective identities, and the hyper-policing of our people.

Elimination also requires that Natives in border towns like Albuquerque are seen as nuisances and are commonly referred to as "drunk Indians" or "transients." Both stereotypes are criminalized, although by definition neither is illegal. Police and settlers often tell us to "Go back to the reservation!" or "You're not from the community!" In those moments, Natives become a criminal element, as if we're the ones who don't belong. It's what Native bodies off-reservation represent that makes us a threat. Native bodies off-reservation represent the unfinished business of settler colonialism; we're physical reminders that this is not settler land—this is stolen Native land. Despite their best efforts to kill us off, confine us to sub-marginal plots of land, breed us white, or to beat or educate the Indian out of us, we remain. We remain because we resist.

We remain as evidence that this is still, and will always be, Native land. We represent a challenge to the legitimacy of the colonial project of border towns and cities because we refuse to quit being Indians when we leave the reservation. We refuse to obey colonial borders. We refuse to disappear and to be quiet.

The Red Nation represents the unification of Natives outside of the institutions of power—taking the struggle back where it belongs: in the hands of the people. Our ancestors did not establish corporate foundations and boards. They fought for their dignity, lands, and lives. They expect the same from us. Corporate and colonial state institutions still dominate our present condition and, as a result, they structure and contain the free will and humanity of Native people. We have to transcend these power structures that, by design and intention, ultimately limit and strangle our lives. To achieve this new humanity, we have to refuse the false promise of capitalistic development—which is commonly disguised as tribal economic self-determination—and state-sponsored colonial reconciliation—which is commonly disguised as community healing and individual self-fulfillment. You cannot heal from a system that continues to violate and kill the land and our relatives unless you dismantle that system. Although seductive, these "solutions" do nothing more than carry on, and carry out, the same power structure that Native people have been resisting for the last five centuries: colonialism and capitalism. The healing of our wounds can only happen if we annihilate profit-making and colonial enterprises.

Instead of nonprofits, we need anti-profits organizing independent of corporate influence and state co-optation, and embedded in the true power of every society: the common people. The poor. The oppressed. The marginalized. In the Lakota language, we call our common people *ikce wicasa*. In Native societies, our common people are those who face the highest rates of violence and discrimination: our youth, our women, our LGTBQ, and our poor relatives. In other words, the broad swath of Native societies today. This is the common experience of Native people.

The current landscape of struggle pits organizations and groups of people against each other, vying for control over resources made scarce by austerity measures and corporate monopolies. Our struggle is not for funding streams or profit-making off the misery of the powerless. We see how organizations and movements mimic corporate and bourgeois competition over brands, logos, name recognition, clientele, and power. We refuse to participate in this corporate model that dominates community organizing. Instead, we organize according to a principle of unity to unite Native peoples and all oppressed peoples in a common struggle beyond national borders and racial and gender identities. That's what separates revolutionary organizing and Native liberation struggles from entities that pit marginalized populations against each other, to compete for funding and resources, without attacking the true source of our collective misery: colonialism and capitalism.

We share an enemy that we must unite against. This is the organizing philosophy of The Red Nation.

Capitalism is the enemy of all life. Climate change, because it envelops the entire planet, makes all life precarious. Poor, oppressed, and Indigenous peoples, however, bear the brunt of rising seas, record droughts, and abnormal weather patterns. As Native people, our kinship with human and nonhuman relatives is fundamental to our being. As I speak, an alliance of Lakota and non-Lakota are laying their bodies on the line to halt a crude oil pipeline from crossing the major fresh water source for millions on the Great Plains, the Missouri River. Our relatives and allies are enacting the sacred duty of the Lakota belief of *Wotakuye*, or kinship. Kinship, in this way, is unconditional because it is revolutionary love. It is the love for our human and nonhuman relatives and the love for the land that will always trump profit. But the land can no longer sustain us if capitalism continues to stalk the earth in search of new markets, bodies, and resources. For life to live on this planet, capitalism must die. For us Lakotas, it is the *owe wasicu*, the way of the fat-taker capitalist, that must die for our people to live.

The Great Spirits have declared: capitalism is organized crime and must be destroyed. It is our obligation to act accordingly.

As Native people, we possess an essential tradition to sustain us—a tradition of resistance. From this tradition of resistance arises The Red Nation. In Lakota, we call ourselves and all Native peoples, *Oyate Luta*, the Red Nation. We are red because we come from the red earth. We are a nation because we have our own laws, language, territory, and customs that have persisted since time immemorial. We claim the land and the land claims us. . . .

Four of five Natives do not live on reservation lands, but that doesn't mean that they have relinquished their treaty rights or their sovereign political identities as Native peoples. It means that we exercise our rights to live where and how we want in our own homelands because that is the ultimate definition of self-determination and sovereignty, collective independence, and autonomy. It is important to remember that no people in the history of this world were ever granted their freedom by begging for it from their oppressors. They had to fight for it. They had to win it. Freedom is actualized not given. . . .

It is time to name the systems that kill us—capitalism and colonialism—and call for their destruction so that our people may live. We will not apologize for this, relatives. It is the only right thing left to do. The Red Nation is a movement for life, not death. And for us to live, capitalism and colonialism must die.

Join us in this movement for life!

In the spirit of Popé and in the spirit of Crazy Horse!

Hecetu Welo!

• • •

Kimberlé Williams Crenshaw is the cofounder and executive director of the African American Policy Forum, and the founder and executive director of the Center for Intersectionality and Social Policy Studies at Columbia Law School, as well as a professor at UCLA Law School. She is popularly known for her development of "intersectionality," "Critical Race Theory," and the #SayHerName Campaign. She gave this speech at the TEDWomen 2016 conference.

Kimberlé Williams Crenshaw, "The Urgency of Intersectionality" (October 27, 2016)

I'd like to try something new. Those of you who are able, please stand up. OK, so I'm going to name some names. When you hear a name that you don't recognize, you can't tell me anything about them, I'd like you to take a seat and stay seated. The last person standing, we're going to see what they know. OK?

All right. Eric Garner. Mike Brown. Tamir Rice. Freddie Gray.

So those of you who are still standing, I'd like you to turn around and take a look. I'd say half to most of the people are still standing. So, let's continue.

Michelle Cusseaux. Tanisha Anderson. Aura Rosser. Meagan Hockaday.

So, if we look around again, there are about four people still standing, and actually I'm not going to put you on the spot. I just say that to encourage transparency, so you can be seated.

So those of you who recognized the first group of names know that these were African Americans who have been killed by the police over the last two and a half years. What you may not know is that the other list is also African Americans who have been killed within the last two years. Only one thing distinguishes the names that you know from the names that you don't know: gender.

So let me first let you know that there's nothing at all distinct about this audience that explains the pattern of recognition that we've just seen. I've done this exercise dozens of times around the country. I've done it to women's rights organizations. I've done it with civil rights groups. I've done it with professors. I've done it with students. I've done it with psychologists. I've done it with sociologists. I've done it even with progressive members of Congress. And everywhere, the awareness of the level of police violence that Black women experience is exceedingly low.

Now, it is surprising, isn't it, that this would be the case. I mean, there are two issues involved here. There's police violence against African Americans, and there's violence against women, two issues that have been talked about a lot lately. But when we think about who is implicated by these problems, when we think about who is victimized by these problems, the names of these Black women never come to mind.

Now, communications experts tell us that when facts do not fit with the available frames, people have a difficult time incorporating new facts into their way of thinking about a problem. These women's names have slipped through our consciousness because there are no frames for us to see them, no frames for us to remember them, no frames for us to hold them. As a consequence, reporters don't lead with them, policymakers don't think about them, and politicians aren't encouraged or demanded that they speak to them.

Now, you might ask, why does a frame matter? I mean, after all, an issue that affects Black people and an issue that affects women, wouldn't that necessarily include Black people who are women and women who are Black people? Well, the simple answer is that this is a trickle-down approach to social justice, and many times it just doesn't work. Without frames that allow us to see how social problems impact all the members of a targeted group, many will fall through the cracks of our movements, left to suffer in virtual isolation. But it doesn't have to be this way.

Many years ago, I began to use the term *intersectionality* to deal with the fact that many of our social justice problems like racism and sexism are often overlapping, creating multiple levels of social injustice.

Now, the experience that gave rise to intersectionality was my chance encounter with a woman named Emma DeGraffenreid. Emma DeGraffenreid was an African American woman, a working wife, and a mother. I actually read about Emma's story from the pages of a legal opinion written by a judge who had dismissed Emma's claim of race and gender discrimination against a local car manufacturing plant. Emma, like so many African American women, sought better employment for her family and for others. She wanted to create a better life for her children and for her family. But she applied for a job, and she was not hired, and she believed that she was not hired because she was a Black woman.

Now, the judge in question dismissed Emma's suit, and the argument for dismissing the suit was that the employer did hire African Americans and the employer hired women. The real problem, though, that the judge was not willing to acknowledge was what Emma was actually trying to say, that the African Americans that were hired, usually for industrial jobs, maintenance jobs, were all men. And the women that were hired, usually for secretarial or front-office work, were all white. Only if the court was able to see how these policies came together would he be able to see the double discrimination that Emma DeGraffenreid was facing. But the court refused to allow Emma to put two causes of action together to tell her story because he believed that, by allowing her to do that, she would be able to have preferential treatment. She would have an advantage by having two swings at the bat, when African American men and white women only had one swing at the bat. But of course, neither African American men or white women needed to combine a race and gender discrimination claim to tell the story of the discrimination they were experiencing. Why wasn't the real unfairness law's refusal to protect African American women simply because their experiences weren't exactly the same as white women and African American men? Rather than broadening the frame to include African American women, the court simply tossed their case completely out of court. . . .

Many years later, I had come to recognize that the problem that Emma was facing was a framing problem. The frame that the court was using to see gender discrimination or to see race discrimination was partial, and it was distorting. For me, the challenge that I faced was trying to figure out whether there was an alternative narrative, a prism that would allow us to see Emma's dilemma, a prism that would allow us to rescue her from the cracks in the law, that would allow judges to see her story.

So, it occurred to me, maybe a simple analogy to an intersection might allow judges to better see Emma's dilemma. So, if we think about this intersection, the roads to the intersection would be the way that the workforce was structured by race and by gender. And then the traffic in those roads would be the hiring policies and the other practices that ran through those roads. Now, because Emma was both Black and female, she was positioned precisely where those roads overlapped, experiencing the simultaneous impact of the company's gender and race traffic. The law—the law is like that ambulance that shows up and is ready to treat Emma only if it can be shown that she was harmed on the race road or on the gender road but not where those roads intersected.

So, what do you call being impacted by multiple forces and then abandoned to fend for yourself? *Intersectionality* seemed to do it for me.

I would go on to learn that African American women, like other women of color, like other socially marginalized people all over the world, were facing all kinds of dilemmas and challenges as a consequence of intersectionality, intersections of race and gender, of heterosexism, transphobia, xenophobia, ableism, all of these social dynamics come together and create challenges that are sometimes quite unique. But in the same way that intersectionality raised our awareness to the way that Black women live their lives, it also exposes the tragic circumstances under which African American women die.

Police violence against Black women is very real. The level of violence that Black women face is such that it's not surprising that some of them do not survive their encounters with police. Black girls as young as seven, great grandmothers as old as ninety-five have been killed by the police. They've been killed in their living rooms, in their bedrooms. They've been killed in their cars. They've been killed on the street. They've been killed in front of their parents and they've been killed in front of their children. They have been shot to death. They have been stomped to death. They have been suffocated to death. They have been manhandled to death. They have been tasered to death. They've been killed when they've called for help. They've been killed when they were alone, and they've been killed when they were with others. They've been killed shopping while Black, driving while Black, having a mental disability while Black, having a domestic disturbance while Black. They've even been killed being homeless while Black. They've been killed talking on the cell phone, laughing with friends, sitting in a car reported as stolen and making a U-turn in front of the White House with an infant strapped in the backseat of the car. Why don't we know these stories? Why is it that their lost lives don't generate the same amount of media attention and communal outcry as the lost lives of their fallen brothers? It's time for a change.

So what can we do? In 2014, the African American Policy Forum began to demand that we "say her name" at rallies, at protests, at conferences, at meetings, anywhere and everywhere that state violence against Black bodies is being discussed. But saying her name is not enough. We have to be willing to do more. We have to be willing to bear witness, to bear witness to the often painful realities that we would just rather not confront, the everyday violence and humiliation that many Black women have had to face, Black women across color, age, gender expression, sexuality, and ability.

So we have the opportunity right now . . . to collectively bear witness to some of this violence . . . . And as we sit with these women, some who have experienced violence and some who have not survived them, we have an opportunity to reverse what happened at the beginning of this talk, when we could not stand for these women because we did not know their names.

So at the end of this clip, there's going to be a roll call. Several Black women's names will come up. I'd like those of you who are able to join us in saying these names as loud as you can, randomly, disorderly. Let's create a cacophony of sound to represent our intention to hold these women up, to sit with them, to bear witness to them, to bring them into the light. . . .

Aiyana Stanley-Jones, Janisha Fonville, Kathryn Johnston, Kayla Moore, Michelle Cusseaux, Rekia Boyd, Shelly Frey, Tarika [Wilson], Yvette Smith . . .

Say Her Name! Say Her Name! Say Her Name! . . .

For all the names I'll never know . . .

Say Her Name! Say Her Name! Say Her Name! . . .

I said at the beginning, if we can't see a problem, we can't fix a problem. Together, we've come together to bear witness to these women's lost lives. But the time now is to move from mourning and grief to action and transformation. This is something that we can do. It's up to us.

• • •

The political prisoner and Native American activist Leonard Peltier was born on the Anishinabe/Chippewa Turtle Mountain Reservation in North Dakota. Moved by the treatment of Indigenous peoples, Peltier joined the American Indian Movement (AIM) and in 1972 took part in the Trail of Broken Treaties. Imprisoned since 1977, charged with the murder of two FBI agents in a shootout on the Pine Ridge Indian Reservation in South Dakota in June 1975, a charge he has always denied, Peltier is still fighting for his freedom. In 2016, on Thanksgiving Day—known to Indigenous activists as the "Day of Mourning"—he wrote of the resistance of the Standing Rock Sioux Tribe against the Dakota Access Pipeline.

Leonard Peltier, "Our Day of Mourning" (November 30, 2016)

Greetings my relatives,

Here we are again. This time the year is 2016. It has been more than forty-one years since I last walked free and was able to see the sun rise and sit and feel the earth beneath my feet. I know there have been more changes than I can even imagine out there.

But I do know that there is a struggle taking place as to whether this country will move on to a more sustainable way of life. This is something we wanted to have happen back in the seventies.

I watch the events at Standing Rock with both pride and sorrow. Pride that our people and their allies are standing up and putting their lives on the line for the coming generations, not because they want to but because they have to. They are right to stand up in a peaceful way. It is the greatest gathering of our people in history and has made us more connected than ever before. We need to support each other as we make our way in these times.

Water is life and we cannot leave this issue for our children and grandchildren to deal with when things are far worse for the natural world than they are now.

And Mother Earth is already in struggle.

And I feel sorrow for the water protectors at Standing Rock because these last few days have brought a much harsher response from the law enforcement agencies there and our people are suffering.

At least they are finally getting attention of the national media.

My home is in North Dakota. The Standing Rock people are my people. Sitting Bull lies in his grave there at Fort Yates. My home at Turtle Mountain is just a few hours north of Standing Rock, just south of Manitoba, Canada.

I have not seen my home since I was a boy, but I still hold out hope of returning there for whatever time I may have left. It is the land of my father and I would like to be able to live there again. And to die there.

I have a different feeling this year. The last time I felt this way was sixteen years ago, when I last had a real chance for freedom. It is an uneasy feeling. An unsettling one. It is a hard thing to allow hope to creep into my heart and my spirit here in these cold buildings of stone and steel.

On one hand, to have hope is a joyful and wonderful feeling, but the downside of it for me can be cruel and bitter.

But today I will choose hope.

I pray that you will all enjoy good health and good feelings and I thank all of you from the bottom of my heart for all you have done and continue to do for me and for our Mother Earth.

Please keep me in your prayers and thoughts as these last days of 2016 slip away.

I send you my love and my respect for all of you who have gathered in the name of Mother Earth and our unborn generations. I stand with you there in spirit.

Doksha.

In the Spirit of Crazy Horse,

Leonard Peltier

Chapter 6

"1,459 Days of Resistance": Resisting Trumpism and the Far Right

Angela Y. Davis, Speech to the Women's March on Washington (January 21, 2017)

Addie Bean, "Dear Donald Trump" (January 21, 2017)

Rebecca Solnit, *The Mother of All Questions* (2017)

Bhairavi Desai, "A Moment of Urgency" (February 16, 2017)

Julian Brave NoiseCat, "Standing Rock Is Burning but Our Resistance Isn't Over" (February 23, 2017)

Luticha Doucette, "If You're in a Wheelchair, Segregation Lives" (May 17, 2017)

Keeanga-Yamahtta Taylor, Keynote at Hampshire College's 2017 Commencement Ceremony (May 20, 2017)

Linda Sarsour, "Islamophobes Are Attacking Me Because I'm Their Worst Nightmare" (July 9, 2017)

Steven Salaita, "Don't Let Fear Be the Lesson" (July 25, 2017)

Victoria-Lola M. Leon Guerrero, "An Open Letter from Guam to America" (August 10, 2017)

Jack Christian and Warren Christian, "The Monuments Must Go" (August 16, 2017)

Susan Bro, "They Tried to Kill My Child to Shut Her Up" (August 16, 2017)

Khury Petersen-Smith, Speech at the Fight Supremacy! Boston Counterprotest and Resistance Rally (August 19, 2017)

● ● ●

In a turn of events that shocked the political establishment, Donald Trump became the forty-fifth president of the United States in 2016, despite losing the popular vote to Hillary Clinton by nearly three million votes. Having campaigned on openly racist, misogynist, anti-immigrant, and Islamophobic rhetoric, his election emboldened the far right and contributed to a rise in hate crimes. In some cases, assailants repeated Trump's precise language or directly referenced him by name. These attacks culminated in a rally by white supremacists in Charlottesville, Virginia, that left social justice activist Heather Heyer dead.

People did not take these attacks lying down. Angela Y. Davis declared at the historic Women's March in Washington, DC, on the day after Trump's inauguration, "The next 1,459 days of the Trump administration will be 1,459 days of resistance—resistance on the ground, resistance in the classrooms, resistance on the job, resistance in our art and in our music." Her words proved prophetic, as protesters fought back against Trump's rapid series of executive orders in unprecedented numbers. Thousands mobilized at airports to resist Trump's ban on refugees from Muslim-majority countries and rallied in DC, again, in a March for Science. Just weeks after the deadly Charlottesville attack, tens of thousands of people descended on Boston to stop the far right from marching again, forcing the bigots who showed up to take refuge in a nearby gazebo until the police escorted them to safety.

• • •

This is Angela Y. Davis's speech to the historic Women's March on Washington, January 21, 2017, by many accounts the largest demonstration in US history.

Angela Y. Davis, Speech to the Women's March on Washington (January 21, 2017)

At a challenging moment in our history, let us remind ourselves that we—the hundreds of thousands, the millions, of women, trans people, men, and youth who are here at the Women's March—we represent the powerful forces of change that are determined to prevent the dying cultures of racism and heteropatriarchy from rising again.

We recognize that we are collective agents of history and that history cannot be deleted like web pages. We know that we gather this afternoon on Indigenous land. And we follow the lead of the first peoples, who, despite massive genocidal violence, have never relinquished the struggle for land, water, culture, their people. We especially salute today the Standing Rock Sioux.

The freedom struggles of Black people that have shaped the very nature of this country's history cannot be deleted with the sweep of a hand. We cannot be made to forget that Black lives do matter. This is a country anchored in slavery and colonialism, which means, for better or for worse, the very history of the United States is a history of immigration and enslavement. Spreading xenophobia, hurling accusations of murder and rape, and building walls will not erase history.

No human being is illegal. The struggle to save the planet, to stop climate change, to guarantee the accessibility of water from the lands of the Standing Rock Sioux, to Flint, Michigan, to the West Bank and Gaza; the struggle to save our flora and fauna, to save the air—this is ground zero of the struggle for social justice.

This is a women's march. And this women's march represents the promise of feminism as against the pernicious powers of state violence. An inclusive and intersectional feminism that calls upon all of us to join the resistance to racism, to Islamophobia, to anti-Semitism, to misogyny, to capitalist exploitation.

Yes, we salute the Fight for 15. We dedicate ourselves to collective resistance. Resistance to the billionaire mortgage profiteers and gentrifiers. Resistance to the health care privateers. Resistance to the attacks on Muslims and on immigrants. Resistance to attacks on disabled people. Resistance to state violence perpetrated by the police and through the prison industrial complex. Resistance to institutional and intimate gender violence, especially against trans women of color.

Women's rights are human rights all over the planet, and that is why we say, "Freedom and justice for Palestine!"

Over the next months and years, we will be called upon to intensify our demands for social justice, to become more militant in our defense of vulnerable populations. Those who still defend the supremacy of white male heteropatriarchy had better watch out.

The next 1,459 days of the Trump administration will be 1,459 days of resistance—resistance on the ground, resistance in the classrooms, resistance on the job, resistance in our art and in our music.

This is just the beginning. And, in the words of the inimitable Ella Baker, "We who believe in freedom cannot rest until it comes."

• • •

Addie Bean, an eleven-year-old in Denver, Colorado, shared this open letter to Donald Trump with the *Colorado Independent* after marching in local protests against the incoming president.

Addie Bean, "Dear Donald Trump" (January 21, 2017)

There is a glass wall that divides men and women. It can be seen through wages, the government, and everyday scenarios. It is strong and everlasting and very part of everyday life. It is ridiculous.

Donald Trump, women in your eyes are defined in terms of child-birth, appearance, weight, and most importantly, their husbands. A woman without a man is like a solar system without a sun. Nothing to hold her together, nothing to steady her, and nothing to rotate around.

To you, Donald Trump, women are like flat objects, toys, dolls, too emotional and too indecisive, incapable of being anything other than a woman. A woman is a gas station, used to fill a tank and then left empty. Something to walk on and touch and mold. A woman is weak and fat and never good enough.

"Why do you starve yourself?" "Because you said I was fat."

"Why do you cut yourself?" "Because you said I wasn't worthy."

"Why are you acting like someone you're not?" "Because you said you can't stand the person I am."

These are the things men say to us, and these are the things you say to us, and these are the reasons we are broken.

You step up and say it's okay to rape women, and it's okay to treat them like slaves, and all the cruel, vain, hurtful things you say to them are okay because there's nothing they will do about it. People look up and listen to you, Donald Trump. We listen to the things men tell us because we want to be good enough. But it's beyond that. It's beyond the numbers on scales and the dye burning hair and the words we can't say. It's because little girls are taught to wear pink and play with dolls and play family, and husband and wife. It's because you've taught us we can only be happy as trophy wives with a man by our sides.

But can't you see? Happiness is beyond picture-perfect fantasies and lies and kisses and slaps and whispers. It's beyond picket fences and mowed lawns and clean houses. Happiness is something that we find within ourselves and something we carry inside, not something we go looking for, but something we unleash.

Women unleash fires that burn so bright they ignite whole cities. Women are so full they overflow, so strong they burst, so loud they crack skies. Women are a force of grit, and fire and light. And so much more.

We will not back down.

So, Donald Trump, when you are sexist, and racist and immature and childish, remember this: We are strong. We can endure and retaliate and triumph. We can make a difference. We are uniting and backlashing and screaming.

Good luck trying to stamp out my fire. And, most importantly, good luck trying to stop the change that's coming. Because no matter how many fits and tantrums you throw and no matter how much money you spend, you are not going to stop us from shattering the world, and the walls you build in it. Your attempts are only like oil to my fire, allowing it to spread and take form and burn.

Sincerely,

Addie Bean, 11, Denver

• • •

Writer, historian, and activist Rebecca Solnit is the author of more than twenty books on feminism, popular power, social change and insurrection, wandering and walking, hope and disaster, including *Men Explain Things to Me* and the book from which this essay is taken, *The Mother of All Questions*.

Rebecca Solnit, *The Mother of All Questions* (2017)

Silence is golden, or so I was told when I was young. Later, everything changed. Silence equals death, the queer activists fighting the neglect and repression around AIDS shouted in the streets. Silence is the ocean of the unsaid, the unspeakable, the repressed, the erased, the unheard. It surrounds the scattered islands made up of those allowed to speak and of what can be said and who listens. Silence occurs in many ways for many reasons; each of us has his or her own sea of unspoken words.

"We are volcanoes," Ursula K. Le Guin once remarked. "When we women offer our experience as our truth, as human truth, all the maps change. There are new mountains." The new voices that are undersea volcanoes erupt in open water, and new islands are born; it's a furious business and a startling one. The world changes. Silence is what allows people to suffer without recourse, what allows hypocrisies and lies to grow and flourish, crimes to go unpunished. If our voices are essential aspects of our humanity, to be rendered voiceless is to be dehumanized or excluded from one's humanity. And the history of silence is central to women's history.

Words bring us together, and silence separates us, leaves us bereft of the help or solidarity or just communion that speech can solicit or elicit.

Being unable to tell your story is a living death and sometimes a literal one. If no one listens when you say your ex-husband is trying to kill you, if no one believes you when you say you are in pain, if no one hears you when you say help, if you don't dare say help, if you have been trained not to bother people by saying help. If you are considered to be out of line when you speak up in a meeting, are not admitted into an institution of power, are subject to irrelevant criticism whose subtext is that women should not be here, or heard. Stories save your life. And stories are your life. We are our stories, stories that can be both prison and the crowbar to break open the door of that prison; we make stories to save ourselves or to trap ourselves or others, stories that lift us up or smash us against the stone wall of our own limits and

fears. Liberation is always in part a storytelling process: breaking stories, breaking silences, making new stories. A free person tells her own
story. A valued person lives in a society in which her story has a place.

Violence against women is often against our voices and our stories. It is
a refusal of our voices, and of what a voice means: the right to self-determination, to participation, to consent or dissent, to live and participate,
to interpret and narrate. A husband hits his wife to silence her; a date
rapist or acquaintance rapist refuses to let the "no" of his victim mean
what it should, that she alone has jurisdiction over her body; rape culture
asserts that women's testimony is worthless, untrustworthy; anti-abortion
activists also seek to silence the self-determination of women; a murderer
silences forever. These are assertions that the victim has no rights, no
value, is not an equal. These silencings take place in smaller ways: the
people harassed and badgered into silence online, talked over and cut out
in conversation, belittled, humiliated, dismissed. Having a voice is crucial.
It's not all there is to human rights, but it's central to them, and so you
can consider the history of women's rights and lack of rights as a history of
silence and breaking silence.

Speech, words, voice sometimes change things in themselves when
they bring about inclusion, recognition, the rehumanization that undoes
dehumanization. Sometimes they are only the preconditions to changing
rules, laws, regimes to bring about justice and liberty. Sometimes just
being able to speak, to be heard, to be believed are crucial parts of membership in a family, a community, a society. Sometimes our voices break
those things apart; sometimes those things are prisons. And then when
words break through unspeakability, what was tolerated by a society
sometimes becomes intolerable. Those not impacted can fail to see or feel
the impact of segregation or police brutality or domestic violence: stories
bring home the trouble and make it unavoidable.

By voice, I don't mean only literal voice—the sound produced by
the vocal cords in the ears of others—but the ability to speak up, to
participate, to experience oneself and be experienced as a free person
with rights. This includes the right not to speak, whether it's the right
against being tortured to confess, as political prisoners are, or not to
be expected to service strangers who approach you, as some men do to

young women, demanding attention and flattery and punishing their absence. The idea of voice expanded to the idea of agency includes wide realms of power and powerlessness.

The struggle of liberation has been in part to create the conditions for the formerly silenced to speak and be heard.

Silence is what allowed predators to rampage through the decades, unchecked. It's as though the voices of these prominent public men devoured the voices of others into nothingness, a narrative cannibalism. They rendered them voiceless to refuse and afflicted with unbelievable stories. Unbelievable means those with power did not want to know, to hear, to believe, did not want them to have voices. People died from being unheard. Then something changed.

If the right to speak, if having credibility, if being heard is a kind of wealth, that wealth is now being redistributed.

● ● ●

On January 28, 2017, protesters converged on airports around the country seeking to defend refugees and migrants impacted by President Donald Trump's executive order imposing an anti-Muslim travel ban. The New York Taxi Workers Alliance called on drivers to refuse to pick up riders at JFK Airport. In an interview with journalist Sarah Jaffe, Bhairavi Desai spoke about this critical protest and the history of taxi worker organizing.

Bhairavi Desai, "A Moment of Urgency" (February 16, 2017)

I am Bhairavi Desai. I am the executive director of the New York Taxi Workers Alliance. We are a workforce that is largely Muslim and Sikh and almost universally immigrant. Over 94 percent of the drivers in New York City are immigrants, and across the country we are a largely immigrant workforce. When the executive order came down, there was a definite sense of urgency and a lot of anger. We really were just starting to talk about all the different members we knew who would be affected and the fact that even though the majority of our Muslim members are not from one of the seven countries in the executive order, still the hysteria around Islamophobia and the fact that fear leads to hate crimes is a major concern of ours. We felt that we really needed to act.

On Saturday, the day after the executive order was signed, when we saw folks coming out to the airport and protesting, it just felt like the most natural thing to do was for us to stand in solidarity and participate in that action in the best way that we know how, which was by striking and holding down that lot.

I think people were really touched that here was a workforce on the front lines of these hateful policies and also the economic margins of what we have seen is a growing sector of the economy which is piecemealing and turning a full-time profession into part-time gigs. People out there know that taxi drivers are really hardworking and that people really struggle day to day to make ends meet. The idea that they would put their incomes on the line and it would be a workforce that is so vulnerable, particularly in these times, to surveillance and deportations and further policing, that they would be the ones to stand up. It seemed to really touch people and we were so moved by their reaction. I think it was a beautiful start to solidarity with our movement.

A few years ago, people will recall, there was a lot of controversy in New York City that down the street from Ground Zero an Islamic Center had opened. Many of the well-known Islamophobes had taken up the issue as their main cause and created a lot of hysteria around it. Folks like Sarah Palin, who at the time was more relevant than today, heavily weighing in. The rhetoric was quite hateful and strong. Well, in the midst of all of that, one of our members, Ahmed Sharif—this is during Ramadan—he picks up a fare, a pretty young guy. [He] started talking to him and at one point the passenger asked Ahmed, "Are you Muslim?" And when Ahmed answered "yes," [the passenger] took out a knife and he slashed him across the neck.

We have seen through the years, right after 9/11 I remember, so many neighborhoods, primarily immigrant neighborhoods where taxis would be parked and overnight the tires would be slashed. The yellow cab went from being kind of a cultural icon, a symbol of New York City, to a symbol of Muslim workers. We would see profanities carved into the taxi with a knife. Already, drivers are twenty times more likely to be killed on the job than other workers. We are one of the most visible immigrant and Muslim workforces. Our members tend to be on the frontlines of that hate and violence.

I remember, after 9/11, I remember our members being subject to a lot of verbal abuse and physical assaults, and at the same time they lost so much work, because all of these streets were closed down and they still had to pay for their lease out of pocket. We did a survey and we found that one out of four drivers had received an eviction notice from their home. People were in debt by as much as $25,000 because they were paying for everything out of pocket and just borrowing money and taking out credit cards.

At the same time, they were contending with the fact that this country was beginning to discuss military action within the Middle East in the same countries where many of the members were from. You can't keep somebody whole and ignore a large part of their life and particularly one when it comes to something as deeply rooted as racism and workplace violence, which given that we represent a workforce that's in the public, the two often intersect in drivers' daily lives.

One of the most beautiful things that happened out of the defense of our strike, every single day, we are still getting postcards in the mail from across the country. It is so lovely. You see that each family member has signed their own name because you see the different handwriting on different postcards coming in. And emails. It has been amazing to see. It is such a wonderful feeling, particularly for us, because we are a workforce that is isolated by the nature of the job itself. When you consider 94 percent immigrant, mostly people of color, non-employees on the edge of the economy, we have been politically isolated for so long. It is an amazing feeling for us when the larger community opens their eyes and their hearts to our struggle.

• • •

Here Julian Brave NoiseCat describes the enduring specter of colonialism faced by Indigenous peoples, and the fearless resistance mounted by protestors at the Standing Rock Sioux reservation against the Dakota Access Pipeline.

Julian Brave NoiseCat, "Standing Rock Is Burning But Our Resistance Isn't Over" (February 23, 2017)

Just north of the Standing Rock Sioux reservation, water protectors set their makeshift and traditional structures ablaze in a final act of prayer and defiance against Energy Transfer Partners' Dakota Access Pipeline, sending columns of black smoke billowing into the winter sky above the Oceti Sakowin protest camp.

The majority of the few hundred remaining protesters marched out, arm in arm ahead of the North Dakota authorities' Wednesday eviction deadline. An estimated one hundred others refused the state's order, choosing to remain in camp and face certain arrest in order to defend land and water promised to the Oceti Sakowin, or Great Sioux Nation, in the long-broken Fort Laramie Treaty of 1851.

On these hallowed grounds, history tends to repeat itself. In 1890, police murdered Sitting Bull on the Standing Rock reservation out of suspicion that he was preparing to lead the Ghost Dance movement in an uprising. Two weeks later the United States Cavalry massacred more than three hundred Lakota at Wounded Knee. Over 126 years later, the characters and details of the stories that animate this landscape have changed, but the Cowboys and Indians remain locked in the same grim dance.

The first whirlwind month of Donald Trump's presidency has brought the injustices of racism, capitalism, and patriarchy long festering beneath the surface of American society out into the open. The eviction of Oceti Sakowin from their treaty lands forces us to confront another foundational injustice, one rarely if ever discussed in contemporary politics—colonialism.

For many, it is contentious and even laughable to suggest that colonialism endures in the present. In the American popular imagination, colonialism ended either when the thirteen colonies declared independence from Britain in 1776, or when John Wayne and the Sixth Cavalry blasted away Geronimo and the Apaches in *Stagecoach*.

Colonialism, according to these narratives, is history.

The eviction of Oceti Sakowin suggests otherwise. But in order to see the big picture in all its unjust and ghastly detail, we must take in the full shame of America's treatment of the Standing Rock Sioux and the first people of this land.

At Standing Rock, 41 percent of citizens live in poverty. That is almost three times the national average. The reservation's basic infrastructure is chronically underfunded. Schools are failing. Jobs are few and far between, and 24 percent of reservation residents are unemployed. Healthcare is inadequate. Many depend on unsafe wells for water. Roads are often unpaved. Housing is in short supply, substandard and overcrowded. If the people of Standing Rock did not take in their beloved family and friends, there would be mass homelessness.

Dakota Access Pipeline's price tag of $3.8 billion is nearly $1 billion more than the entire budget of the Bureau of Indian Affairs. Energy Transfer Partners CEO Kelcy Warren is said to be worth $4.2 billion. The pipeline will pour even more wealth into his pockets.

Meanwhile, Standing Rock will remain in poverty on the margins. The most expensive piece of infrastructure in their community will not be the schools, homes, or hospitals they desperately need. Instead it will be a pipeline that they have vehemently opposed.

This is how the first people of this land live in the forgotten Bantustans of the American West.

This system, an essential foundation of the United States, is rooted in the theft of Indigenous land and the ongoing disavowal of Indigenous sovereignty. Indigenous presence must be confined, erased, and then forgotten, so that the United States may continue to live upon and profit mightily from lands taken from Indigenous people.

The erasure of Indigenous people explains why Dakota Access was rerouted from upstream of Bismarck south to Standing Rock. It explains why pipelines can be hammered through Native communities without regard to their treaties and Indigenous, constitutional, and human rights. It explains why a multi-billion-dollar pipe can be drilled through Standing Rock before long-needed basic infrastructure is built. It explains how, after months of unprecedented protests and visibility, Trump can claim that he received no complaints about the pipeline. It explains how Oceti Sakowin can be wiped off the map.

It is impossible to describe the totality of this picture of land theft, containment, poverty, oppression, policing, and extraction as anything other than colonialism.

But from the moment that colonialism ensnared land and life, Indigenous people fought it—none more than Sitting Bull and his kin, the Oceti Sakowin.

They have lit a fire on the prairie in the heart of America as a symbol of their resistance, a movement that stands for something that is undoubtedly right: water that sustains life, and land that gave birth to people. In its ashes there is the potential for a more just future for this land, this water, and all the nations and people who share it.

• • •

Luticha Doucette is a disability justice activist in Rochester, New York, who describes herself as a "queer, quirky, disabled Black femme . . . committed to helping organizations examine equity across race, gender identity, and disability in policies, practices, procedures, and relationships." She wrote this essay on ableism and the "intersection of race, poverty, and disability" for the New York Times.

Luticha Doucette, "If You're in a Wheelchair, Segregation Lives" (May 17, 2017)

Last year, the former chief of the Santa Fe, New Mexico, police department, Donald Grady II, said something that stuck with me. "There's a thing that we call freedom of movement," he said in an interview with *The Atlantic*, "which is really revered in this country—that we should have the right to move freely without impingement from the police simply because." He was speaking as both a Black man and a police officer about the ways racial discrimination can limit a basic right. But I related to this on more than one level.

As a Black woman with incomplete quadriplegia and chronic pain, and as a full-time manual wheelchair user, my own ability to move freely is frequently restricted. Too often, both the lack of accessibility in public spaces and the ingrained ableism of many nondisabled people bars my way.

Let's say I want to go out to dinner downtown. Even if I can enter an establishment—which I often can't—very rarely is the accessible seating in a visible place, if it is there at all. Once inside, I am often relegated to a corner, the aisle, a back room. In brew pubs with high tables and high chairs, trying to have conversations at eye level with other people's crotches while nursing my beer leads me to feel less like an adult and more like Oliver Twist. No one wants to try the new hot spot in town and then be seated at the kids' table.

If I arrive somewhere by myself, I am often greeted with shock when I make clear that I have no caregiver with me. If I am with a companion—a nondisabled friend or a date—it is assumed that this person is my caregiver. Sometimes it seems that people believe accessibility is having your own chaperone who goes and asks for the accessible entrance.

These are just a few variations on the sort of ableism that people with physical conditions like mine face every day. Ableism is at work when disability is not an inclusive part of the design process, where the space flows and is welcoming to all bodies. Instead, accommodations are tacked on haphazardly, leading to hostile and hard-to-navigate spaces. With the passage of the Americans with Disabilities Act in 1990—which sets standards of compliance for buildings in public spaces—progress has been made, but inclusive thinking and design are still the exception, not the norm.

Today, segregation and limiting the movement of disabled persons in public spaces is commonplace and accepted. Even in our nation's capital, I have to use the back entrance at the National Gallery of Art. As a Black woman I am keenly aware of the irony of being ushered through back ways, sketchy hallways, side entrances, and kitchens to enter restaurants, bars, and other establishments. My favorite bar up the street has its accessible entrance down an alley, with a steep ramp that leads to a door in the bowels of the building. There's no signage, no security cameras, and I once saw a bloody towel covering the fire alarm. At another local restaurant, I have to enter from a side door, through the kitchen and then to the dining room. It is a running joke with my friends that if the accessible entrance is not up front, you're going to end up needing a map to find your way through.

Some aspects of this situation, though, are too painful to joke about. Much of what people with disabilities like mine must suffer conjures the historically painful specter of racial segregation. Even at my job, where I work for the city as a researcher in a government building, there is an entrance with a double doorway for those walking in, then next to it, hidden around a pillar, a sliding door for wheelchair users. The other exterior doors have stairs leading up to them. My employer did a wonderful job in doing a walk-through with me to identify ways to solve the problem, but this raises a key point: the building was built in a time when people with disabilities were almost entirely hidden from society, and architects did not consider how such a person would use the building. This makes retrofitting an even bigger challenge. All this eerily mirrors the segregation of Blacks in the workplace, where separate doors were not unusual. We need to be just as vigilant about disability inclusion as we are about racial inclusion.

In the social justice space, ableism would be categorized as a macroaggression. Disability comes with its own unique challenges and trials, but the inability to engage with, and move freely through, our communities, or not being able to easily visit friends' and relatives' homes—and the social isolation that follows—because inclusive design is so uncommon, is a gross violation of our rights and is detrimental to our health.

Our freedom of movement is hindered in other ways. How we move as disabled people often leads to poor encounters with the police. We are often taken for drunks, our caregivers are harmed, or even shot; we are perceived as threats and beaten when trying to communicate in sign language, or worse, killed. In March, a report published by the Ruderman Family Foundation highlighted that half of police shootings have involved a disabled person. They were also people of color. Yet these deaths are rarely spoken of in the context of the person's disability.

To make things worse, the intersection of race, poverty, and disability is often ignored. Black Lives Matter has come under much deserved criticism by Black and Latinx disability rights activists for lack of inclusion in their "woke" spaces. We cannot be fully woke if we refuse to acknowledge our disabled brothers and sisters. My city has some of the highest poverty rates for minorities and for the disabled. A recent study ranked Rochester 147th out of 150 American cities in a list of best and worst places to live if you are disabled. Yet, those in poverty who are disabled live in the highest-poverty census tracts, have very low education levels, no access to jobs, and a shortage of affordable, accessible housing, and lack the resources to move within their communities, which have poor transportation options. They very rarely have the opportunity to live somewhere else, nor can they fully engage with the myriad initiatives designed to lift people out of poverty.

For me, freedom of movement also encompasses the ability to move in environments without people coming up to me and touching me or invading my personal space. Black women know the violating feeling when someone decides to touch our hair without permission as we go about our daily lives. Disability adds another layer to it. A poignant moment was during prep for an MRI. My hair was ripped out by a white female technician because she was "curious about its softness." My Blackness was singled out and my disability used against me. She took a moment where I was vulnerable and exploited that.

But these body-autonomy violations are a regular occurrence. People push my chair without asking, and often in the wrong direction, and shove me in the back as a way of "helping" me propel my chair—my movement and autonomy are constantly being challenged. And just as Black men experience people moving to the other side of the street or white women clutching their purses on the assumption that they are a threat, I too experience people jumping out of the way or pulling their children to them in fear as they loudly proclaim that they don't want to be hit by a wheelchair, even when I'm several feet from them. To be treated as something to avoid but also something to be touched at will creates an odd juxtaposition that is unique to the Black disabled experience.

Navigating the world as a Black woman is difficult, but I refuse to give up the fight to dismantle structural racism and structural ableism. At the core of the civil rights movement, Black Lives Matter, and the disability-rights movement is the idea of autonomy and agency over one's life. We are fighting for the right to not be judged based on external sets of unrealistic expectations. The rights afforded to us in the Constitution are not fully granted to us if we are constantly obstructed by structural biases. To that end, I would paraphrase Chief Grady's definition to be even more inclusive: We should have the right to move freely without impingement from *anyone or anything*. Simply because.

• • •

Keeanga-Yamahtta Taylor, the author of the essential book *From #BlackLives-Matter to Black Liberation*, delivered the keynote at Hampshire College's commencement in 2017. When her statement that "the most powerful politician in the world is a racist, sexist megalomaniac" was broadcast on Fox News, she was subjected to racist epithets and death threats that forced her to cancel speaking engagements she had planned soon after.

Keeanga-Yamahtta Taylor, Keynote at Hampshire College's 2017 Commencement Ceremony (May 20, 2017)

I wasn't going to say this but . . . I applied to Hampshire College my senior year of high school and didn't get in so . . . it's good to finally be here. . . .

When I received the invitation to deliver your commencement address a few months ago, I was very moved. I'm a professor in African American Studies and I teach at an elite Ivy League university but I don't consider myself an academic. I have always been an organizer who tries to communicate the urgency of our political moment through the lens of history and the concerns of ordinary people. . . .

Let me start by saying I'm not here to tell you what to do with your lives, but I will tell you what I think is necessary to be in this world we live in right now. Today is recognition of the sacrifices that you and your families have made to finish college, but you are graduating into a world of uncertainty and one that is increasingly dangerous. These dangers manifest themselves in a variety of ways. Perhaps the most extreme illustration now resides in the White House. The president of the United States, the most powerful politician in the world, is a racist, sexist megalomaniac.

It is not a benign observation but has meant tragic consequences for many people in this country. From the terror-inducing raids in the communities of undocumented immigrants; to his disparaging of refugees in search of freedom and respite; he has empowered an attorney general who embraces and promulgates policies that have already been proven to have a devastating impact on Black families and communities; he thinks that climate science is fake; and his eagerness to take the country into war can only be interpreted as a callous disregard for its steep price in both money and human life. This list could continue but suffice to say that Donald Trump has fulfilled the campaign promises of a campaign organized and built upon racism, corporatism, and militarism.

But we would be remiss to think that the new president has appeared from nowhere, inexplicably into our otherwise fine democracy. Indeed, it is impossible to understand how we got into this predicament without understanding the deep wells of bitterness, resentment, and anger that have been bubbling beneath the surface of our society for some time. This is not just another partisan battle over race or class decided the presidential election, rather, it is recognizing, simply, that the political and economic status quo in this country have failed, over and over again, to deliver a better way to the vast majority of people in this country.

For too long, civility and good manners in electoral politics have passed as effective governance, hiding the mundane, daily struggles of ordinary people. For too long, the quietude of the status quo has been misinterpreted as indifference to inequality and injustice that pervades our country. For millions of people, the status quo is increasingly intolerable. It gnaws away at the tiny threads that millions of people are hanging onto in their daily struggles to make the ends meet. We live in a celebrity culture that glorifies the rich and famous while ignoring the daily struggles of ordinary people. Their struggles and their lives have been rendered invisible. Imagine if we had a press, a popular culture, or a political class that was curious about the lives of regular people. If we did, what would we find about the status quo?

We would find the deepening crisis of opioid addiction as tens of thousands of people risk and succumb to overdose to escape the uncertainty and pain of life in the world as it is today. The status quo is found in the suffocating racism and poverty in Chicago that has created the conditions for debilitating gun violence in city streets that has taken hundreds of Black and Brown lives; the status quo is found in the shocking reality that life expectancy has declined for working class white women, while 55 percent of Black workers, mostly Black women, in this country live on less than $15 an hour in meaningless jobs. The status quo is found in the fact that hundreds of thousands of undocumented immigrants have been deported through raids. It's found when the US military drops something called the mother of all bombs, the largest non-nuclear weapon in the military's arsenal, that we have a media that is more concerned and interested in the size of the bomb than the human lives that have been destroyed by it. That is the status quo.

It is the normalization of brutality and racism and oppression in our society so much so that it's expected we have no reaction to the daily atrocities that are happening in our country. But when our political system, not this or that party, but our political system is led by a billionaire president and a Congress that is composed mostly of white men who are millionaires, is it any wonder that many people, most people have been left behind?

Given this reality that becomes more surreal with each passing day, it is easy to be discouraged, but you shouldn't be. Now is the time for defiance. And I don't mean a kind of cheap resistance that is only about voting for a different party in the midterm elections in 2018. By defiance, I mean a refusal to accept the world the way it is and instead begin to demand the world we want. It is the kind of defiance that was on display when three to four million of us around the country, rose up to demonstrate the day after the inauguration of Donald Trump, in the largest day of protest in the history of this country.

But saying no and even defiance in and of itself is not enough. To win the world we want to live in and not just changing the guard from a corrupt political party to an inept one, there are four things we need:

The first is history. History reminds us that regular people, not the elites, not the wealthy or the well-connected, but regular people have won against more trying odds than those that we face today. We know that some fifty years ago ordinary Black people from across the South: students, sharecroppers, women, boys and girls, garbage men and house-keepers organized and led a struggle to bring an end to racial apartheid in the South. History reminds us that every important progressive reform, from the end of slavery, to the eight-hour workday, to the right to vote and beyond has come from the struggles of ordinary people.

And yes, struggle is the second thing. The willingness to engage in struggle is to understand that injustice will not simply wither away because it's bad or because it's wrong. Acknowledging the existence of injustice and oppression is not enough. It must actively be opposed. When Trump's first illegal Muslim travel ban was attempted, thousands of ordinary people flooded the airports around this country. And because of those protests and the defiance they represented, that ban was stopped, not once but twice. It is not enough just to be outraged. Injustice has to actually be defied.

Our movements must also be imbued with the spirit of solidarity. What is solidarity? It is the willingness to engage in struggle even when a particular issue might not affect you personally. Most of the people who went to those airport demonstrations were not personally affected by the travel ban, but they were morally outraged. Solidarity means recognizing someone else's suffering and taking on the burden of fighting to end it or even recognizing it, not as a point of difference but as an opportunity for connection.

The revolutionary socialist Eugene Debs spoke most passionately to this when he was being sentenced to prison in 1918 for opposing the First World War; he was going around the country making antiwar speeches. And at his sentencing for sedition he said to the judge, "Your Honor, years ago I recognized my kinship with all living beings, and I made up my mind that I was not one bit better than the meanest on earth. I said then, and I say now, that while there is a lower class, I am in it, and while there is a criminal element, I am of it, and while there is a soul in prison, I am not free." That is the meaning of solidarity.

And perhaps most importantly, we need hope. Hope is not blind faith. Instead, it is the deep desire and belief that our world can and should be better and different, than what currently exists. Hope comes from having some knowledge of history that we have struggled before and we won and we can do it again. But it isn't based on knowledge and facts alone; it is also about imagination and dreams. We have never lived in a world of justice, peace, and freedom. We can only imagine what that world would be like. This is why hope is important. Because in our various movements and struggles it is all too easy to define what we oppose and what harm we wish to end. But we also have to take the time to think about what it is that we want, and not just as an immediate demand, but fundamentally, what do we want for our planet, what do we want for our species. . . .

History, struggle, solidarity and hope—unto themselves they don't guarantee us a better world but without them we don't stand a chance. There are never guarantees that we will win in our movements, but, really, we have nothing to lose but our chains, be they mental, physical, or spiritual. A life of activism and struggle can be exhilarating, frustrating, challenging, but always interesting. Keep reading, keep questioning, listen more intently, and learn from the experiences and mistakes of others.

Another world is possible, a world free of racism, sexism, transphobia, religious bigotry, a world free of borders is possible if we are willing to fight for it.

• • •

Brooklyn-born Palestinian Muslim American organizer Linda Sarsour has long been targeted because of her fierce and unapologetic defense of Palestinians, Muslims, immigrants, the incarcerated and formerly incarcerated, and others. She served asnational cochair of the historic 2017 Women's March on Washington, which led to even greater efforts to silence her by supporters and followers of President Trump, who she defiantly responded to in this essay.

Linda Sarsour, "Islamophobes Are Attacking Me Because I'm Their Worst Nightmare" (July 9, 2017)

This week, conservative media outlets took a speech I gave to the largest gathering of Muslims in America out of context and alleged that I had called for a violent "jihad" against the president. I did not. Sadly, this is not a new experience for me. Since the Women's March on Washington, which I had the privilege of cochairing with inspirational women from across the country, my family and I have received countless threats of physical violence. These ugly threats come from people who also spout anti-Muslim, xenophobic, and white-supremacist beliefs. Their sole agenda is to silence and discredit me because I am an effective leader for progress, a Palestinian American and Brooklyn-born Muslim woman. In short, I am their worst nightmare.

I began my work as director of the Arab American Association of New York in the wake of the horrific attacks of 9/11. As crisis after crisis struck Arab and Muslim communities, from the backlash to the "Ground Zero mosque" to the anti-Muslim hearings held by Rep. Peter King (R-NY) to the rampant surveillance of New York City's Muslim communities, I became more vocal about Islamophobia's terrible impact on my community, city, and country. Because of that, I became a target of the Islamophobia industry, a well-funded group of organizations and spokesmen who fuel anti-Muslim sentiment through misleading narratives, propaganda, local policies, and the vilification of Muslim activists and public figures.

But the post-9/11 environment did not prepare me for the onslaught of vitriol that has come my way since January. First came a campaign to remove me as the commencement speaker at City University of New York's School of Public Health and Health Policy. With hired security at my side, I gave a speech that focused on the rise of hate crimes and xenophobia and the importance of choosing to never be bystanders in the face of injustice. I honored Ricky John Best, Taliesin Myrddin Namkai-Meche, and Micah Fletcher, who saved two young African American women, one of them Muslim, in Portland when they were attacked by a white supremacist. Both Best and Namkai-Meche lost their lives that day.

Now comes the malicious twisting of the speech I gave at the Islamic Society of North America's fifty-fourth annual convention.

In my speech—you can watch the unedited version here—I sent not a call to violence, but a call to speak truth to power and to commit to the struggle for racial and economic justice. I was speaking to an all-Muslim audience; as an American, I should be free to share and discuss scripture and teachings of my beloved Prophet. My statements were clear, and my activism track record is even clearer: my work has always been rooted in nonviolence as espoused by the Rev. Martin Luther King Jr.

Most disturbing about this recent defamation campaign is how it is focused on demonizing the legitimate yet widely misunderstood Islamic term I used, "jihad," which to the majority of Muslims and according to religious scholars means "struggle" or "to strive for." This term has been hijacked by Muslim extremists and right-wing extremists alike, leaving ordinary Muslims to defend our faith and in some cases silenced. It sets a dangerous precedent when people of faith are policed and when practicing their religion peacefully comes with consequences.

Nevertheless, the attacks from xenophobes and the conservative media have continued. It saddens me deeply that my three children are frightened. It angers me that I have to think about securing my physical safety even while walking through the neighborhoods of Brooklyn.

Every day, I speak about women's issues, Indigenous rights, the necessity to fight for Black lives and against the Muslim and refugee bans. I believe wholeheartedly that we must fight injustice and inequality—through marches and direct actions, through policy changes, and through our own voices permeating media spaces. My views are not unique or special, and many activists around the country express them as well. The reasons I am subjected to such particularly public vitriol are simple: I am a Palestinian American woman in a hijab who has become a familiar presence and name in American living rooms when it comes to nonviolent resistance and activism. Indeed, those targeting me have an even broader agenda: to silence and discredit racial-justice activists altogether because we are awakening the masses.

But I refuse to be intimidated. I will not walk away from the people and communities whom I love deeply. I will continue to raise my voice for justice and equality for all, organize communities who want to defend the rights of Black people, stand against policies that target and marginalize Muslims, and advocate for health care for all people. Dissent is the highest form of patriotism, and I intend to continue to push my country to respect the rights of all its citizens. I will not be silenced.

• • •

Palestinian American scholar Steven Salaita had been offered a tenured faculty position at the University of Illinois. However, the offer was revoked over his tweets expressing outrage at the 2014 bombardment of Gaza, one of Israel's deadliest massacres of Palestinians in recent history. Palestine solidarity activists rallied to Salaita's defense and the university eventually agreed to a settlement, but he remains unofficially blacklisted from academia. In a post to social media, Salaita said the price he paid for speaking out was worth it.

Steven Salaita, "Don't Let Fear Be the Lesson" (July 25, 2017)

A few thoughts on leaving academe. . . . I'm still young and energetic. I don't intend to slosh around in self-pity. Whatever I end up doing, I will maintain the spirit of noncompliance that defined my time in academe. If you take any lesson from my ouster, please don't let it be fear or caution. Docility is a gift to those who profit from injustice. Academe can no longer afford this luxury.

People still ask if I would go back in time and change anything. I would not. If my behavior were dishonorable, then I might have something to regret. I condemned a brutal ethnocratic state. On this count, I will die unapologetic. And insofar as we are forced to contemplate life in binaries, I prefer unemployment to subservience. My heart is with those who struggle for dignity amid terrible oppression. I spare no loyalty to a bourgeois industry that rewards self-importance and conformity.

Despite every node of my disposition screaming at me not to say what I'm about to say, I again surrender to my lesser judgment: I leave academe feeling that, no matter my copious shortcomings, I managed to remain a decent human being. Zionists have worked overtime to incriminate me, but they've never found anything incriminating—not from a lack of diligence, but because there's nothing to find but plain-spoken disdain for settler colonization. I haven't always been a good professor—I'm disorganized and forgetful and reclusive and unresponsive and an easy grader—but I've never compromised my ethics or sold out colleagues and students in order to ingratiate myself to power.

Thank you for entertaining my self-indulgence. If my words sound incompatible with the demands of nuance and discretion that predominate in academic culture, then it's because I'm no longer of the culture and thus unconstrained by its emphasis on disinterest and diplomacy. I can speak according to the whims of my conscience. This is what happens when you manage to survive a punishment. You become free.

• • •

In 2017, North Korean dictator Kim Jong-Un threatened a missile strike on the US military base in Guam. President Trump warned that he would retaliate with "fire and fury," raising the specter of nuclear war and annihilation. In an open letter, Victoria-Lola M. Leon Guerrero, cochair of the Independence for Guam Task Force, took the opportunity to assert the people of Guam's right to self-determination.

Victoria-Lola M. Leon Guerrero, "An Open Letter from Guam to America" (August 10, 2017)

Dear America,

I am glad that you are finally paying attention to what is happening in Guam. Many of you, as I am reading online, are asking for the first time, "What is Guam?" Every day growing up here, we have been told all about you. I am sorry that it is only when we are the subject of bombs that you even attempt to say the word Guam; there are so many more interesting things I wish you would want to know about us. We, on the other hand, are not as surprised by the latest bomb threat. We are quite used to hearing Guam and bomb in the same sentence. Every month or so, when another missile is tested, or rhetoric fired, we hear how North Korea, or China, or Russia could bomb Guam. I have even saved pictures of China's infamous "Guam Killer" bombs on my computer so our Independence group can use it in Independence 101 presentations as an example of why we need to get free NOW. Yes, there are people in Guam who want independence from you. But there are also people in Guam who hear these threats of bombs and cower to the hype. They start to believe that we need your mighty military bases and beg for more, because then we would not be bombed, right? But you have been the source of all our bomb problems.

The worst bombs that have ever been dropped on Guam were yours near the end of World War II. At the beginning of the war, you left us defenseless to the Japanese, knowing full well that they were planning to invade Guam all along. You safely boarded your white military wives on ships and sent them home months before the attack, but did nothing to protect us. That's right, the last time an invading nation that you said you would protect us from attacked, you surrendered in two days and left twenty thousand people to suffer, many falling victim to the most atrocious of war crimes. But we are strong and we survived not just that ugly war but also the losses that came after. When you returned in 1944, you leveled our island with your bombs, leaving most families without a home to return to. We were scattered and displaced so you could build your enormous bases. And we were so grateful to you that our people served and continue to serve your military and die for your freedom in higher numbers per capita than you.

Today you occupy nearly one-third of our island, and station bombers and nuclear-powered submarines here to flex your might to our neighbors. You play endless war games emitting fumes and dumping waste into our air, water, soil, bodies. We breathe in the fallout when you test your bombs on our sister islands upwind—those clouds make their way down here. We eat fish from the waters you bomb around us. Grieve the beached whales who rot at the shore, led astray by your sonar testing. We are being made to sacrifice—with no consent (and for many of us, against our will)—access to sacred ancient villages and a thousand acres of a lush limestone forest habitat that you want to destroy to build a firing range for your Marines. You fly bombers over my home at ungodly hours. Come on, America, I am raising babies here. Little ones, who notice when your flag is flown above theirs, and don't like it. Who hide under the slide at their playground and tell their friends to duck when your blaring B-1s, B-2s, be everything in their safe zone. There is a sign on the road that reads, "Slow down, children at play."

Will you please slow down and allow my children to play? I want them to grow up here. This is their/my/my mama's mama's mama's homeland. There is no other place in the world I want them to be. I understand that for many "Americans," you had to flee your homeland. That America became your better life, or at least the promise of it. That many of you long for your homeland and can't return. And sadly, many of you don't think enough about the Indigenous Americans whose lands and lives were stolen to manifest this destiny. But this land, this beautiful island everyone wants to bomb because of you, is my land, not yours. And I don't want to flee. I left my land once for your college education. But I ached for home the entire time. As soon as I got my degrees, I came back to use them here. My home is my better life. I am nourished by my land, where my family grows our own food. I am raising bright babies, with the jungle as their backyard, and this is the life my ancestors wanted for me and for them. I want to go to sleep peacefully knowing that my family is safe in our home. So please, stop all this bomb talk. And instead, ask yourself why Guam is still your colony in 2017.

• • •

In 2017, the mobilization of white supremacists to Charlottesville, Virginia, ignited a national debate on whether to remove monuments to Confederate soldiers. The majority of these monuments, of which there are approximately seven hundred around the United States, were not built in the aftermath of the Civil War, but during the Jim Crow era (between 1890 and 1950). In an open letter, William Jackson Christian and Warren Edmund Christian, the great-great-grandsons of Confederate General Thomas Jonathan "Stonewall" Jackson, joined calls to remove their ancestor's statue from the famous Monument Avenue in Richmond, Virginia.

Jack Christian and Warren Christian, "The Monuments Must Go" (August 16, 2017)

Dear Richmond Mayor Levar Stoney and members of the Monument Avenue Commission,

We are native Richmonders and also the great-great-grandsons of Stonewall Jackson. As two of the closest living relatives to Stonewall, we are writing today to ask for the removal of his statue, as well as the removal of all Confederate statues from Monument Avenue. They are overt symbols of racism and white supremacy, and the time is long overdue for them to depart from public display. Overnight, Baltimore has seen fit to take this action. Richmond should, too.

In making this request, we wish to express our respect and admiration for Mayor Stoney's leadership while also strongly disagreeing with his claim that "removal of symbols does [nothing] for telling the actual truth [nor] changes the state and culture of racism in this country today." In our view, the removal of the Jackson statue and others will necessarily further difficult conversations about racial justice. It will begin to tell the truth of us all coming to our senses.

Last weekend, Charlottesville showed us unequivocally that Confederate statues offer preexisting iconography for racists. The people who descended on Charlottesville last weekend were there to make a naked show of force for white supremacy. To them, the Robert E. Lee statue is a clear symbol of their hateful ideology. The Confederate statues on Monument Avenue are, too—especially Jackson, who faces north, supposedly as if to continue the fight.

We are writing to say that we understand justice very differently from our grandfather's grandfather, and we wish to make it clear his statue does not represent us.

Through our upbringing and education, we have learned much about Stonewall Jackson. We have learned about his reluctance to fight and his teaching of Sunday School to enslaved peoples in Lexington, Virginia, a potentially criminal activity at the time. We have learned how thoughtful and loving he was toward his family. But we cannot ignore his decision to own slaves, his decision to go to war for the Confederacy, and, ultimately, the fact that he was a white man fighting on the side of white supremacy.

While we are not ashamed of our great-great-grandfather, we are ashamed to benefit from white supremacy while our Black family and friends suffer. We are ashamed of the monument.

In fact, instead of lauding Jackson's violence, we choose to celebrate Stonewall's sister—our great-great-grandaunt—Laura Jackson Arnold.

As an adult Laura became a staunch Unionist and abolitionist. Though she and Stonewall were incredibly close through childhood, she never spoke to Stonewall after his decision to support the Confederacy. We choose to stand on the right side of history with Laura Jackson Arnold.

Confederate monuments like the Jackson statue were never intended as benign symbols. Rather, they were the clearly articulated artwork of white supremacy. Among many examples, we can see this plainly if we look at the dedication of a Confederate statue at the University of North Carolina, in which a speaker proclaimed that the Confederate soldier "saved the very life of the Anglo-Saxon race in the South." Disturbingly, he went on to recount a tale of performing the "pleasing duty" of "horse whipping" a Black woman in front of federal soldiers. All over the South, this grotesque message is conveyed by similar monuments. As importantly, this message is clear to today's avowed white supremacists.

There is also historical evidence that the statues on Monument Avenue were rejected by Black Richmonders at the time of their construction. In the 1870s, John Mitchell, a Black city councilman, called the monuments a tribute to "blood and treason" and voiced strong opposition to the use of public funds for building them. Speaking about the Lee Memorial, he vowed that there would come a time when African Americans would "be there to take it down."

Ongoing racial disparities in incarceration, educational attainment, police brutality, hiring practices, access to health care, and, perhaps most starkly, wealth, make it clear that these monuments do not stand somehow outside of history. Racism and white supremacy, which undoubtedly continue today, are neither natural nor inevitable. Rather, they were created in order to justify the unjustifiable, in particular slavery.

One thing that bonds our extended family, besides our common ancestor, is that many have worked, often as clergy and as educators, for justice in their communities. While we do not purport to speak for all of Stonewall's kin, our sense of justice leads us to believe that removing the Stonewall statue and other monuments should be part of a larger project of actively mending the racial disparities that hundreds of years of white supremacy have wrought. We hope other descendants of Confederate generals will stand with us.

As cities all over the South are realizing now, we are not in need of added context. We are in need of a new context—one in which the statues have been taken down.

• • •

Susan Bro, the mother of Heather Heyer, killed by a white nationalist who deliberately drove his car into a demonstration against the far right in Charlottesville, Virginia, on August 12, 2017, gave this speech at Heyer's funeral, delivering a moving call to action in the wake of the tragic death of the thirty-two-year-old activist.

Susan Bro, "They Tried to Kill My Child to Shut Her Up" (August 16, 2017)

My child's famous Facebook post was, "If you're not outraged, you're not paying attention." She paid attention. She made a lot of us pay attention. Oh my gosh, dinner with her we knew was going to be an ordeal of listening. And conversation, and perhaps disagreement. But it was gonna happen.

And so my husband would say, "OK, I'm going to go out in the car and play my video game for a while." And so we'd sit and we'd chill. And she and I would talk. And I would listen. And we would negotiate. And I would listen. And we would talk about all the stuff. We talked about politics, we talked about anything that caught her eye that she felt was fair, unfair. She'd talk about her feelings about the police and how things were going. I mean, she just talked. The girl loved to talk. And she was single, so there was nobody listening at home, so Mama got a lot of it. And that was wonderful.

You never think you're gonna bury your child, you never think to take those pictures. They asked me for pictures for this, and I struggled. I had pictures from her childhood, but I had to go to Facebook to find pictures of my child, because we were always together. I saw her a couple of times a month at least and we would text each other fairly often, and we would Facebook message at bedtime, "I love you. You doing OK?" "Yep, I love you."

So I have no regrets on that part. Take pictures of the ones that you love because you don't know when they're not going to be there.

But here's what I want to say to you today: This could be a storm in a teacup and it could all be for nothing. I could have said, "Let's not do this publicly, let's have a small, private funeral." But you know, that's not who Heather was.

Anybody who knew Heather said, "Yep, this is the way she had to go. Big and large." Had to have the world involved, because that's my child. She's just that way. Always has been, and will continue to be.

Because here's the message: Although Heather was a caring and compassionate person, so are a lot of you. A lot of you go that extra mile. And I think that's the reason that what happened to Heather has struck a chord. Because we know that what she did is achievable. We don't all have to die, we don't all have to sacrifice our lives.

They tried to kill my child to shut her up. Well guess what? You just magnified her.

So here's what I want to happen: You ask me, "what can I do?" So many caring people, pages and pages and pages of stuff I'm going through, I'm reading pages and pages and pages of how she's touching the world. I want this to spread. I don't want this to die.

This is just the beginning of Heather's legacy. This is not the end of Heather's legacy. You need to find in your heart that small spark of accountability. What is there that I can do to make the world a better place? What injustice do I see?

And you might want to turn away—"I don't really want to get involved with that. I don't want to speak up. They'll be annoyed with me. My boss might think less of me."—I don't care. You poke that finger at yourself, like Heather would have done, and you make it happen. You take that extra step. You find a way to make a difference in the world.

My child had a high school education; my child was no saint. She was hard to raise, because everything was a negotiation—not kidding—but you know what? She was a firm believer in whatever she believed. And let's do that. Let's find that spark of conviction, let's find in ourselves that action. Let's spread this. Let's have the uncomfortable dialogue.

It ain't easy sitting down and saying, "Well why are you upset?" It ain't easy sitting down and going, "Yeah, well I think this way, and I don't agree with you, but I'm gonna respectfully listen to what you have to say." We're not going to sit around and shake hands and go "Kumbaya." And I'm sorry, it's not all about forgiveness. I know that's not a popular trend.

But the truth is: We are gonna have our differences. We are going to be angry with each other. But let's channel that anger not into hate, not into violence, not into fear, but let's channel that difference, that anger, into righteous action.

Right now, down the road, there's a blood drive going on in Heather's name. Right now, there are people who are here willing to listen to one another and talk to one another. Last night in New England, they had a peaceful rally in Heather's name to have some difficult dialogues. If you ever want to see what one of those dialogues looked like, look at her Facebook posts. I'm telling you, they were rough sometimes, but they were dialogues, and the conversations have to happen. That's the only way we're gonna carry Heather's spark through.

So remember in your heart: If you're not outraged, you're not paying attention. And I want you to pay attention, find what's wrong, don't ignore it, don't look the other way. You make a point to look at it and say to yourself, "What can I do to make a difference?" and that's how you're going to make my child's death worthwhile.

I'd rather have my child, but, by golly, if I got to give her up, we're gonna make it count.

• • •

Khury Petersen-Smith is a socialist activist and coauthor of the 2015 Black for Palestine statement signed by over 1,100 artists, activists, and scholars. One week after white supremacists had mobilized to Charlottesville, he spoke at the "Fight Supremacy!" counter-protest in Boston, where an estimated

25,000–40,000 people turned out against a planned "free speech" rally by the far right.

Khury Petersen-Smith, Speech at the Fight Supremacy! Boston Counter-Protest and Resistance Rally (August 19, 2017)

Are these our streets?
[*Crowd responds, "Yes!"*]
Is this our city?
[*Crowd responds, "Yes!"*]
Donald Trump says, "Make America Great Again." Today, we are gonna make white supremacists go hide again.

If you know the first thing about this country, you know that white supremacy is nothing new. You know that this country was based on stolen land and stolen people. Now that they have some friends in the White House, they [white supremacists] are walking out. They're in the open and marching with torches and with smiles on their faces. And what we're here to say is that if you come to Boston, we're gonna march down to the Common and wipe that smile off your face.

We are the resistance. I remember a couple of months ago, Hillary Clinton said, "I'm proud to be part of the resistance." What we know is that resistance is not something you say, it's something you do. We are the resistance we've been waiting for. And we're gonna stand up for each other because we know what it's like to walk alone if you're Black, if you're Brown, if you're queer, if you're a woman. We know what it's like to be alone. And we're saying today, you don't have to walk alone.

I remember last Saturday after the horrific attack in Charlottesville, a bunch of us gathered on the Common and there were many of us, and many people spoke. But the two speakers in my mind were Jewish, and they got up and they said, I grew up learning about the Holocaust. And I wondered if this happened again, would somebody hide me? Who would hide me? And what I'm here to say is, not only will I hide you if you're Jewish, not only will I hide you if you're undocumented, not only will I hide you if you're a Muslim, but you don't have to hide.

What I'm saying is I will do everything I can to make sure you don't have to hide, and I know that you will, too. We are used to looking over our own shoulders and watching our backs. But what I'm saying is we're gonna watch each other's backs.

So, these fascists picked the wrong town to come to. We're gonna march down and show them what Boston thinks of white supremacy.

And we're gonna show them that not only are we here to stand against them, but we want to stand for some things too. Let me say real quick. I'm a socialist, all right? I am for Black liberation, a world without capitalism, without borders, and so on. Now, if you're down with that, you should march with the socialists. We're marching together, but we don't have to agree on every single thing to unite and fight the Nazis with the biggest, broadest front. And we will show them today that if you think you can come to Boston, you will lose, and you will always lose in Boston.

Chapter 7

"We Will Not Be Silenced": #MeToo and the Ongoing Resistance to Trump

• • •

Donald Trump's election—despite his bragging about sexual assault in a now infamous *Access Hollywood* recording and facing accusations by at least twenty-six women of sexual harassment or assault—was widely viewed as a major setback for women and survivors of sexual violence. Then, in 2017, the #MeToo movement marked a watershed, toppling powerful men at the top of society from institutions that had long enabled their abuses and offering the hope that survivors who spoke out might actually be believed.

The following year, the nation was rocked by the deadliest school shooting in history, in which seventeen students were killed at Marjory Stoneman Douglas High School in Parkland, Florida. Fed up with "thoughts and prayers" from politicians and the inability or unwillingness of adults in power to pass gun control legislation, students and survivors of the attack took to the streets and demanded action. That same year, a wave of teachers' strikes signaled a revival of the labor movement and won major victories across the South, including in states that had overwhelmingly voted for Donald Trump. This defied mainstream discourse about the irredeemable backwardness of "red states."

Meanwhile, Latinx, Jewish, and Japanese protesters (including those whose family members had been interned in Japanese concentration camps during World War II) spoke out against horrific conditions inside immigrant detention centers and Trump's policy of forcibly separating immigrant children from their parents at the border. They united under the slogan "never again."

● ● ●

Playwright and activist V, formerly Eve Ensler, is best known for her groundbreaking 1996 play *The Vagina Monologues*. She wrote the following essay for the *Guardian* following Donald Trump's election.

V, "Even with a Misogynist Predator-in-Chief, We Will Not Be Silenced" (August 23, 2017)

The first time I ever performed *The Vagina Monologues*, I was sure somebody would shoot me. It might be hard to believe, but at that time, twenty years ago, no one said the word vagina. Not in schools. Not on TV. Not even at the gynecologist. When mothers bathed their daughters, they referred to their vaginas as "pookis" or "poochis" or "down there." So when I stood on stage in a tiny theatre in downtown Manhattan to deliver the fictional monologues I had written about vaginas—after interviewing over two hundred women—it felt as if I were pushing through an invisible barrier, and breaching a very deep taboo.

But I did not get shot. At the end of each performance of *The Vagina Monologues* there were long lines of women who wanted to talk to me. At first, I thought they wanted to share stories of desire and sexual satisfaction—the focus of a big part of the play. But they were lining up to anxiously tell me how and when they had been raped, or assaulted, or beaten, or molested. I was shocked to see that once the taboo was breached, it released a torrent of memories, anger and sorrow.

And then something I never could have expected took place. The show was picked up by women all over the world who wanted to break the silence in their own communities about their bodies and their lives.

Memory one. Oklahoma City, the very heart of the Republican heartland. A tiny warehouse. The second night, word has gotten out about the play and there are too many people and not enough seats, so people arrive with their own lawn chairs. I am performing under what is essentially a light bulb. In the middle of a monologue, there is a great scuttling in the crowd. A young woman has fainted. I stop the play. The audience takes care of the woman, fanning her and getting her water. She stands up and declares what the play has emboldened her to say, for the first time: "I was raped by my stepfather." The audience hugs her and hold her as she weeps. Then, at her request, I continue with the show.

Memory two. Islamabad, Pakistan. *The Vagina Monologues* is banned. So I attend an underground production where brave Pakistani actors are performing the play in secret. There are women who have come all the way from Taliban Afghanistan in the audience. Men are not allowed to sit in the audience, but instead sit in the back, behind a white curtain. During the performance, women cry and laugh so hard their chadors fall off.

Memory three. Mostar, Bosnia. The performance is to commemorate the restoration of the Mostar Bridge, which was destroyed in the war. The crowd is comprised of both Croats and Bosnians, who had been slaughtering each other so recently, and there is tension and uncertainty. Women read a monologue about the rape of women in Bosnia. The audience weeps, wails, screams out. The actors stop. Audience members console each other, hold each other and weep together—Croats holding Bosnians, and vice versa. The play resumes.

Memory four. Lansing, Michigan. Lisa Brown, a state representative, is reproached and silenced by state legislature for using the word "vagina" in protesting a proposed bill restricting abortion. You are not allowed, she is told, to say that word. Two days later I fly to Lansing and join Lisa Brown and ten female house members on the steps of the Statehouse for an emergency performance of *The Vagina Monologues*. Close to five thousand women attend, demanding that our body parts be named and recognized in our own democratic institutions. The taboo is broken. We can speak and be seen.

Shortly after the play was launched, with a group of other feminists, I helped form a movement called V-Day, to stand with all the women (cisgender, transgender, and gender nonconforming in all our colors) who were carrying out these fights across the world. Since then V-Day activists, through their productions of the monologues have raised more than $100 million to support centers and shelters for rape and violence survivors, to fund hotlines, to confront rape culture.

And now, twenty years later, I wish for nothing more than to be able to say that radical anti-racist feminists have won. But patriarchy, alongside white supremacy is a recurrent virus, like herpes. It lives dormant in the body politic and is activated by toxic predatory conditions. Certainly in the United States, with an openly racist and misogynist predator-in-chief, we are in the midst of a massive outbreak. Our job, until a cure is found, is to create hyper-resistant conditions that build our immunity, and will make more outbreaks impossible. It starts where *The Vagina Monologues*, and so many other acts of radical feminist resistance, begin—by speaking out. By saying what we see. By refusing to be silenced.

They tried to stop us even saying the names of some of the most precious parts of our bodies. But here's what I learned. If something isn't named, it is not seen, it doesn't exist. Now more than ever it's time to tell the crucial stories and say the words, whether it's vagina, "My stepfather raped me," or, "The president is a predator and a racist." When you break the silence you realize how many other people have been waiting for permission to do the same thing. We will not be silenced again.

• • •

Ash-Lee Woodard Henderson is an Affrilachian (Black Appalachian) and co-executive director of the famous Highlander Research and Education Center in New Market, Tennessee, which played a crucial role in training civil rights activists like Martin Luther King Jr., Rosa Parks, and members of the Student Nonviolent Coordinating Committee.

Ash-Lee Woodard Henderson, "How We Can Organize the South to Save the Country" (September 1, 2017)

As is true for most born, bred, and rooted Southerners, my relationship to the US South, its people, the land, its complex and often misunderstood histories, shapes my understanding of every single experience in my life. So in the context of 45 and crew's accession to executive power, and the attention of folks from all over the country being focused on recent white supremacist violence in Charlottesville, people are beginning to talk about and observe what's happening down South. The reminder that white supremacy and nationalism as a politic still exists, as well as the organizations and institutions that perpetuate those politics, visibility of what that looks like in the South at its ugliest, has once again sparked the attention of politicized people and stirred the spirits of people across the country.

In a time where people of good will are hungry for strategies to win, tactics to move those strategies, concrete direction, entry points, and actions that regular, everyday people can plug into, it's critically important that those of us who have committed our lives to the liberation of our people move with intentionality about accurately describing what's happening in this moment. Questions that impact strategy development and the tactics that we choose. What's happening right now? Where is it happening? Is this the first time it's happened? What's the impact? Who's impacted? What's our liberatory and utopian vision? How can we, while centering the most marginalized and directly impacted, resist and respond to the crisis while building the communities and alternatives that our people deserve?

Those aren't the questions I'm getting though—not from enough comrades in the region, not from folks outside the region that are making assessments of the role of Southerners, declarations about why the conditions are as they are in the region, what should be done to fix it and how the fixing it should take place. Maybe that's not where we need to start in the conversation about how to organize the South to save the country anyhow, in an effort of meeting folks not from the region and those of us who are who've been taught to hate ourselves where we're at. Shouting, "As goes the South, so goes the nation," or spitting facts to justify why Southern organizing and action is important and valuable isn't what's needed right now. Maybe being my Southern self, sharing my Southern perspective, is useful.

I wonder if folks can wrap their imaginations around the many different ways it can feel, what it means, how it looks to live where white Nazis, nationalists, and supremacists can be your neighbor. I wonder if folks recognize that although that's very obviously a possibility in the South where white supremacist infrastructure has always been more resourced that the social movements to dismantle systemic oppression in all its ugly forms, that possibility is also just as real in the North and West.

I find inspiration in the beauty of this land, the radical legacies and twenty-first-century manifestations of resistance of Southern people, the expressions of Black queer feminism, living into the beauty and challenges that come with family (blood and chosen), and so much more, very similarly to how folks find joy, love, and community outside the region. For every story of terror, fear, lived realities that drove Black people out of the South, fleeing Jim Crow and chattel slavery, there is a sacred story of love and resistance and winning that keeps me rooted and grounded and staying to fight for this place and our people here. Our people deserve the world we envision, and that world requires us to birth and build it. I deserve to experience that world in the place that I was born. This beautiful, fertile, sacred place shouldn't be abandoned or conceded to the right or to white supremacists, and doesn't have to be. So many of us choose to stay and fight and build. Knowing Nazis can be our neighbors. Klansmen are our judges. White supremacist cops run rampant in our streets.

It means that organizers and activists have to be creative, risk-taking but intentional and prepared. We have to study what's been done before and who's done it (both in terms of folks fighting for liberation and building beloved community, but also folks who have done the opposite). We have to be creative in moments of chaos. We have to trust and listen to our people. We have to love them in action. We have to develop multi-tactical strategies with multiple entry points for folks. We need to train up a new generational cohort of freedom fighters with lots of different kinds of skills to build and sustain contemporary movement infrastructure. It's about knowing the intellectual laziness of reducing the enemy to poor, or rural, or poor and rural white folks, but not the rich white folks and policy-makers that sustain systemic oppression with great power and access to resources. It looks like doing the everyday grind to build bases, which might not look like getting every person to every meeting or action, but they'll big-up our work at their church and at their dinner tables every day.

It looks like having a leadership development pipeline that moves those folks from evangelists to mobilizers and popular educators, from there to organizers and activists that can develop strategies for rapid response needs and long-term visions. It feels like not being frozen by fear, exhausted by sacrifice, but finding great healing and joy in what has always sustained our people down here, art and culture, the land, faith and spirit, and fighting like hell for the living.

• • •

In 2017, the #MeToo hash tag went viral when Hollywood actors—a majority of them women—courageously spoke out about their experiences of sexual assault by powerful men in the industry. The spread of #MeToo inspired survivors around the country to tell their own stories, leading to the resignations or firings of high-ranking men who in previous years had been shielded from accountability. The hashtag also prompted conversations about the pervasiveness of sexual violence for members of marginalized communities and low-wage workers. In solidarity with Hollywood survivors, Alianza Nacional de Campesinas, an organization of current and former women farmworkers, wrote the following statement.

Alianza Nacional de Campesinas, "700,000 Female Farmworkers Say They Stand with Hollywood Actors Against Sexual Assault" (November 10, 2017)

Dear Sisters,

We write on behalf of the approximately 700,000 women who work in the agricultural fields and packing sheds across the United States. For the past several weeks we have watched and listened with sadness as we have learned of the actors, models, and other individuals who have come forward to speak out about the gender-based violence they've experienced at the hands of bosses, coworkers, and other powerful people in the entertainment industry. We wish that we could say we're shocked to learn that this is such a pervasive problem in your industry. Sadly, we're not surprised because it's a reality we know far too well. Countless farmworker women across our country suffer in silence because of the widespread sexual harassment and assault that they face at work.

We do not work under bright stage lights or on the big screen. We work in the shadows of society in isolated fields and packinghouses that are out of sight and out of mind for most people in this country. Your job feeds souls, fills hearts, and spreads joy. Our job nourishes the nation with the fruits, vegetables, and other crops that we plant, pick, and pack.

Even though we work in very different environments, we share a common experience of being preyed upon by individuals who have the power to hire, fire, blacklist, and otherwise threaten our economic, physical, and emotional security. Like you, there are few positions available to us and reporting any kind of harm or injustice committed against us doesn't seem like a viable option. Complaining about anything—even sexual harassment—seems unthinkable because too much is at risk, including the ability to feed our families and preserve our reputations.

We understand the hurt, confusion, isolation, and betrayal that you might feel. We also carry shame and fear resulting from this violence. It sits on our backs like oppressive weights. But, deep in our hearts we know that it is not our fault. The only people at fault are the individuals who choose to abuse their power to harass, threaten, and harm us, like they have harmed you.

In these moments of despair, and as you cope with scrutiny and criticism because you have bravely chosen to speak out against the harrowing acts that were committed against you, please know that you're not alone. We believe and stand with you.

In solidarity,

Alianza Nacional de Campesinas

• • •

Boston activist Siham Byah, who had lived for more than twenty years in the United States and had a valid work permit, was detained during a visit to an Immigration and Customs Enforcement office in November 2017, and then deported to Morocco soon after Christmas. Her eight-year-old son, Naseem Byah, who was taken away from his family by the Massachusetts Department of Children and Families (DCF), wrote this letter to be read at a rally in support of his mother.

Naseem Johnson Byah, "I Need My Mom, My Family, and My Home" (December 14, 2017)

Hello, my name is Naseem Johnson Byah, and I am eight years old. I am in third grade and I go to school in Nahant. My favorite colors are orange, yellow, and gold. I love playing video games, and three of my favorites are

Minecraft, Roblox, and Monster Legends. I like to read a lot and I am very advanced for my grade level. I was one year old when I was taught to read by my mom, and we've spent hours reading together ever since.

On November 7, I walked to school like I usually do. After school, I walked home to find out that my mom was gone. After that, DCF came to my house with a police officer. They told me that I couldn't stay with Aziz and that I had to go somewhere else. I felt panicked and sad and scared when I heard that I couldn't stay.

I didn't get to talk to my mom for eleven days and I didn't know the truth until my friends were talking about it at school. Even though my foster parent is very nice, I will always still need my mom, my family, and my home.

I miss and love Mom to pieces and need her in my life to be happy. My mom is not a criminal and please don't send her back to Morocco. My mom is a good person and loves to help others. Please do not punish her for that. Me and my mom do lots of things together and have tons of memories. Without these memories, I am nothing. I love her and miss her so much. Thank you for your time.

● ● ●

X González is an advocate of gun control and survivor of the deadliest school shooting in US history, which claimed the lives of seventeen students at Marjory Stoneman Douglas High School. González rose to national prominence for their passionate speech at the March for Our Lives, where they excoriated lawmakers' failure to enact gun law reform, despite the cost to students' lives.

X González, "We Call BS" (February 17, 2018)

We haven't already had a moment of silence in the House of Representatives, so I would like to have another one. Thank you.

Every single person up here today, all these people should be home grieving. But instead we are up here standing together because, if all our government and president can do is send thoughts and prayers, then it's time for victims to be the change that we need to see.

Since the time of the Founding Fathers and since they added the Second Amendment to the Constitution, our guns have developed at a rate that leaves me dizzy. The guns have changed but our laws have not.

We certainly do not understand why it should be harder to make plans with friends on weekends than to buy an automatic or semi-automatic weapon. In Florida, to buy a gun you do not need a permit; you do not need a gun license; and, once you buy it, you do not need to register it. You do not need a permit to carry a concealed rifle or shotgun. You can buy as many guns as you want at one time.

I read something very powerful to me today. It was from the point of view of a teacher. And I quote: "When adults tell me I have the right to own a gun, all I can hear is my right to own a gun outweighs your students' right to live. All I hear is 'mine, mine, mine, mine.'"

Instead of worrying about our AP [Advanced Placement] Gov[ernment] Chapter 16 test, we have to be studying our notes to make sure that our arguments based on politics and political history are watertight. The students at this school have been having debates on guns for what feels like our entire lives. AP Gov. had about three debates this year. Some discussions on the subject even occurred during the shooting while students were hiding in the closets. The people involved right now—those who were there, those posting, those tweeting, those doing interviews and talking to people—are being listened to for what feels like the very first time on this topic that has come up over one thousand times in the past four years alone.

I found out today there's a website, shootingtracker.com. Nothing in the title suggests that it is exclusively tracking the USA's shootings— and yet, does it need to address that? Because Australia had one mass shooting in 1999 in Port Arthur—[and after the] massacre introduced gun safety—and it hasn't had one since. Japan has never had a mass shooting. Canada has had three and the UK had one—and they both introduced gun control. And yet here we are, with websites dedicated to reporting these tragedies so that they can be formulated into statistics for your convenience.

I watched an interview this morning and noticed that one of the questions was, "Do you think your children will have to go through other school shooter drills?" And our response is that our neighbors will not have to go through other school shooter drills. When we've had our say with the government—and maybe the adults have gotten used to saying "it is what it is"—but if us students have learned anything, it's that if you don't study, you will fail. And in this case if you actively do nothing, people continually end up dead. So, it's time to start doing something.

We are going to be the kids you read about in textbooks. Not because we're going to be another statistic about mass shooting in America, but because, just as David [Hogg] said, we are going to be the last mass shooting. Just like *Tinker v. Des Moines*, we are going to change the law. That's going to be Marjory Stoneman Douglas in that textbook, and it's going to be due to the tireless effort of the school board, the faculty members, the family members, and most of all the students. The students who are dead, the students still in the hospital, the students now suffering PTSD, the students who had panic attacks during the vigil because the helicopters would not leave us alone, hovering over the school for twenty-four hours a day.

There is one tweet I would like to call attention to. So many signs that the Florida shooter was mentally disturbed, even expelled for bad and erratic behavior. Neighbors and classmates knew he was a big problem. [You] must always report such instances to authorities again and again. We did, time and time again. Since he was in middle school. It was no surprise to anyone who knew him to hear that he was the shooter. Those talking about how we should have not ostracized him, you didn't know this kid, OK. We did. We know that they are claiming mental health issues, and I am not a psychologist, but we need to pay attention to the fact that this was not just a mental health issue. He would not have harmed that many students with a knife.

And how about we stop blaming the victims for something that was the student's fault, the fault of the people who let him buy the guns in the first place, those at the gun shows, the people who encouraged him to buy accessories for his guns to make them fully automatic, the people who didn't take them away from him when they knew he expressed homicidal tendencies? And I am not talking about the FBI. I'm talking about the people he lived with. I'm talking about the neighbors who saw him outside holding guns.

If the president wants to come up to me and tell me to my face that it was a terrible tragedy, and how it should never have happened, and maintain telling us how nothing is going to be done about it, I'm going to happily ask him how much money he received from the National Rifle Association.

You want to know something? It doesn't matter. Because I already know. Thirty million dollars. And divided by the number of gunshot victims in the United States in the one and one-half months in 2018 alone, that comes out to being $5,800. Is that how much these people are worth to you, Trump? If you don't do anything to prevent this from continuing to occur, that number of gunshot victims will go up and the number that they are worth will go down. And we will be worthless to you.

To every politician who is taking donations from the NRA, shame on you.

If your money was as threatened as us, would your first thought be, "How is this going to reflect on my campaign? Which should I choose?" Or would you choose us? And if you answered "us," will you act like it for once? You know what would be a good way to act like it? I have an example of how to *not* act like it. In February of 2017, one year ago, President Trump repealed an Obama-era regulation that would have made it easier to block the sale of firearms to people with certain mental illnesses.

From the interactions that I had with the shooter before the shooting, and from the information that I currently know about him, I don't really know if he was mentally ill. I wrote this before I heard what Delaney [Tarr] said. Delaney said he was diagnosed. I don't need a psychologist, and I don't need to be a psychologist, to know that repealing that regulation was a really dumb idea.

Republican Senator Chuck Grassley of Iowa was the sole sponsor on this bill that stops the FBI from performing background checks on people adjudicated to be mentally ill, and now he's stating for the record, "Well, it's a shame the FBI isn't doing background checks on these mentally ill people." Well, duh. You took that opportunity away last year.

The people in the government who were voted into power are lying to us. And us kids seem to be the only ones who notice—and our parents—to call BS.

Companies [are] trying to make caricatures of the teenagers these days, saying that all we are [is] self-involved and trend-obsessed—and they hush us into submission when our message doesn't reach the ears of the nation.

We are prepared to call BS. Politicians who sit in their gilded House and Senate seats funded by the NRA telling us nothing could have been done to prevent this, we call BS. They say tougher gun laws do not decrease gun violence. We call BS. They say a good guy with a gun stops a bad guy with a gun. We call BS. They say guns are just tools like knives and are as dangerous as cars. We call BS. They say no laws could have prevented the hundreds of senseless tragedies that have occurred. We call BS. That us kids don't know what we're talking about, that we're too young to understand how the government works. We call BS.

If you agree, register to vote. Contact your local congresspeople. Give them a piece of your mind.

● ● ●

In 2018, Katie Endicott was among the twenty thousand West Virginia teachers who went on a nine-day statewide strike—and won. Among the central issues behind the strike were rising healthcare costs and some of the lowest teacher salaries in the country. Teachers from all fifty-five West Virginia counties refused to return to work until they secured a 5 percent pay raise for themselves and all state employees. Their victory in a state that voted for Trump in a landslide, and in a "right-to-work" state (where the law restricts the right of workers to strike), inspired the "teacher strike wave," which spread to other so-called "red states" between 2018 and 2019. Below, Endicott describes the exciting buildup to the strike.

Katie Endicott, "How the Spark Became a Flame in West Virginia" (March 12, 2018)

On Martin Luther King Jr. Day, there was a rally. That's a holiday that West Virginia schools have off, and teachers went to the rally in Charleston.

My little boy had the flu, so I stayed with the kids while my husband went to the rally.

When he came home, he was so dejected because he said there were only about 150 teachers there. And when he talked to state senators and delegates, they were telling him: You should be scared, you have no idea what is coming your way.

They said there were some crazy bills that are going to really affect you all, so you need to be thinking about how you're going to approach things.

That was on January 15, and I told him he really needed to tell people, because people in my school didn't know. He was wondering why people weren't outraged, and I said I didn't think people knew about all of these bills, so you need to tell them—tell them that there were lawmakers pulling you into their offices and telling you that this is going to turn really ugly.

So he made a Facebook Live video with a colleague, telling everyone what he had heard, and it went viral. It was crazy—there were people from all across the state messaging me.

The reaction to that Facebook video was just unbelievable. It got all our teachers in Mingo County really riled up.

We started having meetings at the school level, and it was quickly apparent that we were going to have to have an emergency meeting for the whole county, because there was a lot of miscommunication and misinformation.

We scheduled a meeting for January 23, not knowing who would show up. Hundreds of people did. That's basically our county—all of our bus drivers, office workers, our teachers and cooks. We had our union reps, and we had Senator Richard Ojeda and Delegate Mark Dean.

My husband kicked the meeting off, and he reiterated what he said in the Facebook video. From there, our union leaders took questions, and Senator Ojeda took us to church. He gave an impassioned plea that we have to stand up for ourselves, and you can't take this.

The meeting lasted two and a half hours. Several board members were there, and they spoke up and told us: We have your back.

There came a point where we asked everybody in the media to leave because we had to the use the "s" word—the strike word. It was very apparent that people were angry and frustrated, and some kind of action was at least going to have to be discussed.

We said what does everyone think about a "blue flu" day [in which everyone calls in sick and stays home]? Everybody was in support.

Our union reps were there, and I think they were surprised. They said: Let me tell you about all the legal repercussions, you may lose your seniority, you might lose your job, you're definitely going to lose a day of pay. But everyone was still on board.

The momentum and energy in the room was intense. We decided we needed to plan the day of the "blue flu" and make sure that people knew. We wanted to use this like a bargaining chip—if the plan for that day got out, it might end up making some positive changes because they knew this resistance was a reality.

I stood up sometime near the end of the meeting and said: "The eyes of West Virginia are on us. In 1990, the last time the teachers went on strike, it was Mingo County that started the strike. So everyone is wanting to know what does Mingo County think?"

If we had the courage to step out, I knew that other counties would follow us—that we wouldn't be alone. In fact, there were two or three people from other counties who heard we were having an emergency meeting, and their counties weren't meeting, so they came to ours, just to see what we were going to do.

I said that we can't leave here until we choose a day. We can talk about it, but talking about it and doing it are two different things. We voted with a show of hands, and there wasn't one person in the building who voted against it.

We decided February 2—that was the day. Wyoming County had

already said they would be on board for it. From that point, Logan, Lincoln, McDowell, and all these other counties started having their own meetings, and our people were invited to go to those meetings and speak, and we did. At one point, I didn't even see my husband for several days. I told him he was on tour, because he was going to other meetings and having dinner with people. It was a grassroots movement. We were organizing it.

Some people were saying that they didn't think our union reps were really on board for this—that they thought it was too early. We would tell them: you don't work for the union, the union works for you. They're going to back you.

We took a lot of flack at first from other counties because we're smaller, and we do have that reputation of being hotheads or whatever. The mine wars and all of that started down here. Union strikes, we're known for that.

But other counties were saying we weren't giving them enough time, that they needed more time to organize. We talked about that in our leadership meetings: Do we stop? Do we wait on other counties to get organized, or do we just go ahead and do it?

We decided, no, let's just go ahead and do it. The day before I went, someone looked at me and said are you really going to go to the Capitol with four counties? They will laugh you out. You need at least forty-five to make a difference.

I said I don't believe that. I think that it wouldn't matter if it was one county. It's going to start a movement. Wait and see if other counties don't start jumping on board and following our lead.

And sure enough, it happened. It was like a domino effect. We started seeing Lincoln County and Boone and Cabell—they organized their own one-day work stoppage after they saw what we did and how effective it was. It was amazing to see that.

At that point, our union planned this massive rally. Things were spiraling because everyone in the state was now informed, and everyone was willing to take some kind of action. We were organized, and we were ready.

We said in Mingo County that we held ten thousand votes, because every time we decided to do something everybody would have to vote. We voted on Fed Up Friday—that was what we called that one-day work stoppage—and then we had to vote multiple times after that.

Another vote we took was to have our state union leaders call a state work stoppage if they felt it was necessary. At that point, we knew that out of fifty-five counties, it was almost unanimous that everyone wanted to go out. When they had the rally on Saturday, they announced that February 22 and 23 would be work stoppages across the state.

We were fired up. We were so excited that it was going to be all fifty-five counties. Someone has to start the spark, and the spark has to be fanned into a flame. But once it's fanned into a flame, you're not going to be able to put it out.

In our school, our county and neighboring counties, based on what my friends have told me, it was almost unanimous once again. Everybody was saying that if we're going out for those two days, we're not coming back until it's finished.

We stayed fifty-five strong, and nothing was going to break that. Even if some individuals wanted to break it—some individuals higher up—the membership refused to let it break.

Yesterday [after returning to work] was maybe the most exciting day I've had as a teacher. The energy level was amazing. The teachers were excited. Usually, this is a time when we're sort of suffering from burnout.

Of course, we were also exhausted. Most of our teachers went to the Capitol six or seven or eight days, and it's a two-hour drive one way for us. There were several days when me and my colleagues would wake up around 5:30 a.m. to go to the Capitol. We would be there from maybe 8 a.m. to 6 p.m., and then we would drive two hours back home, go to sleep and then get right back up the next morning at 5:30 and do it all again.

We're exhausted physically, but at the same time we're exhilarated emotionally. Our kids were amazing. They were clapping for us, high-fiving and giving hugs and telling us we were heroes. That was energizing—to know that our students were paying attention, and that they understood why we were doing it.

That to me is probably one of the most amazing things: this wasn't just us standing together, it was us standing together with our students and our parents and all of them supporting us. That made a huge difference.

One of the things we said from the beginning was that we weren't just standing up for ourselves, and not just for our state. We wanted to stand up for teachers all across the nation. Because we know that this can be a thankless job, and we don't get the respect we deserve.

We aren't viewed as the professionals that we are. That's not a West Virginia problem; that's a society problem. We said from the beginning that we wanted to stand for all teachers.

We're hoping this is just the beginning of a much larger movement and that people wake up. We hope that legislators wake up—that they understand we've put them on notice now. They can't just throw money at an election, get in there and just slide some of these bills through and play politics as usual.

During my planning period today, there were teachers coming by and talking about Oklahoma and Kentucky and Pittsburgh and these different places [also going on strike].

We're watching. We want to encourage them. We've been sending messages to people that we know are from that state. We've been telling them: people are going to tell you about all of the risks, but look at us.

We can tell you: if you stand together, if you do this together, they will not break you. You will break them.

• • •

At eleven years old, Naomi Wadler was the youngest speaker at the March for Our Lives in Washington, DC, organized in response to the mass shooting at Marjory Stoneman Douglas High School. While the Florida shooting galvanized calls for gun-law reform, Wadler urged the crowd of thousands to remember Black victims of gun violence, especially Black girls whose deaths had previously been overlooked.

Naomi Wadler, "I Speak for Black Girls Victimized by Guns Whose Stories Don't Make the Front Page" (March 24, 2018)

My name is Naomi, and I'm eleven years old. Me and my friend Carter led a walkout at our elementary school on the fourteenth. We walked out—we walked out for eighteen minutes, adding a minute to honor Courtlin Arrington, an African American girl who was the victim of gun violence in her school in Alabama after the Parkland shooting.

I am here today to represent Courtlin Arrington. I am here today to represent Hadiya Pendleton. I am here today to represent Taiyania Thompson, who, at just sixteen, was shot dead in her home here in Washington, DC. I am here today to acknowledge and represent the African American girls whose stories don't make the front page of every national newspaper, whose stories don't lead on the evening news. I represent the African American women who are victims of gun violence, who are simply statistics instead of vibrant, beautiful girls full of potential.

It is my privilege to be here today. I am indeed full of privilege. My voice has been heard. I am here to acknowledge their stories, to say they matter, to say their names, because I can, and I was asked to be. For far too long, these names, these Black girls and women, have been just numbers. I am here to say "Never again" for those girls, too. I am here to say that everyone should value those girls, too.

People have said that I am too young to have these thoughts on my own. People have said that I am a tool of some nameless adult. It's not true. My friends and I might still be eleven, and we might still be in elementary school, but we know. We know life isn't equal for everyone. And we know what is right and wrong. We also know that we stand in the shadow of the Capitol. And we know that we have seven short years until we, too, have the right to vote.

So I am here today to honor the words of Toni Morrison: "If there is a book that you want to read, but it hasn't been written yet, you must be the one to write it." I urge everyone here and everyone who hears my voice to join me in telling the stories that aren't told, to honor the girls, the women of color who are murdered at dispro-portionate rates in this nation. I urge each of you to help me write the narrative for this world and understand, so that these girls and women are never forgotten.

• • •

In 2016, San Francisco 49ers quarterback Colin Kaepernick refused to stand for "The Star Spangled Banner" in protest of police terrorism. When asked about his position, Kaepernick replied, "I am not going to stand up to show pride in a flag for a country that oppresses Black people and people of color. To me, this is bigger than football and it would be selfish on my part to look the other way. There are bodies in the street and people getting paid leave and getting away with murder." For this, Kaepernick faced extreme backlash and was ultimately denied employment by the NFL, along with teammate Eric Reid, who also kneeled during the anthem. Kaepernick's protest inspired athletes at all levels, from high school to college to professional sports, to "take a knee" for justice, and he continues to "advance the liberation of Black and Brown people through storytelling, systems change, and political education." Here is the speech Kaepernick gave after winning Amnesty International's Ambassador of Conscience Award.

Colin Kaepernick, Amnesty International's Ambassador of Conscience Award Speech (April 21, 2018)

It is only fitting that I have the honor of Eric Reid introducing me for this award. In many ways, my recognition would not be possible without our brotherhood. I truly consider him to be more than a friend—Eric, his wife, his children—they are all a part of my family.

Not only did he kneel by my side during the national anthem throughout the entire 2016 NFL season, but Eric continued to use his platform as a professional football player to protest systemic oppres-sion, specifically police brutality against Black and Brown people.

Eric introducing me for this prestigious award brings me great joy.

But I am also pained by the fact that his taking a knee, and demonstrating courage to protect the rights of Black and Brown people in America, has also led to his ostracization from the NFL when he is widely recognized as one of the best competitors in the game and in the prime of his career.

People sometimes forget that love is at the root of our resistance.

My love for Eric has continually grown over the course of our ongoing journey. His brotherhood, resilience, and faith have shined brightly in moments of darkness. My love for my people serves as the fuel that fortifies my mission. And it is the people's unbroken love for themselves that motivates me, even when faced with the dehumanizing norms of a system that can lead to the loss of one's life over simply being Black.

History has proven that there has never been a period in the history of America where anti-Blackness has not been an ever-present terror. Racialized oppression and dehumanization is woven into the very fabric of our nation—the effects of which can be seen in the lawful lynching of Black and Brown people by the police, and the mass incarceration of Black and Brown lives in the prison industrial complex. While America bills itself as the land of the free, the receipts show that the United States has incarcerated approximately 2.2 million people, the largest prison population in the history of humankind.

As police officers continue to terrorize Black and Brown communities, abusing their power, and then hiding behind their blue wall of silence, and laws that allow for them to kill us with virtual impunity, I have realized that our love, that sometimes manifests as Black-rage, is a beautiful form of defiance against a system that seeks to suppress our humanity—a system that wants us to hate ourselves.

I remind you that love is at the root of our resistance.

It is our love for twelve-year-old Tamir Rice, who was gunned down by the police in less than two seconds that will not allow us to bury our anger. It is our love for Philando Castile, who was executed in front of his partner and his daughter, that keeps the people fighting back. It is our love for Stephon Clark, who was lynched in his grandma's backyard, that will not allow us to stop until we achieve liberation for our people.

Our love is not an individualized love—it is a collective love. A collective love that is constantly combating collective forms of racialized hate. Chattel slavery, Jim Crow, New Jim Crow, massive plantations, mass incarcerations, slave patrols, police patrols, we, as a collective, since the colonization of the Americas have been combating collective forms of systemic racialized hate and oppression.

But I am hopeful. I am inspired.

This is why we have to protest. This is why we are so passionate. We protest because we love ourselves, and our people.

It was James Baldwin who said, to be Black in America, "and to be relatively conscious is to be in a rage almost all the time." My question is, why aren't all people? How can you stand for the national anthem of a nation that preaches and propagates "freedom and justice for all," that is so unjust to so many of the people living there? How can you not be in rage when you know that you are always at risk of death in the streets or enslavement in the prison system? How can you willingly be blind to the truth of systemic racialized injustice? When Malcolm X said, "I'm for truth, no matter who tells it. I'm for justice, no matter who it is for or against. I'm a human being, first and foremost, and as such I'm for whoever and whatever benefits humanity as a whole." I took that to heart.

While taking a knee is a physical display that challenges the merits of who is excluded from the notion of freedom, liberty, and justice for all, the protest is also rooted in a convergence of my moralistic beliefs, and my love for the people.

Seeking the truth, finding the truth, telling the truth, and living the truth has been, and always will be what guides my actions. For as long as I have a beating heart, I will continue on this path, working on behalf of the people.

Again . . . Love is at the root of our resistance.

Last but certainly not least; I would like to thank Amnesty International for the Ambassador of Conscience Award. But in truth, this is an award that I share with all of the countless people throughout the world combating the human rights violations of police officers, and their uses of oppressive and excessive force. To again quote Malcolm X, when he said that he "will join in with anyone—I don't care what color you are—as long as you want to change this miserable condition that exists on this earth," I am here to join with you all in this battle against police violence.

• • •

Malinda Limberhand is the mother of Hanna Harris, a member of the Cheyenne tribe who, in 2013, then aged twenty-one, disappeared from the Northern Cheyenne Indian Reservation in Lame Deer, Montana, and was later found murdered. As Limberhand explains, countless missing and murdered Native women and girls have seen their cases ignored, neglected, and marginalized, leading to growing calls for meaningful attention to this pressing issue.

Malinda Limberhand, "A Mother's Walk for Justice" (May 5, 2018)

I want to thank all of you for joining our "Walk for Justice for Missing and Murdered Native Women and Girls." Each one of you by being here today is taking action to say enough is enough. Together we are raising our voices calling for justice for our Native women and girls. We are saying to this state, country, and the world that the lives of Native women and girls are important.

Hanna went missing on July 4, 2013. Like in so many cases of missing Native women, the system was slow to respond. We as her family, friends, and community had to conduct the search for Hanna. And this is what happens across Indian tribes when a Native woman or girl goes missing or disappears.

This failed response is not acceptable and must change.

Today's walk and the other walks being held are so important to telling our story. We are telling the world Native women do matter. We are telling the world the disappearance of a Native woman or girl must be responded to and not ignored.

As a mother of a Native woman who became one of the missing and murdered, I am committed to organizing to make these changes happen. I do this for my daughter and all our missing and murdered Native women.

This is not a new problem. It is an old problem.

Traditionally Native women were respected. Today, we face levels of violence greater than any other group of women. This violence touches every family. Every tribe has Native women who are missing or have been murdered. Since Hanna went missing and was found murdered, I have become very aware of how large a problem we face as Native women and as Indian tribes.

The Department of Justice has found that in some tribal communities, American Indian women face murder rates that are more than ten times the national average.

Hanna was just twenty-one years old when she went missing. Her future was stolen and her beautiful son denied his mother. Like Hanna, murdered Native women will not live to see their potential or dreams come true. Their tribes will not see their talents and contributions.

As a mother, nothing will replace the loss of my daughter, but I know that by organizing today's walk and working to support the National Day of Awareness, this will create changes that will help others. And Hanna and so many others will not be forgotten.

To end this problem, we must understand it.

Many Native women go missing or are murdered by a rapist, abuser, sex trafficker, or, as in the movie *Wind River*, oil rig worker. These men rape, abuse, beat, and murder Native women because we are seen as "unprotected." They know nothing will be done.

Acceptance of violence against Indian women is not new. It goes back to the Indian wars and the boarding schools when violence was used by the government. It also goes back to an old standard of not doing anything when an Indian woman was raped, beaten, or murdered. It is an old problem we continue to live with today.

Bad people commit these horrible crimes against Native women, but it is the system that allows it to happen generation after generation. This needs to stop. The system must change. And that is why I am here today.

A National Day of Awareness for Missing and Murdered Native Women and Girls will help shed light on this horrible reality.

I thank Senators [Steve] Daines and [Jon] Tester for leading the way for passage of the Senate resolution declaring May 5, 2018, Hanna's birthday, as a National Day of Awareness for Missing and Murdered Native Women and Girls.

Our movement is growing. In 2017 and 2018, more than two hundred organizations joined with the National Indigenous Women's Resource Center to support these resolutions.

To all those walking across Indian tribes, I say thank you!

Today we wear red to honor our missing and murdered Native women and girls!

Please take pictures and post your actions on social media! Tell the world of these crimes!

Together we must stand for justice and safety for our daughters, granddaughters, sisters, mothers, grandmothers!

We must stand for all Native women and girls!

• • •

Carol Anderson is a best-selling author, professor, and historian of African American Studies. In 2013, the Supreme Court gutted key provisions of the 1965 Voting Rights Act, arguing that protections for Black voters no longer applied to "current conditions," opening the door to further attacks on the right to vote, particularly for Black voters.

Carol Anderson, "Voting While Black" (June 7, 2018)

The recent spate of whites calling 911 on African Americans for barbecuing while Black, waiting in Starbucks while Black, sleeping at Yale while Black ad nauseam has led to a much-needed discussion about the policing of public spaces.

Yet, there's another important public space where blackness has been policed and we have been far too silent about it: the voting booth. And the implications are just as far-reaching and devastating, and, despite Chief Justice John Roberts's claim, not some relic of a bygone past.

The twenty-first century is, in fact, littered with the bodies of Black votes. In the 2000 presidential election, which George W. Bush won in the sunshine state by 537 ballots, Florida kept African Americans from the polls or ensured that their votes would never be added to the state's tally. The policing was multi-tentacled. On Election Day, there were faulty voting machines, purged voter rolls (purges that targeted minorities), and locked gates at polling places that should have been opened. There was also a Florida Highway Patrol checkpoint at the only road leading to the polls in key, heavily Black precincts in Jacksonville. Then there were the piles of ballots, especially in counties with large minority populations, left uncounted. The US Civil Rights Commission "concluded that, of the 179,855 ballots invalidated by Florida officials, 53 percent were cast by Black voters. In Florida," the commission's report continued, "a Black citizen was ten times as likely to have a vote rejected as a white voter."

That targeting of African Americans was just as egregious in North Carolina after the US Supreme Court gutted the necessary protection of the Voting Rights Act in 2013. The catalyst for North Carolina's assault was simple: Black people had dared access their Fifteenth Amendment rights. Since 2000, African American voter registration had increased by 51.1 percent in the state, and Blacks also had a higher voter turnout "rate than white registered voters in both the 2008 and 2012 presidential elections."

Effective Black access to that public space, the voting booth, triggered, as the federal court noted, a targeting of African American voters "with almost surgical precision." The state required IDs which its research showed a disproportionate number of Black people did not have. And, as ThinkProgress reported, the GOP slashed the number of early voting sites in Guilford County, which is nearly 30 percent African American, from "16 in 2012 to a single location" in 2016. As a result, the magazine noted, "turnout so far is down 85 percent." There was a similar elimination of early voting sites in Mecklenburg County, home to the city of Charlotte and 15 percent of the state's African American population. Pleased with what they had accomplished, North Carolina Republicans "celebrated" mowing down Black access to the voting booth.

In Indiana, once it became clear that Black people could determine the outcome of an election, like when Barack Obama carried the state in 2008, the Republicans mobilized to cut off African Americans' access to the polls. Similar to North Carolina, Indiana's GOP realized how essential early voting was to Black voter turnout. The Republican-dominated legislature mandated that counties with more than 325,000 residents could only have one early voting location unless approved on a bipartisan basis. The governor, Mike Pence, signed this into law in 2013. Once again, the targeting was clear. Only three counties in Indiana have more than 325,000 people and account for 72 percent of the state's Black population. The result, as the *Indianapolis Star* reported, is that Marion County, including the state's largest city, Indianapolis, lost two of its sites and was reduced to only one early voting precinct, which was inaccessibly located downtown with no available parking. Not surprisingly, by design, in the 2016 election, early voting in the county plummeted by 26 percent.

Georgia is also adept at policing Black citizens who dare to vote. In 2010, when African Americans in Brooks County organized a massive voter turnout drive and elected the first majority-Black school board in its history, the secretary of state, Brian Kemp, had a dozen African American activists and school board members arrested and, over the course of a long grueling four-year period, dragged through the courts. Although, in the end, there were zero convictions for voter fraud, there was a chilling effect as lives were ruined, jobs lost, and a hard lesson on the costs of voting made abundantly clear.

Then, in 2014, Kemp put his crosshairs on the New Georgia Voter Project, an organization determined to register some of the seven hundred thousand African Americans in the state who were not yet on the voter rolls. When the group signed up more than one hundred thousand to vote, Kemp immediately took to the airwaves insisting: "We're just not going to put up with fraud." That claim, spoken often and wrongly by Republican stalwarts from Kris Kobach to Donald Trump, is the lie used to justify voter suppression techniques. Yet, as the law professor Justin Levitt has documented, between 2000 and 2014, there have only been thirty-one cases of voter identification fraud out of one billion votes. Kemp, in his own way, acknowledged the lie when, behind closed doors, he explained to a group of fellow Republicans: "Democrats are working hard . . . registering all these minority voters. . . . If they can do that, they can win these elections in November." He, therefore, used the power of his office to launch a very public multiyear investigation that would, once again, aim to intimidate and dissuade African Americans from registering to vote.

In 2016, pummeled by voter suppression in more than thirty states, the Black voter turnout plummeted by 7 percentage points. For the GOP, that was an effective kill rate. For America, it was a lethal assault on democracy.

● ● ●

When Hurricane Maria hit Puerto Rico in September 2017, it destroyed the homes, farms, and businesses; took out power and communications; led to widespread shortages of essential goods, including water; and caused the deaths of thousands. Like Hurricane Katrina in Louisiana, the storm had the greatest impact on the most vulnerable people and exposed deep structural problems in Puerto Rico. And in the aftermath of the storm, investors, corporations, and the rich sought to turn the devastation to their advantage. Here Mercedes Martínez, the president of the Puerto Rican Teachers Federation, speaks to Daniel Denvir of *The Dig* podcast about the impact of Hurricane Maria on Puerto Rican society.

Mercedes Martínez, "Hurricane Maria Just Uncovered What's Been Happening in Puerto Rico for Decades" (June 12, 2018)

Puerto Rico is still devastated after Hurricane Maria. Actually, Hurricane Maria just uncovered what's been happening in Puerto Rico for decades, since we've been a US colony and a Spanish colony, as well. We now have the fiscal board, which is imposing severe austerity measures against the working class, against our children. Yesterday was the last day of the semester and 265 schools are set to shut down permanently, affecting 55,000 students. Eighty-four percent of the schools set to be shut down are in rural areas of extreme poverty.

We still have 60 percent of residents with no electricity. We have people still dying every day in our country, as a recent Harvard study exposed, because of government negligence over the energy problem that we have here.

Law 80 is going to be abolished. It's a law that can defend private working employees from unjustified layoffs, so they get just compensation. They are proposing to lower the minimum wage for our youth twenty-five years and under. They are proposing to increase tuition fees at the University of Puerto Rico and shut down different campuses. So, it's disaster capitalism on steroids while we are living here in Puerto Rico right now.

La Junta, or the oversight control fiscal board, is a dictatorship. It was appointed by the US Congress during Barack Obama's presidency. Obama approved the law, called PROMESA [the Puerto Rico Oversight, Management, and Economic Stability Act]. It was written to create ways to allow the Puerto Rican people to pay an odious debt of $72 billion.

They created this fiscal board just as they did in Detroit. The fiscal board is supposed to implement severe austerity measures against the people of Puerto Rico, so we can repay a debt that has not been audited. We are requesting for the debt to be audited.

The Junta, or the oversight fiscal board, is composed of seven members, unelected officials, who can overrule our laws and budget, who submit fiscal plans, who approve anything that happens in our country. So that is not democracy. That is a dictatorship of seven unelected officials who are governing our country.

They are not here to put behind bars all the corrupt politicians or the bondholders, the people that put the Puerto Rican people into debt. It's very curious to see that two of the members of the oversight fiscal board were involved in the bonds that were [issued] on behalf of Puerto Rican people when they worked at Santander Bank and the Banco Gubernamental de Fomento para Puerto Rico, which is the bank of the government of Puerto Rico.

They are responsible for these bonds that were [issued] on behalf of our people. They are, as we say here, playing pitcher and catcher on both bases. They created the debt—and we have to pay for it, while they get benefits.

A week after the hurricane, teachers themselves reopened the schools. They reconditioned the schools, machete and chainsaws in hand, and put the roofs back on the schools. And we sent [Puerto Rico Education Secretary Julia] Keleher a letter saying, open at least the lunchroom, because children have no electricity. Children have no water in the houses. You have gas stoves and you have food there that you can feed the entire community. Open them up and we will cook. She denied that, so a lot of parents occupied even the lunchrooms after the hurricane, to be able to feed the children and all the community members.

Then, as two weeks passed, the schools were ready to reopen in the majority of the cases, thanks to the work of the people. Because only the people will save the people. The government did not appear—not federal, not state.

Hundreds of thousands of people have already left the island. One study showed that 6 percent of the people that left aren't coming back to our country. It's obvious that they want to depopulate our country.

If you close a school in a rural area where it's the only school, and the closest school is fourteen kilometers away and people have no cars, you are making them leave the mountains and you are making them leave our country, and you have no jobs. Last year, more than 45,000 jobs in the private sector were lost in our country.

They're pushing people out of our country to allow the rich to come here and create their own towns, their own cities, their own Puerto Rico. They're coming here trying to buy the land and have their own private hospitals, their private schools, their private land, their private anything.

Prior to the hurricane, there were huge mobilizations. Students of the University of Puerto Rico had a strike for seventy-two days and they won one of their claims against the tuition fee increase. On May 1 last year, around eighty thousand people flooded the streets of San Juan, particularly on what is called the Gold Mile, which is where the bankers are, protesting against these severe austerity measures, and were able to stop a lot of them.

The governor of Puerto Rico amended the penal code in Puerto Rico to implement many more years of incarceration for people that protest if they commit a crime—people that block the streets, people that block the entrance of the schools for the occupations. So, they are trying to make people feel scared to protest.

This May 1 was amazing as well. The banks were shut down. The biggest mall in Puerto Rico was shut down. Police brutality has been implemented against all of those who struggle. We saw this on May 1, where tear gas, rubber bullets, 1,100 cops were sent to demonstrations of the working class, of university students, environmentalist groups, feminists. They are trying to implement terror, but people are fighting back.

We have been arrested for doing civil disobedience to ask the government to open the schools. But we are not scared. They think that they are going to drive us away or scare us through these terrorizing policies and police brutality against the people of Puerto Rico. They are wrong. We have nothing else to lose.

• • •

Victor Ricardo Plua gave the following speech at a youth rally in Brownsville, Texas, demanding an end to the Trump administration's barbaric—though not unprecedented—policy of separating children from their families at the US border.

Victor Ricardo Plua, "Don't Put Children in Cages! Reunite Families Now!" (June 28, 2018)

My name is Victor Ricardo Plua. I am nine years old. Every day, when I wake up in the morning, I say good morning to my parents, my grandma and grandpa. I love my grandpa. He has taken care of me since I was born. Now that I am older, my grandpa picks me up from school, drives me to jiu-jitsu practice, and teaches me how to build things.

My grandpa came to this country to have better opportunities. He was a farmworker, a construction worker, and washed cars. These are jobs that are hard to do, that are sometimes paid less than minimum wage. My grandpa has contributed to this country like any other citizen.

But, unfortunately, this country does not want people like him to live here. This is why I am afraid. I am afraid that my grandpa will be deported and I will never see him again. So, every night, before I go to bed, I pray to God for everything that I have, and I pray that I will have another day with my grandpa.

This is why I'm here today, because I do not agree with what this government is doing to my community. They are treating us like criminals. No family, no child should live in a world filled with fear—fear of guns, of shootings, of bullying, of being beaten, deported, or torn apart from their families.

To all children, to all the families who are being hurt, who are angry and sad like me, you are not alone. We are not alone. Our love and voice is our strongest weapon. And together we have the power to change what this government is doing, to make sure that we live in a world without fear and harm. Humanity has no borders!

• • •

Winona LaDuke is the cofounder and executive director of Honor the Earth, a Minnesota-based environmental justice organization led by Indigenous women. She is an Anishinaabekwe (Ojibwe) enrolled member of the Mississippi Band Anishinaabeg, who lives and works on the White Earth Reservations. LaDuke has twice run as the vice presidential running mate of consumer advocate Ralph Nader, in 1996 and again in 2000, both times on the Green Party ticket. In 2018, LaDuke described her reasons for opposing a permit to divert water for the Line 3 oil pipeline replacement project.

Winona LaDuke, "Militarizing Minnesota over Line 3"
(October 3, 2018)

On September 24, the Duluth City Council discussed purchasing
$82,721 worth of riot gear for the second time. Water Protectors, the
NAACP, church representatives, and many others packed the City
Council to oppose the riot gear purchase. The decision was tabled for
the second time.

It's an interesting moment in Duluth. Two years ago, the Duluth
City Council passed a resolution opposing the use of excessive force at
Standing Rock during the DAPL protest. There, over $38 million was
spent by North Dakota authorities, who brought in more than 1,200
police and National Guard from across the country, as well as using
Tiger Swan, a paramilitary security force. Now we are talking riot gear
for Duluth. As Tara Houska, Honor the Earth's campaigns director,
noted, there has not been a riot in Duluth for one hundred years. Well,
nearly so.

The last riot in Duluth was the 1920 lynching of three Black men—
Elias Clayton, Elmer Jackson, and Isaac McGhie. Charged with an
unsubstantiated rape on June 15, three young Black men who had come
to town with a traveling circus were arrested. Word spread through the
town, and that evening the three were taken from jail and lynched by
a white mob. Crowd estimates were between one thousand and ten
thousand people (apparently they were sort of bad at counting in those
days). That was the last riot.

Times are changing, the militarization of police is on the increase,
and pressure by Chilean mining and pipeline companies to militarize
northern Minnesota is bearing fruit. On June 28, this year, the Minnesota Public Utilities Commission issued a rogue decision—overriding
all recommendations of state agencies, tribes, and sixty-eight thousand
Minnesotans, and approved a Certificate of Need for the Enbridge Line
3. During that meeting, Commissioner John Tuma asked Enbridge if
the company would underwrite the police expenses required to put in
the Canadian pipeline. Since then, riot gear requests have increased.

In mid-September, Fond du Lac tribal police guarded an informational meeting for band members on Enbridge's Line 3 Agreement with the tribe. The controversial decision to sign with Enbridge has been opposed by Tribal Water Protectors and was done without community forums. Debra Topping attended the meeting and was handing out literature asking for a referendum vote on the proposal when she was pushed aside, searched, and asked for a tribal ID by the police. Details of the agreement are not public, but the estimated $250 million deal is good money, no question. The deal has committed the Fond du Lac band to insure the project's future in their territory. Apparently, that means using tribal police to control tribal members. The question is, at what cost?

Meanwhile, in Mexico, an Indigenous leader opposing the First Majestic Silver mining operation was assassinated. First Majestic is a Canadian company. Margarito Díaz González, a leader of the Huichol people, was killed on September 8. This killing marks one of many in Mexico, where environmental and Indigenous leaders have been assassinated for their opposition to mining and dam projects. The Mexican Human Rights Council condemned the murder and asked authorities to investigate, since Díaz González had been a leading opponent not only to the Majestic Silver Mine, but also to the La Marona dam.

The La Marona dam would flood Wirikuta, one of the most sacred places in the Huichol world. Annually, thousands of Huichol conduct pilgrimages to this place, now threatened to be flooded for the benefit of a Canadian mining corporation. First Majestic and other mining corporations have leases to over 70 percent of Huichol territory.

Canadian mining corporations in particular have procured bad human rights records internationally, often using local militaries and goon squads to carry out the terrorizing of communities and murders. This last year, new lawsuits were filed in Toronto, seeking to hold Canadian corporations accountable for human rights violations. As the *Guardian* reports:

> The case centers on allegations dating back to 2007, when the women say hundreds of police, military and private

security personnel linked to a Canadian mining company descended on the secluded village of Lote Ocho in eastern Guatemala. . . . [S]ecurity personnel had set dozens of homes ablaze in a bid to force the villagers off their ancestral lands, according to court documents.

On January 17, the men were out in the fields, . . . and the women were alone. The eleven women say they were raped repeatedly by the armed men. Choc Cac—three months pregnant at the time—was with her ten-year-old daughter when she was seized by the men, some of whom were in uniform. Twelve of the men raped her, she said. She later suffered a miscarriage.

The women link the violence to the nearby Fenix mine. . . . At the time, the subsidiary was controlled by Vancouver-based Skye Resources. In 2008, Skye was acquired by Toronto's Hudbay Minerals, which sold the mine to a Russian company in 2011.

That's how it goes. The United Nations has also singled out Canadian mining companies and called on authorities to better regulate the sector.

Canadian mining corporations control most of the mining leases in the Great Lakes and in Minnesota. Perhaps we should be concerned.

Meanwhile back in Minnesota, law enforcement will have a bottomless tab open with a Canadian multinational corporation to cover any costs related to quelling resistance to the pipeline. If Fond du Lac's new relationship with Enbridge is any example, we may stand to be a bit worried about civil society. If Duluth's need for riot gear is an indication of our future, we should wonder what a human life is worth in Minnesota. And, if the rights of corporations should supersede the rights of people.

No time like the present to remember Elias Clayton, Elmer Jackson, and Isaac McGhie, the victims of the mob lynching. No time like the present to protect Minnesota from militarization paid for by Canadian corporations.

Chapter 8

"Our Resistance Must Be Intersectional"

African American Policy Forum, "Our Fights Are Connected; Our Resistance Must Be Intersectional" (November 2, 2018)
Marc Lamont Hill, "Our Solidarity Must Be a Verb" (November 28, 2018)
aja monet, Smoke Signals Studio Artists Manifesto (February 1, 2019)
Microsoft Workers 4 Good, "We Did Not Sign Up to Develop Weapons" (February 22, 2019)
Isra Hirsi, Haven Coleman, and Alexandria Villaseñor, "Adults Won't Take Climate Change Seriously. So We, the Youth, Are Forced to Strike" (March 7, 2019)
Lenny Sanchez, "Why I'm Striking Against Uber" (May 8, 2019)
Ta-Nehisi Coates, "Testimony to the House on Reparations" (June 19, 2019)
Rev. Dr. William J. Barber II, et al., "Pastoral Letter on the El Paso Shootings" (August 8, 2019)
Xiuhtezcatl Tonatiuh Martinez, "To Fight for a Just Climate Is to Fight for Everything That We Love" (September 9, 2019)
Stacey Park Milbern, "We Need Power to Live" (October 10, 2019)
Jamaica Heolimeleikalani Osorio, "For All the Aunties, but Especially for Mary Maxine Lani Kahaulelio" (October 28, 2019)
Tarana J. Burke, "The #MeToo Movement's Success Took a Decade of Work, Not Just a Hashtag. And There's More to Do" (December 31, 2019)
Antonia Crane, "Dispatch from the California Stripper Strike" (February 8, 2021)
Maggie Trinkle, "I (Don't) Want a Wife" (April 16, 2020)

• • •

The concept of "intersectionality" was developed by legal scholar Kimberlé Williams Crenshaw in 1989, but the term has gained widespread usage in recent years, with activists seeking to build intersectional movements. In "The Urgency of Intersectionality," which we include in chapter 5, Crenshaw defines intersectionality as an attempt "to deal with the fact that many of our social justice problems like racism and sexism are often overlapping, creating multiple levels of social injustice." Those who fall at the intersections of multiple marginalized identities, such as people who are both Black and female, face unique consequences that go unaddressed when we tend to treat systems of oppression like racism and sexism as entirely separate.

The end of the second decade of the new century saw a growing insistence within social movements on the interconnectedness between the struggles for Black and Palestinian liberation; the battles for workers' control of their own workplaces and for immigrant justice; the efforts to end racist violence at home and militarism abroad; and the goals of disability and climate justice. Such connections underscore the importance of solidarity in strengthening all our fights.

● ● ●

Cofounded in 1996 by Kimberlé Williams Crenshaw, the African American Policy Forum (AAPF) "connects academics, activists and policymakers to promote efforts to dismantle structural inequality." In 2018, the organization released this important statement urging that "we must do much, much more than vote" and "must forge solidarity at every juncture that Trumpism has exploited, recognizing, in particular, the unique ways that anti-Black racism, xenophobia and anti-Semitism have historically worked together in the United States."

African American Policy Forum, "Our Fights Are Connected; Our Resistance Must Be Intersectional" (November 2, 2018)

We at AAPF are anguished as we know are many of you at the successive acts of inhumanity that have rocked the country over the past two weeks. Between last Wednesday's racially motivated murders of Maurice Stallard and Vickie Jones at a Kroger grocery store in Kentucky, and Saturday's mass shooting at a Pittsburgh synagogue, racist terror has claimed thirteen lives. If the explosives that MAGA fanatic Cesar Sayoc allegedly mailed to prominent political and media figures (and frequent Trump targets) had not been intercepted, that already sobering figure might be even higher. And this political mobilization of hate is likely the tip of the iceberg.

The violence of last week and its white supremacist markings confirm fears that many of us have expressed repeatedly about how Donald Trump's presidency has unleashed and emboldened the forces of hate. The drumbeat leading to this awful moment has been a steady one, including Trump's insistence on an equivalency between violent white nationalists in Charlottesville, Virginia, and those who peacefully protested against them; his denigration of African nations as "shithole countries"; his reference to Mexican immigrants as "criminals and rapists"; and his effort to ban those from Muslim-dominant countries from entering the United States. It includes his suggestion that a Black protester at one of his rallies "should have been roughed up," his coded references to a "corrupt, globalist ruling class," and the daily digital demagoguery that spreads fear and outright lies to his most fervent supporters. It includes his decision to send troops to the border to threaten Central Americans lawfully seeking asylum, demonstrating an alarming willingness to use military force to insulate his political power.

As we watch these shocking developments, it becomes abundantly clear that politics as usual will not provide protection against the rapid unraveling of even the most symbolic expressions of core democratic principles. Those who rest their faith in the separation of powers overlook the negligence of the Senate and potentially the courts in drawing any meaningful lines to constrain this president. In the face of all of this, calling for President Trump to offer solace to the nation in our time of grief is about as reasonable as asking the fox to eulogize the missing chickens when he's visibly belching feathers.

So there's no question that we have to get out and vote to create the possibility for significant checks on the anti-democratic policies and rhetoric that are unfolding everywhere. Absolutely everybody must call many bodies to go to the polls. We must outvote the forces of suppression in droves if we are to overcome efforts to suppress the power of our communities.

But we must do much, much more than vote. We have to think and act differently about the traumas we are all facing.

The Trump playbook relies upon a powerful mobilization of racism, anti-Semitism, xenophobia, transphobia, sexism, and homophobia. They are not singular forces, but related and reinforcing. The Pittsburgh shooter downloaded this poisonous discourse, blaming Jews for traitorous support of dehumanized "others"—racially denigrated interlopers who pose a threat to whiteness—because of the Tree of Life's work helping refugees. He and Sayoc were vehement believers in the white nationalist mythology about wealthy Jews like George Soros as the "puppet masters" behind Black activism, a worldview that erases African American agency and presents Jews as disloyal and disruptive to social order. Both of course echo the familiar, wild-eyed venom of self-declared white supremacist Dylann Roof, who murdered nine African Americans in their place of worship, Mother Emanuel church in Charleston, South Carolina, because, he said, Black people "are raping our women and taking over our country." This before coldly gunning down Susie Jackson, who at eighty-seven was the senior person among those lost. Like ninety-seven-year-old Tree of Life worshipper Rose Mallinger, Jackson survived the more overt racism and anti-Semitism of the twentieth century only to become a casualty of its modern-day reverberations.

To counter this multi-fronted white supremacist project, we must forge solidarity at every juncture that Trumpism has exploited, recognizing, in particular, the unique ways that anti-Black racism, xenophobia, and anti-Semitism have historically worked together in the United States. We need an intersectional consciousness to build coalitions that can withstand and contain the rise of white nationalism and its entire family of evils.

Because although these forms of discrimination are intrinsically linked, our struggles against them are all too often disparate and siloed. While Saturday's act of anti-Semitic terror is consistent with a broader history of Jewish persecution, it's also in keeping with a statistical increase in all hate crimes. Hate crimes trended upward in 2014, 2012, 2010, and 2008. Election years—including midterms—often precipitate a spike. After a steep uptick near the 2016 election, hate crimes continued to rise by 12 percent in thirty-eight of the nation's largest cities in 2017. African Americans, Jews, Latinx, and LGBT people were among the most frequently targeted groups. The self-deputization of scores of white people to surveil and police Black people and immigrants in public and private spaces across the country is a symptom of the same malady.

The events of last week are not, then, the miner's canary, an indication of potential trouble, but rather the *confirmation* that our society's toxicity, unnamed and unchecked, will metastasize to every part of the body politic. The assassination of eleven Jews in worship, days after the murder of two Black people for being Black, tragically recalls the 2015 murder of nine African American church parishioners in Charleston, SC, and reminds us that the threat of racist terrorism is a malignancy that cannot be arrested by hope, song, or forgiveness alone.

In the spirit of acknowledging our linked fates, we want to remember the fallen thirteen of last week, and the nine who lost their lives in worship before them. The proper memorialization of their lost lives demands that we say all of their names, and carry out a resistance robust and inclusive enough to support all of the communities mourning their loss.

The Fallen Thirteen

Maurice Stallard
Vickie Jones
Irving Younger
Melvin Wax
Rose Mallinger
Bernice Simon
Sylvan Simon
Jerry Rabinowitz
Joyce Fienberg
Richard Gottfried
Daniel Stein
Cecil Rosenthal
David Rosenthal

The Charleston Nine

Cynthia Marie Graham Hurd
Susie Jackson
Ethel Lee Lance
DePayne Middleton-Doctor
Clementa C. Pinckney
Tywanza Sanders
Daniel Simmons
Sharonda Coleman-Singleton
Myra Thompson

• • •

Marc Lamont Hill is an author, activist, and media personality. Here is the speech he gave before the United Nations in solidarity with the people of Palestine, for which he was fired from his job as a commentator on CNN.

Marc Lamont Hill, "Our Solidarity Must Be a Verb" (November 28, 2018)

Mr. Secretary General, chairman, ambassadors, and your excellencies—good afternoon. It is with great honor and humility that I accept the opportunity to speak before you. As a scholar, as an activist, and as a citizen, I am profoundly interested in the plight of the Palestinian people as well as the broader ethical, moral, and political implications of their struggle for freedom and justice, as well as equality. As such, this annual convening represents a critical intervention. It also represents a site of possibility. On the other hand, it shows considerable irony. As you well know, this year marks the seventieth anniversary of the Universal Declaration of Human Rights. This declaration was produced out of the rubble and contradictions of World War II, and it was intended to offer a clear ethical and moral outline of the basic rights and freedoms to which all human beings, irrespective of race, religion, class, gender, or geography, are entitled. . . . For this reason, it is indeed ironic and sad that this year also marks the seventieth anniversary of the Nakba, the great catastrophe in May 1948 that resulted in the expulsion, murder, and to date permanent dislocation of more than a million Palestinians. For every minute that the global community has articulated a clear and lucid framework for human rights, the Palestinian people have been deprived of the most fundamental of them. . . .

I promise you that I will not exhaust all of my time by enumerating every human rights violation perpetrated by the Israeli government. These are well-known and have been well-documented by every credible human rights organization in the world. Rather, I would like to speak to you about the urgency of the current moment.

As we speak, the conditions on the ground for Palestinian people are worsening. In recent decades, the Israeli government has moved further and further to the right, normalizing settler colonialism and its accompanying logics of denial, destruction, displacement, and death. Despite international condemnation, settlement expansion has continued. At the same time, home demolitions and state-enforced displacement continue to uproot Palestinian communities. For Gazans, the eleven-year Israeli (and Egyptian) blockade by land, air, and sea has created the largest open-air prison in the world.

With only 4 percent potable water, electricity access that is limited to four hours per day, 50 percent unemployment, and the looming threat of Israeli bombs, Gaza continues to constitute one of the most pressing humanitarian crises of the current moment. In the West Bank, conditions are not much better. Unemployment is generally around 18 percent, with frequent loss of income due to Israeli military closures, making it impossible for Palestinian workers to get access to jobs. Settlements and the extra land allocated for them, as well as closed military zones and other restrictions, make it impossible for Palestinian towns to grow.

And in the midst of it all, Prime Minister Netanyahu's administration has become increasingly indifferent to critique, censure, or even scorn from the international community for its practices. Perhaps the most glaring example of this indifference as well as the urgency of the current moment is the recently passed Nation State Law. Through this basic law, the Israeli state has officially rejected Arabic as an official state language. It has described settlement expansion both inside and outside of the Green Line as a national value, and it has reinforced the fact that Israel is not a state of all of its citizens.

As an American, I am embarrassed that my tax dollars contribute to this reality. I am frustrated that no American president since the start of the occupation has taken a principled and actionable position in defense of Palestinian rights. And I am saddened, though not surprised, that President Trump's administration has further emboldened Israel's behavior through its recent actions.

In May of this year, President Trump officially moved the US embassy to Jerusalem, which he recognized as the undivided capital of Israel. This choice not only flew in the face of international law and precedent, but also constituted a powerful provocation and a diplomatic death blow. In late August, President Trump then permanently reneged on America's commitment to funding UNRWA [the United Nations Relief and Works Agency for Palestine Refugees in the Near East], a move that now leaves millions of Palestinian refugees in medical, economic, and educational peril. Moreover, the move serves as a political strong-arm tactic, whereby the United States is unilaterally attempting to resolve, through the Trump administration, the final status of Palestinian refugees.

While President Trump's policies have been the most dramatic, it is important that I stress to you, to reiterate to you, that they are not wildly out of step with American policy. Cuts to UNRWA is an idea that has been raised in Washington for years, dating back at least to the George W. Bush administration.

President Trump's decision to move the US embassy in Israel from Tel Aviv to Jerusalem caused enormous controversy, but he was merely implementing a bipartisan law Congress passed in 1995. And in so doing, he executed what has already been official United States policy and fulfilled a promise made by every United States president and presidential candidate, Democrat and Republican, for a very long time.

With regard to the question of Palestine, Donald Trump is not an exception to American policy. Rather, Donald Trump is a more transparent and aggressive iteration of it.

As I mentioned at the beginning of my remarks, the words offered today by everyone in this room are a necessary component of our resistance efforts. We need powerful, counterintuitive, dangerous, and courageous words. But we must also offer more than just words. Words will not stop the village of Khan al-Ahmar, with its makeshift schools created by local Bedouin villagers, from being demolished in violation of the Fourth Geneva Convention. Words will not stop poets like Dareen Tatour from being caged in Israeli jails for having the audacity to speak the truth about the conditions of struggle on her own personal Facebook page. Words will not stop peaceful protesters in Gaza from being killed as they fight for freedom against Israel's still-undeclared borders.

Regarding the question of Palestine, beyond words, we must ask the question: what does justice require? To truly engage in acts of solidarity, we must make our words flesh. Our solidarity must be more than a noun. Our solidarity must become a verb.

As a Black American, my understanding of action, and solidarity action, is rooted in our own tradition of struggle. As Black Americans resisted slavery, as well as Jim Crow laws that transformed us from a slave state to an apartheid state, we did so through multiple tactics and strategies. It is this array of tactics that I appeal to as I advocate for concrete action from all of us in this room.

Solidarity from the international community demands that we embrace boycott, divestment, and sanctions as a critical means by which to hold Israel accountable for its treatment of Palestinian people. This movement, which emerged out of the overwhelming majority of Palestinian civil society, offers a nonviolent means by which to demand a return to the pre-1967 borders, full rights for Palestinian citizens, and the right of return as dictated by international law.

Solidarity demands that we no longer allow politicians or political parties to remain silent on the question of Palestine. We can no longer, in particular, allow the political left to remain radical or even progressive on every issue—from the environment to war to the economy—except for Palestine.

Contrary to Western mythology, Black resistance to American apartheid did not come purely through Gandhian nonviolence. Rather, slave revolts and self-defense and tactics otherwise divergent from Dr. King or Mahatma Gandhi were equally important to preserving safety and attaining freedom. If we're to operate in true solidarity with the Palestinian people, we must allow the same range of opportunity and political possibility. If we are standing in solidarity with the Palestinian people, we must recognize the right of an occupied people to defend itself.

We must prioritize peace. But we must not romanticize or fetishize it. We must advocate and promote nonviolence at every opportunity, but we cannot endorse a narrow politics of respectability that shames Palestinians for resisting, for refusing to do nothing in the face of state violence and ethnic cleansing.

At the current moment, there is little reason for optimism. Optimism, of course, is the belief that good will inevitably prevail over evil, that justice will inevitably win out. In the course of human history—and certainly, even in the course of the United Nations—there is no evidence of such a proposition. Optimism is unsophisticated. Optimism is immature. Optimism is what my students have when they take examinations that they did not study for. Some become quite religious at that time. But regardless of their strategies of optimism, the outcome is far from guaranteed or even likely.

What I'm challenging us to do, in the spirit of solidarity, is not to embrace optimism but to embrace radical hope. Radical hope is a belief that despite the odds, despite the considerable measures against justice and peace, despite the legacy of hatred and imperialism and white supremacy and patriarchy and homophobia, despite these systems of power that have normalized settler colonialism, despite these structures, we can still win. We can still prevail.

One motivation for my hope in the liberation and ultimate self-determination of the Palestinian people comes in August of 2014. Black Americans were in Ferguson, Missouri, in the Midwest of the United States, protesting the death of a young man named Michael Brown, an unarmed African American male who had been killed by a law enforcement agent. And as we protested, I saw two things that provided hope for the Palestinian struggle.

One was that for the first time in my entire life of activism, I saw a sea of Palestinian people. I saw a sea of Palestinian flags in the crowd saying that we must form a solidarity project. We must struggle together in order to resist, because state violence in the United States and state violence in Brazil and state violence in Syria and state violence in Egypt and state violence in South Africa and state violence in Palestine are all of the same sort. And we finally understood that we must work together and not turn on each other, but instead turn to each other.

And later that night when the police began to tear-gas us, Mariam Barghouti tweeted us from Ramallah. She, along with other Palestinian youth activists, told us that the tear gas that we were experiencing was only temporary. They gave us tips for how to wash our eyes out. They told us how to make gas masks out of T-shirts. They gave us permission to think and dream beyond our local conditions by giving us a global solidarity project.

And from those tweets and social media messages, we began then to organize together. We brought a delegation of Black activists to Palestine, and we saw the connections between the police in New York City who are being trained by Israeli soldiers and the type of policing we were experiencing in New York City. We began to see relationships of resistance, and we began to build and struggle and organize together. That spirit of solidarity, a solidarity that is bound up not just in ideology but in action, is the way out.

So, as we stand here on the seventieth anniversary of the Universal Declaration of Human Rights and the tragic commemoration of the Nakba, we have an opportunity to not just offer solidarity in words but to commit to political action, grassroots action, local action, and international action that will give us what justice requires—and that is a free Palestine from the river to the sea.

• • •

aja monet is a poet, storyteller, and organizer who "follows in the long legacy and tradition of poets participating and assembling in social movements." monet cofounded Smoke Signals Studio, a political home for artists and organizers in Little Haiti, Miami, Florida. In 2019, Smoke Signals Studio shared a call to "create a different world from this rotting one, to be more than entertainer or escapist, to offer the people presence and alternative values."

aja monet, Smoke Signals Studio Artists Manifesto (February 1, 2019)

The role of the artist is to make the revolution irresistible.
—TONI CADE BAMBARA

It has become easier for people to imagine the end of the world than to imagine the end of capitalism.
—MARK FISHER

Meaningful art transforms, alters, and incites. Making art as a form of expression, a practice for truth-telling and rooted in assembly is powerful. Art is a realm of dreams, imagination, and possibility. It offers us the majestic consciousness of feeling, the undeniable truth, and a sense of community. Great art encourages us to delve beneath the surface of human consciousness and to make the invisible visible.

We seek artists intent on challenging, not reinforcing the Western status quo. We seek marvelous art rather than the mundane.

We seek surrealist artists, poets, and visionaries. To create a different world from this rotting one, to be more than entertainer or escapist, to offer the people presence and alternative values. We seek poetic revolution and freedom dreams.

Solidarity is not a luxury, it is vital and necessary for our survival and our creativity. With every thread of our being, artists must confront and oppose individualism.

Throughout history, our art and culture have been used as a commodity and vehicle to entrench and export capitalist values: individualism, patriarchy, materialism, and the like.

In today's social media celebrity culture, artists are forced—more than ever—to become brands to cultivate a network of influence and support from corporate "gatekeepers" and private (corporate) patrons. They soon find themselves with less creative freedom, with others making money off of their projects and guiding their voices toward the safety of conformity or the false pretenses of "trends." This commodification of art changes the process, dehumanizes the artist, and erodes their relationship with their community.

The most precious artistic investment is time. Yet, in this labor-driven economy, idle time is a sin. Therefore artists, poets, philosophers are most troubled by the inability to decide their own relationship to time and labor with the intent of process. If there is not time or space to engage in an artistic process, to meditate, to reflect, to wander in thought and emotional honesty, then the resulting art communicates a sentiment of coercion, mass production, and propaganda. It can exhibit little effort, poor execution, and a need for outside validation,

We all have something to offer. What are your gifts and what is your purpose? This is how you decide your offering to the community.

Every artist should write an artist statement. What do you seek to understand, what do you want your art to accomplish, and what medium(s) best communicates your values? What does your time mean to you? At heart everyone is an artist but not everyone can make art because we are not all afforded the time to reflect, imagine, and create. How do we use art to democratize the people's relationship to time?

Every artist must ask themselves, what is their relationship to money? Is it our agreed metric of value? What are new values we can create? More people are questioning capitalism, the worth of money versus the importance of time, energy, and process.

All Western propaganda claims that a world without capitalism is bland, lackluster, without creativity, innovation, or risk. We are taught that a society founded on socialist principles will wipe out individualism, art, and imagination.

We seek artists willing to animate a world that shows us new values and forms of expression toward communal needs.

We must resist mediocrity for the sake of representational art. All art demands complication, nuance, and depth; gravitate toward the soul, the feeling, and spirit.

Should our art fail, we will create new forms of expression. Ultimately art is not absolute, what comes of art is what we are willing to uncover, reveal, and resolve within. What we are willing to create determines the contribution and importance of our art.

This is an oath for our future and the preservation of collective values. This is a commitment against capitalism and its exploitation of art and therein our humanity.

Will You Join Us?

• • •

In November 2018, Microsoft Corporation entered a $479 million contract to supply the US military with its licensed technology. The army's stated goal was to repurpose Microsoft's HoloLens augmented reality headsets to "increase lethality by enhancing the ability to detect, decide, and engage before the enemy." In response, a group of employees formed Microsoft Workers 4 Good, whose mission is "to empower every worker to hold Microsoft accountable to their stated values." Below is a letter they released, addressed to the company's CEOs and signed by more than fifty employees, demanding that tech workers have a say in how the technology they develop is used. This open letter followed earlier protests in 2018 by tech workers at Google and Microsoft against their companies' contracts with the military and US Immigration and Customs Enforcement.

Microsoft Workers 4 Good, "We Did Not Sign Up to Develop Weapons" (February 22, 2019)

Dear Satya Nadella and Brad Smith,

We are a global coalition of Microsoft workers, and we refuse to create technology for warfare and oppression. We are alarmed that Microsoft is working to provide weapons technology to the US military, helping one country's government "increase lethality" using tools we built. We did not sign up to develop weapons, and we demand a say in how our work is used.

In November, Microsoft was awarded the $479 million Integrated Visual Augmentation System (IVAS) contract with the United States Department of the Army. The contract's stated objective is to "rapidly develop, test, and manufacture a single platform that Soldiers can use to Fight, Rehearse, and Train that provides increased lethality, mobility, and situational awareness necessary to achieve overmatch against our current and future adversaries." Microsoft intends to apply its Holo-Lens augmented reality technology to this purpose. While the company has previously licensed tech to the US military, it has never crossed the line into weapons development. With this contract, it does. The application of HoloLens within the IVAS system is designed to help people kill. It will be deployed on the battlefield, and works by turning warfare into a simulated "video game," further distancing soldiers from the grim stakes of war and the reality of bloodshed.

Intent to harm is not an acceptable use of our technology. We demand that Microsoft:

1. Cancel the IVAS contract;
2. Cease developing any and all weapons technologies, and draft a public-facing acceptable use policy clarifying this commitment;
3. Appoint an independent, external ethics review board with the power to enforce and publicly validate compliance with its acceptable use policy.

Although a review process exists for ethics in AI, AETHER, it is opaque to Microsoft workers, and clearly not robust enough to prevent weapons development, as the IVAS contract demonstrates. Without such a policy, Microsoft fails to inform its engineers on the intent of the software they are building. Such a policy would also enable workers and the public to hold Microsoft accountable.

Brad Smith's suggestion that employees concerned about working on unethical projects "would be allowed to move to other work within the company" ignores the problem that workers are not properly informed of the use of their work. There are many engineers who contributed to HoloLens before this contract even existed, believing it would be used to help architects and engineers build buildings and cars, to help teach people how to perform surgery or play the piano, to push the boundaries of gaming, and to connect with the Mars Rover (RIP). These engineers have now lost their ability to make decisions about what they work on, instead finding themselves implicated as war profiteers.

Microsoft's guidelines on accessibility and security go above and beyond because we care about our customers. We ask for the same approach to a policy on ethics and acceptable use of our technology. Making our products accessible to all audiences has required us to be proactive and unwavering about inclusion. If we don't make the same commitment to be ethical, we won't be. We must design against abuse and the potential to cause violence and harm.

Microsoft's mission is to empower every person and organization on the planet to do more. But implicit in that statement, we believe it is also Microsoft's mission to empower every person and organization on the planet to do good. We also need to be mindful of who we're empowering and what we're empowering them to do. Extending this core mission to encompass warfare and disempower Microsoft employees, is disingenuous, as "every person" also means empowering us. As employees and shareholders we do not want to become war profiteers. To that end, we believe that Microsoft must stop in its activities to empower the US army's ability to cause harm and violence.

• • •

Inspired by then-sixteen-year-old Greta Thunberg's weekly "School Strike for Climate," Isra Hirsi (aged sixteen), Haven Coleman (aged twelve), and Alexandria Villaseñor (aged thirteen) cofounded US Youth Climate Strike. Here is their call to join the March 15, 2019, global day of protest, in which 1.5 million students in 123 countries walked out of school to demand immediate action to stop climate change.

Isra Hirsi, Haven Coleman, and Alexandria Villaseñor, "Adults Won't Take Climate Change Seriously. So We, the Youth, Are Forced to Strike" (March 7, 2019)

We, the youth of America, are fed up with decades of inaction on climate change. On Friday, March 15, young people like us across the United States will strike from school. We strike to bring attention to the millions of our generation who will most suffer the consequences of increased global temperatures, rising seas, and extreme weather. But this isn't a message only to America. It's a message from the world, to the world, as students in dozens of countries on every continent will be striking together for the first time.

For decades, the fossil fuel industry has pumped greenhouse gas emissions into our atmosphere. Thirty years ago, climate scientist James Hansen warned Congress about climate change. Now, according to the most recent Intergovernmental Panel on Climate Change report on global temperature rise, we have only eleven years to prevent even worse effects of climate change. And that is why we strike.

We strike to support the Green New Deal. Outrage has swept across the United States over the proposed legislation. Some balk at the cost of transitioning the country to renewable energy, while others recognize its far greater benefit to society as a whole. The Green New Deal is an investment in our future—and the future of generations beyond us—that will provide jobs, critical new infrastructure, and most importantly, the drastic reduction in greenhouse gas emissions essential to limit global warming. And that is why we strike.

To many people, the Green New Deal seems like a radical, dangerous idea. That same sentiment was felt in 1933, when Franklin D. Roosevelt proposed the New Deal—a drastic piece of legislation credited with ending the Great Depression that threatened (and cost) many lives in this country. Robber barons, ordinary citizens, and many in between were enraged by the policies enacted by the New Deal. But looking back at how it changed the United States, it's impossible to ignore that the New Deal brought an end to the worst economic disaster in history by creating fundamental programs like Social Security and establishing new regulatory agencies such as the Securities and Exchange Commission. The Works Progress Administration mobilized workers across the nation to build important infrastructure—including thousands of schools—that has improved Americans' everyday life for generations.

Change is always difficult, but it shouldn't be feared or shied away from. Even for its detractors, Roosevelt's New Deal ended up working out quite well. The United States led the world's economy throughout the many decades since. The changes proposed in the Green New Deal will help ensure our entire species has the opportunity to thrive in the decades (and centuries) to come. As the original New Deal was to the declining US economy, the Green New Deal is to our changing climate. And that is why we strike.

The popular arguments against the Green New Deal include preposterous claims that it will ban airplanes, burgers, and cow flatulence—claims that are spread even by some of the most powerful leaders in our nation like Senate Majority Leader Mitch McConnell. Although these outlandish claims are clearly false, they reveal a larger truth apparent in the American, and world, populations: Instead of taking action on the imminent threat of climate change, our leaders play political games. Because adults won't take our future seriously, we, the youth, are forced to. And that is why we strike.

The alarming symptoms of Climate Denialism—a serious condition affecting both the hallways of government and the general population—mark our current historical crossroads of make-it-or-break-it action on climate change. Although there are many reasons for this affliction—such as difficulty grasping the abstract concept of a globally changed climate, or paralysis in the face of overwhelming environmental catastrophe—the primary mode of Climate Denialism contagion involves lies spouted by politicians, large corporations, and interest groups. People in power, like Senator McConnell and the Koch brothers, have used money and power to strategically shift the narrative on climate change and spread lies that allow themselves and other fossil fuel industry beneficiaries to keep the fortunes they've built on burning fossil fuels and degrading the environment.

The current US president is a rabid climate change denier himself. President Trump pulled out of the historic Paris Agreement and repeatedly tweets about weather phenomena that he claims somehow disprove the existence of climate change—despite the fact that his own administration has reported the facts of climate change and its impact on the United States.

We are also concerned that top Democrats demonstrate their own lack of urgency about the existential threat of climate change. California senator Dianne Feinstein's recent dismissal of a group of schoolchildren visiting her office to beg her support for the Green New Deal was very disturbing for us young people. Feinstein will not have to face the consequences of her inaction on climate change. She suggested that the children one day run for the Senate themselves if they wish to pass aggressive climate legislation. Sadly, that may not be an option for us, if she and other Democrats, like House Speaker Nancy Pelosi, continue to dismiss the pleas of our generation. Faced with politicians on both sides of the aisle who belittle and ignore us, we're forced to take a stand, and we're doing it together on a global scale. And that is why we strike.

We strike because our world leaders haven't acknowledged, prioritized, or properly addressed the climate crisis. We strike because marginalized communities across our nation—especially communities of color and low-income communities—are already disproportionately impacted by climate change. We strike because if the societal order is disrupted by our refusal to attend school, then influential adults will be forced to take note, face the urgency of the climate crisis, and enact change. With our future at stake, we call for radical legislative action—now—to combat climate change and its countless detrimental effects on the American people. We strike for the Green New Deal, for a fair and just transition to a 100 percent renewable economy, and to stop creation of new fossil fuel infrastructure. We strike because we believe the climate crisis should be called what it really is: a national emergency, because we are running out of time.

• • •

Lenny Sanchez is a founding member of the Independent Drivers Guild (IDG) in Chicago, Illinois. In a blog post, he explained why he joined Uber and Lyft drivers, who are key pillars of the so-called "gig" economy, on May 8, 2019, in an international one-day strike ahead of Uber's anticipated multibillion-dollar IPO (initial public offering) before the New York Stock Exchange.

Lenny Sanchez, "Why I'm Striking Against Uber" (May 8, 2019)

Today, I'm doing what Uber drivers all around the world are doing: I'm going on strike.

I'm far from alone. What started on a Chicago street corner last September has blossomed into an international movement: we're now joined by thousands of rideshare drivers—in New York, Atlanta, and Los Angeles, but also in Scotland, South America, and Africa, as we turn off our apps and refuse rides.

Why are we striking? Because Uber pays drivers a pittance, while its executives become multimillionaires in the company's initial public stock offering, which is expected to raise $90 billion. Uber founder Travis Kalanick will rake in at least $6 billion, even though he's left the company. Ari Emanuel, the brother of Chicago's mayor, Rahm, invested early in Uber so he will also make a fortune.

How little does Uber pay its drivers? Pennies on the mile. They say they skim 20 percent off every ride, but the truth is they take as much as 80 percent from many drivers. That's because in addition to charging commissions, they've become loan sharks, too.

Truth is, nowadays Uber is little more than a payday loan on wheels. They target low-income, minority, and immigrant drivers who don't understand what they're giving away when they sign up with Uber.

No credit? No problem, says Uber! We'll set you up with a car lease and get you on the road in no time. All you have to do is agree to make a weekly payment from what you earn, and commit to make 150 to 200 rides a week for the company.

The problem is, to meet these quotas a driver has to work six days of twelve hour shifts to clear $600, if he's lucky. They feel enslaved. That's why the turnover rate for rideshare drivers is so high. Some even take their own lives.

I remember when I first started driving, eight years ago: As a new dad, we needed extra income for childcare. Back then, Uber used to advertise that full-time drivers could make $90,000 a year—all on their own time. That sounded great, so I signed up!

And it was great, for a while. I bought a new vehicle, and drove mostly in upscale neighborhoods and to the airport. But as Mayor Emanuel began to flood Chicago's streets with rideshares, Uber's profits in the city—and mine—began to plummet.

Uber moved its Chicago offices into impoverished neighborhoods, where now they prey on poor and desperate drivers. But they don't serve those communities—they compel drivers to work in gentrified areas, to keep prices there low. Riders in low-income neighborhoods have to pay the highest rates. Nothing is like Uber says it is.

That's why one morning last September, a handful of us gathered on the Chicago street corner of LaSalle and Jackson to say we'd had enough. A couple of hours later, we had seventy-five drivers. Now we have the whole world with us.

Knowing that we're no longer alone fills my heart with hope. But the road ahead looks rough, and not only for drivers: because if Uber is richly rewarded by investors for taking advantage of its workers, other industries will follow. We'll all become independent contractors, whether we like it or not.

"We'll pay you $15 an hour," they'll tell us. But what they won't say is that you'll be stripped of all benefits, your power to organize, and your voice—forever.

That's why we're standing together against Uber.

● ● ●

Ta-Nehisi Coates is a best-selling author and winner of the 2015 National Book Award for nonfiction. He gained wide recognition for his incisive article "The Case for Reparations" and for his autobiographical book *Between the World and Me,* which reflects on the experience of being Black in the United States. In 2019, Coates spoke before the House Judiciary Committee in support of House Resolution 40, titled the "Commission to Study and Develop Reparation Proposals for African Americans Act." In his speech, Coates references George Stinney Jr., a Black youth who was only fourteen years old when he was executed in South Carolina in 1944; Isaac Woodard, a Black army veteran who was blinded after being beaten by police in South Carolina; Sally Hemings, a woman who was one of the hundreds of the enslaved owned by Thomas Jefferson, the third president of the United States, and mother to a number of his children; Black Wall Street, the thriving Black community in Tulsa, Oklahoma, targeted for destruction by racists during the 1921 Tulsa Race Massacre; and Fort Pillow, the site in Tennessee of a Confederate massacre in April 1864 of Union soldiers who were attempting to surrender, including hundreds of Black Union troops.

Ta-Nehisi Coates, "Testimony to the House on Reparations" (June 19, 2019)

Yesterday, when I asked about reparations, Senate Majority Leader Mitch McConnell offered a familiar reply: America should not be held liable for something that happened one hundred and fifty years ago, since none of us currently alive are responsible. This rebuttal proffers a strange theory of governance that American accounts are somehow bound by the lifetime of its generations. But well into this century, the United States was still paying out pensions to the heirs of Civil War soldiers. We honor treaties that date back some two hundred years despite no one being alive who signed those treaties.

Many of us would love to be taxed for the things we are solely and individually responsible for. But we are American citizens, and thus bound to a collective enterprise that extends beyond our individual and personal reach. It would seem ridiculous to dispute invocations of the founders, or the Greatest Generation, on the basis of a lack of membership in either group. We recognize our lineage as a generational trust, as inheritance, and the real dilemma posed by reparations is just that:

a dilemma of inheritance. It is impossible to imagine America without the inheritance of slavery.

As historian Ed Baptist has written, enslavement "shaped every crucial aspect of the economy and politics" of America, so that by 1836 more than $600 million, almost half of the economic activity in the United States, derived directly or indirectly from the cotton produced by the million-odd slaves. By the time the enslaved were emancipated, they comprised the largest single asset in America: $3 billion in 1860 dollars, more than all the other assets in the country combined.

The method of cultivating this asset was neither gentle cajoling nor persuasion, but torture, rape, and child trafficking. Enslavement reigned for two hundred and fifty years on these shores. When it ended, this country could have extended its hallowed principles—life, liberty, and the pursuit of happiness—to all, regardless of color. But America had other principles in mind. And so, for a century after the Civil War, Black people were subjected to a relentless campaign of terror, a campaign that extended well into the lifetime of Majority Leader McConnell.

It is tempting to divorce this modern campaign of terror, of plunder, from enslavement, but the logic of enslavement, of white supremacy, respects no such borders, and the god of bondage was lustful and begat many heirs. Coup d'états and convict leasing. Vagrancy laws and debt peonage. Redlining and racist GI bills. Poll taxes and state-sponsored terrorism.

We grant that Mr. McConnell was not alive for Appomattox. But he was alive for the electrocution of George Stinney. He was alive for the blinding of Isaac Woodard. He was alive to witness kleptocracy in his native Alabama and a regime premised on electoral theft. Majority Leader McConnell cited civil rights legislation yesterday, as well he should, because he was alive to witness the harassment, jailing, and betrayal of those responsible for that legislation by a government sworn to protect them. He was alive for the redlining of Chicago and the looting of Black homeowners of some $4 billion. Victims of that plunder are very much alive today. I am sure they'd love a word with the majority leader.

What they know, what this committee must know, is that while emancipation dead-bolted the door against the bandits of America, Jim

Crow wedged the windows wide open. And that is the thing about Senator McConnell's "something": It was one hundred and fifty years ago. And it was right now.

The typical Black family in this country has one-tenth the wealth of the typical white family. Black women die in childbirth at four times the rate of white women. And there is, of course, the shame of this land of the free boasting the largest prison population on the planet, of which the descendants of the enslaved make up the largest share.

The matter of reparations is one of making amends and direct redress, but it is also a question of citizenship. In HR 40, this body has a chance to both make good on its 2009 apology for enslavement, and reject fair-weather patriotism, to say that a nation is both its credits and its debits. That if Thomas Jefferson matters, so does Sally Hemings. That if D-Day matters, so does Black Wall Street. That if Valley Forge matters, so does Fort Pillow.

Because the question really is not whether we will be tied to the somethings of our past, but whether we are courageous enough to be tied to the whole of them. Thank you.

● ● ●

Rev. Dr. William J. Barber II, president of Repairers of the Breach, cochair of the Poor People's Campaign: A National Call for Moral Revival, and leader of the Moral Mondays protest movement in North Carolina, was among a number of faith-based organizers who issued this powerful call after the shootings in Dayton, Ohio, and El Paso, Texas, in the summer of 2019.

Rev. Dr. William J. Barber II, et al., "Pastoral Letter on the El Paso Shootings" (August 8, 2019)

One week ago, we were in El Paso at the invitation of the Border Network for Human Rights to highlight the violence that their community has been suffering. We heard stories of families separated, asylum seekers turned away, and refugees detained like prisoners of war. We heard how their community has been militarized and how poor border communities have been especially targeted. We promised that we would do everything in our power to compel the nation to see this violence. Just a few days later, a terrorist opened fire in El Paso. And then another attack occurred in Dayton.

In reflecting on these outbreaks of violence, our hearts are broken. This moment demands a moral reckoning with who we are and who we want to become as a nation.

The truth is that, while every generation has worked to push us toward becoming a more perfect union, we have also tolerated lies that beget violence. America's founding fathers spoke of liberty, while drafting documents that called Native Americans savages; accepted the enslavement of Africans; and ignored the voices of women. This hypocrisy created space for slaveholder religion to bless white supremacy, pseudoscience to justify eugenics, a sick sociology to pit people against one another, and predatory policies to scapegoat non-white immigrants and blame poverty on the poor.

Politicians who try to denounce the racism of an individual, but do not denounce racist policies refuse to deal with the depths of the problems we face. We cannot address the violence of white nationalism without stopping the policies of white nationalism and the lies that are told to justify them. In 1963, George Wallace began to spew racist rhetoric from the governor's office in Alabama. By the end of that year, Medgar Evers was dead, four girls in a church were dead, and a president was dead because these words and these policies were a breeding ground for violence. It always has been that way. Whenever we've had these words and policies, they have also unleashed this kind of violence.

For this reason, we call on President Trump, members of Congress and presidential candidates, our people on the ground in movements and communities of struggle, people who have embraced the lies of white nationalism, and our religious leaders and people of faith and conscience to revive the heart and soul of this country.

Mr. President, we recognize that you are a symptom of our decaying moral fabric and you have ignited a modern-day wildfire. The coals of white nationalism are always smoldering in our common life, and they have fueled the violence of Indigenous genocide, slavery, lynching, and Jim Crow. Stop stoking the fires of violence with racist words and policies. Mr. President, you must repent in word and deed if your leadership is to bring us together, rather than tearing us apart.

To members of Congress and our elected representatives, we ask you to ensure our domestic tranquility. You can take immediate action to stop the president's racist attacks on immigrants. You can act to ensure voting rights, pass gun reform to keep weapons of war out of our communities, end federal programs that send military equipment to our local and state police departments, pass immigration reform that allows us all to thrive and build up the country, ensure good jobs and living wages and relief from our debts, and guarantee health care and social programs that meet our needs. The lies of white nationalism have prevented action on all of these issues, and those who have enabled the president or remained silent are culpable.

As you return to Washington, DC, we call on Congress to honor the August 28 anniversary of the March on Washington and the murder of Emmett Till by passing an omnibus bill that offers a comprehensive response to the systemic racism that connects the issues facing 140 million poor and low-wealth people in this country.

To all candidates running for president in 2020, we call on you to address both the violence of racism and the policies of racism and white nationalism in the public debates. We ask you to connect these policies of systemic racism to poverty, ecological devastation, the war economy, militarism, and a distorted moral narrative that accepts, justifies, and perpetuates systemic violence.

To our movements and organizations on the ground, do not go back to your silos; instead we must build a moral fusion movement. We have been organizing in separate streams, often along lines of race, issue area, or geography, but we need much more than our own fights can win. This is not the time to become entrenched in those divisions. We need to come together across race, gender, sexual orientation, religion, issue, geography, and other lines of division to make a fight for everything we need and make sure we are all in—nobody is out.

To those who have embraced the lies of white nationalism and racism, we humbly recognize the power of fear. We live in a time when many people do not know if they will have work today or health care tomorrow. Many families do not know what agency is coming for them or their children. We do not know who to trust and have been left to fend for ourselves and whoever we believe to be on our side. Let us find strength in our pain, mourn our losses, and remember that we are all part of a common human family. Let us reject every attempt by politicians and corporate interests to pit us against one another. Let us confess that white nationalism is a myth that has not served most people, even those it claims to protect. Let us fight for each other and for a world where everyone can thrive.

To our religious leaders and people of faith, we call on you to offer moral leadership in the public square. If you have condoned the lies of white nationalism or remained silent, you have failed to keep your sacred vows. We ask you to recall the struggles of our ancestors so we can work together to build up a more perfect union in our common life.

We call on all people of faith and conscience to sign on to this letter and share it throughout your networks. Let us prevent this violence from defining who we are as a nation and people.

Forward together, not one step back.

• • •

Indigenous youth activist and musician Xiuhtezcatl Tonatiuh Martinez spoke alongside other young organizers in New York at an event organized by the writer Naomi Klein, responding to a challenge to speak, from the perspective of the year 2029, about how the world changed radically after people embraced the vision of a Green New Deal.

Xiuhtezcatl Tonatiuh Martinez, "To Fight for a Just Climate Is to Fight for Everything That We Love" (September 9, 2019)

Pialli, nanotoka Xiuhtezcatl Tonatiuh. My name is Xiuhtezcatl Tonatiuh and I'm a descendent of the Mexica people of Mexico Tenochtitlan, Mexico City. I'm an artist, a climate warrior, and the youth director of Earth Guardians.

When I was a little boy, my father taught me a poem that was passed down from our ancestors that says,

> *Tinexcayu totiuh xochime*
> *Tinexcayu totiuh cuicame*
> *Por lo menos dejemos flores, por lo menos dejamos cantos.*

At the least we have left flowers, at the least we have left songs. This line in the poem reminds me that although our people were colonized, our temples destroyed, and our ceremonies forbidden, our legacy would live on in flowers and songs, in the hearts of the people. Even in the face of the complete collapse of my ancestors, society and way of life, we believed in a vision where the younger generation would carry on the ways of our people, until we could live freely in this world again. Survival, resilience, and the strength of my ancestors runs in my blood. And when our generation was faced with the greatest threat humanity has collectively seen, the climate crisis, I remembered the prayers of my elders, and knew my place in the movement that brought us into the thriving world we're living in today.

It's been ten years since everything changed. Ten years since the last mass burning of the Amazon, since the world was silent about the acidification of our oceans and the melting of our ice caps. Ten years since the Supreme Court ruled in our favor to uphold our constitutional rights and force the US government to play its part in restoring the balance in our climate. Ten years since nations globally began to implement fearless, just climate recovery plans from the pressure of the collapsing planet and the millions of people led by the youth that flooded the courts and the streets to demand action.

And we couldn't have made it here without the voices of Indigenous and frontline communities as the spearhead of our movement. As Indigenous peoples, resistance has always been woven into our existence. Fighting to protect our land, our water, our air, our children, and our culture have become a part of who we are. We taught our allies in the movement that this struggle is not separate from us. To fight for a just climate is to fight for everything that we love. We reminded the world that as the present generation, everything we do is in honor of our ancestors, of those we lost in the struggle, and in honor of future generations. We reminded the world that we are not separate from nature, from water, or from each other.

Twenty-nineteen became the year where we began to tear down the barriers and borders that separated our people, our movements, and our stories. Climate action became woven into every aspect of our society. I remember that time so clearly. It wasn't just activists and politicians who were building the future. Artists, creatives, storytellers, actors, and athletes began realizing their part in these movements to shape culture and reach the masses. Entrepreneurs, designers, architects, and poets began to reimagine what our society could look like if we used this great time of crisis, as humanity's most unifying moment. I remember the shows I played for thousands of people, and how we transformed those arenas into places of celebration and unity. Our generation began to change the culture of our movements that year. The idea of being an activist was left behind. We realized that it is within our power as humanity, an identity that belongs to us all, to change the story and to build the world we've always known was possible.

The place the world is in is a result of us striking the balance between technology, innovation, culture, and the ancient wisdom and teachings of the original peoples of this earth. Here we are, ten years after changing everything to redefine our legacy. Carried on in flowers and songs.

• • •

Stacey Park Milbern (1987–2020) was a queer, mixed-race Korean and white disability justice activist, organizer, and writer based in Oakland, California. In the wake of California's record-shattering wildfires, she spoke about the intersections between environmental and disability justice. She died at just thirty-three years old due to complications from surgery, leaving behind a legacy grounded in the belief that disabled people are not broken for having to navigate an ableist society—in fact, they are among those best equipped with the creative tools and solutions for society's problems.

Stacey Park Milbern, "We Need Power to Live" (October 10, 2019)

Whether it is fascism or environmental climate crisis created by greed, disabled people—especially disabled people of color—are, as disability justice activist Patricia Berne says, the canary in the coal mine. How we are treated is often an indicator that there is a big problem. We saw that with Nazi extermination. We saw that with the current administration cutting food stamps, housing, and health services.

Right now when there is a climate emergency, people who live in nursing homes and institutions get left behind. Oftentimes staff, families, and community members want to rescue them, even physically fighting nursing home administrators, but are barred because of policy. It is not uncommon for people in institutions to die because they were not rescued. Many advocates are fighting for what we call the right to be rescued. The. Right. To. Be. Rescued.

This week in the Bay Area disabled people and elders without power are having difficulty breathing, moving, eating, and staying alive. A friend is going without her nebulizer treatments. A neighbor didn't have a way to store his insulin. Another community member is homebound because she needs power to open and close their garage. Countless numbers of people are being forced to throw out groceries without knowing where the money will come to replace them. Blind people are crossing the street without there being traffic lights or audible signals that tell them when to cross. Lack of streetlights makes people even more vulnerable. Community members are going without medications they need. Have you tried communicating in American Sign Language in the dark? Not easy. I myself use life-sustaining medical equipment, my ventilator, sixteen hours a day. My doctor completed extensive paperwork telling PG&E why I need power to live. (Let me say that again—my doctor completed extensive paperwork telling PG&E why I need power to live. There are so many more disabled people impacted by the power apocalypse than the medical baseline program—the eligibility requirements for the program are significant and require a disabled person to have a healthcare provider.) On Tuesday I called PG&E to ask for protocol for medical baseline users. I was on hold for two hours and twenty minutes. I hadn't received any notice from PG&E but saw my house on every map as about to lose power. When I was finally connected, the representative confirmed there was nothing really in place. He literally told me, "This is why we let the public know so you would have time to prepare." To PG&E, my life is not important.

All across the Bay, disabled people are providing mutual aid to one another. We are calling our friends and community regularly to check in. We are helping each other find housing and evacuate. We are sourcing generators, ice, and medication. We are making sure people are getting updates in a format accessible to them. We are hosting and transporting people, stranger and friend alike. The world might not care if we live or die but we do.

Disabled queer artist Alli Yates says disabled wisdom saves lives. Do you remember last year when no one could breathe and Mask Oakland disseminated thousands of masks? That was the work of disabled people too. We live and love interdependently. We know no person is an island, we need one another to live. No one does their own dental work or cuts their own hair. We all need support. Hierarchy of what support is okay to need and what isn't is just ableism.

Go home and check on your neighbors. Rest. Reflect on why we must combat capitalism, racism, classism, and ableism that thinks so little of humanity that some people are reduced to expected losses. There is a lot to do and it's going to take all of us.

• • •

Jamaica Heolimeleikalani Osorio is a queer Kanaka Maoli wahine poet, activist, and scholar born and raised in Pālolo Valley working to build "a Hawai'i whose future is decolonial, deoccupied, demilitarized, and bursting with possibility." In this poem, she speaks of the elders in this struggle, including Mary Maxine Lani Kahaulelio, a community organizer and aloha 'āina advocate since the late 1970s. Kahaulelio organized for welfare rights and supported communities against evictions in Chinatown and Waiāhole on O'ahu, and in her demilitarization work she has fought to protect Kaho'olawe, Pōhakuloa, and other sacred places.

Jamaica Heolimeleikalani Osorio, "For All the Aunties, but Especially for Mary Maxine Lani Kahaulelio" (October 28, 2019)

Aunty says
She climbed a ninety-foot cliff in the dark
Traced the scars of a long-forgotten waterfall
Cried as she felt the green disappearing under her fingertips
And I learn
That *aloha* is courage steeped in mourning

Aunty says
This arrest bond is the most important paper I own
She holds it out like a certificate of her lineage
And I learn
To be born kanaka means to take pride in the fight
Means to understand the polity of our bodies

Aunty says malama kou kino
Says don't take no fucking shit from nobody
Not even our own men
And I learn that there are so many violences that will come for me

Too many to count
Too many to turn to metaphor
Too violating to write into this poem

Aunty says she sees hope in me
And I watch her overflow
Says she dreamed of this day
And I learn
That genealogy is a promise to take your place amongst your greatest
  heroes in this moʻolelo

Aunty says I love you
And I stand in her shadow, expanding
And every fear in me evaporates
Every doubt casts itself aside
Every whisper that does me no service is carried away
And I become
Everything she dreamed I could be

I become an aunty too
A mauna—
My moʻopuna will stand in the malu of

● ● ●

Tarana J. Burke is a community organizer from the Bronx, New York, who started
#MeToo in 2006 to help break the silence around sexual violence. A decade
later, the hashtag reemerged when dozens of women came forward to accuse
film producer Harvey Weinstein of rape and sexual assault. In this essay, Burke
contends that to include all survivors, especially people of color, The "me too"
Movement must return to its roots.

Tarana J. Burke, "The #MeToo Movement's Success Took a Decade of Work, Not Just a Hashtag. And There's More to Do" (December 31, 2019)

In 2009—three years after I launched the organization The "me too" Movement—I met a sixteen-year-old girl who was enrolled in the Arise Academy in Philadelphia as part of my side gig running a small nonprofit, JustBe, Inc., which focused on the health and wholeness of young women of color through self-discovery, leadership development, critical media literacy and racial and gender justice training. Hers was a fairly new charter school, and the first in the country devoted to students in foster care and adjudicated youth; this particular girl had a two-year-old son and was pregnant with twins.

Her first child had been conceived as a result of being trafficked by a "friend" of her family who molested her for several years and convinced her it was a relationship; he was her mom's age. When I met her, she was leaving school daily, being picked up and taken to New York to "dance" at a strip club and then driven back to Philly in the wee hours of the morning. She did her homework on the ride there and slept on the way back. A neighbor in the apartment she lived in—provided by the city's Department of Human Services—watched her son when her mom couldn't. She came to school only when she could, which put her in jeopardy both of being truant and of losing her benefits. She was also desperately trying to find alternate housing at the time because DHS rules said only two children were permitted to live in the apartment; the twins she was carrying meant she was about to have three.

She wasn't the typical survivor I encountered, but she certainly wasn't the only one experiencing that kind of abuse and exploitation. I spent weeks in 2009 trying to find resources for that child and eventually found something more suitable than the suggestion given by her caseworker (which was to give up one of her kids).

It took eleven more years and a community of folks who recognized that girls like her, as well as my work and the work of others like me, needed to be inserted into a global conversation about gender equity and sexual violence.

The young girls and women who were served by The "me too" Movement's work in its early years look very different from the ones who many identify with the movement—or the hashtag—today. And before the last few years, it had felt like sexual assault survivors, supporters, and activists had been screaming into the abyss for decades, waiting for the world to wake up.

But since 2017, that conversation has been carried farther and wider than we have ever seen in the fight to combat sexual violence. And, although we have yet to see sexual violence addressed as the global public health crisis it is, we have to acknowledge that we are louder, stronger, and braver now than we've ever been.

A decade ago, I could see the impact JustBe and The "me too" Movement were having on the lives of the girls with whom I worked. It was challenging to find the means to sustain this organization and expand our reach. And I wasn't alone: I knew many other women who were trying to interrupt sexual violence in their communities with little to no support, while organizations such as A Long Walk Home in Chicago, and Girls For A Change in Virginia helped find resources from any and everywhere. It didn't deter us; we were committed to this work.

We knew that sexual violence wasn't plaguing only our communities; sexual violence is a global problem, doing harm to people in nearly every community. However, the challenges we faced as women of color to raise awareness and undo the pathologies that allowed this harm to take place were compounded by our marginalized identities and lived experiences.

This past decade brought about shifts in societal consciousness, culture and policy—the kinds most people thought weren't possible in our lifetime. At critical points of forward movement, however, comes pushback, threatening to undo all the accomplishments we've struggled to achieve.

For instance, Americans experienced most of the two terms of the nation's first Black president, and then the most divisive election in our lifetime, resulting in the election of a self-proclaimed sexual assaulter. We saw anti-capitalist demonstrations spearheaded by Occupy Wall Street and protests that resisted racism and exploitation, often under the umbrella of Black Lives Matter, sweep across the country. But we also witnessed way too many Black lives be taken without explanation or recourse and mass incarceration rates remain at sky-high levels.

Even as the #MeToo hashtag was trending, Black women and girls were (and are) going missing from their neighborhoods at alarming rates and it seemed no one was looking for them, while some of our most powerful celebrities and public figures continue to profit from the very audiences they harm.

I see both the ongoing injustices and the various movements for change as connected and intertwined; we had enough of the status quo and we were going to make real change happen. Survivors have not only been on the front lines of these historical moments, but they simultaneously endured re-traumatization and erasure within these movements.

The "me too" Movement is an iteration of a decades-old fight to end sexual violence, but what makes it so different, powerful, and effective is that it speaks to the needs of all survivors. It addresses sexual violence as a systemic issue—and it explains how other systemic issues, such as anti-Black racism, capitalism and classism, poverty and housing impact survivors. It also provides space for survivors to lead us in the right direction.

But we can't stop now. Today, the criminalization of sex work, strict abortion laws, and a lack of protections against trafficking seek to punish women for merely surviving. Rape-kit backlogs, the gender pay gap, and this administration's dismantling of Title IX protections for students facing sexual violence and workplace sexual harassment have weakened accountability measures and will keep predators in power. Climate change, unjust immigration laws, and even potential unemployment breed all forms of gender-based violence.

These correlations are not anomalies anymore; instead, the intersections are becoming part of the mainstream consciousness, thanks to the incredible collective work of influencers and activists working to advance missions, such as Time's Up, the National Women's Law Center, and the National Domestic Workers Alliance. Cross-movement alliances have applied political pressure to change laws and place the onus for systemic change back on the powerful—where it belongs.

And at the same time, we have to acknowledge that those on the margins of movements—Black, Brown, and Indigenous women and girls, trans women and gender nonconforming survivors—are still organizing and fighting for their right to live with dignity and be protected. We still live in a world that demonstrates that, unless you have access and privilege, your right to heal is subjective.

I still carry the stories of Black women and girls from my days of running JustBe, Inc., and am constantly receiving new ones, like the story of Chrystul Kizer, the seventeen-year-old Black girl charged with murdering a man whom police were investigating for sex trafficking—including of her. I hear the same fear and fire in the voices of those who disclose their survivor status to me when I'm out speaking in front of large audiences. I know our victories and our tribulations intimately because, just like the millions of us who get up and make a conscious effort to survive each day, I too am impacted by every headline, every testimony, and every judicial decision. At every turn, I'm ready to be both affirmed and aggravated, but never apathetic.

As we enter the next decade, I want us to all find our place in the movement to end sexual violence, because we all have a role to play. I look forward to knowing that the movement doesn't rely on the level of celebrity and notoriety of the accused or accuser, but that it instead builds on the changed thinking, behavior, and solutions created by those most impacted.

• • •

Antonia Crane is a sex worker, author, and activist who founded the labor rights group Strippers United. In the following essay, originally published in the anthology *We Too: Essays on Sex Work and Survival* and excerpted in n + 1 online, Crane describes a 2019 strike by strippers at the Crazy Girls Club in Hollywood, California, demanding an end to wage theft and sexual harassment on the job.

Antonia Crane, "Dispatch from the California Stripper Strike" (February 8, 2021)

It's 9 p.m. on a Friday night in 2019 and I'm headed to Crazy Girls, a topless club in Hollywood—the same busy intersection that, two days from now, will be blocked off for the Oscars where the African American actors Regina King, Hannah Beachler, and Ruth Carter will be celebrated this season. Lady Gaga will encourage female artists to stand up no matter how many times they get knocked down.

Crazy Girls has a metal detector outside that customers and dancers walk through, like airport security. This one is flanked by two bulky male bouncers in white Pumas. Tonight I won't walk through the metal detector, because I'm not here to strip or to watch the dancers, even though I'm standing in my sky-high stiletto work shoes with red rhinestone hearts carved into the soles.

Nine on Friday is early for a stripper, but not for our allies, and we need our allies tonight. We're staging a wildcat strike action to interrupt the unfair labor practices at Crazy Girls. I dump a big red plastic tub on the sidewalk—it's filled with bottles of water, chocolate almonds, and protein bars. Our friends from Democratic Socialists of America (DSA)-LA, Sex Workers Outreach Project Los Angeles (SWOPLA), Me Too, 5050by2020, and other groups hold bright pink signs that we made together the night before. We ate a homemade dinner while making the sparkly neon signs, which read, "Heels On, Walk Off." We gathered in an art gallery and learned how to silkscreen T-shirts with bright pink stilettos that say "Stop Wage Theft" in Russian, Spanish, and English. Domino Rey, one of the other Soldiers of Pole—a trio of organizing strippers of which I am one third—is already speaking to a local news channel. Her black hair is pulled tightly into braids and her eyes blaze in the lights that flood down from the media van. She's talking to the seasoned news anchor, a striking brunette, about wage theft and our strike.

"We no longer should have to pay to work. We shouldn't have to pay house fees. We shouldn't have to give any sort of percentage of our tips to management or any other employees and we want to stop the sexual harassment and assault in the club," Domino Rey said.

In all radical labor movements, history is made when ordinary workers disrupt the system that seeks to exploit and silence them. Because of social stigma, wage theft, and sexual assault, the strip club has always been a difficult and dangerous work environment. Today, the stakes have reached a desperate tipping point, even though, technically, thanks to a recent court ruling, we have more legal rights than ever: we have the right to discuss the job while on the job, the right to organize and gather, and the right to unionize, which will give us a voice in the workplace—instead of only a body to be gazed at.

Tonight, we strike. As employees, we can do so because of a California Supreme Court ruling, *Dynamex Operations West, Inc. v. Superior Court of Los Angeles*, that changed the classification of employees in California and made it harder for employers to classify their workforce as "independent contractors." The Dynamex case involved a workforce of delivery drivers, but it is only the latest in a long history of misclassification-of-employment cases fought by seasonal workers, car washers, and others.

While the Dynamex ruling gives us the right to strike more easily and organize more publicly, the ruling has also forced California strip club owners to reckon with the fact they have to pay us minimum wage as well as pay federal and state taxes. The way club owners have implemented the new law has fostered desperation and fear. They've been doling out paychecks for zero dollars or with fictional hours worked. They have created a hostile environment by targeting "problem girls," ones who dare question the random fees and fines, coercive "release of claims" contracts, and confusing bribes from management. In essence, strip clubs are charging strippers more fees in order to get us to pay our own minimum wage. The problem isn't the new labor law itself, but the way employers are implementing it, which makes being an employee seem like a bad deal.

What this looks like on the shop floor is management demanding we hand over the first hundred dollars we earn for the night, or the income from our first five lap dances. Strippers earn the great majority of their income not from their stage performances, but from individual lap dances. Imagine you are an employee at a car wash. Your boss tells you to hand over the cash you earned for the first ten cars you wash. After those ten cars, you get paid. Strip club owners, managers, and bouncers steal our earnings like it's the most natural thing in the world. Now that we're employees, they are snatching and grabbing every last dollar they can before we workers revolt.

Now we are revolting. The rumblings of revolutions begin small: a tiny flickering lamp shedding light on a system designed to keep an almost entirely femme workforce vulnerable by leveraging our financial need.

Rebelling against oppressive, exploitative, racist companies and being frightened of losing my job is nothing new to me. Back in 1995, when I worked at an all-nude peep show in San Francisco called the Lusty Lady, we punched time clocks and took ten-minute water and wig-change breaks. Back then, although we aimed to stop blatant discrimination in our workplace, our main rallying point was to stop customers from filming us naked without our knowledge or consent. Imagine your legs spread wide showing every layer of pink in front of a window with a stranger's head bobbing up and down. Then imagine a red light glowing from a camera recording your clit for a nonconsensual closeup. We wanted management to remove the one-way glass in certain booths and wanted them to ban cameras. After a two-year labor war, we became SEIU Local 790: The Exotic Dancer's Alliance.

Where we were then and where we are now are not much different.

This is what it's like to be a stripper today: lap dancing for free, being pressured to hustle faster to pay your own wages and getting sent home if it doesn't happen fast enough, and being coerced and bullied by bouncers and managers to hand over money that you've earned with your time and body, all while employers continue to avoid providing any employee benefits that you are legally entitled to—like a safe and sane work environment, free from wage theft, assault, and abuse. A monied government official came into the club where I still dance topless. He grabbed me and held me in a choke hold. I grabbed his forearms. I tried to elbow him. I said, "Let me go," over and over. Management was nowhere to be found. When he laughed and released me, I told him to give me $200, then walked away. But there is not enough money in the world to be this exposed, disposable, and unprotected at work.

This is the very business model that we need to explode—the one that club owners have operated for decades under an assumption that strippers' bodies are the product that they are pushing: a product of which they are owed a cut. We strippers do not rent a space or a chair, like hairdressers. We don't rent a stage or a room. We don't sling alcohol. We are not working on commission. We are entertainers. As lap dancers, we have more in common with actors and comics than with bartenders and barbers, because we are a live show. There is no question whether or not strippers should be classified as employees— we are employees. And now we can unionize. The question is: how are we going to protect workers from abusive labor practices, like employers charging women to work for them? It's not audacious for the state to regulate the private sector, but it is audacious for these strip club owners to get away with wage theft, racketeering, assault, labor violations, tax evasion, and abuse for decades. Our bodies are not the property or product of strip clubs, and they never have been.

Corporate strip clubs like Déjà Vu (where Stormy Daniels is the current spokesperson) are the worst offenders. They are notorious for taking a 60 percent cut—or more—of dancers' tips. Daniels and other strippers who dance at Déjà Vu have voiced their preference for independent contractor status, which is contrary to the current change of law in California. How- ever, the term "independent contractor" is intrinsically deceitful. Inde- pendent contractors cannot legally discuss money while on the job and cannot cooperate to set prices due to antitrust laws. The labor commission- er's office has no jurisdiction over independent contractors. Management is under no legal obligation to comply with contractors' demands. The economic incentives for employers to misclassify workers as independent contractors are colossal, as employers under this model evade regulations governing wages, hours, safe and sane working conditions, and other legal protections all workers have under the law.

Most importantly, stripping is women's work. We rely on our tips, which invites different questions that have to do with how we value women's physical and financial autonomy in the workplace. Critics of the Dynamex decision consider regulating the private sector a bad thing, but it can be a useful and powerful tool for workers—and there is nothing suspect about forcing clubs to allow workers employee status.

It's time we ask better questions, like: How would strippers like to experience autonomy in their workplace? And what does a safe and sane workplace look like in a strip club? I ask these questions of young strippers who are vibrating with rage, and it's as if they've never been asked what they want before. The thing about normalizing stigma and exploitation is that eventually you accept your powerlessness. Or you stand up and resist. It's almost 10 p.m. when a petite Latina in sweats and an extra-high ponytail approaches the main entrance of Crazy Girls. I reach into my back pocket, into which I've tucked tubes of clear lip gloss with "soldiersofpole.com" written in black Sharpie—an offering to alert her and her coworkers who are on the schedule tonight that we are here, and we can unionize. As I walk toward her to hand her the lip gloss, two bouncers stand between us. One of them interrupted our chant earlier, yelling out, "You girls can come back and audition on Tuesday." I meet the dancer's eyes, then the bouncer quickly spirits her inside Crazy Girls, where she may be told to ignore us. Later her tips will be confiscated by a "counter" and she will have to wait until 4 a.m. to get a minuscule portion of them. She may be drugged by a customer, sexually harassed by a manager. And she may be fired if she speaks up. I suppose this is why I'm still here, in red glitter stilettos, still stripping and still fighting, twenty-three years after we successfully unionized the Lusty Lady: to keep reaching my hand out, to remind her and all strippers we can change things again. We can, we can, we can.

We are.

• • •

Judy (Syfers) Brady wrote the classic satirical feminist manifesto "I Want a Wife," which appeared in the first issue of *Ms.* magazine in 1971, based on a speech at a rally in San Francisco on August 26, 1970. Fifty years later, writer and conservationist Maggie Trinkle penned this homage and rejoinder.

Maggie Trinkle, "I (Don't) Want a Wife" (April 16, 2020)

I've been on the single motherhood scene a while now, not all that fresh from my years-ago divorce. I have two teenagers who, of course, are with me most of the time.

So, upon receiving my honorary pandemic home-teaching credential, I decided our first history assignment would be to reflect on Judy Brady's iconic manifesto "I Want a Wife," first delivered fifty years ago at a San Francisco rally to mark the fiftieth anniversary of American women's suffrage.

It occurred to me nothing much has changed. In fact, it's gotten worse.

So, I don't want a wife anymore. I just want a goddamn functioning society. Why do I want a functioning society?

Because if society just operated like us ladies do, I wouldn't need a wife, nobody would, and we'd all be better off, and here's why:

For most of my life, I bought into the trope that women are supposed to do it all and make it seem effortless—so it's only fair that society finally fulfills its side of the bargain.

After throwing a helluva brunch with endless dietary accommodations and bottomless gluten-free Bloody Marys to honor our mothers' generation's hard work, I want a society that finally fixes the decades-long stagnant 61 to 80 cent wage gap.

I want a society where divorce doesn't still result in a 20 percent decrease in standard of living for women and children, while men's increase by 30 percent—and while mothers still carry the burden of child-rearing.

I want a society that nurtures our children, that values education and ensures they have a safe social life without the fear of mass shootings or the trauma of lockdown drills. I want a society that helps them process the existential threat of a pandemic, which causes them to change on a dime how they've been indoctrinated to learn their entire lives. I want a society that does not, in the face of said global crisis, expect me to be the default proxy teacher while my ex-husband focuses on work.

I want a society that will not shame me when my kids don't brush their teeth, or when they play on their phones during dinner because the second shift is still a thing, and I'm now even more tired from taking on a third shift running a virtual high school in between a fourth shift as household pandemic expert that specializes in sterilizing all incoming groceries—and burning cardboard boxes on my "off" hours, while teaching myself how to sew masks because my underlying medical-conditioned self hopes to leave the house someday.

I want a society that—should I have a health scare—will provide medical care if I take reasonable time to heal, without burdening my business, losing my job or home, declaring bankruptcy, or dying because I can't afford treatment despite a lifetime of hard work, leaving my children behind far too soon. I want a society that collectively deals with things beyond our control or imagination, like pandemics or the sixth mass extinction.

When I go into society with friends, I want a world that doesn't shame me for wanting a social life while also being a mother. I want a society that knows that sometimes I need solitude, or a night out by myself without fear of violence or harassment.

I want a society that supports complete access to birth control—because it's proven that all genders and future generations benefit when we have control over if/when we have families.

When I meet people I want to entertain, I want a society that hasn't created such unattainable standards that nobody will care if my home doesn't spark minimalist joy or if I didn't get hors d'oeuvres even though I knew you were coming, like, over a week ago.

I want a society that knows that you bearing witness to my exhaustion from getting less sleep than any other generation before us is a gift. Because we're just now figuring out that Title IX and *Roe v. Wade* wasn't enough to send us on our merry way.

I want a society where I can cry in the driveway of my father's trailer and not feel I failed him for not keeping him home longer before I held him as he passed at a care facility. And in the aftermath, I want a society that forgives the latchkey-generation children of divorce for our choices because someday we will have to do this all over again. I want a society that doesn't make me puke from the guilt I feel for setting my children up to inherit this same fate, despite everything I worked so hard to avoid.

I want a society that just gives women a rest already.

My God—what divorcée, ex-wife or mother *wouldn't* want a functioning society?

Chapter 9

"The Real Pandemic Here Is Capitalism"

Astra Taylor, "The Real Pandemic Here Is Capitalism" (March 26, 2020)
Christian Smalls, "Dear Jeff Bezos, Instead of Firing Me, Protect Your
   Workers from Coronavirus" (April 2, 2020)
Adam Kaszynski, "You Could Start Making Parts for Ventilators within
   Twenty-four Hours" (April 9, 2020)
Emily Pierskalla, "I Want My Death to Make You Angry" (April 13, 2020)
Stacy Davis Gates, "They're Not Going to Save Us. We Are Going to Save
   Us" (May 1, 2020)
Sujatha Gidla, "'We Are Not Essential. We Are Sacrificial'" (May 5, 2020)
Lateef McLeod, "Disability Justice and COVID-19" (May 8, 2020)
Jill Nelson, "Trump = Plague" (May 11, 2020)

● ● ●

In late 2019 and early 2020, news started to filter out about a deadly new strain of coronavirus, severe acute respiratory syndrome coronavirus 2 (SARS-CoV-2), which widely came to be known as COVID-19. President Trump consistently minimized the threat of the disease. On February 27, 2020, he said, "It's going to disappear. One day—it's like a miracle—it will disappear." The pandemic, though, would claim more than one million lives in the United States alone—and nearly seven million globally as of the publication of this book.

People who were deemed "essential workers" were compelled to work in life-threatening conditions without proper masks or other protective gear. The health of the economy was a higher priority for politicians than the health of people. Trump overrode the advice of medical professionals and scientists to peddle bogus theories about the pandemic that increased the spread of the disease and caused more deaths. In this environment, far-right conspiracy theories thrived, which made it harder to manage the spread of the disease and which encouraged other forms of violence.

The pandemic both highlighted and exacerbated the many injustices of US capitalism in the twenty-first century. Disability justice organizers were among the most prominent voices pointing to the need for fundamental change in how our society manages work and provides healthcare. While far more radical measures were needed, people pressured the government to at least temporarily postpone rents and student debt payments, provide free testing and vaccines, and share vaccines more globally. Workers began to organize to demand different priorities. And, despite the risks, people also began to take to the streets again to demand change.

● ● ●

In March 2020, the US government finally began to enforce measures to prevent the spread of COVID-19, leading to a profound disruption of daily life, and organizers were forced to move discussions online. In one of the earliest teach-ins of the pandemic, documentary filmmaker, writer, and political organizer Astra Taylor, a cofounder of Debt Collective, named the real pandemic: an economic system that places profit before people.

Astra Taylor, "The Real Pandemic Here Is Capitalism" (March 26, 2020)

The real pandemic here is capitalism. An unfathomable amount of people are going to die, deaths that can be prevented, because they do not have adequate health care. It's not a question of paying for things, it's a question of who's going to profit.

On a state level, on a city level, internationally, we're seeing all kinds of things happening: evictions have been halted, prisoners let out, transit made free. Meals are being distributed, and workers are finally getting paid time off and sick leave. There have been protests in Chile and beyond. In Uganda, rents aren't being collected. Other places around the world understand that it's not the economy that needs to be saved. It's the economy that's killing us right now.

In 2008, there was a massive economic crisis caused by bankers basically playing with mortgages and in the years since they've basically just been rewarded for their bad behavior. Corporations pushed money out the door to their shareholders and enriched themselves, and poor people have just become more vulnerable.

The majority of Americans are in debt. We don't have any wealth. Our debts are other people's assets that they buy and sell and trade and profit from. People literally have less than nothing. People are not going to be able to pay rent and people should feel no shame about that, they should feel outraged.

There's going be a moment where this goes from bad to worse. People are going to go into medical debt as a result of COVID. These debts are immoral. Nobody should have to go into debt because they're sick. Debtors need to collectively come together and demand higher wages and public goods, including universal health care.

● ● ●

Christian Smalls, from Newark, New Jersey, was a thirty-one-year-old assistant manager at the Staten Island Amazon warehouse before he was fired by the company for organizing his coworkers to protect themselves during the coronavirus pandemic. A leaked memo revealed that company executives had plotted to make Smalls the face of a massive anti-union campaign, deriding him as "not smart or articulate." He went on to become the head of the Amazon Labor Union and was part of the first successful unionization effort in the company's history, achieving a breakthrough victory for the union at Staten Island's JFK8 Fulfillment Center in April 2022—a victory that inspired workers at other Amazon warehouses and in other workplaces around the country to unionize. Smalls sent this open letter to Amazon founder Jeff Bezos, who at the time was the richest person in the world, after his termination.

Christian Smalls, "Dear Jeff Bezos, Instead of Firing Me, Protect Your Workers from Coronavirus" (April 2, 2020)

Dear Jeff Bezos,

When I applied to work at Amazon, the job description was simple. It said you need to have a high-school diploma or a GED and you have to be able to lift fifty pounds. That's it. Now, because of COVID-19, we're being told that Amazon workers are "the new Red Cross." But we don't want to be heroes. We are regular people. I don't have a medical degree. I wasn't trained to be a first responder. We shouldn't be asked to risk our lives to come into work. But we are. And someone has to be held accountable for that, and that person is you.

I have worked at Amazon for five years. Until I was fired last week from the Staten Island warehouse in New York City, I was a manager assistant who supervised a team of about sixty to one hundred "pickers," who pick items off the shelves and put them on conveyor belts to get sent out for shipment.

At the beginning of March, before the first confirmed case of coronavirus at the facility, I noticed people were getting sick. People had different symptoms: fatigue, light-headedness, vomiting. I told HR. I said: Hey, something's wrong here. We need to quarantine the building. I wanted us to be proactive not reactive. Management disagreed and assured me they were "following CDC guidelines."

The lack of protections worried me. Inside the warehouse, there are gloves, but they are not the right kind. They are rubber instead of latex. There are also no masks. Hand sanitizer is scarce. There are limited cleaning supplies. People are walking around with their own personal hand sanitizer, but good luck finding one in a local grocery store.

Because of those conditions, I didn't feel safe, so I took paid time off to stay home and avoid getting sick. Eventually, though, I ran out of paid time off and I had to go back to work. Other colleagues don't have that option. Many of my coworkers and friends at the Amazon facility have underlying health conditions. Some have asthma or lupus or diabetes. Others are older people, or pregnant. They haven't gone to work in a month, so they haven't been paid. They're only doing that to save their lives: if they get the virus they could be dead. One of my friends, who has lupus, is living with his relatives so he doesn't have to pay rent. Can you imagine if he couldn't do that? He'd probably be homeless.

Another problem is that Amazon has imposed mandatory overtime to keep up with the demand of everyone ordering online. The result is that Amazon employees are going to work sick as dogs just so they can earn $2 per hour on top of their regular pay. Do you know what I call that? Blood money.

Workers who want to make extra money are doing up to sixty hours of work a week and risking their lives. Some are working even if they are sick. When people are coughing and sneezing they say, oh, it's just allergies. It's a scary time to be in the warehouse right now.

When I went back to work last Tuesday morning, I spoke to a team member who looked really ill. She told me she feared she had corona and had tried to get tested. I told her to go home and get some rest. Then, two hours later, we had a managers' meeting. That's when we were told we had a first confirmed sick employee. The crazy thing was, management told us not to tell the associates. They were being very secretive about it.

I thought the secrecy was wrong, so as soon as I left the meeting I told as many people as I could about the situation. Shortly after that, I started emailing the New York State Health Department, the governor, the CDC. I called the local police department. I did everything I could to close that warehouse down so that it could be properly sanitized but the government is too overwhelmed to act right now. That's when I realized I would have to do something myself.

I decided to start spreading awareness among the workers in the building. I had meetings in the common areas and dozens of workers joined us to talk about their concerns. People were afraid. We went to the general manager's office to demand that the building be closed down so it could be sanitized. We also said we wanted to be paid during the duration of that time. Another demand of ours was that people who can't go to work because of underlying health conditions be paid. Why do they have to risk catching the virus to put food on the table?

This company makes trillions of dollars. Still, our demands and concerns are falling on deaf ears. It's crazy. They don't care if we fall sick. Amazon thinks we are expendable.

Because Amazon was so unresponsive, I and other employees who felt the same way decided to stage a walkout and alert the media to what's going on. On Tuesday, about fifty to sixty workers joined us in our walkout. A number of them spoke to the press. It was beautiful, but unfortunately I believe it cost me my job.

On Saturday, a few days before the walkout, Amazon told me they wanted to put me on "medical quarantine" because I had interacted with someone who was sick. It made no sense because they weren't putting other people on quarantine. I believe they targeted me because the spotlight is on me. The thing is, it won't work. I am getting calls from Amazon workers across the country and they all want to stage walkouts, too. We are starting a revolution and people around the country support us.

If you're an Amazon customer, here's how you can practice real social distancing: stop clicking the "Buy Now" button. Go to the grocery store instead. You might be saving some lives.

And to Mr. Bezos, my message is simple. I don't give a damn about your power. You think you're powerful? We're the ones that have the power. Without us working, what are you going to do? You'll have no money. We have the power. We make money for you. Never forget that.

• • •

Adam Kaszynski is a member of IUE-CWA Local 201 in Lynn, Massachusetts, and a machinist at General Electric. Workers at his plant launched a protest on March 30, 2020, demanding that they be allowed to use the company's idled manufacturing facilities to make desperately needed ventilators for coronavirus patients. Kaszynski spoke to journalist Sarah Jaffe about their demands.

Adam Kaszynski, "You Could Start Making Parts for Ventilators within Twenty-four Hours" (April 9, 2020)

There's been deindustrialization happening . . . and we've been told, "It's inevitable, it's trade, it's competition." We've seen our plant go from thousands and thousands of people and we are down to about 1,200 members.

You used to not be able to park in the plant. Now, half the thing is a parking lot. There are idle buildings and some idle capacity. We have plants all over the country like that.

[The union has been] fighting to keep union jobs and manufacturing jobs in the United States for as long as we've been here. Right now, there's an opportunity for these lifesaving ventilators and where there's skilled manufacturing workers and idle capacity. It feels like a perfect fit.

We decided to picket outside of the plant in Lynn and outside of GE headquarters to raise this demand.

Manufacturing is what workers in these facilities do. It would be totally possible for GE to make the kinds of investments in manufacturing in these plants that would make ventilator production possible. Where there is idle capacity on machines right now, you could start making metal parts for ventilators within twenty-four hours.

As far as the assembly and the electronics and everything, that could take a little bit more time, but there is a huge demand for these things and there are layoffs happening. There is no reason why engineers cannot say, "Here are the programs," or "Here are the blueprints for the parts that we need in these ventilators," and we could get up and running very quickly on at least the metal components.

I think GE posted $95 billion in revenue last year, so anything is possible.

The way that I look at it is that in every crisis these corporations come out of it on top. They shift the way things work to their benefit. NAFTA was a crisis for us. What did they use it for? They used it to ship US union manufacturing jobs overseas to non-union places.

Union workers are tired of watching the rich and corporations take advantage of crisis to screw us over.

[We] have a different vision of how the world should work. That is, when there is something you can do that is productive for society, that is needed, and you have the skills to do it, profit should not be the overwhelming motive for what we produce. It can be keeping jobs, it can be saving lives, it can be all sorts of things besides what it has been.

We've been trying to get out in front of this crisis and say, "We have a solution. We have a way of dealing with this crisis that is different than the way that you always deal with a crisis, which is to make money and profit off of it."

Our typical tools are pretty limited right now because of the virus. We've gotten overwhelming calls and support of solidarity from around the world over our demands. But it is also hard to ask people to come out and support a picket line while distancing.

I feel like the network that people are building by having this discussion and other discussions [about] the COVID-19 pandemic and how unions and workers should respond is building the basis for a revitalized labor movement. Without unions, you don't have a voice at all to say anything collectively. Without that, there is no conversation, there is no moving the needle on any of this.

Everybody needs sick time right now, right? Everybody needs PPE. Everybody needs protections if they are laid off, to be able to come back to their job. These are things that unions provide people. I'm hoping that we can get ahead of this crisis and use it to build our unions and use it to revitalize our best shot at getting a world that isn't strictly controlled by corporations in the interest of a small elite.

● ● ●

Emily Pierskalla was a registered nurse at Hennepin County Medical Center in Minneapolis and a member of the Minnesota Nurses Association. At a time when many people were applauding nurses and "essential workers" as "heroes" but failing to provide adequate protection or support to them in their work, where they daily risked their lives because of COVID-19, she wrote this public letter.

Emily Pierskalla, "I Want My Death to Make You Angry" (April 13, 2020)

What is it like being a nurse in a pandemic? Every day I bounce through the stages of grief like a pinball. The ricochet and whiplash leaves my soul tired and bruised.

Denial: I have spent less and less time in the denial stage. Still, I see many of my loved ones, politicians, and laypersons still stuck in this phase.

Anger: When our elders and immuno-suppressed folks are referred to as disposable members of society, when the pocketbooks of stockholders are considered more important than human lives, when we've known for decades this pandemic was coming, I burn with anger, anger at the system that prioritizes profits over health. It's the system that regularly runs out of "essential" and "critical" supplies seasonally. I have anger knowing the fragility of our supply chain has been exposed time and time again, especially after the earthquakes in Puerto Rico, and yet nothing was done to reinforce them.

Bargaining: The governing bodies bargaining with supply chain availability over scientific evidence. A paper bag is given magic powers to somehow preserve masks that are already expired and soiled. Droplet precautions are now satisfactory for airborne illnesses (but don't you dare leave Scotch tape on the walls).

Depression: Heaviness in my heart knowing my coworkers and friends will become unwilling sacrifices so the system can continue in its self-destructive path. And there's grief for the many people I will not have the resources to care for and save.

Acceptance: I have accepted that I will be infected with COVID-19 at some point. I am not scared of getting sick. I am scared of infecting those who will not survive. I check every day on our state's available hospital beds and ventilators. I wonder, if my illness becomes severe, will there be resources left for me?

And then I'm tagged in another social media post praising me for being "a hero." And I'm instantly flung back into the pinball machine as my emotions ricochet through the stages.

If I die, I don't want to be remembered as a hero.

I want my death to make you angry too.

I want you to politicize my death. I want you to use it as fuel to demand change in this industry, to demand protection, living wages, and safe working conditions for nurses and ALL workers.

Use my death to mobilize others.

Use my name at the bargaining table.

Use my name to shame those who have profited or failed to act, leaving us to clean up the mess.

Don't say, "Heaven has gained an angel." Tell them negligence and greed has murdered a person for choosing a career dedicated to compassion and service.

● ● ●

Educator and labor organizer Stacy Davis Gates became president of the Chicago Teachers Union in 2022. She gave this speech at a virtual May Day rally organized by Haymarket Books, in the early days of the COVID pandemic, arguing that "COVID has shown us that everything is connected."

Stacy Davis Gates, "They're Not Going to Save Us. We Are Going to Save Us" (May 1, 2020)

It's very important in this moment that we understand who the workers are. And the center of gravity has to be with female workers in this moment.

We're frontline workers, we're heads of household, we're mothers. And so that makes this pandemic and what's happening with frontline workers even more insidious. Because not only are frontline workers dying every day, they're leaving behind whole families.

I'm wearing an SEIU [Service Employees International Union] t-shirt intentionally in this moment. SEIU healthcare, a very close ally of ours in the Chicago Teachers Union, their nursing home workers have sent notice to forty nursing homes to say that they're going on strike. And they're not just going on strike for wages and benefits. They're going on strike because they need to live. They need to be available to their families. And then to make it even more personal, these women—these Black women, these Brown women, these working women—they're mothers. Which means that they are the mothers of our students in the Chicago Public Schools. And this across-sector organizing, this across-sector solidarity, is the only thing that's going to save us in this moment.

Look, I know that we talk a lot about Trump and what he's not doing. We're lifting up governors in this moment, we're talking about local politicians in this moment. But let me be very clear about what this moment is and isn't. They're not going to save us. We are going to save us.

And so, the moment that people have been opining about, reading books about, studying about—we're here. We have got to take this moment and clarify the needs of the many. And the needs of the many are different from the needs of those who are on Wall Street. So, when we say recovery, recovery is not a $1,200 check. Recovery is: I have free healthcare. Recovery is that I have a union in every single workplace to make sure that I'm supported and I'm protected. Recovery means I don't lose my home to foreclosure. Recovery means that I don't get kicked out or evicted because I cannot meet my obligations because I'm unemployed. Recovery means that we are going to try and form this in a multiracial, multiethnic coalition led by women to make sure that we are in a position to not just reimagine—I'm sick of imagining—but that we are implementing a society that prioritizes people, their humanity, and their safety.

We're here. We're here. We don't have to theorize it anymore. We're here. Center Brown people who are still in cages at the border. Center Black men and women who have been put in cages across this country. Center the worker who is ringing you out at the grocery store, delivering packages to your home every day and your mail every day.

We have to center this across sectors. We have to center this with women—and we have to center this with Brown and Black leadership, as well.

Look, we've been here before. In 2008, there was the great recession. And the great recession resulted in massive foreclosures, folks out of work. But on the flip side, it was also a time where the greatest concentration of power and wealth happened. I say it all the time. In Chicago, we have Cottage Grove on the South Side. On the West Side, you know we have Homan Avenue. Those places never recovered from 2008. However, Wall Street [did] and quite frankly the stock market is doing just fine.

What we have to do in this moment is identify the fact that the people, the many, they need it. The second thing that we need to do is identify who is unorganized and who we haven't invited to our party. Labor for so long has been a caricature of white men with hard hats and not the nurses or the CNAs [certified nursing assistants] in hospitals saving lives right now, or the laundry workers or environmental services cleaning up the rooms to make it safe for everyone.

So, if we have to do one thing in this moment, it's not just thank a worker. It's to identify who the workers are who have our backs right now. And those are the very people who have our backs right now. They are making it work. And so [don't] just say, "Thank you." . . . Within the labor movement, we have to prioritize who gets to talk, and not just be a shill or a mascot—but who gets to make strategic decisions? Who gets to lead? Who gets to invite other people into the tent and make it more diverse and make it bigger?

For so long we've missed our opportunity to advocate effectively for our immigrant communities. And immigrants are not just coming from south of the border. They're also coming from Africa. They're also coming from the Caribbean. They're also the people who are taking care of the kids of the 1 percent right now and risking their lives to even do that.

We really have to be clear in the labor movement right now. . . . And if we are not centering it with the train operators and the bus drivers, then we're missing a moment. The best thing our members, our educators can do right now is make a call home and ask parents how they're doing. Ask families what can we do with them and for them, and then ask them to sign onto a pledge that all of us get to recover—not just Wall Street.

And then, ultimately, we're going to have to be in a position to shut all of this down. We know that it can get shut down because we're all on Skype right now as a result of the shutdown.

We have to make a decision, not the virus. *We* have to make a decision, not Wall Street. *We* have to make a decision, not the wealthy landowners who have been making decisions for a long time.

We also have to make a decision to trust each other, too. We have to make a decision to trust those who are doing the work, to hear them, and to create policy and strategy that reflects their needs. . . .

COVID has shown us that everything is connected. Everything is connected. And so our bargaining, our labor, it has to be about common good. It has to be about the 360 degrees of a person's existence in this world.

In order for us to fight the power, in order for us to organize with each other, we have to see the humanity in one another. We have to break down the barriers and say, "Look, everyone deserves healthcare. Everyone deserves shelter. Everyone deserves a living wage. And I deserve to be safe when I go into my work site." Those are things that we can organize around, regardless of region, geography, gender, race, or ethnicity.

• • •

Indian-American author Sujatha Gidla, who wrote *Ants Among Elephants: An Untouchable Family and the Making of Modern India*, was a New York City subway conductor at the time she penned this essay.

Sujatha Gidla, "'We Are Not Essential. We Are Sacrificial'" (May 5, 2020)

When I heard that a coworker had died from COVID-19—the first in the Metropolitan Transportation Authority—on March 27, I thought, "It's starting." More deaths followed in quick succession, frequently more than once a day. Some of those people I used to see every day and fist bump.

On Facebook, when bad news comes, my coworkers and I express grief and offer condolences to the families. But our spontaneous response is the numb curiosity of an onlooker. We knew this was coming. We knew many among us wouldn't make it through the pandemic.

Every day I see posts on the MTA workers' group pages striking a jaunty tone: "Oh Lord, here we go. I got the symptoms, see you all in fourteen days. Or not."

We work at the epicenter of the epicenter, with a mortality rate substantially higher than that of first responders. Common sense tells you that subway trains and platforms are giant vectors of this virus. We breathe it in along with steel dust. As a conductor, when I stick my head out of the car to perform the required platform observation, passengers in many stations are standing ten inches from my face. At other times, they lean into the cab to ask questions. Bus drivers, whose passengers enter right in front of them, are even worse off.

My coworkers want doors locked on the two cars where the crew rides. Bus drivers want to let passengers enter through the back doors. We want hazard pay and family leave for childcare.

In mid-March, a bulletin came out mandating that conductors make an announcement every fifteen minutes. Wash hands, soap and water, sanitizer, elbow-sneeze. "Together we can help keep New York safe."

The irony was that we didn't have soap and water. At my terminal at that time, the restrooms were closed for three days after a water main break. Most employee restrooms are in similarly bad shape. Crew rooms are packed.

The MTA takes stern action against workers seen without goggles or cotton knit safety gloves. Yet we had to work without protection against the coronavirus.

At first we were warned not to wear masks. The MTA said it would panic the public. It said masks were dangerous for us. Later it said we could wear masks we bought ourselves. But by then there were few masks for sale.

One week after the pandemic was declared, a vice president of TWU Local 100 came to my terminal to give a talk. I rose to my feet in outrage and asked why we weren't receiving masks. I was told healthy people didn't need masks and that doctors needed them more. Aren't doctors healthy? No answer. How about rubber gloves and hand sanitizer? No answer.

Finally, the MTA agreed to supply us with personal protective equipment. When signing in, we get an N95 mask and three small packets of wipes the size of those used before a shot at the doctor's office. This is meant to last three days. We also get a small container to fill with hand sanitizer from a bottle in the dispatcher's office.

The masks are cheaply made. My co-workers complain that the masks pinch their noses. The straps break easily. Many masks must be secured with duct tape.

Or so I have heard. Two days after the vice president's visit, I developed severe body aches, chills, and a dry cough. On March 27, I woke up at 6 a.m. to go to the bathroom and collapsed. I made a quick call to a close friend and then dialed 911. An ambulance took me to NYU Langone Medical Center, where I was treated and discharged. I stayed isolated for fourteen days, after which I felt better. My coworkers told me about a place where I could get tested. On April 15, I tested positive. Further quarantine. My direct-deposit statement shows $692: less than half my wages for the first pay period and nothing thereafter. (I had used up all of my sick days).

The third death I heard about was a Black coworker I used to see every day who once saw me reading Michelle Alexander's *The New Jim Crow*. He wanted to know why a woman from India was interested in the condition of Black people. From then on, whenever we ran into each other we hugged and cheek-kissed.

I used to talk to another coworker across the platform when his N train and my R train reached Atlantic Avenue. He was one of only two Orthodox Jews in the rapid transit operations. A train buff, he once noticed that a cable that connects one car to another had come loose and was hanging dangerously near the third rail. He may have saved lives that day. Now he's dead, too.

We are stumbling upon dead bodies. I know of two cases. A train operator nearly tripped over one while walking between cars. The other person was sitting upright on a bench right outside the conductor's window and discovered to be dead only at the end of an eight-hour shift after my coworkers kept noticing the person on each trip.

The conditions created by the pandemic drive home the fact that we essential workers—workers in general—are the ones who keep the social order from sinking into chaos. Yet we are treated with the utmost disrespect, as though we're expendable. Since March 27, at least ninety-eight New York transit workers have died of COVID-19. My coworkers say bitterly: "We are not essential. We are sacrificial."

That may be true individually, but not in our numbers. Hopefully this experience will make us see clearly the crucial role we play in keeping society running so that we can stand up for our interests, for our lives. Like the Pittsburgh sanitation workers walking out to demand protective equipment. Like the GE workers calling on the company to repurpose plants to make ventilators instead of jet engines.

I took my second test on April 30. It was negative. Tomorrow, I will go back to work.

• • •

The COVID-19 pandemic revealed and exacerbated the ways in which disabled people are often treated as disposable and less deserving of care within the US healthcare system and society at large. In a virtual panel—part of the Grounding Movements in Disability Justice series—the Black poet, scholar, and disability justice activist Lateef McLeod discussed disability oppression in the context of the pandemic and what a society based around disability justice might look like.

Lateef McLeod, "Disability Justice and COVID-19" (May 8, 2020)

Good evening, everyone, I am Lateef McLeod. . . . I am here today to address the issue of COVID-19 and disability justice. If you give a preliminary look at both of these subjects, you would say that the two was pulling society in two opposite directions. There is COVID-19, a ruthless and deadly pandemic, who is mercilessly killing our loved ones, especially our disabled folks, poor, and Black and Brown people of color that in our communities. The virus is revealing how stark and harsh our hierarchies are in this society and the heartlessness in which our society deals with the most vulnerable in society. Then there is disability justice, which is a praxis that advocates for a community where those that the society marginalized are the center of our movements. Through the words of Mia Mingus, disability justice professes that access is love and is advocating for a world in which everyone has what they need to live a sustainable and fulfilled life in a community that they choose.

Now if you just glimpsed at the news in the last month, you have seen how horrid this country has handled the COVID-19 crisis in the last month. Currently, there is still a lack of testing to determine who has the virus and need medical care. There are medical providers who are caring for the sick without proper personal protective equipment (PPE). There are people with disabilities who are in danger of being denied care because doctors might prioritize the care of an able-bodied people over them. People with complex communication needs, that they had before COVID-19 or because of COVID-19, are having challenges communicating with medical care providers so that they could help direct their care. Also, in this country there is not a unified message among our governmental leadership as to whether to open back up the country or to keep the shelter-in-place ordinances intact, which leaves Americans confused on what will happen next. All horrible and disastrous things that we have to deal with in the dystopian reality we currently live in. Now let us pose the question how could the country handle the crisis differently if it was led by disability justice principles as the ones stated in the Sins Invalid's disability justice primer, *Skin, Tooth, and Bone: The Basis of Movement Is Our People*? First, we can look at disability justice having an anticapitalist politic where medical care is not run on a profit margin but is organized and is prepared for giving care to those who need it. Disability justice is looking for a medical care industry that does not ration care to those that doctors deem are more productive in society, namely temporary able-bodied people that the capitalists see as more valuable as workers. Disability justice proudly exclaims that everyone is valuable and that no one is disposable. Also because of the disability justice principle of leadership from the most impacted we need to listen to the most vulnerable in this crisis and both amplify their voices and make sure their needs are met. As a result, if we had more of a disability justice mindset, we would see more people getting access to care when they need it, and no one being denied care. We also would have invested more in our medical health care system so that health care providers would have all the equipment and resources that need to take care of those who are sick. Also, keeping in mind the most vulnerable to commutable diseases in this country, we should listen to scientists and health professionals for when it would be safe to venture out in public again.

What the COVID-19 pandemic crisis also reveals is that to protect our lives, we need a society and an economy that values our lives and work for us. We do not need to sacrifice our lives in going to work to prop up the economy. The people who own the most capital wants the economy open again because they know that the economy, as it is constructed now, will benefit them and not us. As the lieutenant governor of Texas, Dan Patrick, clearly expressed, they would have us die to open back up the economy so that they can increase their wealth. We can also see this response mirrored in the capitalists who fund these reactionary conservative activists to protest state and local governments to open up so we can all, supposedly, get back to work. This asinine response may not make sense at first glance, but if you frame it in the Protestant work ethic and the myth of American capitalism this reaction becomes predictable. For centuries there has been a myth in this country that if you work hard and dedicate yourself to your goals you will be prosperous. This myth was used to stigmatize those who were not prosperous as lazy and thus deserving of poverty and destitution, which included many people of color and disabled people. The stigmatization ultimately led to the eugenics movement where capitalists tried to eradicate people of color and disabled people from the human genome. Thus, we circle back today where many of our Black and Brown and disabled comrades are dying from this COVID-19 virus, and we have this virulent reactionary movement that are advocating for the economy to be open so we can all die at a larger percentage. This should make us question our relationship to work. Is work so essential and important that we should let many people die so that we can get back to doing labor? I thought we went to work to sustain our lives and those of our loved ones in our community. However, if we get back to work too quickly, we might have the opposite effect than we intended.

So, as I close, I want to say that the COVID-19 crisis has shown how a wider acceptance of a disability justice praxis is sorely needed in this country. We should throw away the notion that everyone should be able-bodied in this society and construct the infrastructure needed to care for everyone in this country, regardless of how their body or mind works. We need to shift the paradigm from how everyone can work for a living to thinking about how we can care for one another and meet each other's needs. There are several people with disabilities doing this work currently, and I would like to shout out the organization BADD CRIPS for the work they are doing in mutual aid. This priorities paradigm shift goes to addressing what society we want to continue to live as human beings. Do we want to continue to live in this capitalist society where everyone has to work to prove their worth to society, or do we want to live in society where everyone has their needs met regardless of who they are and are free to realize their full potential? This is a question that we need to ask before the economy opens back up so that we can push society in the direction we want it to go when it does.

● ● ●

Jill Nelson is a writer, activist, and journalist. Nelson was arrested on April 16, 2020, when she wrote "Trump = Plague" in chalk on an abandoned building in the Washington Heights neighborhood of New York City. She was held for more than five hours in jail.

Jill Nelson, "Trump = Plague" (May 11, 2020)

I went out to go to the drugstore and the supermarket, essential trips. I was walking from the drugstore down to Broadway to go to the supermarket, when I saw a green boarded-up, empty, for-rent building. It was covered with plywood. I had a piece of chalk in my pocket, and I wrote "Trump = Plague."

Before I could even step back, cops swooped in . . . "What are you doing? What are you doing? You're under arrest." They searched me, asked me if I had weapons, told me to take my hands out of my pockets—it was a cold day, so I said no—frisked me, shoved me into a police car and took me to the 33rd Precinct, where they put me in a cell and left me there for five-and-a-half hours.

I took my shoes off. I had had a mask, a fabric mask I had made, on, but I demanded that they give me one of their more professional masks. They didn't allow me to make any phone calls. I was never read my rights.

It was absurd, absolutely absurd, a total waste of time, energy. And this is in a community that has one of the highest rates of COVID, has many people who are poor and working poor. And there's something the police could have been doing besides attacking me for writing the truth. I have yet to have anyone disagree with what I said . . . .

"Trump = Plague" . . . sums . . . up, to me, what's going on, how it is, what's happening in this country and in the world. And we have a president who is aiding and abetting and telling us that as people of color, and older people, we should just die, get out there and die for capitalism. It's ridiculous. There are so many disparities in healthcare, in treatment, in coverage.

You know, I think the police are out of control. I think the mayor is afraid of the police. Instead of saying what he ought to say, which is, "Now I see how you feel, people of color," he's fronting for the police, as always. Apparently, the only person he worries about is [his son] Dante. . . .

You know, I'm sixty-seven years old. I was politicized by the killing of Clifford Glover when I was eighteen. This notion that it's only a few bad apples and that this isn't policy and that the police are there to serve and protect, I don't buy it. I don't buy it. I don't see it. I can't see how arresting me or rushing down those young men in Brooklyn serves any purpose. It doesn't make us safer.

And I frankly feel that COVID-19 has been racialized, really, and it's now being used as a way to further oppress people of color. It's just absolutely wrong. The police aren't doing their job. What a waste. . . .

COVID-19 has been weaponized and racialized and is being used to further oppress Black and Latinx people. And we have to resist . . .

You know, we cannot just sit by and act as if this is acceptable or anything goes to survive. It's not enough, to me, to bang pots and make cheer and clap at 7:00 every night.

We have to, as Norman said, get out there, demonstrate and resist this militarization of our city, of our country, and the racialization of this alleged great fight against COVID-19. . . .

I think it is, as it has always been in America, open season on people of color. And we see COVID-19 and the stress in the nation being used as a cover for that same thing. . . . It ties into these scenes we see of armed white men with swastikas and Confederate flags converging in front of statehouses and demanding that governors reopen. I mean, this is the Civil War, with this as just the latest battle.

Chapter 10

Abolition and the Uprising for Black Lives

Natasha Cloud, "Your Silence Is a Knee on My Neck" (May 30, 2020)
Olivia Olson, "This Is What's Really Happening in Minneapolis" (June 3, 2020)
8toAbolition, "#8toAbolition: Abolition Can't Wait" (June 7, 2020)
Mariame Kaba, "Yes, We Mean Literally Abolish the Police: Because Reform
    Won't Happen" (June 12, 2020)
Ianne Fields Stewart, "Today Is the Last Day of Trans Oppression" (June 14, 2020)
Imani Perry, "Racism Is Terrible. Blackness Is Not." (June 15, 2020)

• • •

The horrifying police killing of George Perry Floyd Jr., a forty-six-year-old Black man, unfolded in public view on May 25, 2020. Minneapolis police officer Derek Chauvin knelt on Floyd's neck for more than eight minutes, despite him stating repeatedly "I can't breathe" and calling out for his mother—and even after he had become unresponsive—while other officers stood by. His murder was captured on video by a seventeen-year-old bystander, Darnella Frazier. As news of another Black person being killed by police spread, protests erupted locally, with bus drivers in the Amalgamated Transit Union refusing to transport arrested protesters to jail. Soon people mobilized nationally, then globally.

These protests further escalated when local activists in Louisville, Kentucky, organized for justice after the police killing of Breonna Taylor, a twenty-six-year-old Black woman, on March 13, 2020. Taylor, a nurse, was shot in her home by officers executing a falsified "no-knock" warrant. Activists in the #SayHerName movement helped bring national attention to Taylor's case and its connections to the many other women, trans, and gender nonconforming people whose lives have been taken by the police.

The multiracial uprising for Black lives in summer 2020 took place in towns and cities across the country, involving, by one estimate, 15 to 26 million people. Within this broader set of actions, a bold group of abolitionists pushed for fundamental changes to the institutions that uphold racism and violence. They called for divesting from programs that cause harm and investing in the actual needs of communities, such as better schools, health care, jobs, and clean water.

● ● ●

The police killing of George Perry Floyd Jr. helped spark a summer of massive protests. One of the people who spoke out early in this new uprising for Black lives was Natasha Cloud, a WNBA player for the Washington Mystics. Her moving essay in *The Players' Tribune*, whose title references the brutal manner in which Floyd was murdered, reflected the leading role of WNBA players in spotlighting issues of racial justice on and off the court.

Natasha Cloud, "Your Silence Is a Knee on My Neck" (May 30, 2020)

To tell you the truth, I was planning on writing about something else. Had a whole other article mapped out, about this upcoming WNBA season, and what this moment means for the W—and stay on the lookout for that. Coming soon.

But not right now.

Because right now . . . there's only one thing that's on my mind. Right now, if we're being really real? As a Black person in America, there's only one thing that could possibly BE on my mind.

And that's fearing for my life.

It's fearing for my life, and for the life of every other person who is guilty of nothing more than belonging to a race that this country has been built on oppressing. It's wanting to stay alive—in a time where the reality for a lot of people is that my staying alive doesn't matter.

It's 2020, man. That was supposed to be the future, you know what I mean? Growing up, if you said "the year 2020," that felt like some Star Trek shit. It felt like this endless possibility. But what you realize as you get older is that if you're a Black kid in America, the future . . . it just isn't about possibility like that. You start to notice how many forces there are in place to make sure that 2020 isn't really all that much different from 2010. Or 2000. Or 1990. Or 1920. You start to understand how the systems of power in this country, they're not built to create possibility or opportunity for Black people—they're built to lock them out.

America's systems of power exist to lock in the white status quo.

America's systems of power exist so that, in 2020, George Floyd can have a knee forced on his neck by a white police officer, by someone whose job it was to serve and protect him, for almost nine minutes in broad daylight—nine minutes in broad daylight—even after he had become unresponsive. America's systems of power exist so that an acceptable response to a cop killing George Floyd is to make excuses for the cop. America's systems of power exist so that George Floyd, a Black murder victim, can be blamed for his own damn murder.

But you know what crushes me most of all?? It's how the systems of power in this country are built so strong, and with such prejudice, that in order for white supremacy to flourish—people don't even have to actively be about white supremacy. They don't have to carry the burden of being openly racist, or waste their energy on being loudly oppressive. It's not like that at all.

All they have to do is be silent.

That's what's so scary about it to me. That's what's so crazy about it, and so frustrating. And if I'm being honest, that's what pisses me off. Because it's like—those racist cops who keep killing us? There's way too many of them, that's for sure. But we're going to keep on speaking out, keep on shining a light at their behavior . . . and eventually we're going to get them the hell out of the paint. Relatively speaking, that one's easy. But you know what's not as easy?? You know what's harder to shine a light on? The millions of people who are helping to protect those racist cops, and who are helping to insulate those in power, by staying "neutral." That right there is what's exhausting to me. It's all the people who think that—in 2020!!—they can still somehow just politely opt out of this shit.

And those are the people who I wanted to write this for.

Because those are the people with the ability to really change things. And to me the first step in getting those people to change their behavior—it's getting them to understand the meaning of their behavior. It's getting them to see that this "both sides" wave they think they're riding . . . it doesn't exist. It never existed, of course—but especially not now. Not in this moment. Not with these deaths so fresh and so raw.

I'm writing this because I have a platform. It may not be the biggest platform in the world . . . but it's bigger than a lot of people have. It's what I've got. And the only thing I feel like using that platform for right now is to send a message to the so-called "neutral" people out there. It's to tell them that we're changing up the definitions of some of these words they've been hiding behind.

It's to tell them that "seeing both sides" means having blood on their hands—and "opting out" means leaving innocent people to die.

It's to tell them that neutrality about Black lives might as well be murder.

It's to tell them that their silence is the knee on George Floyd's neck.

And by the way—I'm so proud to be an athlete right now. I'm so unbelievably proud to be a part of this community. The way that so many different athletes from so many different sports (and so many different backgrounds) have been finding their voices through all of this, and standing up against racial injustice, and making a real impact . . . it's a beautiful thing.

When I see Jaylen Brown organizing a walk to the MLK memorial. When I see Amanda Zahui B. speaking out and *inspiring* people. When I see Stephen Jackson mourning the loss of his "twin" with this combination of anger and grace. That's powerful to me.

But it's like I said: what's really going to move the needle here is everyone getting involved—and by that I mean all athletes. Because there's no room for any of that silence or "neutrality" in the athlete community either. Those old excuses about not wanting to lose sponsorships, or not wanting to alienate certain types of fans, or how "racists buy sneakers too" or whatever?? We don't have time for that. Not when lives are being lost.

We need to meet this moment with accountability, and solidarity, and leadership.

And I know it can be done.

Man—like, when I see Elena Delle Donne posting on her IG story the other day?? You have no idea what that does to my spirits, or what that means to me. I saw Elena's post, and I was just like . . . Ahhh, I fucking *knew* my teammate would have my back. I knew it. And that felt so good. That's the MVP of our league, one of the most famous white basketball players alive, and now everyone is seeing how real she is. How she didn't hesitate—she got in there. And it was like, even that *one* post on its own, it took just a little bit of the weight off my shoulders. It made me feel just a little less powerless in this world.

It also laid down the gauntlet, I think, for other athletes.

And if it didn't? Then I hope this article does.

Because there's no new information to wait for. There's no other side to hear from. There's no safe space, no neutral territory to chill in and sit these issues out. Athletes, if you're reading this . . . know that we see you. I'll repeat that: *we see you.* I love y'all—and like I said, I'm so proud to be one of y'all. But you're being judged right now the same as everyone else—and if you're silent, you are part of the problem.

If you're silent, I don't fuck with you, period.

Because I'm just out here trying to stay alive.

And your knee is on my neck.

● ● ●

The protests that emerged in the Twin Cities following the police killing of George Floyd were dynamic, defiant, and determined. Local activist Olivia Olson shared her inspiring view of the solidarity and community at the heart of these demonstrations in a series of Facebook posts.

Olivia Olson, "This Is What's Really Happening in Minneapolis" (June 3, 2020)

This is what's really happening in Minneapolis:

Our communities are standing up, protecting one another, and organizing for a different world.

- Neighbors are (literally) painting over an area where violence and death spilled, with murals, chalk art, flowers, songs, dancing, and also tears.
- Neighbors are taking turns guarding George Floyd's memorial site from white supremacist groups, from the police, and from the National Guard.
- Neighbors are coming together to organize extended moments of silence throughout the city every single day. To remember George Floyd. To remember all of the Black and Brown bodies terrorized and taken by the police.
- Neighbors are organizing mass protests every day to fight for the justice of George Floyd and for the end of violence against Black and Brown communities.
- Neighbors are gathering in public parks to be with one another, to comfort one another, to dream of another world, and to organize defense units against violent white supremacist groups, against the police, and against the national guard.
- Neighbors are blocking off side streets and creating makeshift barricades to protect vulnerable residential areas from the violence of white supremacist groups, the police, and the National Guard.
- Neighbors are going door to door to check on each other, to make sure everyone has enough food and water, basic necessities, and emotional support.
- Neighbors are organizing pop-up community food drives all over the city, on almost every block.
- Neighbors are turning abandoned Targets and other large abandoned corporate buildings into community food shelves.

- Neighbors are turning abandoned hotels (the Sheraton Hotel) in the middle of the city into housing units for now homeless communities.
- Neighbors are organizing donations for local immigrant, Indigenous, Asian, Latinx, and Black owned businesses to rebuild after destruction.
- Neighbors are volunteering and taking shifts to stay awake throughout the night to be on the lookout for (more) violence caused by the police, by the National Guard, and by white supremacist groups and to protect one another, especially their Black and Brown neighbors.
- Neighbors are opening their doors to anyone and everyone that feels unsafe or needs to seek sanctuary at any time.
- Neighbors are organizing community crisis hotlines and groups on social media to coordinate emergency needs throughout the day and into the night (childcare, evacuation support, food and medication needs, emotional support, financial support, transportation support, medical support, and to alert of lethal dangers, and alert of police, National Guard, and white supremacy activities).
- The Minneapolis School Board and the teacher union are cutting ties with the Minneapolis Police Department.
- The University of Minnesota is cutting ties with the Minneapolis Police Department.
- Minneapolis local businesses are making public statements against the Minneapolis Police Department and are in the streets with the community seeking justice.
- The Minneapolis City Bus Union is refusing to work with the police and National Guard to transport arrested community members to jail.

Supporting and bringing in more militarized police to a city that is grieving . . . because of the militarized police . . . is not the answer.

Let's remember the power of our beautiful communities.

• • •

In June of 2020, the liberal reform group Campaign Zero released a policy platform called #8CantWait. While some praised their demands on social media,
others pointed out that the campaign's proposals, such as de-escalation training
and banning chokeholds, had already been implemented by police departments
around the country and had not resulted in fewer police killings of Black people.
In fact, most of these reforms had already been implemented by the Minneapolis Police Department, and had failed to prevent George Floyd's murder. Rather
than reducing the deadly presence of police in Black and Brown communities, the
proposed reforms would require increased funding for policing. Based on their
conviction that policing cannot be reformed, abolitionist organizers responded
with #8toAbolition, a resource for activists who strive for "a world without police,
where no one is held in a cage, and all people thrive and be well."

8toAbolition, "#8toAbolition: Abolition Can't Wait" (June 7, 2020)

#8TOABOLITION
A WORLD WITHOUT PRISONS OR POLICE,
WHERE WE CAN ALL BE SAFE

DEFUND THE POLICE	DEMILITARIZE COMMUNITIES	REMOVE POLICE FROM SCHOOLS	FREE PEOPLE FROM PRISONS & JAILS

WE BELIEVE IN A WORLD WHERE THERE ARE
 ZERO POLICE MURDERS BECAUSE THERE ARE ZERO POLICE.

REPEAL LAWS CRIMINALIZING SURVIVAL	INVEST IN COMMUNITY SELF-GOVERNANCE	PROVIDE SAFE HOUSING FOR EVERYONE	INVEST IN CARE, NOT COPS

ABOLITION CAN'T WAIT.

• • •

Mariame Kaba is an organizer, educator, and curator, and founder and director of Project NIA, a grassroots organization working to end youth incarceration. She is the author of *We Do This 'Til We Free Us: Abolitionist Organizing and Transforming Justice*. In summer 2020, as abolitionist ideas and calls to "Defund the Police" gained popularity—and were widely contested—she put forward a clear argument about the ways police reform efforts have consistently failed and why, instead, we need a radically different approach based on the political framework of abolitionism.

Mariame Kaba, "Yes, We Mean Literally Abolish the Police: Because Reform Won't Happen" (June 12, 2020)

Congressional Democrats want to make it easier to identify and prosecute police misconduct; Joe Biden wants to give police departments $300 million. But efforts to solve police violence through liberal reforms like these have failed for nearly a century.

Enough. We can't reform the police. The only way to diminish police violence is to reduce contact between the public and the police.

There is not a single era in United States history in which the police were not a force of violence against Black people. Policing in the South emerged from the slave patrols in the 1700s and 1800s that caught and returned runaway slaves. In the North, the first municipal police departments in the mid-1800s helped quash labor strikes and riots against the rich. Everywhere, they have suppressed marginalized populations to protect the status quo.

So when you see a police officer pressing his knee into a Black man's neck until he dies, that's the logical result of policing in America. When a police officer brutalizes a Black person, he is doing what he sees as his job.

Now two weeks of nationwide protests have led some to call for defunding the police, while others argue that doing so would make us less safe.

The first thing to point out is that police officers don't do what you think they do. They spend most of their time responding to noise complaints, issuing parking and traffic citations, and dealing with other noncriminal issues. We've been taught to think they "catch the bad guys; they chase the bank robbers; they find the serial killers," said Alex Vitale, the coordinator of the Policing and Social Justice Project at Brooklyn College, in an interview with *Jacobin*. But this is "a big myth," he said. "The vast majority of police officers make one felony arrest a year. If they make two, they're cop of the month."

We can't simply change their job descriptions to focus on the worst of the worst criminals. That's not what they are set up to do.

Second, a "safe" world is not one in which the police keep Black and other marginalized people in check through threats of arrest, incarceration, violence, and death.

I've been advocating the abolition of the police for years. Regardless of your view on police power—whether you want to get rid of the police or simply to make them less violent—here's an immediate demand we can all make: cut the number of police in half and cut their budget in half. Fewer police officers equals fewer opportunities for them to brutalize and kill people. The idea is gaining traction in Minneapolis, Dallas, Los Angeles, and other cities.

History is instructive, not because it offers us a blueprint for how to act in the present but because it can help us ask better questions for the future.

The Lexow Committee undertook the first major investigation into police misconduct in New York City in 1894. At the time, the most common complaint against the police was about "clubbing"—"the routine bludgeoning of citizens by patrolmen armed with nightsticks or blackjacks," as the historian Marilynn Johnson has written.

The Wickersham Commission, convened to study the criminal justice system and examine the problem of Prohibition enforcement, offered a scathing indictment in 1931, including evidence of brutal interrogation strategies. It put the blame on a lack of professionalism among the police.

After the 1967 urban uprisings, the Kerner Commission found that "police actions were 'final' incidents before the outbreak of violence in twelve of the twenty-four surveyed disorders." Its report listed a now-familiar set of recommendations, like working to build "community support for law enforcement" and reviewing police operations "in the ghetto, to ensure proper conduct by police officers."

These commissions didn't stop the violence; they just served as a kind of counterinsurgent function each time police violence led to protests. Calls for similar reforms were trotted out in response to the brutal police beating of Rodney King in 1991 and the rebellion that followed, and again after the killings of Michael Brown and Eric Garner. The final report of the Obama administration's President's Task Force on 21st Century Policing resulted in procedural tweaks like implicit-bias training, police-community listening sessions, slight alterations of use-of-force policies and systems to identify potentially problematic officers early on.

But even a member of the task force, Tracey Meares, noted in 2017, "policing as we know it must be abolished before it can be transformed."

The philosophy undergirding these reforms is that more rules will mean less violence. But police officers break rules all the time. Look what has happened over the past few weeks—police officers slashing tires, shoving old men on camera, and arresting and injuring journalists and protesters. These officers are not worried about repercussions any more than Daniel Pantaleo, the former New York City police officer whose chokehold led to Eric Garner's death; he waved to a camera filming the incident. He knew that the police union would back him up and he was right. He stayed on the job for five more years.

Minneapolis had instituted many of these "best practices" but failed to remove Derek Chauvin from the force despite seventeen misconduct complaints over nearly two decades, culminating in the entire world watching as he knelt on George Floyd's neck for almost nine minutes.

Why on earth would we think the same reforms would work now? We need to change our demands. The surest way of reducing police violence is to reduce the power of the police, by cutting budgets and the number of officers.

But don't get me wrong. We are not abandoning our communities to violence. We don't want to just close police departments. We want to make them obsolete.

We should redirect the billions that now go to police departments toward providing health care, housing, education, and good jobs. If we did this, there would be less need for the police in the first place.

We can build other ways of responding to harms in our society. Trained "community care workers" could do mental-health checks if someone needs help. Towns could use restorative-justice models instead of throwing people in prison.

What about rape? The current approach hasn't ended it. In fact most rapists never see the inside of a courtroom. Two-thirds of people who experience sexual violence never report it to anyone. Those who file police reports are often dissatisfied with the response. Additionally, police officers themselves commit sexual assault alarmingly often. A study in 2010 found that sexual misconduct was the second most frequently reported form of police misconduct. In 2015, the *Buffalo News* found that an officer was caught for sexual misconduct every five days.

When people, especially white people, consider a world without the police, they envision a society as violent as our current one, merely without law enforcement—and they shudder. As a society, we have been so indoctrinated with the idea that we solve problems by policing and caging people that many cannot imagine anything other than prisons and the police as solutions to violence and harm.

People like me who want to abolish prisons and police, however, have a vision of a different society, built on cooperation instead of individualism, on mutual aid instead of self-preservation. What would the country look like if it had billions of extra dollars to spend on housing, food, and education for all? This change in society wouldn't happen immediately, but the protests show that many people are ready to embrace a different vision of safety and justice.

When the streets calm and people suggest once again that we hire more Black police officers or create more civilian review boards, I hope that we remember all the times those efforts have failed.

• • •

Ianne Fields Stewart is a Black transfeminine actor, storyteller, and activist and is the founder of The Okra Project, which works to address food insecurity in

Black transgender communities. Stewart gave the following speech before a crowd of fifteen thousand people at the 2020 Brooklyn March for Black Trans Lives, the largest such gathering to date.

Ianne Fields Stewart, "Today Is the Last Day of Trans Oppression" (June 14, 2020)

Good afternoon. My name is Ianne Fields Stewart. I use they/them/she/her pronouns.

Today I call upon each and every one of you to make a commitment. Today I urge you to commit, that today is the very last day that transphobia will claim the lives, loves, and joys of Black trans people!

For too long, Black trans people have fought for our humanity, and for too long, cis people have been acting like they don't know what the fuck we talking about.

So today is the last day that a Black trans woman fears for her life, when she names and claims herself, in front of a man, whose hatred of himself is stronger than his love for her.

Today is the last day that a Black trans man fears occupying physical space because he can't find his binder or is without it, and he fears that, because he fears being misgendered, because he fears brutality. It is the last day.

Today is the last day that Black nonbinary people feel forced to fake themselves into a binary that doesn't exist.

Today is the last day that cis people use trans people as an encyclopedia when Google is right there.

Today is the last day. And today, I demand that you commit that there will be no more hashtags. There will be no more elevated rates of incarceration, housing insecurity, and unemployment for Black trans people.

Today I demand that the state be held accountable for our murders. Today I demand that the state be held accountable for continuously ignoring us, abusing us, while profiting off of us in the shadows.

Today we bring that violence into the light and crush it beneath our feet. To summarize I have one simple thing to say: transphobia ends today. And it doesn't end because your nonprofit made a grant off of it. It doesn't end because you put a trans flag on a credit card. It doesn't even end because you said to your white family that trans lives matter. It doesn't end because you fuck us and still misgender us to your friends. Transphobia ends today because if you ain't with us, you are learning today what it means to be against us.

• • •

The George Floyd protests were remarkable for how multiracial they were compared to previous movements against racial injustice. Large numbers of white people seemed to have finally awakened to the problem of anti-Black racism. Black Lives Matter protests spread to former "sundown" towns (those where Black people might be lynched if they were found after dark), and exit polls from the November 2020 election identified racial injustice as the second most important issue facing the country after the economy. In an article for *The Atlantic*, African American Studies scholar Imani Perry pushed back on some of the responses from well-intentioned white people, who tended to only depict Black people as suffering, not proud.

Imani Perry, "Racism Is Terrible. Blackness Is Not." (June 15, 2020)

A lot of kind statements about Black people are coming from the pens and minds of white people now. That's a good thing. But sometimes, it is frankly hard to tell the difference between expressions of solidarity and gestures of absolution. (*See, I'm not a racist, I said you matter!*) Among the most difficult to swallow are social-media posts and notes that I and others have received expressing sorrow and implying that Black-ness is the most terrible of fates. Their worrisome chorus: "I cannot imagine . . . How do you . . . My heart breaks for you . . . I know you are hurting . . . You may not think you matter but you matter to me." Let me be clear: I certainly know I matter. Racism is terrible. Blackness is not.

I cannot remember a time in my life when I wasn't earnestly happy about the fact of my Blackness. When my cousins and I were small, we would crowd in front of the mirrors in my grandmother's house, admiring our shining brown faces, the puffiness of our hair.

My elders taught me that I belonged to a tradition of resilience, of music that resonates across the globe, of spoken and written language that sings. If you've had the good fortune to experience a holiday with a large Black American family, you have witnessed the masterful art of storytelling, the vitality of our laughter, and the everyday poetry of our experience. The narrative boils down quite simply to this: "We are still here! Praise life, after everything, we are still here!" So many people taught us to be more than the hatred heaped upon us, to cultivate a deep self-regard no matter what others may think, say, or do. Many of us have absorbed that lesson and revel in it.

One of the classic texts in African American studies is Zora Neale Hurston's 1928 essay "How It Feels to Be Colored Me." Her playful yet profound articulation resonates for me now. She wrote:

> I am not tragically colored. There is no great sorrow dammed up in my soul, nor lurking behind my eyes. I do not mind at all. I do not belong to the sobbing school of Negrohood who hold that nature somehow has given them a lowdown dirty deal and whose feelings are all but about it. . . . No, I do not weep at the world—I am too busy sharpening my oyster knife.

Some of her words, I must admit, are too hopeful, at least for me right now. In fact, I *do* weep at the world; I am, in a sense, part of the sobbing school; and I am skeptical that my lone oyster knife can cut any of the rot out of this nation. But, like Hurston, I refuse to see the story of who I am as a tragedy.

Joy is not found in the absence of pain and suffering. It exists through it. The scourges of racism, poverty, incarceration, medical discrimination, and so much more shape Black life. We live with the vestiges of slavery and Jim Crow, and with the new creative tides of anti-Blackness directed toward us and our children. We know the wail of a dying man calling for his mama, and it echoes into the distant past and cuts into our deepest wounds. The injustice is inescapable. So yes, I want the world to recognize our suffering. But I do not want pity from a single soul. Sin and shame are found in neither my body nor my identity. Blackness is an immense and defiant joy. As the poet Sonia Sanchez wrote in a haiku about her power—and her struggles:

> Come windless invader
> I am a carnival of
> stars a poem of blood

People of all walks of life are protesting the violent deaths handed out by police officers. This is extraordinary both because the victims were Black—and when does Black death elicit such a response?—and because Americans in general have a hard time dealing with death. Think about how uncomfortable many Americans are with grief. You are supposed to meet it with a hidden shamefulness, tuck yourself away respectably for a season, and then return whole and recovered. But that is not at all how grief courses through life. It is emetic, peripatetic; it shakes you and stops you and sometimes disappears only to come barreling back to knock the wind out of you.

Black Americans right now are experiencing a collective grief, one that unfolds publicly. And we are unable to tuck it away. I do think Hurston would have to admit this too, were she around today. She wrote her essay before *Brown v. Board of Education*, the Montgomery bus boycott, the Birmingham crusade, the March on Washington, Freedom Summer, the Voting Rights Act, the Civil Rights Acts, the rise of Black mayors, the first Black governor, the first Black president. She wrote her essay before we understood how tightly this nation would grasp onto its original sin even after legions of Black people came with razor-sharp oyster knives and hands full of pearls.

Black Americans continue to die prematurely—whether under the knee of a police officer, or struggling for breath on a respirator, or along the stretch of the Mississippi River known as Cancer Alley, or in the shadow of Superfund sites, or in one of the countless other ways we are caught in the spokes. The trauma is repetitive. We weep. But we are still, even in our most anguished seasons, not reducible to the fact of our grief. Rather, the capacity to access joy is a testament to the grace of living as a protest—described by Lorraine Hansberry, who, as one of the greatest playwrights in the history of American theater, wrote *A Raisin in the Sun*. Whenever she recounted the story of Black America in lectures or discussions, she pointed to the extraordinary achievements we attained under obscene degradation. "Isn't it rather remarkable that we can talk about a people who were publishing newspapers while they were still in slavery in 1827, you see?" she said during a speech in 1964.

Some of us who comment on racial inequality these days are averse to such accounts of Black history, thinking them romantic and not frank enough about the ravages of racism. So I hope that no one is confused by my words. American racism is unquestionably rapacious. To identify the achievement and exhilaration in Black life is not to mute or minimize racism, but to shame racism, to damn it to hell. The masters were wrong in the antebellum South, when they described the body-shaking, delighted chuckle of an enslaved person as simplemindedness. No, that laugh—like our music, like our language, like our movement—was a testimony that refused the terms of our degradation. In the footage of the protests over the past several weeks, we have seen Black people dancing, chanting, singing. Do not misunderstand. This is not an absence of grief or rage, or a distraction. It is insistence.

And so, I must turn the pitying gaze back upon any who offer it to me, because they cannot understand the spiritual majesty of joy in suffering. But my rejection of their account also comes with an invitation. If you join us, you might feel not only our pain but also the beauty of being human.

Chapter 11

"Trumpism Can't Be Voted Away"

Viet Thanh Nguyen, "Asian Americans Are Still Caught in the Trap of the 'Model Minority' Stereotype. And It Creates Inequality for All" (June 25, 2020)

Alexandria Ocasio-Cortez, "I Could Not Allow That to Stand" (July 23, 2020)

Melania Brown, "My Sister Layleen Polanco Died Alone in Rikers. Solitary Confinement Is Torture" (July 23, 2020)

Barbara Smith, "How to Dismantle White Supremacy" (August 21, 2020)

Anna Kuperman, "The Emperor Has No Clothes" (September 8, 2020)

Mumia Abu-Jamal, "Inside the Inside of Lockdown America" (September 14, 2020)

Barbara Ransby, "Trumpism Can't Be Voted Away. We Need Radical Social Transformation." (November 18, 2020)

Hakeem Jefferson, "Storming the US Capitol Was about Maintaining White Power in America" (January 8, 2021)

● ● ●

The scale and success of the George Floyd protests forced a national reckoning with white supremacy. As the United States continued to surpass the rest of the world in deaths due to COVID-19, the country witnessed a spike in hate crimes against members of the Asian, Asian American, and Pacific Islander (AAPI) community. These attacks were fueled by racist and xenophobic theories about the origins of the novel coronavirus in China, which were cynically promoted by the Trump administration and repeated in mainstream media. This violence shattered the myth that overt racism against Asian Americans is a thing of the past.

Conditions were nowhere more egregious than inside US prisons, where incarcerated people were denied access to personal protective equipment and soap and lacked the ability to socially distance themselves outside of solitary confinement, a practice widely denounced by human rights organizations as a form of torture. At the notorious Rikers Island jail in New York City, the epicenter of the pandemic in 2020, the rate of infection was eighty-seven times higher than the national infection rate. These conditions sparked resistance within and outside jails and prisons under the hashtag #FreeThemAll.

The November 2020 election of Joe Biden to the presidency represented more a rebuke of Trump than enthusiasm for Biden's centrist agenda, which promised to overturn the worst Trump-era policies but rejected calls for universal healthcare, a Green New Deal, and defunding the police, and other more far-reaching demands to address the deep economic and social crises exacerbated by the pandemic. However, the January 6, 2021, storming of the US Capital, fueled by conspiracy theories about election fraud, made clear that Trumpism would survive the removal of Trump from the White House.

• • •

Here, Viet Thanh Nguyen, who is a Vietnamese refugee and winner of the 2016 Pulitzer Prize for his novel *The Sympathizer,* reflects on efforts throughout US history to control—or exclude—Asian people from the full rights of citizenship, a problem brought again to the forefront by the racist response to the COVID-19 pandemic.

Viet Thanh Nguyen, "Asian Americans Are Still Caught in the Trap of the 'Model Minority' Stereotype. And It Creates Inequality for All" (June 25, 2020)

I am not surprised by the rising tide of anti-Asian racism in this country. Sickened, yes, to hear of a woman splashed with acid on her doorstep; a man and his son slashed by a knife-wielding assailant at a Sam's Club; numerous people being called the "Chinese virus" or the "chink virus" or told to go to China, even if they are not of Chinese descent; people being spat on for being Asian; people afraid to leave their homes, not only because of the pandemic but also out of fear of being verbally or physically assaulted, or just looked at askance. Cataloging these incidents, the poet and essayist Cathy Park Hong wrote, "We don't have coronavirus. We are coronavirus."

Racism is not just the physical assault. I have never been physically assaulted because of my appearance. But I had been assaulted by the racism of the airwaves, the ching-chong jokes of radio shock jocks, the villainous or comical japs and chinks and gooks of American war movies and comedies. Like many Asian Americans, I learned to feel a sense of shame over the things that supposedly made us foreign: our food, our language, our haircuts, our fashion, our smell, our parents.

We told ourselves these were "minor feelings." How could we have anything valid to feel or say about race when we, as a model minority, were supposedly accepted by American society? At the same time, anti-Asian sentiment remained a reservoir of major feeling from which Americans could always draw in a time of crisis.

The basis of anti-Asian racism is that Asians belong in Asia, no matter how many generations we have actually lived in non-Asian countries, or what we might have done to prove our belonging to non-Asian countries if we were not born there. Pointing the finger at Asians in Asia, or Asians in non-Asian countries, has been a tried and true method of racism for a long time; in the United States, it dates from the nineteenth century.

It was then that the United States imported thousands of Chinese workers to build the transcontinental railroad. When their usefulness was over, American politicians, journalists, and business leaders demonized them racially to appease white workers who felt threatened by Chinese competition. The result was white mobs lynching Chinese migrants, driving them en masse out of towns and burning down Chinatowns. The climax of anti-Chinese feeling was the passage of the 1882 Chinese Exclusion Act, the first racially discriminatory immigration law in American history, which would turn Chinese entering the United States into the nation's first illegal immigrant population. The

Immigration and Naturalization Service was created, policing Chinese immigration.

American history has been marked by the cycle of big businesses relying on cheap Asian labor, which threatened the white working class, whose fears were stoked by race-baiting politicians and media, leading to catastrophic events like the Chinese Exclusion Act and the internment of Japanese Americans in 1942.

It is easier to blame a foreign country or a minority, or even politicians who negotiate trade agreements, than to identify the real power: corporations and economic elites who shift jobs, maximize profit at the expense of workers, and care nothing for working Americans. To acknowledge this reality is far too disturbing for many Americans, who resort to blaming Asians as a simpler answer.

Asian Americans have not forgotten this anti-Asian history, and yet many have hoped that it was behind them. Asian Americans have literally wrapped themselves in the American flag in times of anti-Asian crisis; have donated to white neighbors and fellow citizens in emergencies.

None of these efforts have prevented the stubborn persistence of anti-Asian racism. Calling for more sacrifices simply reiterates the sense that Asian Americans are not American and must constantly prove an Americanness that should not need to be proven. Japanese Americans had to prove their Americanness during World War II by fighting against Germans and Japanese while their families were incarcerated, but German and Italian Americans never had to prove their Americanness to the same extent.

Asian Americans are caught between the perception that we are inevitably foreign and the temptation that we can be allied with white people in a country built on white supremacy. As a result, anti-Black (and anti-Brown and anti-Native) racism runs deep in Asian American communities. Frequently, we have gone along with the status quo and affiliated with white people.

And yet there have been vocal Asian Americans who have called for solidarity with Black people and other people of color, from the activist Yuri Kochiyama to the activist Grace Lee Boggs. The very term Asian American, coined in the 1960s by Yuji Ichioka and Emma Gee and adopted by college student activists, was brought to national consciousness by a movement that was about more than just defending Asian Americans against racism and promoting an Asian American identity. Asian American activists saw their movement as also being anti-war, anti-imperialism and anticapitalism.

The legacy of the third-world and Asian-American movements continues today among Asian-American activists and scholars, who have long argued that Asian Americans, because of their history of experiencing racism and labor exploitation, offer a radical potential for contesting the worst aspects of American society.

For many if not all Black, Brown, and Indigenous people, the American dream is a farce as much as a tragedy. Multiculturalism may make us feel good, but it will not save the American dream. Reparations, economic redistribution, and defunding or abolishing the police might.

● ● ●

Alexandria Ocasio-Cortez, often referred to by her initials, "AOC," rose to prominence when she beat Democratic incumbent Joe Crowley in an upset victory, making her, at age twenty-nine, the youngest woman ever to serve in Congress. As a self-described democratic socialist and member of the Democratic Socialists of America (DSA), Ocasio-Cortez's victory came on the heels of Bernie Sanders' 2016 run for president, signaling that "socialism" was no longer a dirty word in the United States. However, her political opponents focused not only on her policies, but regularly criticized her appearance and intelligence, and even sent her death threats. On the floor of the House of Representatives, she gave the following speech calling out the sexism of her fellow legislators.

Alexandria Ocasio-Cortez, "I Could Not Allow That to Stand" (July 23, 2020)

Speaker, I seek recognition for a question of personal privilege.

I would . . . like to thank many of my colleagues for the opportunity to not only speak today but for the many members from both sides of the aisle who have reached out to me in support following an incident earlier this week. About two days ago, I was walking up the steps of the Capitol when Representative [Ted] Yoho suddenly turned a corner and he was accompanied by Representative Roger Williams, and accosted me on the steps right here in front of our nation's Capitol. I was minding my own business, walking up the steps and Representative Yoho put his finger in my face, he called me disgusting, he called me crazy, he called me out of my mind, and he called me dangerous. Then he took a few more steps and after I had recognized his comments as rude, he walked away and said I'm rude, you're calling me rude. I took a few steps ahead and I walked inside and cast my vote. Because my constituents send me here each and every day to fight for them and to make sure that they are able to keep a roof over their head, that they're able to feed their families and that they're able to carry their lives with dignity.

I walked back out and there were reporters in the front of the Capitol and in front of reporters Representative Yoho called me, and I quote, "a fucking bitch." These were the words that Representative Yoho levied against a congresswoman. The congresswoman that not only represents New York's 14th Congressional District, but every congresswoman and every woman in this country. Because all of us have had to deal with this in some form, some way, some shape, at some point in our lives. I want to be clear that Representative Yoho's comments were not deeply hurtful or piercing to me, because I have worked a working class job. I have waited tables in restaurants. I have ridden the subway. I have walked the streets in New York City, and this kind of language is not new. I have encountered words uttered by Mr. Yoho and men uttering the same words as Mr. Yoho while I was being harassed in restaurants. I have tossed men out of bars that have used language like Mr. Yoho's and I have encountered this type of harassment riding the subway in New York City.

This is not new, and that is the problem. Mr. Yoho was not alone. He was walking shoulder to shoulder with Representative Roger Williams, and that's when we start to see that this issue is not about one incident. It is cultural. It is a culture of lack of impunity, of accepting of violence and violent language against women, and an entire structure of power that supports that. Because not only have I been spoken to disrespectfully, particularly by members of the Republican Party and elected officials in the Republican Party, not just here, but the president of the United States last year told me to go home to another country, with the implication that I don't even belong in America. The governor of Florida, Governor DeSantis, before I even was sworn in, called me a whatever that is. Dehumanizing language is not new, and what we are seeing is that incidents like these are happening in a pattern. This is a pattern of an attitude toward women and dehumanization of others.

So while I was not deeply hurt or offended by little comments that are made, when I was reflecting on this, I honestly thought that I was just going to pack it up and go home. It's just another day, right? But then yesterday, Representative Yoho decided to come to the floor of the House of Representatives and make excuses for his behavior, and that I could not let go. I could not allow my nieces, I could not allow the little girls that I go home to, I could not allow victims of verbal abuse and worse to see that, to see that excuse and to see our Congress accept it as legitimate and accept it as an apology and to accept silence as a form of acceptance. I could not allow that to stand which is why I am rising today to raise this point of personal privilege.

I do not need Representative Yoho to apologize to me. Clearly he does not want to. Clearly when given the opportunity he will not and I will not stay up late at night waiting for an apology from a man who has no remorse over calling women and using abusive language toward women, but what I do have issue with is using women, our wives and daughters, as shields and excuses for poor behavior. Mr. Yoho mentioned that he has a wife and two daughters. I am two years younger than Mr. Yoho's youngest daughter. I am someone's daughter, too. My father, thankfully, is not alive to see how Mr. Yoho treated his daughter. My mother got to see Mr. Yoho's disrespect on the floor of this House toward me on television and I am here because I have to show my parents that I am their daughter and that they did not raise me to accept abuse from men.

Now what I am here to say is that this harm that Mr. Yoho levied, it tried to levy against me, was not just an incident directed at me, but when you do that to any woman, what Mr. Yoho did was give permission to other men to do that to his daughters. In using that language in front of the press, he gave permission to use that language against his wife, his daughters, women in his community, and I am here to stand up to say that is not acceptable. I do not care what your views are. It does not matter how much I disagree or how much it incenses me or how much I feel that people are dehumanizing others. I will not do that myself. I will not allow people to change and create hatred in our hearts.

And so what I believe is that having a daughter does not make a man decent. Having a wife does not make a decent man. Treating people with dignity and respect makes a decent man, and when a decent man messes up as we all are bound to do, he tries his best and does apologize. Not to save face, not to win a vote, he apologizes genuinely to repair and acknowledge the harm done so that we can all move on.

Lastly, what I want to express to Mr. Yoho is gratitude. I want to thank him for showing the world that you can be a powerful man and accost women. You can have daughters and accost women without remorse. You can be married and accost women. You can take photos and project an image to the world of being a family man and accost women without remorse and with a sense of impunity. It happens every day in this country. It happened here on the steps of our nation's Capitol. It happens when individuals who hold the highest office in this land admit, admit to hurting women and using this language against all of us.

• • •

Melania Brown is the sister of Layleen Polanco, a twenty-seven-year-old Afro-Latina trans woman who died on Rikers Island in New York City. Corrections officers failed to seek medical attention for an hour and a half after finding her unresponsive in a jail cell, where she was being held in solitary confinement. In an article published for *Think*, Brown described the struggle to win justice for other victims of solitary confinement and for her sister.

Melania Brown, "My Sister Layleen Polanco Died Alone in Rikers. Solitary Confinement Is Torture" (July 23, 2020)

My sister, Layleen Xtravaganza Cubilette-Polanco, died last year at the notorious Rikers Island. While in detention, she suffered an epileptic seizure and died alone in solitary confinement. She was only twenty-seven years old—nowhere close to getting to fully live her life. The system killed her, like it kills so many Black people and other people of color.

To be clear, my sister's death was preventable. The New York City Department of Correction knew about her medical condition and yet, as a new report revealed, pushed to place her in solitary confinement over the objections of medical staff members. They pushed her into solitary in part because they didn't know how to house a transgender woman in Rikers. There, correctional officers laughed as she lay unresponsive nearby instead of getting her the care she needed. Rikers and solitary confinement killed my sister.

At any given time, tens of thousands of people are locked in solitary confinement in the United States, a practice that, when endured for more than a few days, has been classified as torture by the United Nations. America's use of solitary confinement is an international disgrace and a national mark of shame.

But this isn't the first time my family and I have endured pain and loss at the hands of the government. Four years before the death of Layleen, my cousin Miguel Espinal was shot and killed by a uniformed New York police officer. Miguel was unarmed, and no weapon was ever recovered. Today, I'm fighting for him, too.

But really, I'm fighting for the countless people who have been abused behind bars in New York (and around the United States). Andy

Henriquez, a nineteen-year-old from Washington Heights, died in a solitary confinement cell after suffering a tear in his aorta that left him barely able to breathe. He cried out for medical help as he was dying, and other people incarcerated near him yelled and banged on their doors, but no help came. He died alone on the floor of his cell.

Kalief Browder was accused of stealing a backpack when he was sixteen years old and was sent to Rikers Island to await a trial that never happened. He spent a hard three years in Rikers, the majority of it in solitary confinement. Not long after prosecutors dropped all charges against him and he was released, Kalief died by suicide. He couldn't escape the trauma of his time in solitary and all he'd experienced behind bars.

Davon Washington thought he was going to die when he was brutally beaten and locked in solitary confinement in an upstate New York jail. City officials transferred him from Rikers to a jail in Albany to avoid recent restrictions on placing young people in solitary. Guards pummeled Davon, who had been accused of attacking a guard.

They kill us out here and in cages behind bars. The prison system uses solitary confinement to break us down and mentally abuse us. It must stop. This is what the jail and prison system does to Black and Brown people.

Late last month, after a year of rallies in support of my family and increased demands from advocacy organizations and the community, Mayor Bill de Blasio disciplined seventeen Rikers staff in connection with my sister's death. In addition, he said New York City intends to end solitary confinement for all those with serious medical conditions immediately (something the city was already supposed to have been doing under existing rules) and to establish a work group to provide recommendations to end it for all by the fall.

This isn't good enough. It's been over a year since my baby sister died, and not a day goes by when I don't think about her. After the community outcry following Layleen's death, the New York City Board of Correction's jails oversight body announced last year they [would] issue rules to limit solitary. A year later, there have been no changes in the city or the state, and we simply [got] another announcement.

We can't wait any longer for justice for Layleen and the countless others—many of whom we don't even know about—who were traumatized and even killed by the state-sanctioned torture that is solitary confinement. New York City and New York State need to end solitary confinement today.

The mayor said my sister deserves justice. But real justice for my sister means firing all of the Rikers staff whose negligence and indifference killed her. #JusticeforLayleen means never allowing anyone else to suffer what she suffered. It means passing the HALT Solitary Confinement Act in New York, which has majority support in both houses of the Legislature. The Senate majority leader and the Assembly speaker must bring HALT to a vote, and the governor must sign it into law.

Justice for my sister means New York City, the mayor, the Board of Correction, and the city council each have the opportunity, authority, and responsibility to go further and must fully eliminate solitary confinement in all its forms right now.

Justice for my sister is undoing bail reform rollbacks and releasing people from jail during this era of COVID-19. Justice for my sister is repealing the so-called walking while trans law, a loitering law that law enforcement uses to profile and target Black trans and cisgender women for existing in public. Anything less is just lip service.

We have to stand up for what is right. As we fight for the people abused by police on the sidewalk or in their own homes, we cannot forget the people behind bars, in cages, in this city and state. We need to keep protesting. We need to be seen and heard. Black trans lives matter. My sister's life mattered. I will keep spreading my sister's word, and we all must demand that not one more person is tortured to death, by solitary or otherwise.

• • •

Barbara Smith is a Black feminist, socialist activist, writer, and scholar who coauthored the pioneering Combahee River Collective Statement. In an article for *The Nation*, Smith imagines the scale of action this country might take if it were serious about ending racism.

Barbara Smith, "How to Dismantle White Supremacy"
(August 21, 2020)

A few days after police lynched George Floyd, I began writing what became the op-ed "The Problem Is White Supremacy." Filled with grief, I wrote because I needed to do something with my rage and pain. I wrote because I was frustrated with public discussions about race that rarely mentioned—let alone examined—the root cause of this atrocity: white supremacy.

The reason these horrors continue century after century is that the system of racial domination that disadvantages people of color and privileges whites has not been broken. The ruling class dismisses the subjugation, exploitation, and violence because of the unrestricted power and disproportionate wealth that they gain as a result.

After explaining in the *Boston Globe* that the nation's racial quagmire does not result from negative attitudes and the behavior of "a few bad apples" but is instead caused by this overarching system of oppression, I asked the following question:

> What if we launched an initiative on the scale of the Marshall Plan or the space race to eradicate white supremacy? What if it were led by experts with the most detailed knowledge of how white supremacy in tandem with racial capitalism operates, that is, poor and working-class people of color? What if these experts partnered with researchers, advocates, and practitioners to provide exhaustive documentation, analysis, and comprehensive recommendations for ending the scourge of white supremacy once and for all? What if . . . ?

In a country where millions deny the existence of systemic racism, including a cohort that enthusiastically supports white supremacy, it is difficult to imagine such a plan being realized. It would be a major struggle, but one that would move the country closer to being a functional democracy, freed from the terror and hypocrisy that poisons life on both sides of the color line.

If roadblocks could be put aside, how might one begin this paradigm-shifting work? I would start by calling it the Hamer-Baker Plan. Fannie Lou Hamer and Ella Baker did as much to end white supremacy as any persons who ever lived. It feels appropriate to evoke their legacies in the process of envisioning the completion of that task.

The purpose of the Marshall Plan was to rebuild European nations that had been decimated by World War II and to align them politically as US allies in the Cold War. Its goals were both economic and ideological, and the same should be true of the Hamer-Baker Plan, except that its ideological goal would be to consolidate justice, not power and empire. Since white supremacy permeates every facet of life in the United States, the scope of the Hamer-Baker Plan would need to be even more sweeping than the Marshall Plan.

Because racial capitalism has had such grievous repercussions for generations of people of color, economic interventions would be at the forefront of this project. Eradicating poverty; eliminating the racial wealth gap; investing in the infrastructure of Black, Brown, and Indigenous communities whose labor and natural resources have been stolen; and guaranteeing full employment are some of the actions that must be taken to rectify centuries of economic exploitation. The cancellation of student loan and medical debt, stricter sanctions against discriminatory lenders, a viable federal minimum wage, paid family leave, free quality childcare, and pro-union labor laws are examples of policies that can address economic inequality.

It also would make sense to explore reparations as part of the plan's economic agenda.

Ending mass incarceration and shutting down the prison industrial complex would also go a long way toward destroying white supremacy. Prison abolition, defunding the police, and ensuring that all neighborhoods have the level of resources that affluent communities take for granted are solutions that already exist.

As I thought about the possibilities of the Hamer-Baker Plan, I realized that there are already innovative strategies that would be effective in alleviating the day-to-day consequences of structural racism. Here are some that come immediately to mind. The Nurse-Family Partnership pairs first-time, low-income mothers with visiting nurses who help families get a healthy start and work toward economic stability. The Harlem Children's Zone offers wraparound programs for children, from birth through college, assisting their families to overcome poverty and ensuring their academic success. Cure Violence (formerly Cease-Fire) uses a highly effective public health model, including violence interrupters, to end gun violence. The Green New Deal recognizes that environmental devastation disproportionately affects communities of color and that interventions in these communities need to be a priority. It also would be a source of thousands of new infrastructure jobs. Medicare For All would address racial health disparities resulting from the lack of access to affordable quality health care. The severely disproportionate impact of COVID-19 upon communities of color shows the pressing need to establish health care as a human right.

Currently, initiatives that focus on inequality in specific sectors like education, health care, and criminal justice are not aligned with one another, are seldom brought to scale so that they have maximum impact, and may not operate with the conscious goal of challenging white supremacy. The Hamer-Baker Plan would close these gaps and encourage integrated approaches.

For example, if quality education were a priority, there would be an understanding that stable, affordable housing; safe neighborhoods; access to excellent, affordable health care; and minimal exposure to trauma are all critical components of children's educational success. A holistic approach could make it possible for America to have a robust social safety net for the first time, benefiting people of every background.

The Hamer-Baker Plan would not only maximize the effectiveness of existing initiatives, but would also function as a catalyst for imagining new ways to challenge systemic racism. After reading my op-ed, a friend told me that he was ready to sign up for the Anti–White Supremacy Peace Corps (his own concept), and added that his city could really use some help. He was joking, but imagine if there were dedicated organizers fanning out across the country to help communities figure out ways to rid their local schools, courts, workplaces, hospitals, and houses of worship of entrenched white supremacy.

It would be groundbreaking for Hamer-Baker to use an intersectional approach based on the fact that misogyny and heteropatriarchy are integral to the functioning of white supremacy. The plan would consistently take gender, gender expression, and sexuality into account, and create solutions to address the specific impact of racism upon the lives of women, transgender, and queer people of color. New York's Audre Lorde Project exemplifies this approach. Founded in 1994 as a community organizing center for lesbian, gay, bisexual, two-spirit, trans, and gender nonconforming people of color, it has been centrally involved in the fight against police brutality and in coalitions for racial, gender, social, and economic justice.

There are myriad paths that a Hamer-Baker Plan could take. It is far easier to imagine what a plan to end white supremacy might look like than it is to imagine the conditions that would lead to a national consensus that this is what needs to be done. There are more people than we care to admit who look at the video of George Floyd pleading for his life and assume that he did something to deserve being choked to death while handcuffed. Less than three weeks after Floyd's death, police shot Rayshard Brooks in the back as he was running away. After he fell to the ground, the officers kicked him and stood on his body as he struggled for life. Despite being shot eight times, Breonna Taylor did not die immediately, but none of the medically trained officers at the scene made an effort to assist her. As a society, we are a long way from committing to end this nightmare.

Our job is to do everything possible to make that day come sooner. A few suggestions of how to get us to a time when a Hamer-Baker Plan could become a reality:

- Name the problem. Begin using the term "systemic white supremacy" to describe America's racial morass instead of less incisive terms that may feel more comfortable.
- Understand the scope of the problem. Read Black history. Read about the international impact of white supremacy reflected in US imperialism and militarism in non-European countries. Read classic, noncontemporary Black authors besides James Baldwin

and Toni Morrison. Read social science research that provides statistical documentation and analysis of America's rampant inequality.

- Do not accept it when the power structure's response to this period of racial reckoning is platitudes and partial solutions. In 1968, the Kerner Commission report on civil disorders concluded that the primary cause of urban rebellions was white racism. That would have been a great time to launch a Marshall Plan to dismantle white supremacy, especially since the report provided extensive recommendations, but of course this did not occur.

- Using Hamer-Baker as a template, envision what a comprehensive, explicitly anti-racist plan to eradicate systemic racial oppression in your workplace or community would look like, and then work with others to make it happen.

We can be encouraged that one day when a consensus does emerge, it will not come from the top. History indicates that it will come from the streets, from people organizing and demanding that every kind of dehumanization and carnage must stop, and that after more than five hundred years, the system of white supremacy must end.

• • •

With vaccines against COVID-19 still months away, educators at more than thirty-five school districts around the country protested city officials' push to resume in-person learning. Anna Kuperman, an English teacher at Classical High School and a member of the Providence Teachers Union, described the chaos she encountered when her school reopened in September 2020 in an editorial published in her school newspaper.

Anna Kuperman, "The Emperor Has No Clothes"
(September 8, 2020)

Last week I entered my classroom at Classical High School. Everything looked exactly the same as when I left in March. No sign of the deep cleaning or ventilation repair claimed by Providence Superintendent Harrison Peters and Governor Gina Raimondo. Colleagues in other Providence Public School buildings posted pictures of filthy toilets, moldy ceilings, and indoor rain puddles, belying claims that our buildings have been reoutfitted to handle students safely during a pandemic.

Last night I read the Hans Christian Andersen parable "The Emperor's New Clothes." In the story, the Emperor's sycophants repeatedly tell him that his new outfit is divine, when in fact, he is wearing nothing. It takes a child to point out that he is naked. Our leaders continue to insist that our buildings are clean and safe. Their Aramark cronies, advisers, and district leaders continue to mimic their lies. Well, I'm calling it. The Emperor has no clothes. The buildings weren't safe before the pandemic and they aren't safe now.

Some of the preexisting issues at my school, Classical High School, include:

1. Classrooms with no windows
2. No air conditioning. Classrooms reach temperatures in excess of 90 degrees
3. Windows that do not open
4. Unmitigated mold
5. A majority of classrooms with no ventilation system
6. Rooms that become covered with a black dust when their ventilation unit is turned on (no one can tell you when the ducts were last cleaned)

The pandemic shone a spotlight on inequities and exacerbated them. Private schools in Providence are thoroughly prepared with equipment and plans, and have been extra communicative with parents throughout the spring and summer. Providence public school teachers and parents have received communication so confusing or absent that parents are calling me for information to make the right decision for their kids.

And colleagues are calling me, crying, wondering since they signed up to teach in the Virtual Learning Academy, will they be able to return to their position in their current school in 2021? Few understand how VLA, propelled by an online platform called Edgenuity, will work or if it is the right choice for them, because we don't know enough about it.

Providence schools must return to distance learning until the spread of COVID-19 is contained. We can reopen Nathan Bishop Middle School and Providence Career & Technical Academy now to special populations who need to see their teachers and receive services, to Newcomers, to some early grades, and Multi-Language Learners.

Teachers have creative ideas about how to reopen safely. We want to teach in person! We know that distance learning is not ideal; still, it creates a more cohesive learning environment where students stay connected to their school community compared to attending the Virtual Learning Academy or the disruption of switching between in-person and distance learning when flu season hits.

Providence, with over 90 percent students of color and COVID numbers too high to reopen fully, has been disproportionately affected by the pandemic. Prematurely sending kids back to decrepit, under-resourced buildings under the guise of "equity" and "the importance of education" perpetuates health inequities. Any directive for an in-person model before COVID is contained will harm our communities and put our city at an even greater health risk.

The Emperors proclaim: All is fixed. All is safe. Just do your job and all will be fine.

But I'm here to tell you, the Emperor has no clothes.

I am glad that private schools have a plan. It proves it is possible. I am angry that our district does not. It doesn't have to be this complicated and chaotic. Fix the damn schools. Reallocate funds to make it happen. Tear down the funding formula and make a new one that actually works. Take care of our students by investing in our buildings, teachers, counselors, and curricula.

• • •

The award-winning journalist Mumia Abu-Jamal has been incarcerated since 1982, after a trial filled with procedural errors, in which he was convicted of shooting and killing police officer Daniel Faulkner. Abu-Jamal grew up in Philadelphia and became a member of the Black Panthers. He was well known as a crusading journalist and activist when his case went to trial. Despite appeals from numerous human rights groups for a new trial, international protests, and evidence of his wrongful conviction, Abu-Jamal lived on death row in Pennsylvania from 1982 to 2012 and still remains in prison. From prison, Abu-Jamal has recorded a series of radio commentaries and written a number of essays about the racism and injustice of the US criminal legal system and the war on the poor, inside and outside of prison.

Mumia Abu-Jamal, "Inside the Inside of Lockdown America" (September 14, 2020)

When one considers the social implications of COVID-19's rampage throughout America, one must recognize that its greatest impact was upon perhaps 80 percent of America, those who are in what is now called lockdown, unable to leave their homes except to shop for food or, if an essential worker, to work. Millions of Americans had an intimate opportunity to experience lockdown, which for singles or some elders was a strange form of solitary confinement.

For many people in America's prisons, general population, also known as mainline, became close to solitary confinement. For prisoners, jobs, education, recreation, and gyms became shuttered areas off limits to people deeply habituated to daily or regular access to such activities.

As for solitary confinement, it was this in large strokes. But here was solitary with a difference. The difference? This kind of solitary had no release date. Therefore, many prisoners are still in this form of solitary with no cutoff date to date. For how long will COVID-19 reign over the land? No one knows. The idea that some prison official will any-time soon yell "all clear" is laughable.

The nation may see two hundred thousand deaths in the next few weeks and perhaps over six million cases. So the coronavirus is alive and well in America and in the nation's prisons.

When COVID-19 first struck, activists believed it heralded a time of mass releases to rival mass incarceration.

It seems they underestimated the state's addiction to prison as a political staple, not to mention an economic mainstay. What this really means, however, is that many prisons have become more than solitary confinement units. They have become, in the time of COVID, new death rows. So the question is not how many folks will get sick, but how many will die?

The fear, anxiety, and distress is off the charts.

• • •

Barbara Ransby is an award-winning author, historian, and longtime activist. Trump's defeat at the polls led to spontaneous celebrations in the streets, but he lost to Joe Biden by a far slimmer margin than expected and with even more total votes than he garnered in 2016. In an opinion piece for *Truthout*, Ransby urged readers to reckon not only with the conditions that produced Trump, but the failures of the Democratic Party to offer a far-reaching alternative.

Barbara Ransby, "Trumpism Can't Be Voted Away. We Need Radical Social Transformation." (November 18, 2020)

Even as votes are still being counted, a chorus of pundits and politicos have begun attacking the left for allegedly scaring people away from the Democratic Party, jeopardizing Biden's victory and weakening down-ballot races. Nothing could be further from the truth.

Many Democratic candidates had lackluster showings, because they were, in many cases, lackluster candidates, offering nothing new or hopeful. In contrast, bold and forward-thinking progressives, like Cori Bush from St. Louis and Jamaal Bowman from New York, did quite well against the odds.

The Democratic establishment's failure to acknowledge its role in suppressing progressive electoral energy and contributing to the disappointing performance of many down-ballot Democrats reminds me of the title of a song performed by the Black women's a cappella group Sweet Honey in the Rock: "No Mirrors in My Nana's House." Their message was different, but it makes me think . . . there are no mirrors in Nancy Pelosi's House of Representatives.

We do not need a pale centrist agenda to bridge what has wrongly been termed as the Biden-Trump divide. We need a real alternative to both Biden's centrism and Trump's far-right authoritarianism. And we do have an alternative, as long as we don't let the Pelosi-Schumer-Clyburn triumvirate talk us out of it.

Our first task has nothing to do with Trump's base, but our own. In the days ahead, we must not straitjacket our work inside the Democratic Party. We need to strategize and self-organize on all levels.

And by "we" I mean two groups: the eclectic and far-flung motley tribe we call "the left," and the marginalized frontline communities that have borne the brunt of twenty-first-century racial capitalism's wrath, but may not see themselves as explicitly political, one way or another. Those are the two groups that need organizations they can own and shape and feel at home inside of. How do we offer a skeletal frame on which to build that big-tent home, and how do we offer portals of entry to that which is already out there?

We need to hone, polish, and sharpen a palpable set of alternatives to the systems, institutions, and policy platforms that now exist, and as social activist Toni Cade Bambara once said about revolution itself, we need to make it all "irresistible."

We have the cornerstone of this visionary agenda in three sets of movement-generated documents:

1. The Green New Deal (augmented by the Red Deal and the forthcoming Red, Black, and Green New Deal);

2. The Breathe Act, generated by the policy table of the Movement for Black Lives; and
3. The People's Charter, created by the Working Families Party.

These concrete policy proposals are based on values and vision: a commitment to minimize and repair harm, confront systemic racism, place people above profits, respect the rights and dignity of marginalized and oppressed communities, and save the planet.

These progressive policy documents are important. They illustrate in stark terms that movements are not simply protest campaigns; narrowly defined, they are generative spaces where new ideas and creative solutions are incubated. But how do we leverage the power necessary to really enact these game-changing policies? To do so, we need expansive, inclusive organizing efforts at all levels, including the level of self-organization. More specifically, we need to build stronger labor organizations, cooperatives, block clubs, reading groups, freedom circles, coalitions, networks, and parties that connect the different sites of local organizing, while still giving people the self-determining democratic power that local groups provide. At the same time, we have to create on-ramps and portals of entry to the national movement groups that already exist.

We need mass-based membership organizations! We have enough invite-only think tanks, elite policy teams and closed-door leadership circles, and we have too many self-proclaimed celebrity leaders. We need frameworks that say to people, "If you agree with us, here is how you join."

Candidates running for office cannot be the only ones making that offer. The seventy-million-plus people who voted Trump out of office need a real political home. The twenty-three million who marched against racism and police brutality earlier this year need a political home. That said, how that home is built and on what foundation is key. Certain sectors of the left still argue for a "colorblind" unity but that simply won't work. Millions of white people have demonstrated unprecedented willingness to stand up to some of the most egregious examples of racism. The task is to deepen that commitment, not ignore it. Much work to do on all of these fronts.

Our second set of analytical and political tasks is to dissect, demystify, and diffuse Trumpism. Seventy million people were willing to support a guy who calls neo-Nazis "fine people"; who cages Brown children; who pillages the natural environment; who gives perks and pardons to his thuggish cronies; who uses his position to fill his own pockets; who threatens his critics, including media; and who places lives at risk for the sake of ego, vanity, and ambition. What a guy! All the makings of a dictator, and tens of millions of Americans went into the voting booth and chose him. That is disturbing, at the very least.

Trump's political ascendancy, irrespective of his narrow loss at the polls, shows that there is a mass base willing to support a xenophobic, American-style fascist agenda. So, Trump is out of the White House but Trumpism continues. The worst-case scenario is that Trump was just the tester, the raggedy and sloppy dress rehearsal for what may come next. He has emboldened a racist far-right fascist movement that now feels aggrieved and on the move. Thousands of them were in the streets in Washington, DC, last weekend, and they were violent. At least two anti-racist protesters were reportedly stabbed. Despite the jumbled rhetoric of individual liberty, these movements, for the most part, are enamored with a pseudo-strongman leader. Their next hero may be smarter, more conniving, and more effective than Trump. We have to thwart the growth of this dangerous movement. They won't simply be voted away

Part of the work of undermining fascism, and its willing and unwitting enablers, is to disaggregate the movement, as the analysts at Political Research Associates and Southern Poverty Law Center do. Seventy million Trump voters are not a monolith. Some of them clearly embraced Trump's racist, venomous ideas wholeheartedly. Hopefully, they are a minority. Others are outright ignorant, falling for the many lies they see on television. Finally, some Trump supporters are undoubtedly seduced by his rhetoric, embodying a kernel of truth as every lie does, that "the system is rigged," and, stretching the limits of credulity, that Trump is out to help "the little guy," and the average Joe.

Throw in a few hundred congregations of opportunist evangelicals with a skewed and selective brand of morality, and you have Trump's base. So, the "hearts and minds" part of the battle is to expose, confront, and defeat some, shame (yes, shame!) others, and provide a genuine moral and political alternative to those willing to listen.

We have to make the case—for prison abolition, Medicare For All, divesting from police and investing in communities, climate justice, LGBTQ and women's rights, disability rights, housing for all, an end to the debt trap, the redistribution of resources from the few to the many, a just immigration policy and an end to the Muslim ban, peace on our streets and in the world—persuasive and irresistible. We surely won't win all of them, but we can win some of them.

Can we do this? *Sí, se puede.* Over twelve million people voted for Bernie Sanders and Elizabeth Warren earlier this year, two of the most progressive major contenders we have seen in a Democratic Party presidential primary. Neither one was perfect, but both were left-leaning, if not left on most issues, in contrast to the "safe" middle-of-the-roader that won the nomination.

What if half the people who voted for the progressive flank of the party could be energized to organize those who are skeptical about voting altogether, as well as some who voted for what was erroneously framed as the "safe center," and perhaps even win or neutralize some of those who drank the Trump Kool-Aid but are now gagging on it? This work is not primarily about compromise, it is about strategy and struggle and relentless effort.

So, yes, we can. We must. We must roll up our sleeves, get over our aversions, and walk into places of worship, community centers, college campuses, unemployment offices, state fairs, internet chat rooms, and onto street corners. We need to talk, listen, debate, build trust, and win people to a process of vision-building and freedom-making. We cannot pretend to have all the answers, but we do have some of the answers. And we have to offer people an entry point into a radically democratic process of social transformation grounded in process and principles. The other path is not a dead end, but a deadly precipice.

• • •

On January 6, 2021, the president of the United States, despite clearly losing the election, made another desperate attempt to hold onto power. Working hand-in-hand with far-right organizations such as the Oath Keepers, he summoned supporters to Washington, DC, by openly lying about the election being "stolen." Trump and some of his allies had hatched a plan to interrupt the certification by his own vice president of the Electoral College votes during a joint session of Congress. "[I]f you don't fight like hell, you're not going to have a country anymore," Trump told the crowd gathered in Washington, and then urged them to march on the Capitol, which they did. The crowd soon broke through police lines and entered the Capitol, which they began to ransack, leading to the deaths of several people and the evacuation of the Senate floor and the vice president. Trump retreated to the White House and for 187 minutes did absolutely nothing to intervene to stop the violence. While the certification of Joe Biden as president-elect was eventually affirmed the next morning at 3:42 a.m., the consequences of January 6 will be felt for years to come. Shortly after January 6, political scientist Hakeem Jefferson wrote this essay on the role of avowed white supremacists in the attack on the Capitol.

Hakeem Jefferson, "Storming the US Capitol Was about Maintaining White Power in America" (January 8, 2021)

On Wednesday, after weeks of refusing to accept the outcome of the election, President Trump's supporters stormed the Capitol of the United States as members of Congress were meeting to carry out their duties to certify the election results and confirm Joe Biden's victory.

Much will be said about the fact that these actions threaten the core of our democracy and undermine the rule of law. Commentators and political observers will rightly note that these actions are the result of disinformation and heightened political polarization in the United States. And there will be no shortage of debate and discussion about the role Trump played in giving rise to this kind of extreme behavior. As we have these discussions, however, we must take care to appreciate that this is not just about folks being angry about the outcome of one election. Nor should we believe for one second that this is a simple manifestation of the president's lies about the integrity of his defeat. This is, like so much of American politics, about race, racism, and white Americans' stubborn commitment to white dominance, no matter the cost or the consequence.

It is not by chance that most of the individuals who descended on the nation's capital were white, nor is it an accident that they align with the Republican Party and this president. Moreover, it is not a coincidence that symbols of white racism, including the Confederate flag, were present and prominently displayed. Rather, years of research make clear that what we witnessed in Washington, DC, is the violent outgrowth of a belief system that argues that white Americans and leaders who assuage whiteness should have an unlimited hold on the levers of power in this country. And this, unfortunately, is what we should expect from those whose white identity is threatened by an increasingly diverse citizenry.

Let's start here: Scholars interested in the sociological underpinnings of white racism often call our attention to concerns about group status as starting places for understanding white Americans' attitudes toward members of other social groups. In a famous essay from 1958 on the topic, entitled "Race Prejudice as a Sense of Group Position," Herbert Blumer, a noted sociologist, wrote the following:

> There are four basic types of feeling that seem to be always present in race prejudice in the dominant group. They are (1) a feeling of superiority, (2) a feeling that the subordinate race is intrinsically different and alien, (3) a feeling of proprietary claim to certain areas of privilege and advantage, and (4) a fear and suspicion that the subordinate race harbors designs on the prerogatives of the dominant race.

Building on Blumer's early work, other scholars have highlighted the consequences that result when white Americans perceive threats to their dominant position in the social hierarchy. Some research by social psychologists Maureen Craig and Jennifer Richeson, for example, finds that reminding white Americans of changing racial demographics causes them to adopt more negative racial attitudes toward minority groups. These same researchers also find that these reminders lead politically unaffiliated white Americans to report a stronger attachment to the Republican Party and to express greater political conservatism. These findings make sense, as the GOP is widely perceived to be a party that caters to white interests, a perception that predates the election of Trump but that has undoubtedly been strengthened by his ascendance to power in the party. In her award-winning book, "White Identity Politics," Ashley Jardina goes further than any scholar to date in documenting the causes and consequences of white identity, arguing that the increased salience of whiteness as a social category corresponds largely with how demographics have changed in this country. Jardina finds in her research that this, in turn, has created a fear among some white Americans that their hold on power has become increasingly precarious, highlighted most sharply by the ascendance of Barack Obama, a Black man, to the White House.

And most recently, Larry Bartels, a renowned scholar of American politics at Vanderbilt University, wrote the following in his research focused on the erosion of Republicans' commitment to democracy:

> The support expressed by many Republicans for violations of a variety of crucial democratic norms is primarily attributable not to partisan affect, enthusiasm for President Trump, political cynicism, economic conservatism, or general cultural conservatism, but to what I have termed ethnic antagonism. The single survey item with the highest average correlation with antidemocratic sentiments is not a measure of attitudes toward Trump, but an item inviting respondents to agree that "discrimination against whites is as big a problem today as discrimination against Blacks and other minorities." Not far behind are items positing that "things have changed so much that I often feel like a stranger in my own country," that immigrants get more than their fair share of government resources, that people on welfare often have it better than those who work for a living, that speaking English is "essential for being a true American," and that African Americans "need to stop using racism as an excuse."

To summarize Bartels's claims, white Republicans who have come to oppose democracy do so, in part, because they don't like those whom they believe democracy serves. And, more than that, they believe that the interests of nonwhite Americans have been given priority over the interests of their racial group. Many white Americans seem to be asking themselves, Why act in defense of a democracy that benefits "those people"?

So, let's return to the images of Wednesday, when a crowd of white people gathered at the Capitol with American flags and Trump flags and symbols of the Confederacy. For these white Americans, the notion of America itself is likely one that is white, making the American flag they so proudly wield as a symbol also one of white supremacy and white racial domination. Of course, the iconography of the failed Confederacy, alongside other reminders of white racial violence, including the placing of a noose around a tree near the Capitol, are intentional, too. For those who broke glass in windows of the Capitol, who marched in opposition to American democracy, who held up as a model the seditious behaviors of slaveholding states, who threatened the lives of elected officials and caused chaos that lays bare the dangerous situation we are in as a country—these are not political protesters asking their government for a redress of grievances. Nor are they patriots whose actions should be countenanced in a society governed by the rule of law.

Instead, we must characterize them as they are: they are a dangerous mob of grievous white people worried that their position in the status hierarchy is threatened by a multiracial coalition of Americans who brought Biden to power and defeated Trump, whom back in 2017 Ta-Nehisi Coates called the first white president. Making this provocative point, Coates wrote, "It is often said that Trump has no real ideology, which is not true—his ideology is white supremacy, in all its truculent and sanctimonious power." So, when we think about those who gathered in Washington, DC, on Wednesday and who will surely continue their advance in opposition to democratic rule, let it not be lost on us that they do not simply come in defense of Donald Trump. They come in defense of white supremacy.

Chapter 12

The Struggle Continues

Jesse Hagopian, "I'm Not Alone in Pledging to #TeachTruth" (June 12, 2021)

Cheri Renfro, "Dear Frito-Lay" (July 2, 2021)

Red Canary Song, "Radical Healing from State and Community Violence: Mourning with Asian Massage Workers in the Americas" (August 17, 2021)

H. Melt, "I Don't Want a Trans President" (August 23, 2021)

Haley Pessin, "What It Will Take To Defend Abortion Rights" (September 12, 2021)

Leta Hirschmann-Levy, "Never Again—Not for Anyone, Not Just the Jews" (February 24, 2022)

Dissenters, "Dissenters Opposes Imperialist Violence Everywhere" (February 25, 2022)

Dorothy Roberts, "Abolish Family Policing, Too" (June 2022)

Michelle Eisen, "No Contract, No Coffee!" (June 17, 2022)

Melissa Gira Grant, "The Fight for Abortion Rights Must Break the Law to Win" (June 24, 2022)

• • •

The uprising for Black Lives in summer 2020 and the defeat of Donald Trump threatened powerful interests in the United States, generating a mounting backlash against the gains of social movements, not only of recent years but as far back as the 1950s. The right, mobilizing resentment against health guidelines and COVID-19 restrictions, especially mask mandates, weaponized anti-vaccine and other conspiracy theories and escalated attacks on the already weak and limited forms of democracy that exist in the United States. The right targeted teachers, librarians, trans people, parents of trans children, election officials, and others. Against this background, the Supreme Court, with its three new extreme-right members from the Trump era, passed a series of decisions to erode hard-won civil liberties, most drastically overturning the right to abortion.

Meanwhile, President Biden, a centrist establishment Democrat, made clear that his administration would not deliver on the more fundamental changes demanded by protesters, such as full student debt abolition, and was more interested in "reopening" the economy than in truly addressing the needs of a society still experiencing widespread suffering and deaths due to COVID-19. Biden joined in the right's attacks on people calling to "defund the police," in fact directing billions more into policing and the military.

Teachers, parents, workers, and others did not remain silent in the face of these attacks, however. Teachers pledged to teach the truth of this country's history, despite the genuine risks to their livelihood. Abortion rights activists formed new organizations and networks to demand—and win—reproductive justice. Asian American and other abolitionists proposed genuine solutions to state and community violence. Workers made major new breakthroughs in their efforts to form unions at Starbucks and Amazon, despite massive opposition from the companies. In all of these movements, new bonds of solidarity emerged—laying the basis for the hard work of liberation ahead of us.

• • •

On June 12, 2021, teachers in more than forty cities joined a National Day of Action to #TeachTruth in opposition to a slew of new state laws seeking to ban the teaching of Critical Race Theory and about institutional racism, heterosexism, and other forms of oppression. Educator Jesse Hagopian, who works with the Zinn Education Project, *Rethinking Schools*, and Black Lives Matter at School, delivered this speech at the #TeachTruth rally in Seattle, Washington.

Jesse Hagopian, "I'm Not Alone in Pledging to #TeachTruth" (June 12, 2021)

Racists are scared these days, y'all.

You can tell a scared racist because when they can't win a debate, they just try to make it illegal for you to say—or teach—anything that challenges them. I'm proud to stand with all of you today in the #TeachTruth movement.

I want to begin by acknowledging that we are on homeland of the Duwamish people—land that was colonized by the United States. We live in a city named after a Duwamish Chief and yet the Duwamish people still don't have federal recognition. . . . And, now, wait a minute . . . If I was in Tennessee, would it even be legal for me to acknowledge that I was on Native American land that was colonized? That's really how far things have gone these days.

These laws banning the teaching of structural racism, sexism, and oppression are impacting every classroom—because even in states where there isn't yet a bill, this legislation is emboldening people to attack teachers who want to teach the truth. And everyone should know that our neighbors to the east, the state of Idaho, recently passed a bill that declares, "Social justice ideology poses a grave threat to America and to the American way of life." What? They are literally arguing that it's social justice that poses a threat, not racism and sexism.

But you can't understand our country without understanding racism and its intersections with sexism and heterosexism. Consider these facts:

- The average white family has ten times more wealth than the average Black family.
- A Black woman is three times more likely to die from pregnancy or childbirth-related causes than a white woman.
- Black students are over three times more likely to be suspended from school than white students.
- Anti-Asian hate crimes have surged over 169 percent so far this year.

- At least forty-four transgender and gender nonconforming people were violently killed in 2020, with Black transgender women accounting for two-thirds of total recorded deaths since 2013.

Despite these glaring examples, in Iowa, they recently passed a bill which bans teaching that "the United States of America and the state of Iowa are fundamentally or systemically racist or sexist."

According to *Merriam-Webster*, "fundamental" means: serving as an original or generating source. The original source of our country was the genocide against Native Americans and the enslavement of Black people. So you literally can't teach about the founding of this country or its long history without talking about systemic racism.

In Missouri they proposed a bill that would ban teaching The 1619 Project—which frames US history in terms of the enslavement of African people who were brought to North American colonies in 1619. And it bans the Zinn Education Project. And it bans the Black Lives Matter at School curriculum.

But I want to tell you all here today that the fact is they wouldn't be passing these laws to ban the teaching of structural racism and oppression if they weren't scared of something.

So, what are they scared of?

They are scared of the fact that activists built the broadest protest in US history over the spring and summer in the wake of the police killings of George Floyd and Breonna Taylor, which shook this country and exposed the structural nature of anti-Blackness to many.

They are scared of the fact that the BLM at School movement tripled in size this school year.

They are sacred of solidarity. The bill in Arkansas actually suggests banning the teaching of solidarity!

And they are certainly scared of students who can think critically.

The summer uprising was led by youth. The media likes to talk about learning loss from summer break or from remote schooling, but the truth is the students have learned—and taught—the nation so much about the nature of structural racism. These youth who can think for themselves and challenge injustice really scare racists.

But informed Black people have always scared racists.

This isn't the first time that frightened racists have tried to ban education. The first law of this kind was a slave code enacted in 1740 in reaction to the Stono Slave Rebellion 1739 in South Carolina and it made writing illegal for enslaved African people.

But from the time it was illegal to be literate until today, Black people have always led a struggle for racial justice and education.

Enslaved Black people snuck off plantations to teach each other how to read and write, even though it was illegal—they called it "stealing the meeting." The punishment could be maiming or even death if you were caught reading or writing, but Black people did it anyway.

During the Reconstruction era, Black educators built the public school system across the South because they knew there was no full emancipation without education.

During the civil rights movement, Freedom Schools were organized, especially during the "Freedom Summer" campaign of 1964. During Freedom Summer, more than three thousand Black students attended a Freedom School—and the final exam was going and registering to vote or organizing others into the movement—not bubbling in answers on standardized tests.

Then there was the proliferation of the Afrocentric schools around the country in the 1970s and the Black Panther Party's Liberation Schools—like the Oakland Community School that was run by Ericka Huggins.

Today we have the Black Lives Matter at School and other movements for racial justice in education.

It's important to look at this history to help us understand the way forward. But I want to be clear about something. While today's racists may not be so bold as to ban the reading of the word—as they did for my ancestors—they do want to ban the reading of the world.

But I am telling you all that I am going to teach my students about how to read the world—because it desperately needs changing. And I refuse to be intimidated from teaching about the people throughout history who have helped make these needed changes. I am going to teach my students about the ideas and practice of people like Sojourner

Truth, and Harriet Tubman, and Claudia Jones, and Fannie Lou Hamer, and Ella Baker, and Barbara Smith, and Angela Davis. Because a world where kids learn about these freedom fighters and put their ideas in action will be a world with less oppression and more empathy, more dignity, more equity, more democracy.

I'm pledging to you all today that I will refuse to lie to kids—no matter what the law tells me to do. And I'm so glad I'm not alone.

• • •

Cheri Renfro is a worker at Frito-Lay whose viral essay, "Dear Frito-Lay," condemns the company's decision to keep the line moving after a worker died on the job, precipitating a strike.

Cheri Renfro, "Dear Frito-Lay" (July 2, 2021)

Dear Frito-Lay,

So you are "shocked" that your employees voted to strike for the first time at this plant. I'm shocked you are so out of touch with your employees you didn't see this coming. This storm has been brewing for years.

It began when you started giving lump sums instead of raises, when you lowered wages for new hires coming in, when you supported an iron-fisted management that has created a toxic work environment.

Here are a few examples:

- Making us work in dense smoke and fumes during and after a fire because as you stated, "It's just smoke."
- When a coworker collapsed and died, you had us move the body and put in another coworker to keep the line going.
- During the COVID-19 lockdown, a coworker's father passed away in another state. You told her since there wasn't a funeral she didn't qualify for bereavement time. She had to take off two of her own days to grieve.

- We worked during the entire COVID-19 quarantine while office personnel worked from home. We didn't get hazard pay, bonuses, rewards, or recognition.
- We worked through the deep freeze struggling to keep warm and everything running, getting forced over and into the weekend again, while an upper manager received a recognition award for "his dedication to come in on his weekend to keep our plant running."
- How you fill our warehouse with carts of cardboard and product blocking walkways, exits, and work areas. When we point out it's not safe, you shrug your shoulders and say, "It's push week."
- How you bring in inexperienced temporary drivers leading to two injuries, one of them major, and numerous accidents, including a hit to a major structure beam, bending it and damaging the forklift.
- The fact you offer paternity leave to all employees except those at union plants.
- Your negotiator told us that it isn't that Frito-Lay can't afford to give us raises, it's that he is there to protect the stockholder investments.

Meanwhile you have held down our wages year after year by refusing to give us cost-of-living raises. One classification got a total of 20 cents in a decade. We no longer offer competitive wages to balance the stress of unpredictable long hours—twelve-hour days, seven days a week.

The contract you offered actually covered two years, only one of which gave a 41-cent raise and you bragged that it's the highest raise you've given in years.

You have no problem paying for the drug tests, background checks, orientation, and training for 350-plus employees that you hired and lost this past year. You fly in temporary workers, paying for hotel rooms, car rentals, wages, food, and more—training for people who have no investment here.

But you have a problem giving decent living wages to keep loyal employees, already trained, already here. You were a fool to not do more to keep your employees from walking out that door because many are never coming back, not with a job market so rich right now.

After numerous informational pickets and contract offers that we voted down, you said: "That's it! Take it or leave it!" So it was time to do a strike vote.

First, you allowed us time off to vote if we signed a sheet. Then at the last minute, you took down those sheets and said no one is allowed time off to vote.

Your threats and bully tactics only fuel our fire. You have pushed us into a corner and we came out swinging.

And now you're "shocked"?

• • •

On March 16, 2021, a gunman shot and killed eight women, six of whom were of Asian descent, at the Gold Massage Spa in Atlanta, Georgia. The shooting sparked protests around the country to "Stop Asian Hate." While many called for more police to address the rise in anti-Asian hate crimes, sex workers argued that police would only contribute to the violence they face as both Asian women and sex workers. In a statement signed by over three hundred organizations, the group Red Canary Song—a collective of Asian and migrant sex workers and allies—insisted that addressing this violence requires the decriminalization of sex work.

Red Canary Song, "Radical Healing from State and Community Violence: Mourning with Asian Massage Workers in the Americas" (August 17, 2021)

In the wake of the deaths of multiple Asian women massage workers in Georgia, we are sending radical love, care, and healing to all of our community members. We acknowledge the ongoing pain and grief from continued violent assaults on our Asian and Asian American, APIA community, which has been compounded by the alienation, isolation, and violence brought on by racist rhetoric and governmental neglect in reaction to the COVID-19 pandemic. We are concerned that many of those calling for action in this moment have and will continue to endorse violence toward Asian sex workers, massage workers, and survivors.

We reject the call for increased policing in response to this tragedy. The impulse to call for increased policing is even greater in the midst of rising anti-Asian violence calling for carceral punishment. We understand the pain that motivates our Asian and Asian American community members' call for increased policing, but we nevertheless stand against it. Policing has never been an effective response to violence because the police are agents of white supremacy. Policing has never kept sex workers or massage workers or immigrants safe. The criminalization and demonization of sex work has hurt and killed countless people—many at the hands of the police both directly and indirectly. Due to sexist racialized perceptions of Asian women, especially those engaged in vulnerable, low-wage work, Asian massage workers are harmed by the criminalization of sex work, regardless of whether they engage in it themselves.

Decriminalization of sex work is the only way that sex workers, massage workers, sex trafficking survivors, and anyone criminalized for their survival and/or livelihood will ever be safe.

Media coverage that examines the racist or sexist motivations of the killings as independent of each other fail to grasp the deeply connected histories of racialized violence and paternalistic rescue complexes that inform the violence experienced by Asian massage workers. We see the effort to invisibilize these women's gender, labor, class, and immigration status as a refusal to reckon with the legacy of United States imperialism, and as a desire to collapse the identities of migrant Asian women, sex workers, massage workers, and trafficking survivors. The women who were killed faced specific racialized gendered violence for being Asian women and massage workers. Whether or not they were actually sex workers or self-identified under that label, we know that as massage workers, they were subjected to sexualized violence stemming from the hatred of sex workers, Asian women, working class people, and immigrants.

We are asking that the community stand in solidarity with us and all immigrant and migrant massage workers and sex workers. We highlight the following demands from New York–based massage parlor workers:

1. Pay attention to the life and work safety of massage and salon employees!
2. Asian massage workers and businesses come from the community and give back to the community!
3. The legal working rights of Asian massage workers must be protected!
4. The lives of Asian massage workers must not be lost in vain!
5. The legal profession of massage work should be respected and protected by US society!

• • •

H. Melt is a poet, artist, and educator based in Chicago, Illinois, "whose work celebrates trans people, history, and culture." They are the editor of *Subject to Change: Trans Poetry and Conversation* and the author of *There Are Trans People Here*, which includes this poem.

H. Melt, "I Don't Want a Trans President" (August 23, 2021)

I want trans doctors
performing my surgery
trans journalists reporting
the news, trans historians writing
textbooks. I don't want trans capitalists
walking on wall street or trans cops
patrolling my neighborhood. I want
trans musicians playing on my stereo
trans designers crafting my clothes
trans chefs filling my stomach

trans farmers planting my food
& trans gardeners picking
flowers for my funeral.

• • •

Haley Pessin, who coedited this book, gave the following speech at an abortion rights march organized by radical groups at Union Square in New York to protest the Supreme Court's decision to neither strike down nor block Texas's infamous "vigilante law," SB 8, which bans abortions after six weeks, before most people know they are pregnant.

Haley Pessin, "What it Will Take to Defend Abortion Rights" (September 12, 2021)

Some of the big women's rights organizations, Planned Parenthood, National Organization for Women, and some of the other NGOs have called a mass protest to defend abortion rights on October 2. And you know what? I'd say it's about fucking time.

For way too long, the dominant strategy of these groups has not been to mobilize their base for a full-throated defense of abortion, but to fight through the courts, through lobbying, through fundraising, through calling your senator, and worst of all, by downplaying the centrality of abortion rights to women's and gender liberation. They don't even say the word *abortion* sometimes.

But we all know that none of that has been enough to stop the offensive of the Right against our rights. The only way we're going to stop the rollback is by telling that archaic, unaccountable slavery-era institution, the Supreme Court, that we are not going to roll over and hand our rights and futures away, we are going to fight back!

The latest law in Texas is not just an abortion ban. It criminalizes everyone down to the cab driver who might aid and abet a pregnant person who dares to decide what to do with their own body. This reveals what we already know: the Right wants to control the bodies of women and people who can become pregnant by pushing us back to the days before *Roe v. Wade.* In fact, we know these efforts will never actually eliminate abortions—they will make them accessible only to the rich and white.

Poor and working-class people, especially people of color, will be made to have children they do not want or cannot afford to have, while putting their lives at risk. This gives lie to the idea that the Right has the moral high ground because they care so damn much about life. Guess what? They don't care if women and trans people die.

The Democrats are also at fault here because they've treated abortion for years now as if it's a single-issue fight that we can sidestep when it's convenient for winning elections in red states.

This isn't a single-issue protest. This is about gender and economic justice. Abortions cost as much as $300 to $1,500, and that's just in the first trimester. This is unacceptable at a time when people in the United States can't afford an emergency $400 expense and after a pandemic that left many people unable to even afford rent. We have an eviction crisis—we shouldn't have a health care crisis as well.

This is about racial justice. Not only will Texas law have the worst impact on women of color, Texas is also already the state with the highest maternal mortality rate for Black women. We need to say abortion rights are part of what it will take to make Black lives matter in this country.

This is an immigrant justice issue. Last year in Georgia, they sterilized immigrant women at a privately-run ICE detention center. This isn't just about the right not to have kids, it's about the right to have kids if and when we choose. That's reproductive justice!

We need to get our unions on board because from Ireland to Argentina, wherever they've had a successful fight for abortion rights, it's through mobilizing the power of labor and the power of the strike weapon to bring the courts to their knees.

We have history on our side and we have the numbers on our side. It's still the case that 60 percent of people in this country support the right to legal, safe abortion. We need to give them a movement they deserve and we need to give ourselves the movement we deserve by mobilizing in the tens, hundreds, thousands, and millions for safe, legal abortion, free, on-demand, and without apology.

• • •

Leta Hirschmann-Levy is an actor from New York City and a teaching artist with Voices of a People's History of the United States, an education and performance organization cofounded by Howard Zinn. Leta participated in a human rights delegation to the West Bank and Jerusalem in 2011. In 2022, after consecutive bombings of Gaza by the Israeli government and the forced displacement of Palestinians from their homes in Sheikh Jarrah, she wrote the following essay about the real meaning of solidarity with Palestinians, published first in *Mondoweiss*.

Leta Hirschmann-Levy, "Never Again—Not for Anyone, Not Just the Jews" (February 24, 2022)

The first time I was called a "self-hating Jew" was almost fifteen years ago by someone I considered a close friend. I had never heard this epithet before. It stung and I felt confused. Why would she call me that? Why does supporting Palestinian rights and questioning the Israeli occupation of Palestine make me self-hating? And what does that have to do with my Judaism?

Israel/Palestine seemed like a clear-cut situation to me. At the time, I didn't know much about that history but I knew Israel did not exist before 1948 and what did exist was Palestine. How could taking a country away from the people who had been there for centuries be right? And how could we not all condemn such an act?

Fifteen years later I have never felt stronger in my stance as a self-loving anti-Zionist Jew.

I grew up in New York. My grandparents were Holocaust survivors. I was taught "Never again." This lesson, I understood, was meant to apply to all people. I grew up watching my parents fight for the rights of oppressed and marginalized people. In the nineties we boycotted

Nike, to oppose sweatshops and child labor. Shortly after South African apartheid ended in 1994, my parents took my siblings and myself to see Nelson Mandela speak at his first New York appearance. We marched against the Iraq war in 2003. We demonstrated for women's rights and against the racial profiling that was taking place after 9/11. My parents were arrested numerous times for standing up for what they believed in, including against police violence and the murder of Amadou Diallo. I knew that the need to fight for equality and justice for all people followed inexorably from what I learned from my parents and my grandparents. Never again.

So, it was no leap when I got to university and joined an anti-racist student group. The first call to action I took part in was to demand that the university divest from Israel. I had never heard anyone talk about divestment before I joined this group. But freshman year in my Intro to Middle Eastern History class I learned that, unlike the Zionist mythologies that orbit most Americans about a land without people for a people without a land, there were in fact millions of Palestinians living there, in what was called Palestine. I also learned that nearly three quarters of a million of these people had been expelled from their homes and their villages, and those who remained were now second-class citizens in their own land. So of course, we must stand up for their rights and freedoms.

In 2005 Palestinian civil society called for international Boycott, Divestment and Sanctions (BDS) of Israel. There were seven of us in this anti-racist student group and we would follow their call. There was not yet a Students for Justice in Palestine on campus in those days; that would come several years later. Our small but committed group did our best to mobilize community members. We organized a demonstration, which, sadly, did not get much attention. Still, this was a clear anti-racist, anti-colonialist issue to me. At eighteen years old I wondered, why wasn't this issue discussed more on campus?

Some things have changed in the last fifteen years. Universities and colleges across the United States now have chapters of Students for Justice in Palestine as well as Jewish Voice for Peace. And the movement for BDS and support for justice in Palestine has become more public across the country.

What hasn't changed is that criticism of Israel or Zionism is still often equated with anti-Semitism. What hasn't changed is the oppressive, often brutal, treatment of Palestinians at the hands of Israel and backed by the US government. What hasn't changed in my mind is that this is still a clear-cut issue—what was to be "never again" has come again. This time the former victims are the victimizers.

Between my upbringing in a home rooted in social justice, to majoring in Ethnic Studies at college, where I learned more deeply about racism, classism, colonialism, and imperialism, I thought I had a deep understanding of oppression. So, in 2011 when I went to Palestine, I felt I was as prepared as anyone could be. However, what I witnessed was absolutely devastating.

What I saw in the West Bank and in Jerusalem was a complete apartheid system. Palestinians had ID cards saying where they could and could not go, who they could and could not live with. They had to go through checkpoints and were routinely harassed by soldiers, settlers, and Israelis who supported the occupation. They were cut off from water supplies, had no freedom of movement, limited rights of worship or expression, and were often arrested for what we in the United States would call "freedom of speech." There are streets that are for "Jews only." Reminiscent of the Jim Crow "whites only" era in the United States, Palestinians are walled in, fenced in, and often their homes demolished and lands taken. In 1948, at least 750,000 Palestinians were kicked off their land, out of their homes in order to create the state of Israel. The Nakba of 1948, or catastrophe, was the intended outcome of the Zionist project of colonization, the aim of which was to create a Jewish state of Israel. Those expulsions continue today in Sheikh Jarrah and elsewhere. These are not "evictions" but the brute theft of land. And it is one of the many masks that settler colonialism wears as it displaces and erases the native.

As Human Rights Watch stated in 2021, and as Amnesty International recently declared this February 2022, both in well-documented reports, this is in fact apartheid.

Gaza, with all of the Orientalist and Islamophobic rhetoric employed to dehumanize its inhabitants, is in fact the largest open-air prison in the world. Gazans have no freedom to leave should they want or need to. They are largely refugees forced from their homes in what is now called Israel. They cannot freely access clean water; healthcare supplies, building supplies, educational materials; their fishing rights are restricted; they can't leave for weddings or funerals or college. Bombing an open-air prison, bombing schools, hospitals, roadways, and mosques is not "self-defense" no matter how many rockets get sent toward Israel. One cannot "self-defend" when they are the occupier. And Israel has one of the most advanced armies in the world.

We are told Israelis and Palestinians need to compromise. Would we have told Black South Africans they should have compromised more during their period of apartheid? Should they have accepted less than full equality? Would you have hesitated to take an unequivocal stand against South African apartheid?

It is often said that this issue is "complex" or "complicated." But it is not complicated. And if my Jewish roots have taught me anything, it is actually clear as day. Never again. To anybody.

What we are witnessing is an ethnic cleansing. And as a Jew who knows exactly what that looks like from my own family's history I say, Israel does not speak for me. Zionism is racism. Let me say that again. Zionism is racism. The Zionist project is foundationally linked to dehumanizing Palestinians, erasing their culture, stealing their land, displacing them from their homes; an ongoing colonization effort that makes them second- or third-class citizens at best, and confined subjects/inhabitants at worst (as is the case for the approximately five million Palestinians in the West Bank and Gaza Strip).

We cannot pick and choose what marginalized communities we stand in solidarity with if we truly believe in freedom, justice, and liberation for all. If we stood up against sweatshops and against the Iraq war, if we marched on Washington for ALL women's rights, if we stand up for Black Lives, the AAPI community, for LGBTQIA+ rights, then we must stand up for Palestinians. One cannot be pro–Black lives and not be pro-the liberation and freedom of Palestine. No one is free until everyone is free.

I am thrilled to see how much has changed and how much more

awareness there is now than fifteen years ago when I was first called a "self-hating Jew." This is no doubt due to the bravery of Palestinians and the incredible resistance and organizing that is taking place in Palestine and by Palestinians around the globe who are fighting for freedom. May we all continue to follow their lead and let our awareness grow.

The well-documented apartheid system in Israel/Palestine, the theft of land, besiegement, violence, and the Zionist project of colonialism are all very much currently taking place. It is therefore imperative that we continue to understand more clearly how Zionism is intertwined with white supremacy and how our fight against racism in the United States must therefore extend to Israel. May we become more grounded in our understanding of Israel's apartheid system and the need to break it. And may we continue to fight to see the day where Palestinians are not only liberated but receive what is owed to them. Their homeland. Without walls. Without ID cards. Without the violence and terror that is their everyday.

In 2019 I received my German citizenship, owed to me for the displacement and atrocities done to my family during the Holocaust. May I live to see the day my Palestinian friends, and all Palestinians, receive their right of return, their homes, their reparations, their full equality. And may we all see their humanity. Remember the lesson clearly. Never again. To anyone.

• • •

The youth-led anti-war organization Dissenters works "to reclaim our resources from the war industry, reinvest in life-giving institutions, and repair collaborative relationships with the earth and people around the world." In February 2022, soon after Russian troops invaded Ukraine, they issued a clear call for solidarity with Ukraine while cautioning against any uncritical embrace of the US military and other imperial powers.

Dissenters, "Dissenters Opposes Imperialist Violence Everywhere" (February 25, 2022)

In solidarity with Ukrainian people impacted by the violence of Russia's invasion, we are calling for immediate humanitarian aid to Ukraine, evacuation and resettlement support for refugees, *not* military escalation.

We condemn Russia's imperialist invasion and we reject US and NATO escalations that have co-created this crisis. NATO does not exist for the safety of everyday people in Ukraine or anywhere. NATO works to expand the global US empire and western dominance. #AbolishNATO

People across the world are calling to end imperialist war, affirming the right to safety and self-determination for Ukrainians. As we take action here in the United States to stop US aggression, Russian antiwar protesters are rising up in Russia. Our movement is global.

To end all empires, we need a global movement targeting all leverage points. As an internationalist movement based in the United States, Dissenters is grounded in our unique role today and every day: to dismantle the US empire from within and redirect resources.

If you are a young person looking for a political home to help make sense of war, imperialism, and how we resist, we welcome you.

● ● ●

Dorothy Roberts is a writer and professor of race, law, and gender. In the following essay, and in her latest book, *Torn Apart*, she urges police and prison abolitionists to include the child welfare system among the systems that need to be radically transformed.

Dorothy Roberts, "Abolish Family Policing, Too" (June 2022)

Imagine if there were an arm of the state that sent government agents to invade Black people's homes, kept them under intense and indefinite surveillance, regulated their daily lives, and forcibly separated their families, often permanently. The left would put toppling this regime high on its agenda, right? This racist structure exists in the United States today, and yet the left pays little attention to it. The child welfare system—the assemblage of public and private child protection agencies, foster care, and preventive services—is a crucial part of the carceral machinery in Black communities. Many Americans view the child welfare system as a benign social service provider that safeguards children from abuse and neglect in their homes. Though it may bungle its responsibilities, they tell themselves, it is an essential safety net for children whose parents are unable to care for them. The left should be contesting, not buying into, this misguided perspective.

The child welfare system is a powerful state policing apparatus that functions to regulate poor and working-class families—especially those that are Black, Latinx, and Indigenous—by wielding the threat of taking their children from them. In 2018 alone, Child Protective Services (CPS) received referrals of nearly eight million children suspected to be victims of maltreatment. Intake workers weeded out reports regarding 4.3 million of these children as inappropriate for CPS involvement. But the screening process still leaves millions of families subject to state investigation each year.

In cities across the nation, CPS surveillance is concentrated in impoverished Black neighborhoods, where all parents are ruled by the agencies' threatening presence. Fifty-three percent of Black children in America will experience a CPS investigation at some point before their eighteenth birthday. During CPS investigations, caseworkers may inspect every corner of the home, interrogate family members about intimate details of their lives, strip-search children to look for evidence, and collect confidential information from schools, healthcare providers, and social service programs. If caseworkers detect a problem, like drug use, inadequate medical care, or insecure housing, they will coerce families into an onerous regimen of supervision that rarely addresses their needs.

More disruptive still is the forcible family separation that often follows CPS investigations. Every year child welfare agencies take more than 250,000 children from their parents and put them in the formal foster care system. At the same time, these agencies informally separate an estimated 250,000 more children from their parents each year based on so-called "safety plans"—arrangements parents are pressured to agree to in lieu of a formal court proceeding. In 2019, the national foster care population stood at 423,997. Hundreds of thousands more children were removed from their homes and kept in foster care at some point during the year. Black children have long been grossly overrepresented in the national foster care population: although they were only 14 percent of children in the United States in 2019, they made up 23 percent of children in foster care. Most of the money spent on child welfare services goes to keeping children away from their families. In 2019, the federal government alone devoted $8.6 billion to maintaining children in foster care—more than ten times the amount allocated to services aimed at keeping families together.

While President Trump's cruel policy of separating migrant children from their parents at the Mexican border drew national condemnation, hardly anyone on the left connected it to the far more widespread family separation that takes place every day in Black neighborhoods. For centuries, the United States has wielded child removal to terrorize, control, and disintegrate racialized populations—enslaved Africans whose children were considered white people's property and sold away at will, European immigrant children swept up from urban slums by elite charities and put to work on farms, and Indigenous children kidnapped and confined to boarding schools under a federal campaign of tribal decimation. Today's child welfare system still revolves around an ideology that confuses poverty with child neglect and attributes the suffering caused by structural inequities to parental pathologies. It then prescribes useless therapeutic remedies in place of radical social change.

The rhetoric of saving children is a guise to justify expanding the government's power to investigate and regulate communities even beyond what would be permitted by the criminal legal system. Local child welfare agencies collaborate with law enforcement by sharing information, engaging in common trainings, cooperating in investigations, and jointly responding to reports. The prison system and the foster care system converge disproportionately in the lives of incarcerated Black mothers, sometimes ending in termination of their parental rights and the permanent loss of their children.

Although many on the left argue for redistribution of wealth to raise families out of poverty, and for cash assistance, childcare, and other welfare programs to help struggling parents, the child welfare system has been largely overlooked. During the uprisings against police violence in summer 2020, I became increasingly concerned that family policing was absent from most demands to defund the police and dismantle the prison industrial complex. Some activists even recommended transferring money, resources, and authority from police departments to the health and human services agencies that handle child protection. This move would magnify the capacity of these agencies to regulate Black communities. Linking 911 calls to child abuse hotlines would trigger more child maltreatment investigations. Even well-meaning recommendations to deploy social workers to conduct "wellness checks" in homes would increase maltreatment reports, expanding the state's capacity to monitor and separate families.

The abolition of family policing should be at the top of the left's agenda. A growing movement to dismantle the family regulation system led by parents and youth who have been ensnared in it is already charting the way. These activists promote legislation to curtail mandated reporting, guarantee legal representation for parents, and require informed consent for drug testing of pregnant people and their newborns. They advocate for policies that shift government funds away from coercive interventions in families toward putting resources directly in parents' hands. And they are creating community-based approaches to support families and keep children safe. As with prison abolition, the aim is not to reform the child protection system; the aim is to replace it with a society that attends to children's welfare in a radically different way. With a common vision for meeting human needs and ensuring safety, we can build a world where caging people and tearing families apart are unimaginable.

• • •

On January 21, 2022, workers at the Elmwood Avenue Starbucks in Buffalo, New York, made history by becoming the first Starbucks store to unionize. Michelle Eisen, who is a member of the newly formed Starbucks Workers United, gave the following speech at the annual Labor Notes Conference in Chicago, where more than four thousand people were in attendance.

Michelle Eisen, "No Contract, No Coffee!" (June 17, 2022)

I am far from Gen Z, but I am more than happy to fight alongside them in this movement I started with Starbucks in 2010.

I'm a production stage manager in the theater industry and I needed a flexible part-time day job that would provide me with benefits. Enter Starbucks, a self-proclaimed progressive company that said that they cared about the environment, the community, and their workers, who they call "partners." And for a time after I was hired, I believed that to be true. Fast forward to June of 2021. I, like hundreds of thousands of service workers in the United States, had worked through the bulk of the pandemic putting ourselves and our families at risk daily—and in almost all cases the companies that we worked for completely failed us.

We were called "essential," but we were treated like we were disposable. And I was done. I didn't know what I was going to do but I knew I couldn't continue to work for a company that would so blatantly undervalue its partners. At most I probably had a few months left in me, and then shortly after I made that decision. I received a text message from one of my fellow partners, and she asked me if I would like to get a cup of coffee after one of our shifts that week—which is weird, because we literally serve coffee all day—but I agreed and it was at that meeting that she asked me what I thought about Starbucks unionizing, to which I replied I had never thought about it.

I knew very little about organized labor, but I knew that it included very little of the service industry. . . . I asked her to tell me everything she knew, and when she finished, I calmly replied that I was interested but I did not know how much time I was going to be able to commit.

My industry was opening back up for the first time post-pandemic, and I was going to be busy with production work, but I was certainly not going to stand in their way. And then, about a week after we filed our petition, I was called into my first anti-union meeting with Starbucks corporate, and we sat in a circle in a hotel conference room and listened to Rossann Williams, the president of Starbucks North America—at least until today, when she tendered her resignation. And I feel completely comfortable in speaking for my fellow partners when I say we are more than happy to take full credit for that resignation!

But in that meeting, we listened to her tell us that we are all partners and that the company has already done so much for all of us—and what more could we possibly be asking for? And I saw the looks on the faces of my coworkers as we were being bullied and manipulated into voting against our best interests. And that was the moment that I realized that I could not take a passive role in this fight, that not actively working against my coworkers was not the same as standing with them.

They concluded this meeting giving us the "facts" and [said] that if we needed more information about the union, we should contact one of our union reps. So, with my heart pounding, I raised my hand and I said, "I'm a partner organizer, and I would be happy to answer any questions anybody might have about the union."

There was no turning back from there. And on December 9, 2021, we won the first Starbucks union in the United States. And with that, our campaign became a movement. As of today, there are 160 unionized Starbucks in the country, with more joining that every single day. Just for reference, a little over six months ago, there were zero unionized Starbucks in the United States.

Now I'm often told that our campaign is different, that it is not like campaigns of the past. And I think there are aspects of that that are true. But I think it's more accurate to say that what Starbucks workers are doing is an extension of what worker organizers throughout US labor history have already done.

Now we have successfully harnessed social media and video platforms to talk to and connect with workers across the country and the globe—and those have been unbelievable tools for our campaign—but

I think the most important lesson of our success is that the basic essentials of organizing remain the same as they have for one hundred years. Our movement is rooted in our ability to connect with one another on a human level through our shared experiences and our workplaces and our industry. And it is [by] using those tools that have been refined from earlier organizing efforts that we have been able to create a movement that is largely worker-led.

We refer to . . . "partner organizers," which basically just means a worker from an organized store, reaching out and connecting with a worker and helping them organize their store. We also take larger roles in other aspects of the campaign, such as communication media and broader strategy questions. . . .

It takes an immense amount of support to take on a campaign like ours, especially when you're going up against a company like Starbucks, and many unions would think that too big a risk to take. Fortunately for us, Workers United was willing to take on that challenge. We are very lucky to have formed such a collaborative relationship with a union as established as Workers United. Not only is our worker-led movement supported but it is encouraged and even celebrated by both staff and our fellow union members, who have committed $1 million of their dues to a strike and relief fund for our Starbucks campaign. I cannot think of a more fitting example of solidarity.

There is a very pervasive way of thinking that's drilled into most service workers that is that our jobs are unskilled, that we don't deserve fair wages or safe working conditions, and that disrespect is just to be expected on the regular—and if we don't like it, we can work somewhere else. Ask anybody who has ever worked on a floor in one of these cafes. Our jobs are far from unskilled. Our labor is valuable. We bring in billions of dollars a year for Starbucks—and without our labor, the business would simply cease to exist.

So, I hope this movement is a step in the direction of changing that way of thinking. Our asks are simple: listen to our voices when it comes to working conditions, pay us fairly, and invest in our future with the company—because we are Starbucks.

So, that brings us to the final step . . . How do we win this fight?

How do we get a contract? We need to continue to support our fellow workers. We need to continue to organize. We need to stand together and contest Starbucks's anti-union behavior. We need to ask the public to do the same.

We have a pledge going around, if you could all sign, that it is "No Contract, No Coffee!" Help us build our solidarity and support our movement, because we're not only fighting Starbucks, we're fighting the public brand of Starbucks. And if Starbucks was the progressive company that I claimed it would be, it would recognize our rights to organize and be a leader in the industry. . . .

If there's any example of what this movement and the overall labor movement in the country is right now, it's that it's hopeful. So, we will stand together, and we will continue to fight together.

• • •

On June 24, 2022, the Supreme Court overturned *Roe v. Wade*, the fifty-year-old precedent that legalized the right to abortion in the United States. Soon after news of the expected decision was released, Melissa Gira Grant, author of *Playing the Whore: The Work of Sex Work,* argued that abortion rights defenders will need to break unjust laws if they want to win reproductive justice.

Melissa Gira Grant, "The Fight for Abortion Rights Must Break the Law to Win" (June 24, 2022)

I've never lived without *Roe*, and while I can't precisely remember the first time someone working in abortion rights told me to expect that we would lose them soon, I know that it was more than ten years ago. I also know that it takes time to adjust to the unsettling of established rights, of established law—decades of which were demolished in a few brief lines of Justice Samuel Alito's seventy-nine-page majority opinion, issued Friday morning, in *Dobbs v. Jackson Women's Health Organization*: "The Constitution does not confer a right to abortion; *Roe* and

Casey are overruled; and the authority to regulate abortion is returned to the people and their elected representatives." The people who show up later this week to help others get to a clinic, and those who scramble to support women who have had their abortion appointments canceled, have had time to plan for this moment. What many other people in the United States are about to go through is a kind of national catching-up. It will take time.

Yet before anyone had the chance to read the full opinion came a cast of former prosecutors who now work as professional legal commentators, who (fairly) called this, among other things, "a very dark day in America." They are trying to describe how unprecedented this opinion is, while they are reaching for the familiar—to soothe ahead of the pain. They are asking if the era of looking to the court to protect our rights, with *Dobbs*, has ended. It's not just the overturning of *Roe*, I believe, that unsettles. The whole idea of a rule of law that defines and protects rights is, correctly, feeling just as unstable. It's just that this is not at all a new condition.

This did not start today, the power of the courts themselves to jeopardize liberty and obstruct justice. Many people in the United States have already been living outside the era of legally constituted "rights," whether that's due to the courts rolling back abortion rights or the right to vote. Far from breaking with precedent, the decision in *Dobbs* has only brought that condition nearer to more people's lives.

Some will look for a solution to this erosion of rights within the same legal system that eroded them. That is understandable. To expand the court, to impose term limits, to abolish the Electoral College so that we never again end up with a majority of justices appointed by presidents who lost the popular vote—those are solutions, even if they depart from some norms, that still feel somewhat familiar and orderly. They involve clear steps that members of Congress could or could not take, campaign promises made or ignored, calm cable news discussions thereof (in the breaks between the January 6 hearings on attempts to undermine the Justice Department or news of patriot groups whose members have links to former Republican legislators menacing Pride events for kids).

That exaggerated and mostly unmerited hope for what the law can do is why we now have this decision. Locating the demand for abortion access in the courts, for example, made it a fight waged mostly by lawyers, which in turn pushed the movement—including providers and people who have abortions—to the margins. Resources that could have gone to expanding access went to crafting legal arguments that could, at best, slow the onslaught of abortion restrictions instituted by the Christian right. Clinic escorting, community abortion funds, informal networks ensuring access through travel and housing—that's where abortion rights have been fought for by and on behalf of so many more people, and where abortion access will be defended now.

There will still be a legal battle for abortion, one that now moves from the defense of constitutional rights to criminal defense—to challenge the criminalization of both providers and people who have abortions. People have been criminalized for the outcomes of their pregnancies, even with *Roe*: National Advocates for Pregnant Women, or NAPW, has identified at least 1,600 such cases since 1973 involving arrests or other deprivations of liberty, according to executive director Lynn Paltrow. That can include people criminalized for self-managed abortion, a method that will become more commonplace. Farah Diaz-Tello, senior counsel and legal director at the reproductive justice law and policy organization If/When/How, told me that at least sixty people have faced criminal penalties for self-managed abortions between 2000 and the present day, according to the preliminary findings of its research—which she cautioned is very likely an undercount. Groups like If/When/How and NAPW are growing networks of criminal defense attorneys with the expertise to take on these cases, as well as educating health care providers and child welfare workers on how to resist pregnancy criminalization.

Navigating the post-*Roe* world, though, will require going outside the law. As Laurie Bertram Roberts—executive director of the Yellowhammer Fund, an abortion fund based in Alabama, and cofounder of the Mississippi Reproductive Freedom Fund—put it when we spoke in the spring, "You have to be able to move in areas that may make people uncomfortable, that may not be fully 'legal,' while you are striving for what should be legal." For all who have spent decades demanding that courts respect the constitutional right to an abortion—the rule of law itself—will they now do something they have argued against? Will they be willing to violate the law?

Permissions

PROLOGUE

Howard Zinn, "Against Discouragement" (May 15, 2005). 2005 Spelman College commencement address in Atlanta, Georgia. First published in *Original Zinn: Conversations on History and Politics*. Copyright © 2006 by Howard Zinn and David Barsamian. Reprinted by permission of Myla Kabat-Zinn and the Estate of Howard Zinn.

CHAPTER I: FIGHTING WAR AND INJUSTICE
IN THE NEW MILLENNIUM

Anita Cameron, "And the Steps Came Tumbling Down—ADAPT's Battle with the HBA" (2000). Copyright © 2000 by Anita Cameron. Reprinted by permission of the author.

Manning Marable, "Race, Class, and Globalization: The Global Struggle for Democracy" (April 13, 2001). Speech at the opening plenary of the 2001 Socialist Scholars Conference in New York, New York. First published in *International Socialist Review*, no. 19 (August–September 2001), 94–97. Copyright © 2001 by Manning Marable. Reprinted by permission of Sandra Mullings and the Estate of Manning Marable.

Kenny Riley, "We Won't Rest Until They're Vindicated" (July 4, 2001). Excerpts from speech in Madison, Wisconsin, before the South Central Federation of Labor and the Coalition of Black Trade Unionists. First published in *Socialist Worker* (July 20, 2001). Copyright © 2001 by Kenny Riley. Reprinted by permission of the author.

Orlando Rodriguez and Phyllis Rodriguez, "Not in Our Son's Name" (September 15, 2001). Copyright © 2001 by Orlando Rodriguez and Phyllis Rodriguez. Reprinted by permission of the authors.

Monami Maulik, "Organizing in Our Communities Post–September 11th" (2001). Copyright © 2001 by Monami Maulik. Reprinted by permission of the author.

Boots Riley, "Heven Tonite" (November 6, 2001). Copyright © 2001 by Boots Riley. Reprinted by permission of Boots Riley.

Rita Lasar, "To Avoid Another September 11, United States Must Join the World" (September 5, 2002). Copyright © 2002 by Rita Lasar. Reprinted by permission of Matthew Lasar and the Rita Lasar Estate.

Rachel Corrie, Letter from Palestine (February 7, 2003). Published in *Let Me Stand Alone* (2008). Copyright © 2008 by Craig and Cindy Corrie. Reprinted by permission of Craig and Cindy Corrie and W. W. Norton & Company.

Danny Glover, Speech During the World Day of Protest Against the War (February 15, 2003). Copyright © 2003 by Danny Glover. Reprinted by permission of the author.

Amy Goodman, "Independent Media in a Time of War," *Democracy Now!* (April 21, 2003). Copyright © 2003 by Amy Goodman. Reprinted under the CC BY-NC-ND 3.0 license.

Arundhati Roy, "Instant-Mix Imperial Democracy (Buy One, Get One Free)" (May 13, 2003). Copyright © 2003 by Arundhati Roy. Reprinted by permission of the author and Róisín Davis.

Robin D. G. Kelley, *Freedom Dreams: The Black Radical Imagination* (Boston: Beacon Press, 2003).

Toni Smith-Thompson, "If They Don't Want Politics in Sports Then They Need to Take the National Anthem Out" (March 12, 2004). Copyright © 2004 by Toni Smith-Thompson. Reprinted by permission of the author.

Camilo Mejía, "I Pledge My Allegiance to the Poor and Oppressed" (July 3, 2005). Copyright © 2005 by Camilo Mejía. Reprinted by permission of the author.

Cindy Sheehan, "It's Time the Anti-War Choir Started Singing" (August 5, 2005). Copyright © 2005 by Cindy Sheehan. Reprinted by permission of the author.

CHAPTER 2: THE STRUGGLE FOR JUSTICE IN THE AFTERMATH OF HURRICANE KATRINA

Patricia Thompson, Kalamu Ya Salaam, and Father Jerome Ledoux, *Voices from the Storm* (Fall 2005). Copyright © 2022 by Voice of Witness. Reprinted by permission of Voice of Witness.

Howard Zinn, "Don't Despair about the Supreme Court" (October 21, 2005). Copyright © 2006 by Howard Zinn. Reprinted by permission of Myla Kabat-Zinn and the Estate of Howard Zinn.

CHAPTER 3: OCCUPY OPENS A NEW ERA

or any other US government department or agency. Chelsea Manning was not compensated for use of her expressions here.

CHAPTER 4: STANDING UP FOR EACH OTHER

Phillip Agnew, "#OurMarch" (August 28, 2013). Copyright © 2013 by Phillip Agnew. Reprinted by permission of the author.

Airickca Gordon-Taylor, "No Justice, No Peace: Families of Police Brutality Victims Speak Out" (June 28, 2014). Copyright © 2014 by Airickca Gordon-Taylor. Reprinted by permission of Ollie Gordon and the Mamie Till Mobley Memorial Foundation.

Chrishaun "CeCe" McDonald, "Standing Up for Each Other" (March 10, 2014). Copyright © 2014 by Chrishaun "CeCe" McDonald. Reprinted by permission of the author.

Michelle Farber, "We All Have to Be Brave," SocialistWorker.org, May 14, 2014. Copyright © 2014 by Michelle Farber. Reprinted by permission of the author.

Michelle Alexander, "How to Dismantle the 'New Jim Crow,'" Sojourners, July 2014. Copyright © 2014 by Michelle Alexander. Reprinted by permission of the author.

Ursula K. Le Guin, Speech in Acceptance of the National Book Foundation Medal for Distinguished Contribution to American Letters (November 19, 2014). Copyright © 2014 by Ursula K. Le Guin. Reprinted under the CC0 1.0 Universal license.

CHAPTER 5: THE FERGUSON UPRISING, BARACK OBAMA, AND THE LIMITS OF "EQUALITY"

Tef Poe, "Dear Mr. President" (December 1, 2014). Copyright © 2014 by Tef Poe. Reprinted by permission of the author.

Ferguson Action, "About This Movement" (December 15, 2014). Copyright © 2014 by Ferguson Action. Reprinted under the CC0 1.0 Universal license.

Amanda Blackhorse, "This Is What Dehumanization Looks Like" (March 21, 2015). Copyright © 2015 by Amanda Blackhorse. Reprinted by permission of the author.

Ross Gay, "A Small Needful Fact" (April 30, 2015). Copyright © 2015 by Ross Gay. Reprinted by permission of the author.

Bree Newsome, "Now Is the Time for True Courage" (June 30, 2015). Copyright © 2015 by Bree Newsome. Reprinted by permission of the author.

Sins Invalid, "10 Principles of Disability Justice" (September 17, 2015). Copyright © 2015 by Sins Invalid. Reprinted by permission of Patty Berne.

CHAPTER 6: "1,459 DAYS OF RESISTANCE": RESISTING TRUMPISM AND THE FAR RIGHT

CHAPTER 7: "WE WILL NOT BE SILENCED": #METOO AND THE ONGOING RESISTANCE TO TRUMP

CHAPTER 8: "OUR RESISTANCE MUST BE INTERSECTIONAL"

CHAPTER 9: "THE REAL PANDEMIC HERE IS CAPITALISM"

CHAPTER 10: ABOLITION AND THE UPRISING FOR BLACK LIVES

CHAPTER 11: "TRUMPISM CAN'T BE VOTED AWAY"

Viet Thanh Nguyen, "Asian Americans Are Still Caught in the Trap of the 'Model Minority' Stereotype. And It Creates Inequality for All," *Time*, June 25, 2020. Copyright © 2020 by Viet Thanh Nguyen. Reprinted by permission of the author.

Alexandria Ocasio-Cortez, "I Could Not Allow That to Stand" (July 23, 2020). Copyright © 2020 by Alexandria Ocasio-Cortez. Reprinted under the CC0 1.0 Universal license.

Melania Brown, "My Sister Layleen Polanco Died Alone in Rikers. Solitary Confinement Is Torture," *NBC News Digital*, July 23, 2020. Copyright © 2020 by Melania Brown. Reprinted by permission of the author.

Barbara Smith, "How to Dismantle White Supremacy," *The Nation*, August 21, 2020. Copyright © 2020 by Barbara Smith. Reprinted by permission of the author.

Anna Kuperman, "The Emperor Has No Clothes," *Providence Journal*, September 8, 2020. Copyright © 2020 by Anna Kuperman. Reprinted by permission of the author.

Mumia Abu-Jamal, "Inside the Inside of Lockdown America," *Prison Radio*, September 14, 2020. Copyright © 2020 by Mumia Abu-Jamal. Reprinted by permission.

Barbara Ransby, "Trumpism Can't Be Voted Away. We Need Radical Social Transformation," Truthout.org, November 18, 2020. Copyright © 2020. Reprinted with permission.

Hakeem Jefferson, "Storming the US Capitol Was about Maintaining White Power in America," FiveThirtyEight, January 8, 2021. Copyright © 2021 by Hakeem Jefferson. Reprinted by permission of the author.

CHAPTER 12: THE STRUGGLE CONTINUES

Jesse Hagopian, "I'm Not Alone in Pledging to #TeachTruth" (June 12, 2021). Copyright © 2021 by Jesse Hagopian. Reprinted by permission of the author.

Cheri Renfro, "Dear Frito-Lay" (July 2, 2021). Copyright © 2021 by Cheri Renfro. Reprinted by permission of the author.

Red Canary Song, "Radical Healing from State and Community Violence: Mourning with Asian Massage Workers in the Americas" (August 17, 2021). Copyright © 2020 by Red Canary Song. Reprinted by permission.

H. Melt, "I Don't Want a Trans President," *Hooligan Mag*, August 23, 2021. Copyright © 2021 by H. Melt. Reprinted by permission of the author.

Haley Pessin, "What It Will Take To Defend Abortion Rights" (September 12, 2021). Copyright © 2021 by Haley Pessin. Reprinted by permission of the author.

Index

About the Editors

ANTHONY ARNOVE is the editor of several books, including, with Howard Zinn, *Voices of a People's History of the United States* and *Terrorism and War*. He wrote the introduction to the thirty-fifth anniversary edition of Zinn's classic book *A People's History of the United States*. Arnove cofounded the nonprofit education and arts organization Voices of a People's History of the United States; wrote, directed, and produced the documentary *The People Speak*; and has directed stage and television versions of *The People Speak* in Dublin with Stephen Rea, in London with Colin Firth, and across the United States with various arts groups, including Lincoln Center, the Brooklyn Academy of Music, and the Sundance Film Festival. He produced the Academy Award–nominated documentary *Dirty Wars*. Arnove is on the editorial boards of Haymarket Books and Tempestmag.org and is the director of Roam Agency, where he represents authors including Arundhati Roy and Noam Chomsky.

HALEY PESSIN is a writer and socialist activist living in Queens, New York. They have participated in struggles against police brutality and mass incarceration, in solidarity with Palestine, in defense of abortion rights and reproductive justice, and as a legal service worker and union delegate for 1199SEIU (Service Employees International Union). Pessin has spoken at conferences in Switzerland, Australia, Ireland, Quebec, and throughout the United States on the struggle for Black liberation. Their writing has appeared in *New Politics* and at Tempestmag.org, where they currently serve on the editorial board.

Author photographs © Francesca Ruggiero and Eric Soucy.